Programming in the
.NET Environment

Microsoft .NET Development Series

John Montgomery, *Series Advisor*
Don Box, *Series Advisor*
Martin Heller, *Series Editor*

"This Microsoft .NET series is a great resource for .NET developers. Coupling the .NET architects at Microsoft with the training skills of DevelopMentor means that all the technical bases, from reference to 'how-to,' will be covered."
　　　　　　　　　　—JOHN MONTGOMERY, Group Product Manager
　　　　　　　　　　for the .NET platform, Microsoft Corporation

"The Microsoft .NET series has the unique advantage of an author pool that combines some of the most insightful authors in the industry with the actual architects and developers of the .NET platform."
　　　　　　　　　　—DON BOX, Architect, Microsoft Corporation

Titles in the Series

Keith Ballinger, *.NET Web Services: Architecture and Implementation with .NET*, 0-321-11359-4

Don Box with Chris Sells, *Essential .NET Volume 1: The Common Language Runtime*, 0-201-73411-7

Microsoft Common Language Runtime Team, *The Common Language Runtime Annotated Reference and Specification*, 0-321-15493-2

Microsoft .NET Framework Class Libraries Team, *The .NET Framework CLI Standard Class Library Annotated Reference*, 0-321-15489-4

Microsoft Visual C# Development Team, *The C# Annotated Reference and Specification*, 0-321-15491-6

Fritz Onion, *Essential ASP.NET with Examples in C#*, 0-201-76040-1

Fritz Onion, *Essential ASP.NET with Examples in Visual Basic .NET*, 0-201-76039-8

Damien Watkins, Mark Hammond, Brad Abrams, *Programming in the .NET Environment*, 0-201-77018-0

Shawn Wildermuth, *Pragmatic ADO.NET: Data Access for the Internet World*, 0-201-74568-2

http://www.awprofessional.com/msdotnetseries/

Programming in the .NET Environment

- **Damien Watkins**
  Mark Hammond
  Brad Abrams

✦Addison-Wesley

Boston • San Francisco • New York • Toronto • Montreal
London • Munich • Paris • Madrid
Capetown • Sydney • Tokyo • Singapore • Mexico City

The publisher offers discounts on this book when ordered in quantity for special sales. For more information, please contact:

U.S. Corporate and Government Sales
(800) 382-3419
corpsales@pearsontechgroup.com

For sales outside of the U.S., please contact:
International Sales
(317) 581-3793
international@pearsontechgroup.com

Visit Addison-Wesley on the Web:
www.awprofessional.com

Library of Congress Cataloging-in-Publication Data
Watkins, Damien.
  Programming in the .NET environment /
Damien Watkins, Mark Hammond, Brad
Abrams.
      p. cm.
   ISBN 0-201-77018-0 (pbk. : alk. paper)
   1. Microsoft .NET Framework. 2. Internet
programming. 3. Computer software—
Development. I. Hammond, Mark (Mark J.) II./
Abrams, Brad. III. Title.

QA76.625 .W38 2002
005.2'762—dc21
                                    2002026217

For information on obtaining permission for use of material from this work, please submit a written request to:

Pearson Education, Inc.
Rights and Contracts Department
75 Arlington Street, Suite 300
Boston, MA 02116
Fax: (617) 848-7047

ISBN 0-201-77018-0
Text printed on recycled paper
1 2 3 4 5 6 7 8 9 10—MA—0605040302
First printing, November 2002

To our parents, who have made us all that we are today:

Roy and Betty
—Damien

John and Lee
—Mark

Judy and Frank
—Brad

Contents

Foreword

THERE IS NO substitute for experience. This is especially true when the goal of the exercise is to transmit that experience. As you'll see when you start reading *Programming in the .NET Environment*, the authors—Damien Watkins, Mark Hammond, and Brad Abrams—have experience to spare with Microsoft .NET development, as well as the ability to explain clearly what they know.

Damien Watkins was a member of the first wave of outside developers recruited to join Project 7, a joint project between Microsoft and a number of universities to develop the next generation of COM.

Mark Hammond, probably best known for his extensive work on the Win32 extensions to Python, was recruited into Project 7 at about the same time as Damien, when the Project 7 team thought that Python should be one of the first languages ported to the .NET platform.

Brad Abrams is a lead program manager on the .NET Framework team at Microsoft, and leader of the team responsible for the Common Language Specification (CLS). He has been involved with the design and implementation of the .NET Framework from the very beginning.

While the .NET Framework builds on Microsoft's experience with the Win32 API and component-based programming, it is different enough from any of its antecedents that it takes some time for a developer to get used to the environment. There are some fundamental shifts in thinking that have to be made before you can be efficient.

As a simple example, take the area of memory management. In Win32 programming, memory and resource leakage were major headaches. In .NET programming, the garbage-collected managed heap resolves most of those kinds of problems automatically. On the other hand, having garbage collection doesn't absolve the programmer of responsibility for good design—and the explanation you'll find here of how the .NET memory management system works will give you a leg up on designing your structures intelligently.

The CLR's security system provides two different security models, Role Based Security and Evidence Based Security. You're probably familiar with Role Based Security from working with Windows NT roles, users, and groups. Evidence Based Security, on the other hand, is probably a whole new kettle of fish for you. Watkins and his coauthors explain this new model in a concrete way, making it easy for you to take full advantage of this powerful new platform feature.

While the subject of the Framework Class Libraries (FCL) is a huge one, requiring thousands of pages to cover it in detail, you'll find the short introduction to the FCL in this book an excellent way to get started. Again, experience tells: the authors explain the principles behind the library design as well as telling you how to use the classes.

You're in good hands.

—Jeffrey Richter

Preface

DEVELOPING LARGE DISTRIBUTED software systems is a complex and interesting challenge. A number of architectures have emerged to simplify this task and to relieve developers of the burden of dealing with the many interoperability issues associated with creating such systems. This book focuses on one of those architectures, Microsoft's .NET Framework.

An often-asked question is, "So what is new in the .NET Framework?" On one level, the answer is simple: "Not much." To put this answer into context, however, the same may be said of most recent software advancements. For example, C++ represented a significant step forward—but it was actually an amalgamation taking advantage of the object-oriented concepts of Simula 67 and the efficiency of C. Likewise, Java contained very little new science, with the concepts of virtual machines and class libraries having been commonplace for many years. So how, then, do these advancements contribute to the computing body of knowledge? Often they exploit synergy—that is, the combination of known technologies in a new and different manner that allows developers to bring together two powerful concepts in a single architecture. So it is with the .NET Framework. Although significant benefits can be gained by using the framework, many readers will be relieved to see that the environment includes many familiar concepts, although their implementation may have changed.

For example, a major concept pervading the .NET Framework is object orientation. Recently, this paradigm has won enormous acceptance in many areas, ranging from graphic user interface (GUI) development to network programming. The .NET Framework supports all of the object-oriented concepts, including classification, information hiding, inheritance, and polymorphism. What *is* new in the .NET Framework is the elimination of language boundaries that have hampered object orientation in the past. The framework also extends these concepts in concert with other concepts. For example, inheritance can be subject to security constraints; just because you can use a type, it may not follow that you can subtype from that type.

Intended Audience for This Book

It is important to understand the audience for whom this book was written so that you can know whether this book is for you. This book is targeted at software developers who wish to

- Understand the philosophy and architecture of the .NET Framework,
- Produce generic frameworks, libraries, classes, and tools to be used in the .NET Framework, and
- Use multiple languages to develop applications in the .NET Framework.

As this book is geared toward software developers, it not only describes the goals and architecture of the .NET Framework but also demonstrates how the technology implements features and services to meet these goals. Understanding the philosophy and architecture of .NET is important for all distributed system developers, even if they do not use the .NET Framework. Why? Because the .NET Framework represents Microsoft's vision of distributed systems development for the Internet. By understanding the architecture of the .NET Framework, developers gain insight into the issues associated with distributed systems development and Microsoft's solution to these issues.

Once developers have an understanding of the .NET Framework's architecture, the next step is to develop software that takes advantage of it. The .NET Framework is not an abstract programming model, but rather a full-featured system that allows developers to implement their solutions and then make them available to other developers in a robust and secure environment. As the .NET Framework is language agnostic, developers can use the right language to develop parts of a system and then merge these parts together at runtime, regardless of any language differences.

So who is this book *not* for? It is not an introduction to programming; readers should have experience developing software before reading this book. It is also not the definitive guide to all aspects of the .NET Framework or even to any single aspect of the .NET Framework. A book that covered in detail all aspects of the .NET Framework would be almost indigestible. Many books devoted to a single part of the .NET Framework, such as ASP.NET, are available. This book, in contrast, provides a solid overview of fundamental aspects of the .NET architecture. For in-depth information on individual aspects of the framework, such as the security system, readers must refer to other texts or specific documentation.

Organization of This Book

This book has a fairly straightforward organization:

- Chapter 1 describes the basic concepts and gives background information on the issues involved in distributed system development.
- Chapters 2 through 4 are the "runtime section." They describe the issues that can be thought of as "programming in the small"—defining types, storing metadata, and executing programs, for example.
- Chapters 5 through 7 are the "building and deployment section." They deal with the hard issues in distributed systems development—issues such as assembling and developing software from components and deployment challenges. This section also covers the Base Framework, including the libraries used to build applications.
- The appendices contain important peripheral information that does not fit into Chapters 1 through 7. This information includes experience reports from people who have developed compliers for the .NET Framework.

Our Motivation for Writing This Book

"Why are we writing a book?" We have asked this question many times over.

In late 1998, Monash University was asked if it would like to become involved with Microsoft in the development of the "next generation of COM," which was then known as the COM Object Runtime (COR). The invitation to join Project 7, the name for this multinational joint collaboration between Microsoft and a number of universities, came from James Plamondon at Microsoft Research. Why was Monash University chosen? The major reason was because of the association with Bertrand Meyer and his object-oriented programming language Eiffel. Even at this early stage, Microsoft was firmly focused on having the runtime system support as many languages as possible.

Monash University accepted the invitation, and Damien Watkins attended an overview meeting in Atlanta during early 1999. The idea of writing this book was first discussed at that time. Having just seen a preview of COR, which was then known as Lightning, Damien asked James Plamondon whether anyone was writing a book on Lightning. It was clear that a number of books would be required to cover all aspects of Lightning, but Damien wanted to ensure that the small, but hopefully beneficial, involvement of Project 7 members was recorded. With James's encouragement, and after a few years and numerous changes, this book emerged. The appendices in this book are a concrete acknowledgment of the work done by many people outside of Microsoft on Project 7.

Mark Hammond has been involved in Python development since 1991, developing and maintaining the Win32 extensions for Python, which includes the `PythonWin` IDE and the support libraries for COM. Mark had worked with Microsoft since the mid-1990s on Python-related projects, most notably the `ActiveScripting` and `ActiveDebugging` extensions for the Python language. In 2000, Mark released his first book, *Python Programming on Win32*, co-authored with Andy Robinson.

In 1998, recognizing the increasing popularity of the Python programming language, the Project 7 team decided that Python should be one of the initial languages ported to the platform. Mark's history with Microsoft made him the obvious choice for spearheading this effort. His residency in Melbourne, Australia, near Melbourne University and Monash University, meant that a core group of Project 7 participants formed almost exactly on the other side of the world from Seattle. That was how Damien and Mark met.

Brad Abrams was fortunate to be present for the birth of the Common Language Runtime (CLR), cutting his teeth in application programming interface (API) design and working on fundamental types such as `System.Object` and `System.String`. He participated in the earliest design decisions, which would later infiltrate the breadth of the .NET Framework and, in fact, all .NET code. Brad was very enthusiastic about the cross-language support being built into the runtime system while he led the team that developed the Common Language Specification (CLS).

Early in 1998, Adam Smith, a developer from another team, asked an interesting question: If he exposed properties from his library, could Visual Basic (and other languages) consume his API? Brad did what any respectable program manager at Microsoft would do—he called a one-hour meeting to decide which features of the CLR would be available in all languages. That meeting didn't resolve the issue. In fact, answering the question took more than three years and thousands of hours from key architects inside Microsoft, including Anders Hejlsberg, Peter Kukol, Paul Vick, Alan Carter, Scott Wiltamuth, George Bosworth, Lauren Feaux, Ian Ellison-Taylor, Herman Venter, Jonathan Caves, Francis Hogle, Mark Hall, Daryl Olander, Craig Symonds, and Brian Harry. Later, Brad reviewed and honed the CLS with a group of key language innovators outside Microsoft, the Project 7 members. It was through this effort that Brad met Damien and Mark.

As a by-product of working out what was to be included in the CLS, many "best practices" were developed. Brad started writing these best practices down in what would later become the *.NET Framework Design Guidelines* document. This document led the way in the drive for consistency and usability across the APIs exposed in the .NET Framework. The work on the CLS and the *Design Guidelines* document put Brad into a unifying role as Microsoft took disparate internal groups and formed the .NET Framework team. Through this effort, Brad gained an appreciation for the value of the different parts of the .NET Framework as well as the need for consistent usage of concepts across them.

In addition to his day job, Brad joined a very small team charged with creating the CLI and C# language standards, first through the European Computer Manufacturers Association (ECMA) and then through the International Standards Organization (ISO). Once again, the CLS and *Design*

Guidelines received a careful review and fine-tuning from this group; with great help from Jim Miller, they were published as part of the international CLI standard. Brad loves to talk about the .NET Framework and the way it simplifies the lives of developers, so agreeing to do this book was a no-brainer for him!

For us, the major satisfaction gained from working on Project 7, as with all experiences in life, has come not from developing a technology but rather from working with such a large, diverse, and talented group of developers from all over the world.

One final word about the book's title, which pays homage to the truly excellent book *Advanced Programming in the UNIX Environment*, by W. Richard Stevens (Addison-Wesley, 1992). Rich's book is amazing, and he will be sadly missed.

Current Status of the .NET Framework

The .NET Framework has undergone numerous name changes throughout its history. First, it was known as Project 42, then renamed COR, and subsequently called Lightning, COM+2.0, and NGWS (Next Generation Web Services). It was finally renamed the .NET Framework only weeks before its launch at the Professional Developers Conference (PDC) in Orlando in July 2000.[1]

Core elements of the .NET Framework have been standardized by the ECMA. A major reason for standardizing the .NET Framework is to permit other implementations of the framework to be built. Apart from the commercial Windows-based implementation, Microsoft has built `shared-source` implementations for Windows and BSD UNIX; it is hoped that other implementations from different groups will follow. For information on the standardization effort, interested readers should visit the following Web site:

```
http://www.ecma.ch
```

---

[1] An interesting aside about the history of the .NET Framework: Every .NET Framework executable contains the string "BSJB". This magic string refers to some of the original developers of the .NET Framework—Brian Harry, Susan Radke-Sproull, Jason Zander, and Bill Evans.

The .NET Framework standardization effort is detailed at the following Web site:

```
http://www.ecma.ch/ecma1/STAND/ecma-335.htm
```

The C# language standard is found at the following address:

```
http://www.ecma.ch/ecma1/STAND/ECMA-334.htm
```

You can find out more about the shared-source implementations at the following Web site:

```
http://msdn.microsoft.com/net/sscli
```

Acknowledgments

There are so many people whom we wish to thank. First, we thank all those at Microsoft who allowed us to test the .NET Framework, explained their reasoning for building the framework as they did, listened to our feedback, and even modified the system to incorporate our wishes. Although we will accidentally omit many people—and we are very sorry for that—a non-exhaustive list of these individuals would include the following: Nick Abbott, Ihab Abdelhalim, Chris Anderson, Eric Andrae, George Bosworth, Bryan Barnett, Jonathan Caves, Shuk Chan, Steve Christianson, Dennis Crain, Krzysztof Cwalina, Dan Fay, Kit George, Tony Goodhew, David Glance, Carl Grumbeck, Brian Grunkemeyer, Jonathan Hawkins, Mark Hall, Brain Harry, Anders Hejlsberg, Nick Hodapp, Jim Hogg, Rob Howard, Tom Kaiser, Loren Kohnfelder, Pranish Kumar, Ronald Laeremans, Sebastian Lange, Jason McConnell, Erik Meijer, Todd Merrell, Brad Merrill, Jim Miller, Oshoma Momoh, John Montgomery, Anthony Moore, Jon Nicponski, James Plamondon, Peter Plamondon, Susan Radke-Sproull, Jayanth Rajan, Craig Schertz, Don Syme, Clemens Szyperski, Peter Torr, Paul Vick, Scott Wiltamuth, and Eric Zinda.

To all our fellow Project 7 members, who actively participated at the Redmond Development Laboratories, thanks for your valuable insights. Again, a nonexhaustive list would include the following people: Gerry Butler, Chee Yeen Chan, Simon Cuce, John Daintree, Tyson Dowd, Jan Dubois, John Gough, Jürg Gutknecht, Fergus Henderson, Basim Kadhim, Leif Kornstaedt, Bertrand Meyer, Christine Mingins, Nick Nicoloudis,

Nigel Perry, Paul Roe, David Simmons, Raphael Simon, Emmanuel Stapf, Pinku Surana, and Dean Thompson.

The reviewers of the book provided invaluable feedback and eliminated numerous errors from the book—many thanks. We would like to especially express our appreciation to Martin Heller, Michi Henning, Jim Hogg, Laurie McGuire, Erik Meijer, Scott Meyers, Christophe Nasarre, Jeffrey Richter, and Purush Rudrakshala. All the remaining errors belong solely to the authors.

A very special thanks to all those who helped at Addison-Wesley, who turned our words into a book: Kristin Erickson, Jill Hobbs, Curt Johnson, Chris Kief, Debbie Lafferty, Chanda Leary-Coutu, Joan Murray, Robin O'Brien, Simone Payment, Stephane Thomas, and Katherine Tristaino.

Special mentions should also go to the Thai Kitchen and Kim Chi restaurants. Many perplexing issues have been resolved over fine lunches at these establishments.

Most of all we thank our families, who endured our absence and preoccupation for the last four years:

> To my wife: Your love and support strengthen me; your proofreading saves my butt! Philippians 1:3
>
> Brad

***

> To my daughter, Sacha, who has to put up with her dad spending way too much time playing and working on his PC. To everyone at Dave's Jungle Bar, who ensure that I have a life other than computers. To my parents, Lee and John, and my brothers, Paul, Scott, and Jason, for allowing me to grow up in an environment that allowed me to become whatever I wanted. Thanks and love to you all.
>
> Mark

***

> To my wife, Māire, and our five children, Joseph, Jane, John, Leah, and Katherine, for putting up with all those weeks I spent away from you. Now that the book and the thesis are finished we should spend some time together! Love to you all.
>
> Damien

***

1.

Introducing the .NET Framework

.**N**ET IS MICROSOFT's strategy for developing large distributed software systems. A core component of .NET is the .NET Framework, a component model for the Internet. A component model allows separate software components written in different languages to be combined to form a functioning system.

The .NET Framework could be contrasted with Microsoft's Component Object Model (COM), which can be described as a component model for the desktop. COM was not originally designed to address issues associated with large distributed systems, such as security. In contrast, the .NET Framework has been built to address the issues associated with distributed programming from its very inception.

Likewise, the .NET Framework could be contrasted with the Object Management Group's (OMG's) Common Object Request Broker Architecture (CORBA). CORBA can be described as a programming model for the Internet. It provides an object-oriented architecture originally designed to build distributed systems. CORBA, however, was not originally designed as a component architecture, although extensions in CORBA 3 are designed to extend the model in this area.

1

Finally, the .NET Framework could be compared with Java, a programming language for the Internet. Java provides many of the same features that COM, CORBA and .NET do, except that it is designed for a single programming language. By comparison, the other architectures have always had the goal of supporting multiple languages at their core.

This chapter provides an introduction to and overview of the .NET Framework. It highlights one element of the .NET Framework, the Common Language Runtime (CLR), and discusses some of the issues that the CLR was created to address. It also focuses on the fact that the CLR is language agnostic; all .NET languages are equal players as far as the framework is concerned. Note, however, that not all languages expose all of the CLR facilities to developers or fully express their facilities in the CLR. For example, Visual Basic requires language extensions, such as inheritance and exception handling, to better target the CLR. Because Version 1 of the CLR does not support generics, although Version 2 may, CLR does not support facilities such as templates in C++.

Before attempting to understand "what the .NET Framework is," it is important to understand "why .NET is." That is, it is important to identify the issues addressed by the .NET Framework. Armed with this knowledge, it becomes possible to understand why the .NET Framework's architecture is designed as it is and how best to utilize that architecture.

Programming Issues

With the increasing use of distributed systems, interoperability has emerged as a major issue for system developers. Of course, the problems of interoperability have actually been around for many years, and a number of standards and architectures have been developed to address some of these issues, with varying degrees of success. These issues can be generally classified into two broad categories: "programming in the small" and "programming in the large."

Programming in the Small

The "programming in the small" issues can be divided into three general domains: type system issues, metadata issues, and execution issues.

Type System Issues

Often what appears to be a simple objective—for example, passing an integer from one program on one machine to another program on another machine—turns out to be a complicated problem. Many languages have a different notion of what an integer is. Even if both programs are written in the same language, sometimes no accurate definition of what an integer is exists in that language. For example, the C++ language standard states that an integer (`int`) is equal to or greater than a short and is equal to or less than a long on any given platform. It does not define the size (and therefore the range) of the type, however. Thus, an integer may be 16 bits long on one machine, but 64 bits on a second machine. This choice, of course, says nothing about the endianness of either machine.

The situation becomes more complex when one attempts to pass types between different programming languages, even if they reside on the same machine. Some languages, such as C++, see an integer as a sequence of bits; other languages, such as SmallTalk, see an integer as an object; and still other languages, such as Java, allow integers to be either (`int` or `Integer`). The situation becomes even more complicated when you start to pass user-defined types between machines; passing the value of data members is far easier than passing the methods of the type.

Metadata Issues

A type's description is normally stored in a language-specific source file—for example, a header file in C++. When the source file is compiled, many compilers remove a large amount of the type's metadata. As a consequence, little or no type information may remain in the executable file that other compilers can use to inspect the metadata of a type. Recently, the loss of metadata has become a more significant problem as languages and architectures add more support for dynamic type discovery and method invocation. C++ has added runtime type information (RTTI) to partially address this problem in a language-specific manner. COM and CORBA provide type libraries and interface repositories, respectively, as language-independent solutions. Maintaining consistency in this situation, where the type and its metadata are located in separate files and possibly generated at different times, is difficult and error prone.

Execution Issues

When a developer uses a type from another language, how does the run-time environment provide access to the type? Many architectures provide cross-language method invocation, but is this the best result that can be achieved? Certainly, cross-language method invocation is a significantly useful facility, but it is also a complicated scenario. For example, how are program constructs, such as exceptions, mapped from one language or machine to another? Add to the mix the fact that the programs may be executing on different hardware platforms with different operating systems, and the magnitude of the problem becomes evident.

True language interoperability should, in fact, offer more than cross-language method invocation. If a C++ programmer's classes can inherit from other C++ classes developed by other developers and then extend their functionality by overriding method bodies, then a C++ class should be able to inherit from a Python class. Today, however, the object and execution models provided by the languages are sufficiently different that a common execution system cannot be supported.

Programming in the Large

A number of "programming in the large" issues need to be addressed when taking software produced by a number of different developers using different languages, and then attempting to integrate these components into a coherent distributed system. Examples of these issues include, but are not limited to, the following:

- *Naming.* If developers from many sites plan to reuse one another's classes, how do you avoid name clashes?
- *Error handling.* Some languages and architectures use return values to represent error conditions, whereas others use exceptions. What is required is a schema that allows translation while preserving semantics across languages/architectures.
- *Security.* Large distributed systems cross many language, architecture, organizational, and international boundaries. Ensuring that software is not used maliciously in such an environment can prove very difficult.

- *Versioning.* Anyone who has ever dealt with incompatible upgrades of system software, one form of which is commonly known as "DLL hell," understands that the evolution of system architectures is a major issue complicating component-based software development.
- *Scalability.* Scalability is probably the least known and most poorly understood of the issues associated with large distributed systems. What works well for 100 users on an intranet often proves completely inadequate for 1 million users on the Internet.

It can be argued that much of the recent evolution of programming languages and architectures has targeted "programming in the large" issues. Facilities added to C++ that are not found in C, such as namespaces and exceptions, address some of these issues. Likewise, the immutability of interfaces and the use of globally unique identifiers (GUIDs) as names in COM address some of these issues. One goal of the Portable Object Adapter (POA) in CORBA is to provide "scalable high-performance server applications."[1]

Solutions

These programming issues have perplexed developers for a number of years, and several techniques have already been developed to address them. For example:

- Representation standards, such as eXternal Data Representation (XDR) and Network Data Representation (NDR), address the issue of passing data types between different machines. These standards compensate for issues such as big/little endian and different word sizes.
- Language standards, such as ANSI C, allow the distribution of source code across compilers and machines. They permit source code to be recompiled on different machines and with different libraries without the need to modify the source files.

---

[1] Michi Henning and Steve Vinoski (1999), *Advanced CORBA Programming with C++*, Addison-Wesley.

- Architecture standards, such as the Distributed Computing Environment's (DCE) Remote Procedure Call (RPC), OMG's CORBA, and Microsoft's (Distributed) Component Object Model (COM/DCOM), address the issue of calling methods across language, process, and machine boundaries.
- Execution environments, such as those provided by SmallTalk's and Java's Virtual Machines (VMs), allow code to execute on different physical machines by providing a standardized execution environment.

All of these approaches provide significant benefits to the application developer, but unfortunately none has solved—or even attempted to address—all the problems associated with a distributed computing environment. In particular, the issue of language interoperability deserves more attention. Language interoperability entails more than just a standardized calling model, such as those provided by COM and CORBA; it also involves a schema that allows classes and objects in one language to be used as first-class citizens in another language. Achieving this level of interoperability is a major goal of Microsoft's .NET Framework.

Comparing the .NET Framework and IDL-Based Systems

It is an interesting exercise to compare the architecture of the .NET Framework with other distributed architectures that provide many of the same facilities. Both COM and CORBA, for example, address many of the same issues that the .NET Framework tackles. These architectures utilize an Interface Definition Language (IDL), which addresses many of the issues discussed earlier. But how does this interaction happen?

When developing a program with either COM or CORBA, a developer writes an IDL file that represents the interfaces provided or required by the server. The IDL provides the common type system and some built-in types, and it also permits the developer to define his or her own simple types and interfaces. At IDL compile time, the IDL compiler can generate and write metadata to a file. Clients can use this file, which is known as a type library in COM and an interface repository in CORBA, to discover the types and the interfaces they provide. The IDL compiler also generates proxy objects. These objects, which reside in the client and server processes, translate data types between machine architectures and translate between the different execution models of different programming languages.

If COM and CORBA already address these issues, then why would a developer use the .NET Framework? First, both COM and CORBA have some limitations. An IDL is a separate language that must be used in addition to the development language. Although both COM's and CORBA's IDLs are based on C/C++, this fact offers little help to a SmallTalk programmer. Second, the IDLs greatly restrict facilities such as method overloading, and neither provides a rich exception hierarchy.

Third, the metadata files produced by the IDL compilers are not necessarily embedded with the type's definition. This fact leads to any of the following situations:

- A developer may have access to a type (that is, its implementation file), but no metadata (that is, its type library or interface repository entries).
- A developer may have a type's metadata but not the type (the reverse of the previous case).
- A developer may have a type and inconsistent metadata—in other words, the metadata refers to a different version of the type. This situation occurs because an IDL compiler generates the metadata but a language compiler generates the type.

Finally, IDLs deal in interfaces, not types—hence their name. A developer could potentially find an interface that describes a number of methods that perform tasks that the developer wishes to provide and gain access to a type that implements this interface. The developer may then wish to add a single method to this interface. Unfortunately, he or she may not be able to reuse the type that implements the first interface and just add the implementation for the new method. In the .NET Framework, if a developer finds a type that implements all the methods required, he or she can subtype from that type, subject to certain constraints. The developer can then add, or even override, only those methods for which different behavior is required, regardless of the language in which either type is written.

Elements of the .NET Framework

Figure 1.1 shows an extremely simplified view of the architecture and relationships between elements of the .NET Framework. The CLR is the base on which all of the.NET Framework's other facilities are built. In particular, the CLR is responsible for addressing most of the "programming in the small" issues that have been identified with developing distributed systems. On top of the CLR is a Base Framework, a set of class libraries that can be used and shared by any .NET-aware language. The CLR and fundamental parts of the Base Framework are collectively known as the Common Language Infrastructure (CLI); the CLI has been standardized by ECMA.[2]

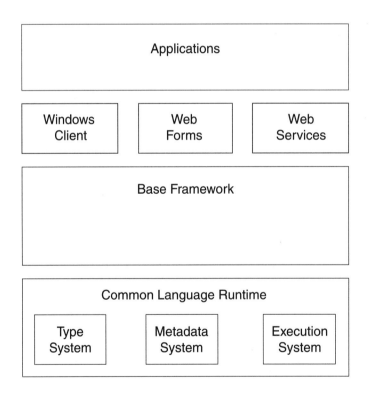

Figure 1.1 *.NET Framework*

---

2   See http://www.ecma.ch/.

Common Language Runtime

The CLR is a core component of the .NET Framework. It consists of three main components:

- A *type system* that supports many of the types and operations found in modern programming languages
- A *metadata system* that allows metadata to be persisted along with types at compile time and then be interrogated by other CLR compilers or the execution system at runtime
- An *execution system* that executes CLR programs, utilizing the metadata to perform such services as memory management

On one level, the CLR may be considered to be the union of the features of many programming languages and architectures. It defines standard types, permits developers to define their own types, and allows developers to specify interfaces and methods for their types. The CLR allows compilers to store metadata with the user-defined types, enabling other languages to inspect, use, and extend these types. In addition, the CLR provides a safe and secure environment for program execution. It readily supports an object-oriented programming style characterized by classification, inheritance, and polymorphism. Similarly, the CLR can support non–object-oriented languages.

If the CLR represents a superset of programming features, then it is clear that most—if not all—programming languages cannot support every facility in the CLR. An agreed minimum subset that almost all languages can support is defined in the Common Language Specification (CLS). The CLS is a set of rules that limits the type system and parts of the execution system to a certain group of the facilities provided by the CLR. The resulting feature set is designed to support interoperability between most programming languages. The CLS is, however, rich enough that nearly all meaningful libraries can be written using only CLS-compliant features. As a simple example demonstrating the relationship between the CLR's type system and the CLS, consider the integer types: The CLR supports both signed and unsigned integers, whereas CLS-compliant languages need to support only signed integers. Note that the CLS refers to only the publicly exposed aspects of a type; internally, a type can use any of the CLR's features while still remaining CLS compliant.

Base Framework

The Base Framework provides a number of fundamental classes, of which every application will use a subset. These classes include `Object`, `String`, and `Type`:

- The `Object` class serves as the base class for all classes. It provides a number of methods, including those that allow developers to access metadata about any type.
- The `String` class represents a Unicode string that can be shared between programming languages and different cultures. Its availability eliminates the need to perform difficult and unnatural conversions between different string types—for example, between `char*` (C++) and BSTRs (Visual Basic) in COM.
- The `Type` class is the fundamental building block that enables executing programs to gain access to the metadata system. An object can be asked for a `Type` object that provides all the information about that type.

These fundamental classes are described in detail in Chapters 2–4.

Exposing the .NET Framework

When designing and building software components, developers must choose carefully how the functionality of their components will be exposed. A number of scenarios must be considered, including the following:

- Producing components that will be installed on client machines with a separate installation process. This approach permits the component to query its environment at installation time and modify its functionality to suit its environment.
- Producing components whose functionality will be downloaded over the Internet and hosted inside an application such as a Web browser. This approach permits the component to expose its functionality to a

large and diverse range of clients but can also limit the component's opportunity to tailor its functionality to individual clients.

- Producing components that will be hosted locally but accessed via remote clients. In situations where the component provides access to a local resource, such as a database, the component may reside locally and be accessed by remote clients. Web Services are an example of this scenario.
- Producing components (or, more likely, a framework) that support all of the preceding scenarios.

Component architectures should support as many of these scenarios as possible. Importantly, an architecture should not arbitrarily restrict the developer from using a user-defined component with any of these models. The .NET Framework provides a number of facilities and services for just this purpose. A brief explanation of some of the major facilities in the .NET Framework for exposing a component's functionality follows; a more extensive and complete discussion appears in the later chapters of the book.

Windows Clients

The `System.Windows.Forms` namespace of the .NET Framework provides types that support the creation of rich graphical user interface (GUI) applications, often called *smart clients,* developed for Windows operating systems. The types found in this namespace are similar in functionality to some of the classes found in the Microsoft Foundation Classes (MFCs) or the Abstract Windows Toolkit (AWT); however, the .NET Framework types can be used from any .NET-compatible language. Such GUI libraries offer enormous support for rapid application development (RAD). A major advantage of these libraries is that they provide the specification and default implementation of GUI applications and require developers only to override the behavior of types when the provided functionality differs from the application's requirements.

A number of useful classes are defined in the `System.Windows.Forms` namespace. For example, the class `System.Windows.Forms.Form` represents a window in a desktop application. The namespace also includes classes to represent buttons, check boxes, combo boxes, controls, dialog boxes, forms, labels, menus, panels, status bars, tab controls, and many other useful windowing elements.

ASP.NET: Web Forms

ASP.NET provides a complete set of types for the development of Web-based applications. It defines types that represent all of the elements of a fully functional Web-based system, ranging from types that represent the visual elements of a Web application to types that provide Web site functionality, such as caching and security. ASP.NET, as the name suggests, is built on top of the .NET Framework and, therefore, offers facilities such as dynamic compilation of Web pages, the ability to script Web pages in many .NET languages, and the ability to reuse .NET types from Web pages. Useful classes defined in ASP.NET include `System.Web.UI.Page`, the base class that defines all the common features and facilities utilized by Web pages. Other classes represent elements such as buttons, list boxes, calendars, and data display controls.

ASP.NET: Web Services

Web Services is an emerging standard for exposing programmatic functionality on the Internet. These services are built on top of open standards and protocols such as HTTP, XML, and SOAP, all of which enable components to communicate independently of the underlying system on which the component resides. The .NET Framework provides types and services to support the creation, deployment, and consumption of Web Services. The namespace `System.Web.Services` defines types such as `WebService`, a class for accessing ASP.NET functionality from Web Services.

This brief overview of some of the means of exposing the functionality of the .NET Framework is intended to whet your appetite to learn more. The remainder of this book describes the features and services provided by the .NET Framework in detail.

Applications and the .NET Framework

In Figure 1.1, at the top of the .NET Framework, you see the word "Applications." This section of the diagram represents the applications that developers will write: desktop applications, ASP.NET Web-based applications, and Web Services. All of these applications will utilize the functionality provided by the lower levels of the diagram. All of these applications run on the .NET Framework, a situation that provides three fundamental benefits:

- Concepts and services remain consistent across all applications. For example, the classes that provide access to a database are the same for all types of applications. This consistency significantly reduces the learning curve when exposing your components via different means.
- The possibility for substantial reuse exists. You can use a well-constructed database access component from many different types of applications without modification (or recompiling).
- The support for multiple programming languages means that choosing any particular programming language does not tie you into language-specific libraries and functionality. This freedom of language choice is similar to the situation when using architectures such as CORBA.

Terminology

Unfortunately, nearly every computing term is overloaded and interpreted differently by many developers. To clarify what basic .NET Framework terms mean in this book, this section defines a number of fundamental and basic terms. These terms are defined from the ground up. For an alphabetical listing that is far more precise and complete, see the Glossary at the end of this book.

The Type System

The *type system* is the part of the CLR that defines all the types that programmers can use. A *type* is a definition, or blueprint, from which a *value* can be instantiated. The CLR contains many types, such as *value types* and *reference types*. Reference types are subdivided into *object types, interface types*, and *pointer types*. An object type is similar to a *class* in many object-oriented programming languages, such as Java.

Types have *members.* These members can be either *fields* or *methods.* As discussed later, *properties* and *events* are special types of methods. Fields and methods can be described as either a *type* or an *instance.* A type field or method can be thought of as coexisting with the type's definition; as a consequence, it can be accessed or invoked even if no values of that type are currently instantiated. Instance fields can be envisioned as existing in objects; as a consequence, access to an instance field always occurs via a value. Instance methods can be invoked only on a value.

The Metadata System

The *metadata system* is the part of the CLR that describes the types in the CLR. Compilers use the metadata to make types available in their own languages, and the execution system uses metadata to manage types at runtime. Metadata is stored in a *binary format.* Tools and programmers can access the metadata via APIs without needing to understand the binary format.

The Execution System

The *execution system* is the part of the CLR that is responsible for loading *assemblies,* controlling execution flow, and managing the garbage collected heap. Logically, an assembly is similar to a DLL; that is, it can be loaded into memory and the types and methods it contains can then be used. Unlike a DLL, however, an assembly is a collection of files and is identified not only by its name but also by other attributes such as its version number. The terms *managed code* and *managed data* qualify code or data that executes in cooperation with the execution engine. Managed code provides the execution system with sufficient metadata to allow facilities such as stack walking to verify security constraints. Managed data provides sufficient metadata to allow the execution engine to support facilities such as automatic lifetime management. Unmanaged code or data is not controlled by the execution engine and, therefore, cannot use the features of the execution system.

Example: Hello World

As stated previously, the .NET Framework is both a specification and an implementation. Given that this book is intended for use by developers, it is about time that we demonstrated some of the framework's abilities. This simple example will highlight just how powerful and flexible the language integration between .NET languages is.

Listing 1.1 defines a `Python` class called `HelloWorldPY`.

Listing 1.1 *Python class:* `HelloWorldPY`

```
class HelloWorldPY:
    def __init__(self):
        self.message = "Hello World from Python!"
    def SayHello(self):
        _com_return_type_="System.Void"
        COR.System.Console.WriteLine(self.message)

if __name__=="__main__":
    AnObject = HelloWorldPY()
    AnObject.SayHello()
```

The class `HelloWorldPY` defines two methods, a constructor (`__init__`) and `SayHello`. Although not explicitly stated, it inherits from the CLR's base class `Object`; this implicit inheritance may seem unusual to some developers, such as those familiar with C++. Nevertheless, many languages and architectures whose type systems have a standard base class also support implicit inheritance from the base class, even if that fact is not explicitly stated in the source code. The constructor sets an instance member called `message` to the value "Hello World from Python!". The first line in the `SayHello` method designates that the method has no return value, `_com_return_type_= "System.Void"`, and the second line writes the value of `message` to the console. Developers familiar with Python will realize that the first line is not *standard* Python; rather, it uses a compiler extension to support the CLR.

Listing 1.2 defines a C++ class called `HelloWorldCPP`, which inherits from the Python class. `HelloWorldCPP` overrides the method `SayHello`, which it inherited from its base class. This implementation of `SayHello` calls its base class's method and writes a single string to the console. The `__gc` keyword is an extension to *standard* C++; it indicates that the class is a managed class and that instances of this class are garbage collected by the CLR. This extended form of C++ is known as the *Managed Extensions for C++*; for brevity, in this book we use the term *Managed C++* to refer to these extensions.

Listing 1.2 C++ class: `HelloWorldCPP`

```
#using <mscorlib.dll>
#using "Python.dll"
#using "HelloWorldPY.dll"

using namespace System;

__gc public class HelloWorldCPP: public HelloWorldPY
{
  public:
  void SayHello()
  {
    __super::SayHello();
    Console::WriteLine("Hello World from C++!");
  }
};
```

Listing 1.3 defines a Visual Basic class that inherits from the C++ class. The Visual Basic class, which is called `HelloWorldVB`, also overrides the method called `SayHello`. Again, in this implementation, the base class's method is called and a string is then written to the console. As compared to Python and Managed C++, Visual Basic does not use language extensions to expose the CLR faculties; instead, the actual language has been extended. As an example of these modifications is the addition of new keywords such as `Inherits`.

Listing 1.3 Visual Basic class: `HelloWorldVB`

```
Imports System
Imports HelloWorldCPP

Public Class HelloWorldVB
Inherits HelloWorldCPP
  Overrides Sub SayHello()
    MyBase.SayHello()
    Console.WriteLine ("Hello World from Visual Basic!")
  End Sub
End Class
```

Listing 1.4 defines a COBOL class that inherits from the Visual Basic class. Like the previous classes, `HelloWorldCOB` overrides `SayHello`, again calling its base class's method and then writing a string to the console.

Unlike the previous classes, the COBOL class uses the COBOL keyword DISPLAY to write the string to the console.

Listing 1.4 COBOL class: `HelloWorldCOB`

```
000010 CLASS-ID. HelloWorldCOB INHERITS HelloWorldVB.
000020 ENVIRONMENT DIVISION.
000030 CONFIGURATION SECTION.
000040 REPOSITORY.
000050     CLASS HelloWorldVB AS "HelloWorldVB".
000060 OBJECT.
000070 PROCEDURE DIVISION.
000080 METHOD-ID. SayHello.
000090 PROCEDURE DIVISION.
000100     INVOKE SUPER "SayHello".
000110     DISPLAY "Hello World from COBOL!".
000120 END METHOD SayHello.
000130 END OBJECT.
000140 END CLASS HelloWorldCOB.
```

Listing 1.5 defines a C# class that inherits from the COBOL class. Like its predecessor classes, `HelloWorldCS` overrides the `SayHello` method, once again calling its base class's method and then writing a string to the console.

Listing 1.5 C# class: `HelloWorldCS`

```
using System;

class HelloWorldCS: HELLOWORLDCOB
{
  override public void SayHello()
  {
    base.SAYHELLO();
    Console.WriteLine("Hello World from C#!");
  }
  public static int Main()
  {
    HelloWorldCS h = new HelloWorldCS();
    h.SayHello();
    return 0;
  }
}
```

The class `HelloWorldCS` provides a function called `Main`, which serves as an entry point so that the C# file can be compiled into an executable file. Compiling and executing the `HelloWorldCS` class produces the following output:

```
Hello World from Python!
Hello World from C++!
Hello World from Visual Basic!
Hello World from COBOL!
Hello World from C#!
```

Of course, the idea of creating classes where each individual function is written in a different language is definitely not the point of the .NET Framework. The benefit of using the framework is that now classes, libraries, and tools built in one language can be used in other languages. For example, developers need not know or care which language the Base Framework is written in—they just use it.[3]

Summary

This chapter provided a very short introduction to the .NET Framework. It concentrated far more on describing which issues are addressed by the .NET Framework than on how it addresses those concerns. This focus was intentional; understanding the issues addressed by .NET offers a far better basis from which to learn the .NET Framework and understand its design and trade-offs. Along the way, the chapter probably raised more questions than it answered. Do not worry: The remainder of this book attempts to answer those questions.

---

[3] Most of the Base Framework is written in C#, but this choice is more an implementation detail than a necessity.

■ 2 ■

The Type System

C HAPTER 1 PROVIDED a high-level overview of the issues involved in building distributed systems. It introduced a solution to these issues, the .NET Framework, and used a simple "Hello World" example to highlight the language interoperability offered by the .NET Framework. But, as is so often the case, the devil lies in the details. Chapters 2 through 4 describe in more depth the three CLR subsystems: the type system (described in this chapter) and the metadata and execution systems (described in Chapters 3 and 4, respectively).

As noted in Chapter 1, the facilities provided by the type, metadata, and execution systems are not new. However, the CLR does provide functionality in addition to the services provided by other architectures, such as COM/DCOM, CORBA, and Java. For example:

- The type system supports many programming styles and languages, allowing types defined in one language to be first-class citizens in other languages.
- The metadata system supports an extensibility mechanism, called custom attributes, that allows developers to extend the metadata annotations.
- The execution system ensures security and supports versioning on types in the CLR.

Using the .NET Framework, developers can both define and share types. Defining and sharing new types in a single language is not particularly challenging; allowing a newly defined type to be used in other languages is much more problematic. This chapter offers a sufficiently detailed understanding of the CLR type system so that developers can appreciate how it achieves type interoperability.

The Relationship Between Programming Languages and Type Systems

The Evolution of Type Systems

Why is a type system necessary at all? Some early programming languages did not provide a type system; they simply saw memory as a sequence of bytes. This perspective required developers to manually craft their own "types" to represent user-defined abstractions. For example, if a developer needed four bytes to represent integer values, then he or she had to write code to allocate four bytes for these integers and then manually check for overflow when adding two integers, byte by byte.

Later programming languages provided type systems, which included a number of built-in abstractions for common programming types. The first type systems were very low level, providing abstractions for fundamental types, such as characters, integers, and floating-point numbers, but little more. These types were commonly supported by specific machine instructions that could manipulate them. As type systems become more expressive and powerful, programming languages emerged that allowed users to define their own types.

Of course, type systems provide more benefits than just abstraction. Types are a specification, which the compiler uses to validate programs through a mechanism such as static type checking. (In recent years, dynamic type checking has become more popular.) Types also serve as documentation, allowing developers to more easily decipher code and understand its intended semantics. Unfortunately, the type systems provided by many programming languages are incompatible, so language integration requires the integration of different types to succeed.

Programming Language-Specific Type Systems

Before attempting to design a type system for use by multiple languages, let's briefly review the type systems used by some of the more popular programming languages.

The C programming language provides a number of primitive built-in types, such as `int` and `float`. These types are said to closely resemble a machine's architecture, as they can often be held in a single register and may have specific machine instructions to process them. The C programmer can also create user-defined types, such as enumerations or structures. Structures are essentially aggregate types that contain members of one or more other types.

The C++ programming language takes the type system of C and extends it with object-oriented and generic programming facilities. C++'s classes (essentially C structures) can inherit from multiple other classes and extend these classes' functionality. C++ does not provide any new built-in types but does offer libraries, such as the Standard Template Library (STL), that greatly enhance the language's functionality.

SmallTalk is an object-oriented language in which all types are classes. SmallTalk's type system provides single-implementation inheritance, and every type usually directly or indirectly inherits from a common base class called `Object`,[1] providing a common root class in the SmallTalk type system. SmallTalk is an example of a dynamically type-checked language.

Like SmallTalk, Java provides an object-oriented type system; unlike SmallTalk, it also supports a limited number of primitive built-in types. Java provides a single-implementation inheritance model with multiple inheritance of interfaces.

The Design Challenge: Development of a
Single Type System for Multiple Languages

Given the variety of type systems associated with these programming languages, it should be readily apparent that developing a single type system for multiple languages poses a difficult design challenge. (Most of the lan-

---

[1]   In Smalltalk, a class can inherit from `nil` rather than `Object`.

guages mentioned previously are object-oriented.) Also, it is clear from the list of requirements that not all type systems are compatible. For example, the single-implementation inheritance model of SmallTalk and Java differs from the multiple-implementation inheritance capabilities of C++.

The approach taken when designing the CLR generally accommodated most of the common types and operations supported in modern object-oriented programming languages. In general terms, the CLR's type system can be regarded as the union of the type systems of many object-oriented languages. For example, many languages support primitive built-in types; the CLR's type system follows suit. The CLR's type system also supports more advanced features such as properties and events, two concepts that are found in more modern programming languages. An example of a feature not currently supported in the CLR is multiple-implementation inheritance—an omission that naturally affects languages that do support multiple inheritance, such as C++, Eiffel, and Python.

Although the CLR's type system most closely matches the typical object-oriented type system, nothing in the CLR precludes non–object-oriented languages from using or extending the type system. Note, however, that the mapping from the CLR type system provided by a non–object-oriented language may involve *contortions*. Interested readers should see the appendices at the end of this book for more details on language mapping in non–object-oriented languages.

CLR–Programming Language Interaction: An Overview

Figure 2.1 depicts the relationship between elements of the CLR and programming languages. At the top of the diagram, the source file may hold a definition of a new type written in any of the .NET languages, such as Python. When the Python.NET compiler compiles this file, the resulting executable code is saved in a file with a .DLL or .EXE extension, along with the new type's metadata. The metadata format used is independent of the programming language in which the type was defined.

Once the executable file for this new type exists, other source files—perhaps written in languages such as C#, Managed C++, Eiffel, or Visual Basic (VB)—can then import the file. The type that was originally defined in Python can then be used, for example, within a VB source code file just as if it were a VB type. The process of importing types may be repeated

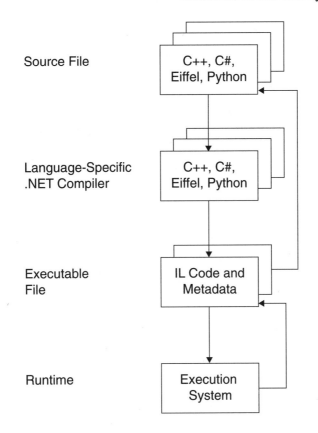

Figure 2.1 *Interaction between languages, compilers, and the CLR*

numerous times between different languages, as represented by the arrow from the executable file returning to another source file in Figure 2.1.

At runtime, the execution system will load and start executing an executable file. References to a type defined in a different executable file will cause that file to be loaded, its metadata will be read, and then values of the new type can be exposed to the runtime environment. This scenario is represented by the line running from the execution system back to the executable files in Figure 2.1.

Elements of the CLR Type System

Figure 2.2 depicts the basic CLR type system. The type system is logically divided into two subsystems, value types and reference types.

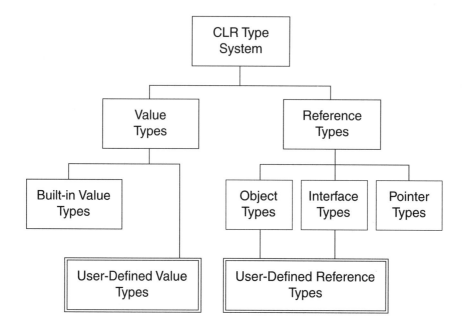

Figure 2.2 *The CLR type system*

A *value type* consists of a sequence of bits in memory, such as a 32-bit integer. Any two 32-bit integers are considered equal if they hold the same number—that is, if the sequence of bits is identical.

Reference types combine the address of a value (known as its identity) and the value's sequence of bits. Reference types can, therefore, be compared using both identity and equality. *Identity* means that two references refer to the same object; *equality* means that two references refer to two different objects that have the same data—that is, the same sequence of bits.

On a more practical level, references types differ from value types in the following ways:

- Value types always directly inherit from `System.ValueType` or `System.Enum`, which itself inherits from `System.ValueType`. The types are always sealed, which means that no other types can inherit from them. Reference types, in contrast, inherit from any class other than `System.ValueType` or `System.Enum`.

- Reference types are always allocated on the garbage collected heap, whereas value types are normally allocated on the stack. Note, however, that value types may be allocated on the garbage collected heap—for instance, as members of reference types.
- Reference types are accessed via strongly typed references. These references are updated if the garbage collector moves an object.

As mentioned previously, in CLR terminology, an instance of any type (value or reference) is known as a *value*. Every value in the CLR has one exact type, which in turn defines all methods that can be called on that value.

In Figure 2.2, note that the User-Defined Reference Types box does not connect with the Pointer Types box. This fact is sometimes misconstrued as meaning that pointers cannot point to user-defined types. This is not the case, however; rather, the lack of a connection means that developers cannot define pointer types but the CLR will generate pointers to user-defined types as needed. This situation is similar to that observed with arrays of user-defined types: Developers cannot define these arrays but the CLR generates their definitions whenever they are needed.

Value Types

Value types represent types that are known as *simple* or *primitive* types in many languages. They include types such as `int` and `float` in C++ and Java. Value types are often allocated on the stack, which means that they can be local variables, parameters, or return values from functions. By default, they are passed by value. Unlike in some programming languages, CLR value types are not limited to built-in data types; developers may define their own value types if necessary.

Built-in Value Types

Table 2.1 lists the CLR's built-in value types. In the table, the "CIL Name" column gives the type's name as used in Common Intermediate Language (CIL), which could best be described as the assembly language for the CLR. CIL is described in more detail in Chapter 4, which covers the execution system. The next column, "Base Framework Name," gives the name for the type in the Base Framework. The Base Framework is often referred to as the Framework Class Library (FCL). As the library contains more than just classes, this name is somewhat inaccurate. Chapter 7 covers the Base Framework in more detail.

TABLE 2.1 CLR Built-in Value Types

CIL Name	Base Framework Name	Description	CLS Support
bool	System.Boolean	Boolean, true or false	Y
char	System.Char	Unicode character	Y
int8	System.SByte	Signed 8-bit integer	N
int16	System.Int16	Signed 16-bit integer	Y
int32	System.Int32	Signed 32-bit integer	Y
int64	System.Int64	Signed 64-bit integer	Y
unsigned int8	System.Byte	Unsigned 8-bit integer	Y
unsigned int16	System.UInt16	Unsigned 16-bit integer	N
unsigned int32	System.UInt32	Unsigned 32-bit integer	N
unsigned int64	System.UInt64	Unsigned 64-bit integer	N
float32	System.Single	IEEE 32-bit floating-point number	Y
float64	System.Double	IEEE 64-bit floating-point number	Y
native int	System.IntPtr	Signed native integer, equivalent to the machine word size (32 bits on a 32-bit machine, 64 bits on a 64-bit machine)	Y
native unsigned int	System.UIntPtr	Unsigned native integer	N

Note that 8-bit integers appear to be named in an inconsistent manner when compared to the other integral types. Normally, the unsigned integers are known as `System.UIntX`, where `X` is the size of the integer. With 8-bit integers, however, the signed version is known as `System.SByte`, where `S` means signed. This nomenclature is preferred because unsigned bytes are used more frequently than signed bytes are, so the unsigned byte gets the simpler name.

Boolean Values

The `bool` type is used to represent true and false values. Unlike some languages that use an integer for this type (so that a value such as 0 represents false and all other values represent true), the CLR designates a specific type for this purpose. This choice eliminates errors that could potentially arise when integer values are taken to signify Boolean values but that interpretation was not the programmer's intention.

Characters

All characters in the CLR are 16-bit Unicode code points.[2] The UTF-16 character set uses 16 bits to represent characters; by comparison, the ASCII character set normally uses 8 bits for this purpose. This point is important for a component model such as the .NET Framework, for which distributed programming over the Internet was a prime design goal of the architecture. Many newer languages and systems for Internet programming, such as Java, have also decided to support Unicode.

Integers

The CLR supports a range of built-in integer representations. Integers vary in three ways:

- Their size can be 8, 16, 32, or 64 bits. This range covers the size of integers in many common languages and machine architectures.

---

[2] Throughout this book, the generic term *character* is used rather than terms from the Unicode standard, such as *abstract character* and *code point.*

- Integers can be signed or unsigned, designating whether the values they hold are positive only or positive/negative.
- Native integers are used to represent the most natural size integer on the execution architecture. Because the CLR is designed to run on a number of different platforms, it needs a mechanism to inform the execution engine that it is free to choose the most efficient representation on the platform that the code executes on—hence the native integer type.

The last point highlights a recurring theme in the design of the CLR—namely, that many issues are left to the execution system to resolve at runtime. While this flexibility does incur some overhead, the execution system can make decisions about runtime values to ensure more efficient execution. Another example of this facility, which is covered in more detail later, involves the layout of objects in memory. Developers may explicitly specify how objects are laid out or they can defer this decision to the execution engine. The execution engine can take aspects of the machine's architecture, such as word size, into account to ensure that the layout of fields aligns with the machine's word boundaries.

Floating-Point Types

CLR floating-point types vary between 32- and 64-bit representations and adhere to the IEEE floating-point standard.[3] Rather than providing a detailed overview of this standard here, readers are referred to the IEEE documentation. Native floating-point representations are used when values are manipulated in a machine, as they may be the natural size for floating-point arithmetic as supported by the hardware of the underlying platform. These values, however, will be converted to `float32` or `float64` when they are stored as values in the CLR. Providing internal representations for floating-point numbers that match the natural size for floating-point values on the machine on which the code executes allows the runtime environment to operate on a number of different platforms where intermediate results may be larger than these types. A native floating-point

---

[3] IEC 60559:1989, *Binary Floating-Point Arithmetic for Microprocessor Systems.*

value will be truncated, if necessary, when the value is stored into a 32- or 64-bit location in the CLR.

Special Issues with Built-in Value Types

In Table 2.1, notice which of the built-in value types are CLS compliant. As stated previously, languages must adhere to the CLS subset of the CLR to achieve maximum interoperability between languages. It is not surprising that types such as `int32` are listed in the CLS whereas types such as `native unsigned int` are not. Note, however, that most unsigned integers are not included in the CLS.

Also, note that not all programming languages will expose all of these value types to developers. Types such as `native int`, for instance, may not have a natural mapping into a language's type system. Also, language designers may choose not to expose a type—instead exposing only CLS-compliant types, for example.

A number of value types are defined in the Framework Class Library. Technically speaking, they are really user-defined types; that is, they have been defined by the developers of the Base Framework rather than being integral CLR value types. Developers using the CLR often do not recognize this distinction, however, so these types are mentioned here. Of course, such a blurry distinction is precisely what the designers of the CLR type system were hoping to achieve. Examples of such types include `System.DateTime`, which represents time; `System.Decimal`, which represents decimal values in the approximate range from positive to negative 79,228,162,514,264,337,593,543,950,335; `System.TimeSpan`, which represents time spans; and `System.Guid`, which represents globally unique identifiers (GUIDs).

User-Defined Value Types

In addition to providing the built-in value types described previously, the CLR allows developers to define their own value types. Like the built-in value types, these types will have copy semantics and will normally be allocated on the stack. A default constructor is not defined for a value type. User-defined value types may be enumerations or structures.

Enumerations

Listing 2.1 gives an example of the declaration and use of a user-defined enumeration.[4] This program defines a simple enumeration representing the months in the year and then prints a string to the console window matching a month name with its number.

Listing 2.1 *User-defined value type:* `EnumerationSample`

```
using System;

namespace Enumeration
{
  struct EnumerationSample
  {
    enum Month {January = 1, February, March,
                April, May, June,
                July, August, September,
                October, November, December}
    static int Main(string[] args)
    {
      Console.WriteLine("{0} is month {1}",
            Month.September,
            (int) Month.September);
      return 0;
    }
  }
}
```

For the first few examples in the book, the C# code used is described so that you will become familiar with how to read C#. Later, such detailed descriptions of the example code are omitted.

The first line in Listing 2.1 is the `using  System` directive, which is included so that types whose names start with "`System.`", such as `System.Console`, can be referenced without fully qualifying those names. While this tactic reduces the amount of typing developers need to do, its overuse can eliminate the advantages gained by using namespaces, so employ this technique judiciously.

---

[4] Although C# is used for most programming examples in this book, this choice was made only because the C-derived syntax is assumed to be familiar to many programmers.

Next in Listing 2.1 comes the definition of a namespace called `Enumeration`. This name has no programmatic significance; we could have used any name for the namespace or even not used a namespace at all. Nevertheless, because components developed within the CLR are designed to be reused in many scenarios, including being downloaded from the Internet, the use of namespaces is strongly encouraged to avoid collisions between the names of components developed by different developers.

Listing 2.1 continues with the definition of the user-defined value type `EnumerationSample`. This value type will hold the program's entry point, the method with which execution will commence. The C# keyword `enum` is used to define an enumeration. In Listing 2.1, this enumeration is called `Month` and contains constants representing each month of the year. The declaration of the enumeration is reasonably straightforward, except for the fact that the enumeration starts the constants with a value of `1`; the default value would be `0`.

`Main` is the entry point for the program. It prints out a single line of output that informs the user that September is the ninth month (`9`) of the year.

Listing 2.1 produces the following output:

```
September is 9
```

Structures

In this book, user-defined value types are called *structures.* Some languages, such as Managed C++, allow users to use a keyword such as `class` when defining either value or reference types. Other languages, such as C#, use a keyword such as `struct` to indicate a user-defined value type and `class` to indicate a user-defined reference type. This choice is largely a language-specific issue, but readers should be aware of these differences and understand the behavior of the language they are using.

Structures can contain any of the following:

- Methods (both static and instance)
- Fields (both static and instance)
- Properties (both static and instance)
- Events (both static and instance)

Methods Methods specify a contract that must be honored by both the caller and the callee. Methods have a name, a parameter list (which may be empty), and a return type. Clients that need to call a method must satisfy the contract when calling the method.

Methods on value types can be either static methods or instance methods:

- Static methods are invoked on the type itself and are callable at any time, even if no values of the type exist.
- Instance methods are always invoked on values of a type.

One limitation on value types is that they cannot define a constructor that takes no parameters, known as a *default constructor* in some languages.

Listing 2.2 demonstrates the definition and use of both static and instance methods on a value type in C#. Both methods write a greeting to the console window. The code starts with a using directive; it allows types whose names would start with System, such as "System.Console," to be referenced more simply: Console. Next comes the declaration of the user-defined namespace, ValueTypeMethods. Note that the CLR does not intrinsically support namespaces; instead, a type T declared in namespace N is known to the CLR as the type N.T. This type, N.T, will reside in an *assembly*; the CLR uses such assemblies to uniquely identify types—not namespaces, as in some languages. (Assemblies are covered in Chapter 5.)

Listing 2.2 *Use of static and instance methods with a user-defined value type*

```
using System;

namespace ValueTypeMethods
{
  struct Sample
  {
    public static void SayHelloType()
    {
      Console.WriteLine("Hello world from Type");
    }
    public void SayHelloInstance()
    {
      Console.WriteLine("Hello world from instance");
    }
```

```
    static void Main(string[] args)
    {
      SayHelloType();
      Sample s = new Sample();
      s.SayHelloInstance();
    }
  }
}
```

The C# keyword `struct` is used to create a value type called `Sample`. This struct has three methods, two of which are static methods: `SayHelloClass` and `Main`. The method `SayHelloInstance` is an instance method and is, therefore, always invoked on values of the type.

The static method `Main` is also the entry point for the program. As far as the CLR is concerned, the entry point for a program need not be called `Main`, although in C# it always has that name. The entry point must be a static method and can be a member of either a value type or a reference type. In Listing 2.2, `Main` calls both the static and instance methods. The entry point function can return a 32-bit value indicating its success or failure; in Listing 2.2, however, `Main` returns `void` (i.e., nothing). (Methods also have visibility and accessibility—topics covered later in this chapter.)

Listing 2.2 produces the following output:

```
Hello world from Type
Hello world from instance
```

Fields A type may contain zero or more fields, each of which has a type. Like methods, fields can be either static or instance. Used to store values, they represent the *state* of a type or value. Every field has a type and a name. For example, a `Point` class may have two fields to represent its *x* and *y* coordinates. These values may exist in every instance of the type, thereby allowing the state to be different within each value. If these fields have private accessibility, which is often the desired situation, then the state of an instance remains hidden and only its other members may access it. (Visibility and accessibility are covered later in this chapter.)

The next section, on properties, gives an example of defining and using fields.

Properties   Languages that target the CLR are provided with support for properties by the CLR; that is, they are not just a naming convention to be followed by developers. This relationship proves particularly useful when the goal is to provide expressive class libraries. The CLR implements properties through the use of some special metadata annotations and methods. To a certain degree, properties are "syntactic sugar": They represent `set` and `get` methods defined on logical fields of a type.

What is a logical field of a type? As an example, a Person type may have properties that represent the Person's Birth Date, Star Sign, and Age. Clearly, storing the actual date of birth is sufficient to allow all the other values to be computed and supplied at runtime. Therefore, Age can be represented as a property—that is, a logical field of a type where an actual member is not used. Properties have a name, a type, and a number of accessor methods. A type, such as the Person type, would be free to implement all of these logical members as properties.

In client code, although they may appear to be accessing public fields when they read and write to these properties, compilers will insert code to call the property's methods. These methods may compute the needed values and provide all the data validation required to ensure the integrity of the member's values. Properties exist in COM and CORBA as well. In CORBA, they are known as *attributes* (the IDL keyword used to describe them).

Listing 2.3 demonstrates the definition and use of a value type with properties and fields in C#. This program first defines a value type called `Point` with properties representing its *x* and *y* coordinates, and then writes and reads values to these properties. The value type is a C# `struct` that has two integers as its data members. Because they are passed by value by default, value types should generally be lightweight; this struct is an example of this requirement.

Listing 2.3 *Use of properties and fields with a user-defined value type*

```
using System;

namespace ValueType
{
  struct Point
  {
```

```
      private int xPosition, yPosition;
      public int X
      {
        get {return xPosition;}
        set {xPosition = value;}
      }
      public int Y
      {
        get {return yPosition;}
        set {yPosition = value;}
      }

    }
    class EntryPoint
    {
      static void Main(string[] args)
      {
        Point p = new Point();
        p.X = 42;
        p.Y = 42;
        Console.WriteLine("X: {0}", p.X);
        Console.WriteLine("Y: {0}", p.Y);
      }
    }
  }
```

The first item in Listing 2.3 is the using System directive, which ensures that types whose names start with "System." can be referenced without the need to fully qualify these names. Next comes the definition of a namespace called ValueType; this name has no particular significance, as we could have used any name for this namespace or even no namespace at all. The definition of the user-defined value type Point follows. This type has two fields, both of type int, which represent the *x* and *y* coordinates of a point.

The value type definition is followed by the definition of two more members, both properties. The definition of the properties looks a little awkward initially. The first part of the definition gives the accessibility, type, and name of the property; this information looks identical to the description of any field. The subsequent lines of the definitions provide the set and get methods for these properties. In fact, using the metadata facilities to look at this struct (as is done in Chapter 3), it becomes apparent that two methods are generated for each property, both with the words `set_` and `get_` prefixed to the names of the properties—for example, `set_X` and `get_X`.

Note two points relating to Listing 2.3:

- The properties map to fields within the type, although such mapping is not strictly necessary.
- Properties are not limited to types such `int`; they can be of any type.

The class `EntryPoint` provides the entry point for this program. This class could have been given any name, but `EntryPoint` was chosen because it describes the class's purpose (rather than for any syntactical reason). Within `Main`, the first line *appears* to allocate a new instance of the `Point` type on the heap; in reality, this is not the case. For developers familiar with other programming languages, this idea is very counterintuitive; as value types are allocated on the stack, the local variable `p` is, in fact, allocated on the stack. Next, the use of the properties is highlighted. Notice how access to the properties appears similar to access to a public field, but the compiler generated code to call the `get_` and `set_` methods as required. Properties also offer "hints" to the just-in-time (JIT) compiler, which may choose to inline the method calls. (The JIT compiler is discussed in Chapter 4.) For simple properties such as the ones defined in Listing 2.3, little (if any) performance overhead is incurred and many reasons exist to prefer properties over publicly exposing instance fields (e.g., the elimination of versioning and data integrity issues).

Listing 2.3 produces the following output:

```
X: 42
Y: 42
```

Events   As with properties, languages that target the CLR are provided with support for events by the CLR; like properties, events are not just a naming convention to be followed by developers. Events are used to expose asynchronous changes in an observed object. At a fundamental level, they are "syntactic sugar" that generates methods and associated metadata.

An event has both a name and a type. The type specifies the method signature that clients must provide for the event's callback method. When types define an event, methods to add and remove listeners are created automatically, named `add_EventName` and `remove_EventName`. Clients register to listen for events. When an event is raised, a callback method is invoked on the affected clients. When a client is no longer interested in receiving notification of events, it can remove itself from the list of listeners on an event source.

Both COM and CORBA support events, albeit somewhat differently. In COM, an interface can be marked as a `source` interface, which means that the methods in the interface need to be implemented by the client and the component will call back to the client through these methods. CORBA uses a similar method—namely, an interface is passed from a client to a server and callbacks are made through the same interface. The CORBA interface is not specifically marked as a callback interface, however, as it is in COM. The approaches employed in COM and CORBA are similar to events in the CLR, except that the CLR registers individual methods to be called back rather than interfaces (which contain a number of methods). CORBA also provides an Event Service that gives full control over events, providing, for example, both push and pull functionality. Unfortunately, a functional equivalent to CORBA Event Service does exist in the CLR.

Listing 2.4 demonstrates the definition and use of events in a value type in C#. This program defines a value type called `EventClass` that exposes an event, creates a value of this value type, attaches listeners, and then invokes the event. Events are tied to the concept of delegates in the CLR. A delegate is best described as a type-safe function pointer. With events, delegates are used to specify the signature of the method that the event will call when it is raised. For example, the definition of `ADelegate` in Listing 2.4 states that `ADelegate` is a delegate (function pointer) that can point at functions that take no parameters and return nothing. The value type `EventClass` defines an event called `AnEvent` of type `ADelegate`; that is, it can register and call back methods whose signature matches that of `ADelegate`.

Listing 2.4 *Use of events with a user-defined value type*

```
using System;

namespace EventSample
{
  public delegate void ADelegate();
  struct EventClass
  {
    public event ADelegate AnEvent;
    public void InvokeEvent()
    {
      if(AnEvent !=null)
        AnEvent();
    }
    static void CallMe()
    {
      Console.WriteLine("I got called!");
    }
    static void Main(string[] args)
    {
      EventClass e = new EventClass();
      e.AnEvent += new ADelegate(CallMe);
      e.AnEvent += new ADelegate(CallMe);
      e.AnEvent += new ADelegate(CallMe);
      e.InvokeEvent();
    }
  }
}
```

Within the class `EventClass`, the event can be raised by calling the event's name, such as `AnEvent()` in the method `InvokeEvent`. When this event is called, all delegates currently listening on the event are called. The sample program attaches three delegates to this event on the instance of the class called `e`. Thus, whenever `e` raises the event, the static method `CallMe` is called three times. Note that the called method does not always have to be a static method as it is in Listing 2.4.

Listing 2.4 produces the following output:

```
I got called!
I got called!
I got called!
```

Sealed Value Types

As mentioned previously, all value types inherit from specific classes—enumerations from `System.Enum` and structures from `System.ValueType`. It is not possible to build an inheritance hierarchy with value types; that is, a value type cannot inherit from another value type. In CLR terminology, a value type is said to be *sealed*. Sealing explains why instance methods are not declared as virtual in value types, because it is not possible to subtype them and, therefore, the definitions of methods cannot be overridden.

By contrast, reference types in the CLR can optionally be declared as sealed, which prohibits subtyping of these types. An example of a reference type that is sealed in the CLR is the `String` class.

Boxed Types

For every value type, including user-defined value types, there exists a corresponding object type, known as its *boxed type*. The CLR automatically generates boxed types for user-defined value types, which means that values of any value type can be boxed and unboxed:

- *Boxing* a value type copies the data from the value into an object of its boxed type allocated on the garbage collected heap.
- *Unboxing* a value type returns a pointer to the actual data—that is, the sequence of bits—held in a boxed object. (In some programming languages, unboxing not only facilitates obtaining the pointer to the data members of a boxed object but also copies the data from the boxed object into a value of the value type on the stack.)

The fact that all value types can be converted to their corresponding object types allows all values in the type system to be treated as objects if required. This situation has the effect of unifying the two fundamentally different types in the CLR, because everything can be treated as a subtype of `Object`. This approach is somewhat similar to that created by the use of COM's `IUnknown` and CORBA's `Object` interfaces, which also act as the base interface in the IDLs. Because a box type is an object type, it may support *interface types*, thereby providing additional functionality to its unboxed representation. Object types, reference types, and interface types are described later in this chapter.

Reference Types

Reference types combine a location and a sequence of bits. The location provides identity by designating an area in memory where values can be stored *and* the type of values that can be stored there. A location is "type safe" in that only assignment-compatible types can be stored in it. (The section "Assignment Compatibility" gives an example of assignment compatibility.)

Because all reference types are allocated on the garbage collected heap and the garbage collector is free to move objects during execution, reference types are always accessed through a strongly typed reference rather than directly. As the garbage collector moves the object, the reference can be updated as part of the relocation process. As shown in Figure 2.2 on page 24, three categories of reference types exist: object types, interface types, and pointer types.

Object Types

Object types represent types that are known as classes in many languages, such as SmallTalk and Java. The built-in object types include `Object` and `String`. The CLR uses the term *object* to refer to values of an object type; the set of all exact types for all objects is known as the *object types*. Because `String` is an object type, all instances of the `String` type are therefore objects. Object types are always allocated on the garbage collected heap. Table 2.2 lists the relevant information for the CLR's built-in object types.

A number of reference types are supplied with the Base Framework. They are not considered to be built-in types because the CLR provides no inherent support for them; instead, these reference types are viewed as being under the user-defined object types that are subtypes of `Object`.

Object

All object types inherit, either directly or indirectly, from the CLR type `System.Object` class. A major facility of the `Object` class is its ability to

TABLE 2.2 CLR Built-in Reference Types: Object Types

CIL Name	Library Name	Description	CLS Support
Object	System.Object	Base class for all object types	Y
String	System.String	Unicode string	Y

enforce a singular rooted inheritance hierarchy on all types in the CLR. Although you may think that this kind of inheritance does not apply to value types, value types can be treated as a subtype of Object through boxing. The libraries make extensive use of the Object type as the parameters to, and the return type of, many functions.

The Object class provides a number of methods that can be called on all objects:

- Equals returns true if the two objects are equal. Subtypes may override this method to provide either identity or equality comparison. Equals is available as both a virtual method that takes a single parameter consisting of the other object with which this object is being compared and a static method that, naturally, requires two parameters.
- Finalize is invoked by the garbage collector before an object's memory is reclaimed. Because the garbage collector is not guaranteed to run during a program's execution, this method may not be invoked.[5] In C#, if a developer defines a *destructor,* then it is renamed to be the type's Finalize method.
- GetHashCode returns a hash code for an object. It can be used when inserting objects into containers that require a key to be associated with each such object.
- GetType returns the type object for this object. This method gives access to the metadata for the object. A static method on the Type class

---

[5] The CLR provides no facility that guarantees the invocation of a destructor method. The IDisposable interface contains a method called Dispose. By convention, clients call this method when they finish with an object.

can be used for the same purpose; it does not require that an instance of the class be created first.

- `MemberwiseClone` returns a shallow copy of the object. This method has protected accessibility and, therefore, can be accessed only by subtypes. It cannot be overridden. If a deep copy is required, then the developer should implement the `ICloneable` interface.

- `ReferenceEquals` returns true if both object references passed to the method refer to the same object. It also returns true if both references are null.

- `ToString` returns a string that *represents* the object. As defined in `Object`, this method returns the name of the type of the object—that is, its exact type. Subtypes may override this method to have the return string represent the object as the developer sees fit. For example, the `String` class returns the value of the string and not the name of the `String` class.

Most of the methods defined on `Object` are public. `MemberwiseClone` and `Finalize`, however, have protected access; that is, only subtypes can access them. The following program output shows the assembly qualified name and the publicly available methods on the `Object` class. (Assemblies are covered in Chapter 5.)

```
System.Object, mscorlib, Version=1.0.2411.0,
 Culture=neutral, PublicKeyToken=b77a5c561934e089
Int32 GetHashCode()
Boolean Equals(System.Object)
System.String ToString()
Boolean Equals(System.Object, System.Object)
Boolean ReferenceEquals(System.Object, System.Object)
System.Type GetType()
Void .ctor()
```

A simple program using the metadata facilities of the CLR generated this output. Chapter 3 describes how to build this approximately 10-line program and explains the significance of the assembly qualified name shown as the first line of output. In brief, the program retrieves the Object class's Type object and then displays its public method's prototypes. The two protected methods are not shown. The preceding output also shows the use of built-in types, such as Boolean, Int32, and String.

Listing 2.5 demonstrates how many classes override the ToString method. The default behavior is to print a string representing the type of the object on which it is invoked—that is the action of the Object class. String and Int32 have both overridden this behavior to provide a more intuitive string representation of the object on which it is invoked.

Listing 2.5 *Overriding the* ToString *method*

```
using System;

namespace Override
{
  class Sample
  {
    static void Print(params Object[] objects)
    {
      foreach(Object o in objects)
        Console.WriteLine(o.ToString());
    }
    static void Main(string[] args)
    {
      Object o = new Object();
      String s = "Mark";
      int i = 42;
      Print(o, s, i);
    }
  }
}
```

One interesting feature of Listing 2.5 relates to the use of the C# params keyword. You can call the Print method with any number of arguments, and these arguments will be passed to the method in an array that holds Object references. Within the Print method, each member of the array will have its virtual ToString method called, so the correct method for each argument will be invoked. You may wonder how the value i of type int is passed given that it is a value type: It is boxed.

Listing 2.5 produces the following output:

```
System.Object
Mark
42
```

The constructor for `Object` *should* be called whenever an object is created; it *must* be called if the goal is to produce verifiable code. Chapter 4 discusses verifiable code in more detail, but for now consider "verifiable code" to mean proven type-safe code. As a simplification of the rules, compiler writers must ensure that a call to the constructor for the base class occurs during construction of all derived classes. This call can occur at any time during the construction of derived classes; it need not be the first instruction executed in the constructor of subtype. Developers should be aware that construction of the base class may not have occurred when a user-defined constructor starts running.

String

Like `Object`, `String` is a built-in type in the CLR. This class is sealed, which means that no type can be subtyped from it. The sealed nature of `String` allows for much greater optimization by the execution system if it is known that subtypes cannot be passed where a type, such as `String`, is expected. Strings are also immutable, such that calling any method to modify a string creates a new string. The fact that the `String` class is sealed and immutable allows for an extremely efficient implementation. Developers can also use a `StringBuilder` class if creating temporary strings while doing string manipulations with the `String` class proves too expensive.

The `String` class contains far too many members to describe them all here. A nonexhaustive list of the general functionality of the class would include the following abilities:

- Constructors: No default constructor exists. Constructors take arguments of type `char`, arrays of `char`, and pointers to `char`.
- Compare: These methods take two strings (or parts thereof) and compare them. The comparison can be case sensitive or case insensitive.

- Concatenate: This method returns a new string that represents the concatenation of a number of individual strings.
- Conversion: This method returns a new string in which the characters within the string have been converted to uppercase or lowercase.
- Format: This method takes a format string and an array of objects and returns a new string. It replaces each placeholder in the format string with the string representation of an object in the array.
- IndexOf: This method returns an integer index that identifies the location of a character or string within another string.
- Insert: This method returns a new string representing the insertion of one string into another string.
- Length: This property represents the length of the string. It supplies only a `get` method—that is, it is a read-only value.
- Pad and Trim Strings: These methods return a new string that represents the original string with padding characters inserted or removed, respectively.

Listing 2.6 is a simple example demonstrating the use of the built-in `String` reference type in C#. This program creates objects of type `string`, converts them between uppercase and lowercase, concatenates them, and then checks for a substring within a string.

Listing 2.6 *Using the* `String` *reference type*

```
using System;

namespace StringSample
{

  class Sample
  {
    static void Main(string[] args)
    {
      String s = "Mark";
      Console.WriteLine("Length is: " + s.Length);
      Console.WriteLine(s.ToLower());
      String[] strings = {"Damien", "Mark", "Brad"};
      String authors = String.Concat(strings);
      if(authors.IndexOf(s) > 0)
```

continues

```
            Console.WriteLine("{0} is an author", s.ToUpper());
        }
    }
}
```

Main begins by defining an instance of the String class called s with the contents "Mark". Normally, you allocate an instance of a reference type by using a language construct such as new. In the CLR and in many languages, such as C#, a string is a special case because it is a built-in type and, therefore, can be allocated using special instructions or different syntax. The CLR has an instruction for just this purpose. Likewise, as shown in Listing 2.6, C# has a special syntax for allocating a string.

The next line accesses a property of the string object called Length, returns an integer representing the number of characters in a string. You have already seen how a property is defined, but now you may wonder how an integer is "added" to a string. Of course, the answer is that it is not. While an int is a value type, a reference type is always created for all value types, known as the boxed type. In this case, code is inserted to box the integer value and place it on the garbage collected heap.

How, then, are a string and a boxed integer concatenated? Again, the answer is that they are not. One of the overloaded concatenation methods on the String class takes parameters of type Object. The compiler calls this method, and the resulting string is added to the first string; this value is then written to the screen. Developers need to be aware that compilers may silently insert a number of calls to provide conversion and coercion methods, such as boxing. The exact behavior is a function of the particular compiler; some compilers will insert these method calls, whereas others will require the developer to call them explicitly. Of course, Listing 2.6 could be rewritten to avoid boxing altogether; again, this choice requires the developer to know and understand the code generated by the particular compiler.

Finally, the program in Listing 2.6 makes a single string containing all the names of the authors of this book and then searches to see whether "Mark" is one of the authors.

Your attention is also drawn to the generation of temporary string objects in Listing 2.6. Note that calls to methods such as ToLower and

`ToUpper` generate temporary string objects that may produce performance problems.

Listing 2.6 produces the following output:

```
Length is: 4
mark
MARK is an author
```

Interface Types

Programming with interface types is an extremely powerful concept; in fact, with COM and CORBA, interface-based programming is the predominate paradigm. Object-oriented programmers will already be familiar with the concept of substituting a derived type for a base type. Sometimes, however, two classes are not related by implementation inheritance but do share a common contract. For example, many classes contain methods to save their state to and from persistent storage. For this purpose, classes not related by inheritance may support common interfaces, allowing programmers to code for their shared behavior based on their shared interface type rather than their exact types.

An *interface type* is a partial specification of a type. This contract binds implementers to providing implementations of the members contained in the interface. Object types may support many interface types, and many different object types would normally support an interface type. By definition, an interface type can never be an object type or an exact type. Interface types may extend other interface types; that is, an interface type can inherit from other interface types.

An interface type may define the following:

- Methods (static and instance)
- Fields (static)
- Properties
- Events

Of course, properties and events equate to methods. By definition, all instance methods in an interface are public, abstract, and virtual. This is the opposite of the situation with value types, where user-defined methods on the value type, as opposed to the boxed type, are always nonvirtual because no inheritance from value types is possible. The CLR does not include any built-in interface types, although the Base Framework provides a number of interface types.

Listing 2.7 demonstrates the use of the IEnumerator interface supported by array objects. The array of String objects allows clients to enumerate over the array by requesting an IEnumerator interface. (Developers never need to define an array class even for their own types, because the CLR generates one automatically if needed. The automatically defined array type implements the IEnumerator interface and provides the GetLength method so they can be used in exactly the same manner as arrays for built-in types.) The IEnumerator interface defines three methods:

- Current returns the current object.
- MoveNext moves the enumerator on to the next object.
- Reset resets the enumerator to its initial position.

Listing 2.7 *Using the* IEnumerator *interface*

```
using System;
using System.Collections;

namespace StringArray
{
  class EntryPoint
  {
    static void Main(string[] args)
    {
      String [] names = {"Brad", "Damien", "Mark"};
      IEnumerator i = names.GetEnumerator();
      while(i.MoveNext())
        Console.WriteLine(i.Current);
    }
  }
}
```

Of course, you could have written the while loop in Listing 2.7 as a foreach loop, but the former technique seems slightly more explicit for demonstration purposes. The program produces the following output:

```
Brad
Damien
Mark
```

Array objects support many other useful methods, such as `Clear`, `GetLength`, and `Sort`. The `Sort` method makes use of another Base Framework interface, `IComparable`, which must be implemented by the type that the array holds. Array objects also provide support for synchronization, an ability that is provided by methods such as `IsSynchronized` and `SyncRoot`.

Pointer Types

Pointer types provide a means of specifying the location of either code or a value. The CLR supports three pointer types:

- Unmanaged function pointers refer to code and are similar to function pointers in C++.[6]
- Managed Pointers are known to the garbage collector and are updated if they refer to an item that is moved on the garbage collected heap.
- Unmanaged pointers are similar to unmanaged function pointers but refer to values. Unmanaged pointers are not CLS compliant, and many languages do not even expose syntax to define or use them. By comparison, managed pointers can point at items located on the garbage collected heap and are CLS compliant.

The semantics for these pointer types vary greatly. For example, pointers to managed objects must be registered with the garbage collector so that as objects are moved on the heap, the pointers can be updated. Pointers to local variables have different lifetime issues. When using unmanaged pointers, objects will often need to be *pinned* in memory so that the garbage collector will not move the object while it is possible to access the object via an unmanaged pointer.

This book will not cover pointer types in detail for two reasons. First, a greater understanding of the .NET platform architecture is needed to

------

[6] Delegates, discussed later, provide an alternative to unmanaged function pointers.

understand the semantic issues relating to pointers. Second, most programming languages will abstract the existence of pointers to such a degree that they will be invisible to programmers.

Example: User-Defined Object Type

User-defined object types are the types that most developers will use to expose their services. These types correspond most closely to classes in many object-oriented languages. As discussed earlier, classes can define different types of members. However, at the fundamental level, only two types of members exist: methods and fields. Abstractions layered over methods include the notions of properties and events. Methods are also specialized to produce constructors, which can be either instance or class constructors (.ctor and .cctor). Once again, on a basic level these constructs are simply methods with added semantics and additional runtime support. This runtime support includes the notion that the class constructor will begin executing before any of its members is used for the first time.[7]

Let's look an example of how to create a user-defined object type. To make the example more complete, Listing 2.8 creates an object type called Point that implements two interfaces—one interface with an event, and one interface with properties—as well as the user-defined object type. After creating the Point type, the program attaches a listener to the event, writes the properties via interface references that fire the event, and then accesses the properties.

---

[7] The language designer chooses which CLR abstractions are exposed to developers and how they are exposed. For example, some languages that target the CLR provide little support for object-oriented programming. Instead, they just provide global functions that communicate by passing data as parameters. These languages may still participate in the CLR, but their global functions will normally be mapped to static functions on a "well-known" class, possibly one with a name like Global. Although the way these languages expose their functionality in the CLR is very interesting, the many variations are beyond the scope of this book. The appendices do describe how many languages map their semantics to the CLR.

Listing 2.8 Creating a user-defined object type

```
using System;

namespace ObjectType
{
  public delegate void ADelegate();
  public interface IChanged
  {
    event ADelegate AnEvent;
  }
  public interface IPoint
  {

    int X {get; set;}
    int Y {get; set;}
  }
  class Point: IPoint, IChanged
  {
    private int xPosition, yPosition;
    public event ADelegate AnEvent;
    public int X
    {
      get {return xPosition;}
      set {xPosition = value; AnEvent();}
    }
    public int Y
    {
      get {return yPosition;}
      set {yPosition = value; AnEvent();}
    }
  }
  class EntryPoint
  {
    static void CallMe()
    {
      Console.WriteLine("I got called!");
    }
    static void Main(string[] args)
    {
      Point p = new Point();
      IChanged ic = p;
      IPoint ip = p;
      ic.AnEvent += new ADelegate(CallMe);
      ip.X = 42;
```

continues

```
        ip.Y = 42;
        Console.WriteLine("X: {0} Y: {1} ", p.X, p.Y);
    }
  }
}
```

The delegate is declared first in the program. It serves as a delegate for functions that accept no arguments and return nothing (void). The returning of void is common with many delegates.

The first interface, which is called IChanged, contains a single event that is of the same type as the delegate. The second interface, which is called IPoint, provides two properties that allow access to two properties known as X and Y. Both properties have get and set methods.

Next comes the definition of the class Point. It would be fair to say that a Point could just as easily be a value type as an object type. Here, however, it is used as a simple abstraction. The class Point inherits from Object, although this relationship is not stated explicitly, and from the two interfaces just defined, IChanged and IPoint. By inheriting from IPoint, for example, the class Point agrees to implement the four abstract methods required for the two properties. The set methods fire the event whenever they are called.

The class EntryPoint provides the entry point for the Main program. This class also provides a static function called CallMe, which matches the prototype of the delegate. The program registers that this method is to be called whenever the event is fired on the Point object named p.

A number of fine points can be emphasized about the program in Listing 2.8. First, only one object is ever created through the activity of the new operator on the first line of Main. The IChanged and IPoint interface types are merely references used to access this Point object. As Point is the exact type for the object, all methods available on the Point class, including the methods in both interfaces, are available through a reference of type Point—in this case, p. This relationship is demonstrated by invoking the methods X and Y in the WriteLine method calls. The interface types can call only the methods in their own interface, even though the object has more functionality.

Listing 2.8 produces the following output:

```
I got called!
I got called!
X: 42 Y: 42
```

Example: Use of Interfaces on Value Types

When considering the use of interfaces on a value type, often the first question asked is, "Can value types support interfaces?" The simple answer is yes; you can call the methods defined in the interface directly on the value type without incurring any overhead. The situation is different, however, if you call the methods through an interface reference. An interface references objects allocated on the garbage collected heap, and value types are normally allocated on the stack—so how does this work? The answer is a familiar one: boxing.

Listing 2.9 demonstrates the use of events and properties in a user-defined interface, `IPoint`. This interface is implemented by a value type, `Point`, and an object type, `EntryPoint`, provides the entry point method. Similar to Listing 2.8, this program creates a value of the value type and then accesses its properties.

Listing 2.9 *Using events and properties in a user-defined interface*

```
using System;

namespace InterfaceSample
{
  public delegate void Changed();

  interface IPoint
  {
    int X
    { get; set;}
    int Y
    { get; set;}
  }

  struct Point: IPoint
  {
```

continues

```
private int xValue, yValue;
public int X
{
  get { return xValue; }
  set { xValue = value; }
}
public int Y
{
  get { return yValue; }
  set { yValue = value; }
}
}
public class EntryPoint
{
  public static int Main()
  {
    Point p = new Point();
    p.X = p.Y = 42;
    IPoint ip = p;
    Console.WriteLine("X: {0}, Y: {1}",
                      ip.X, ip.Y);
    return 0;
  }
}
}
```

Listing 2.9 produces the following output:

```
X: 42, Y: 42
```

The interesting point regarding this program is the use of the interface ip to access the properties of p when calling the WriteLine method. As Listing 2.9 is written, the interface ip can only refer to reference types and p is a value type, so p is silently boxed and ip references the boxed object, which contains a copy of p.

Assignment Compatibility

As the concepts of object types and interface types have now been explained, albeit very simply, the question of assignment compatibility can be addressed. A simple definition of assignment compatibility for reference types is that a location of type T, where T may be either an object type or an interface type, can refer to any object:

- With an exact type of T, or
- That is a subtype of T, or
- That supports the interface T.

Listing 2.10 demonstrates aspects of assignment compatibility. The program starts by creating values of two different types and two interface references:

- A value of type System.Int32 called i
- An Object reference called o
- A String reference called s
- An IComparable reference called ic

Listing 2.10 *Assignment compatibility*

```
using System;

namespace AssignmentCompatibility
{
  class Sample
  {
    static void Main(string[] args)
    {
      System.Int32 i = 42;
      Object o;
      String s = "Brad";
      IComparable ic;

      // OK
      o = s;
      ic = s;

      // OK - box and assign
      o = i;
      ic = i;

      // compiler error
      i = s;
```

continues

```
                    // runtime error
                    s = (String) o;
                }
            }
        }
```

The assignments of s to o and of s to ic are all compatible, so they compile and execute without any errors. The next two assignments are also compatible, so they, too, compile and execute without any errors. The surprise may come with the fact that boxing of i is needed, which the C# compiler performs silently in both cases. Other languages might require explicit code to handle this boxing.

The assignment of s to i is not compatible, so it generates a compile-time error. Unfortunately, downcasting (narrowing) is inherently problematic, making the last assignment difficult to test for compatibility until runtime. The JIT compiler will insert code to check the type of the object referenced by o before performing the assignment. In this case, o refers to a boxed integer type at the time of assignment, so the cast fails and an exception is thrown. Of course, if o did refer to a string, then the cast would execute without throwing an exception.

Assignment compatibility is a crucial mechanism that helps ensure type safety in the CLR. The execution system can validate assignment to a reference to verify that the assignment ensures that the type and the reference are compatible.

Nested Types

You can define types inside of other types, known as nested types. Nested types have access to the members of their enclosing types as well as to the members of their enclosing type's base class (subject to the normal accessibility conditions, as will be discussed shortly). Listing 2.11 demonstrates their use. This program defines three different object types: Outer, Middle, and Inner. Inner contains the entry point and accesses the enumerations defined in its enclosing types.

Listing 2.11 *Nested types*

```
using System;

namespace NestedTypes
{
  class Outer
  {
    private enum Day {Sunday, Monday, Tuesday,
        Wednesday, Thursday, Friday, Saturday};
    class Middle
    {
      private enum Month {January = 1, February,
            March, April, May, June, July, August,
            September, October, November, December};
      class Inner
      {
        static void Main(string[] args)
        {
          Day d = Day.Sunday;
          Month m = Month.September;
          Console.WriteLine(
            "Father's day is the first "
            + d + " in " + m);
        }
      }
    }
  }
}
```

Running this program generates the following output:[8]

```
Father's day is the first Sunday in September
```

Visibility

Visibility refers to whether a type is available outside its assembly. If a type is exported from its assembly, then it is visible to types in other assemblies. Object and String are examples of two types that are exported from their

---

8   Father's Day is the first Sunday in September in Australia.

assemblies. Visibility does not affect members of types, whereas accessibility (discussed next) can be used to limit access to members.

Accessibility

Members of a type can have different *accessibility* levels. Accessibility levels define which other types can access the members of a type. In many situations, it is desirable to limit the accessibility of a member. If one member implements some functionality for a type, such as data validation of field values, then it may be useful to all other members of that type but may be considered an implementation detail of the type. Developers can limit the accessibility of the member so as to prevent clients from using it. This practice helps to localize the effects of change. For example, if the signature of such a privately scoped member changes, then the change will not affect any of the clients of this type. Thus the effect of the change remains limited to this type's definition. Conversely, accessibility may be restricted to a higher level than private but less than public. This choice could, for example, widen the effect of a change, possibly to the type's assembly, but keep it a much smaller effect than changing a publicly available member.

The CLR supports a number of accessibility levels:

- Public: available to all types
- Assembly: available to all types within this assembly
- Family: available in the type's definition and all of its subtypes
- Family or Assembly: available to types that qualify as either Family or Assembly
- Family and Assembly: available to types that qualify as both Family and Assembly
- Compiler-controlled: available to types within a single translation unit
- Private: available only in the type's definition

All members in an interface are public. Types are permitted to widen accessibility. That is, a subtype may make a member more visible, as sometimes occurs with inherited virtual methods, for example. This approach ensures that the method is at least equally visible in the subtype. Use of this widening facility, although legal, is considered problematic at best and should be avoided.

Summary

This chapter provided a detailed view of the type system of the Common Language Runtime. The CLR supports an object-oriented programming style, which is reflected in its type system. The CTS contains two basic types: value types and reference types. Value types are similar to primitive types in many programming languages. Reference types are analogous to classes in many object-oriented languages; they are further divided into object, interface, and pointer types.

All object types inherit from `Object`. Object types may introduce new methods, these methods can be either static or instance; instance methods can also be virtually dispatched. Methods may, of course, follow the rules for properties or events, thereby gaining additional support from the CLR or other tools.

Methods may be overloaded. In other words, a class can have many methods with the same name as long as the types of the methods' parameters are different. When a program calls a method with multiple names, the choice of which method is called depends on the argument list and its correspondence with the available methods' signatures.

Virtual methods may also be overridden. In such a case, subtypes supply methods with exactly the same signatures as the base classes. The compiler may issue instructions to do runtime dispatching of the method call. The method selection is then left until runtime, when the exact type of the object on which the method acts is known.

3.

The Metadata System

C HAPTER 2 DESCRIBED the different types that the CLR supports and demonstrated how developers can define new types as well as use types defined in other languages. The essential facility that enables such type sharing between compilers is the metadata system, which is the focus of this chapter.

Metadata is not a new concept. Language-specific metadata facilities have existed for a number of years; a header file in C/C++, for example, is a metadata facility. A C++ header file may contain the declaration of a new type, such as a structure or class. By including such a header file in their own source files, other developers may program against the new type. A header file is a severely limited metadata facility, for several reasons. First, a C/C++ header file is, of course, language-specific. Second, it does not contain the entire definition of the type; at some point, a linker must resolve the abstract declaration of the type with its implementation, which is usually contained in an object file or a dynamically linked library (DLL). Multilanguage component architectures require much more sophisticated metadata services than these—for example, types must be made available across language boundaries. Previously, this extra sophistication required extra complexity. Today, the CLR provides these facilities with little impact on developers.

The CLR also extends the use of metadata to provide not only information about types but also information about assemblies, the unit of deployment in the .NET Framework. As a consequence, both assemblies and types are self-describing. The execution engine uses this information to ensure correct runtime execution of code—for example, making sure that version requirements are honored.

This chapter begins with a brief description of how other component architectures implement their metadata facilities. Next, it considers how developers may interact with the metadata system. Most developers will not need to know how metadata is created; rather, compilers will automatically generate and persist this information for them. For this reason, the discussion initially concentrates on how developers use and manipulate the metadata system, although an overview of metadata creation appears later in the chapter. This chapter also describes how developers can create their own metadata annotations using custom attributes. It explains how metadata describes assemblies, why and what metadata is generated, and how that metadata is used. In addition, it looks at the meta-programming facilities offered by the .NET Framework. Finally, the chapter provides an overview of how .NET metadata can be translated for use with COM, and vice versa.

Metadata Issues

The metadata system is the essential link that bridges the gap between the type system and the execution engine. Currently, three significant issues exist in regard to the metadata facilities in many software architectures:

- Traditionally, metadata has been found in language-specific files, but providing interoperability between such files across language boundaries is almost impossible. Also, compilers routinely remove most of this information when the source files are compiled. As a consequence, executable files often have little or no metadata about their types available at runtime.
- In many systems, a component's metadata is often not stored with the component. Rather, metadata may be stored in auxiliary files, such as

Interface Definition Language (IDL) files, interface repositories, implementation repositories, type libraries, or the Registry. This situation leads to versioning and inconsistency problems between components and their metadata descriptions.

- Metadata facilities remain primitive. Most allow developers to specify the syntax of an interface but not its semantics. Proof of this problem lies with the number of IDL "extensions" that can be found in many systems, such as TINAC's Object Definition Language (ODL), an extension to CORBA's IDL for use in the telecommunications domain.

It is important that developers understand that CLR compilers describe the types they produce with metadata, for two major reasons:

- Metadata permits types defined in one language to be used in another language. Metadata and the common type system are the facilities that help ensure language interoperability in the CLR.
- The execution engine requires metadata to manage objects. Managing objects includes services such as the layout of objects in memory, memory management, and security.

Although metadata is stored in files in a binary format, developers do not need to understand or program against its binary layout; instead, a number of types and methods are available for reading and writing metadata. These facilities represent a higher level of abstraction that make the metadata facilities more intuitive to developers and provide a layer of insulation against the underlying format.

Saving Metadata About Types: IDL Files

The need to preserve metadata about types has been known for a number of years, and a variety of component architectures already provide solutions to this problem. COM and CORBA, for example, allow developers to describe their components' interfaces in an IDL. IDL files serve as the public interface to the components they describe. The IDL syntax of both COM and CORBA is based on C/C++. The compilation of IDL files produces binary descriptions of the metadata described by the IDL files. In CORBA, this description is known as an interface repository; in COM, it is known as a type library.

A number of limitations arise with the use of IDL files.

- IDL files remain separate from the source files of a type, which may lead to inconsistencies. For example, if an IDL file states that a method takes no parameters but the definition of the method asks for a parameter, then the IDL and source files must be synchronized before clients can successfully program against the type's interface.
- IDL files can be compiled before a type's definition has even appeared, so the binary files produced by the IDL compilers are kept separate from the type's implementation files. Thus a developer might have one file without the other; that is, a developer might have a type library for a type without having the definition of the type available on the system, and vice versa. COM provides one solution to this problem: Type libraries can be embedded in executable files as a resource, which ties the type library to its implementation.

Another approach is to have the language compiler generate the type's metadata directly when compiling the source files, rather than during a separate IDL compilation. In this case, the language compiler can also embed the metadata directly into the implementation file for the type, which is similar to how a type library can be embedded as a resource. This method does not permit a type's metadata to exist with the definition of the type, and vice versa. It also prohibits incompatibility between a type and its metadata description. The CLR uses this technique to manage metadata.

Reflection: Inspection of a Type's Metadata

The act of inspecting a type's metadata at runtime is called *reflection*, and it is a fundamental facility of the CLR. In fact, reflection is so fundamental that the type system's base class, `System.Object`, has a method `GetType` specifically designed to facilitate this inspection. The `GetType` method returns an object of type `Type`—a slightly unfortunate choice, as this overloading of the word *type* can sometimes prove confusing. To distinguish between the two usages, in this chapter the term *type*, with a lowercase *t*, normally means any type in the CLR, such as the `Object` or `String` type. The term `Type`, with a capital *T*, refers to the `Type` class provided by the Base Framework. The `GetType()` method returns a singleton `Type` object for the type on which it was invoked. The `Type` class provides a means for developers to access the metadata of the type it describes.

Reflection Classes

A number of classes are used in the .NET Framework's reflection facilities. This section describes the architecture of these classes and demonstrates how developers use these classes. Note that a full and complete description of all of the functionality of the reflection classes is beyond the scope of this book. Instead, we provide a generalized overview of the structure of these classes; users should then be able to extrapolate the general usage.

The `MemberInfo` and `Type` classes are the foundation for the reflection facilities. The `Type` class provides several methods and properties to permit inspection of a type's metadata. It inherits from the `MemberInfo` class, which in turn inherits from `Object`. Figure 3.1 shows the relationship between fundamental classes in the reflection hierarchy.

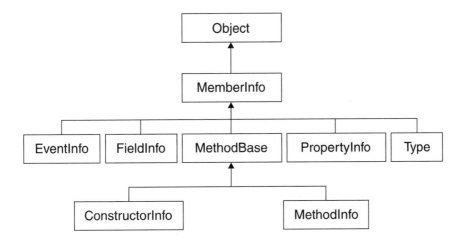

Figure 3.1 *The reflection class hierarchy*

MemberInfo *Class*

The MemberInfo class serves as a base class for many of the reflection "Info" classes—that is, classes whose names end in the word "Info" and are extensively used in the CLR's reflection services.[1] The MemberInfo class is abstract. Subtypes of MemberInfo include the following:

- EventInfo, a class whose objects represent events of a type. Example properties and methods of this type include Name, GetAddMethod, GetRaiseMethod, and GetRemoveMethod.
- FieldInfo, a class whose objects represent fields of the type. Example properties and methods of this type include Name, FieldType, and GetValue.
- MethodBase, a base class for representing methods on a class, such as constructors and methods. Example properties and methods include IsConstructor, GetParameters, and Invoke.
- PropertyInfo, a class whose objects represent properties of the type. Example properties and methods of this type include Name, CanRead, CanWrite, and GetAccessors.
- Type, a class whose objects represent types in the CLR. The Type class is discussed shortly.

MethodBase serves as the abstract base class for the following classes:

- ConstructorInfo, a class whose objects represent constructors available on the type. A ConstructorInfo object exists for each constructor that a class has. Example members of this type include ConstructorName, which is always .ctor; TypeConstructorName, which is always .cctor; and Invoke.
- MethodInfo, a class whose objects represent methods of the type. Example properties and methods of this type include IsAbstract, ReturnType, and GetBaseDefinition, which is used to access the overridden method definition from the class's base type.

---

1 The names of some other classes in the Base Framework also end in "Info"—for example, CultureInfo. The discussion here focuses specifically on those classes related to the reflection services.

One other class is also used by many of the reflection "Info" classes:

- ParameterInfo, a class whose objects represent parameters of a method of the type. This class inherits from Object. Example properties and methods of this type include IsIn, IsOut, and IsDefined.

This common base, MemberInfo, provides a number of methods that can be invoked on all "Info" classes as well as an abstract base class that is used as the return type of many methods. An example of the useful functionality specified by this class is the GetCustomAttributes method of the MemberInfo class. All members of a type can be annotated with custom attributes, which consist of user-defined metadata annotations. (Custom attributes are explained in detail later in this chapter.) The GetCustomAttributes method ensures that developers can access the custom attributes on any subclass of MemberInfo regardless of the subtype with which a developer is dealing. (The list of custom attributes on a member may, of course, be empty.)

Instances of most classes derived from MemberInfo are provided as singletons. For example, when a Type object is required for a type, it will be created once and that same object will be reused whenever a Type object is required for that specific type. The same situation applies to many of the other reflection classes. Thus, if an EventInfo object is created for an event on a certain type, then that object is reused whenever information is needed for that event on the particular type.

Another example of the usefulness of the MemberInfo class as a base class involves the GetMembers method defined on the Type type. It returns an array of MemberInfo objects, so that the array can hold instances of any derived class. As a consequence, a single array can hold Info classes for properties, events, methods, and fields.

Type Class

Like MemberInfo, the Type class is an abstract class. Like the String class described in Chapter 2, it provides a number of methods—far too many to cover individually here. To simplify the description of the functionality offered by the members of the Type class, the methods and properties can be divided into groups based on the services they provide. From a very general viewpoint, the methods could be categorized as follows:

- Get methods: Methods that start with the word Get and return information about one aspect of the type
- Is methods or properties: Methods or properties that return a Boolean value indicating whether the type satisfies a condition
- Properties: Properties of the type, such as AssemblyQualifiedName
- Static fields: Fields holding information required to process the type

Get Methods A number of methods on the Type class are prefixed with the word Get. As this naming convention suggests, these methods return information about an aspect of the type. For example, the GetMethod method returns a MethodInfo object that describes a method defined by the type. GetMethod requires a parameter of type String that supplies the name of the method needed. By comparison, the GetMethods method does not require a string to designate which method is needed; it returns an array of MethodInfo objects that represents all of the publicly available methods for a type.

Is Methods and Properties A number of properties on the Type class return a Boolean value that describes a single aspect of the type. For example, the IsAutoLay property returns true or false to indicate whether the execution engine automatically lays out the type at runtime. Sometimes symmetrically related properties are available. For example, the IsExplicitLayout, IsLayoutSequential, and IsAutoLayout properties indicate whether the developer has specified a specific memory layout for the class. One and only one of these properties can be true for any type.

Properties Each type has a number of properties, one variety of which is the Is properties described previously. Other properties include the required properties AssemblyQualifiedName, BaseType, and FullName. Every type must have these properties, which have only a single value.

Static Fields   Static fields represent values that are shared by all types in the CLR. For example, the EmptyTypes field represents an empty array of Type objects.

For a complete list of the members of the Type class, consult the current definition of Type in the SDK. Table 3.1 briefly describes the functionality of the Type class's methods.

Example: Using Reflection

It is often much easier to understand how the classes function together by working through a simple example. The program fragment in Listing 3.1 builds on many of the concepts already discussed. The code demonstrates the use of the Type object for the Object class. This program accesses the Type object for the System.Object class. It then writes a number of the type's properties to the console as well as a string representing each member that the type has.

Listing 3.1 Use of the Type *object for the* Object *class*

```
using System;
using System.Reflection;

namespace ReflectionSample
{
  class ObjectSample
  {
    static void Main(string[] args)
    {
      Type t = Type.GetType("System.Object");
      Console.WriteLine(t.FullName);
      Console.WriteLine(t.AssemblyQualifiedName);
      Console.WriteLine("GUID: " + t.GUID);
      Console.WriteLine("IsAbstract: " + t.IsAbstract);
      Console.WriteLine("IsClass: " + t.IsClass);
      Console.WriteLine("IsInterface: " + t.IsInterface);
      Console.WriteLine("IsSealed: " + t.IsSealed);
      MemberInfo[] members = t.GetMembers();
      foreach(MemberInfo m in members)
        Console.WriteLine("\t{0}",m);
    }
  }
}
```

TABLE 3.1 Type **Class Methods**

Method Name	Description
BaseType	Returns the base type's Type object; allows dynamic discovery of a type's inheritance hierarchy
FindInterfaces	Returns an array of Type objects representing the interface types supported by the type
FindMembers	Returns an array of MemberInfo objects representing the members of the type
AssemblyQualifiedName	Returns the type's fully qualified name
GetConstructors	Returns an array of ConstructorInfo objects representing the constructors of the type
GetMethods	Returns an array of MethodInfo objects representing the public methods of the type
GetNestedTypes	Returns an array of Type objects representing the nested types of the type
IsAbstract	Returns a Boolean value indicating whether the type is abstract
IsInterface	Returns a Boolean value indicating whether the type is an interface
InvokeMember	Invokes a member of the type
IsPublic	Returns a Boolean value indicating whether the type is publicly accessible
IsSealed	Returns a Boolean value indicating whether the type is sealed
IsValueType	Returns a Boolean value indicating whether the type is a value type

You are already familiar with the Object class. The code in Listing 3.1 uses the Type class's static GetType method to return a reference to the singleton Type object for the Object class. As the sample programs in this book are written in C#, you could use the C# keyword typeof to access the

`Type` object for a type. The static method is used here because not all languages have a `typeof` keyword but all languages should be able to call the `GetType` method from the Framework Class Library.

Next, the program displays some properties, such as the type's full name, its assembly qualified name,[2] and its GUID. A GUID is stored with the class for interoperability with COM but is not a fundamental aspect of identifying a type in the CLR as it is in COM.

Next, the program displays some information about the type: Is it abstract? Is it a class? Is it an interface? Is it sealed?

Finally, the `GetMembers` method is called to retrieve an array of `MemberInfo`-derived classes. Each element in the array represents one member of the type. The program iterates through the array and prints out a string representation for each element.

Listing 3.1 produces the following output:

```
System.Object
System.Object, mscorlib, Version=1.0.3300.0,
Culture=neutral, PublicKeyToken=b77a5c561934e089
GUID: 81c5fe01-027c-3e1c-98d5-da9c9862aa21
IsAbstract: False
IsClass: True
IsInterface: False
IsSealed: False
        Int32 GetHashCode()
        Boolean Equals(System.Object)
        System.String ToString()
        Boolean Equals(System.Object, System.Object)
        Boolean ReferenceEquals(System.Object,
                                System.Object)
        System.Type GetType()
        Void .ctor()
```

Note that if you run the program fragment in Listing 3.1, you may get slightly different output. In particular, the version of the .NET Framework that you are using may differ from that shown here. Essentially, however,

---

[2] You may be puzzled about exactly what an assembly qualified name is and why it is so detailed. This explanation will appear later in this chapter.

the output will provide the same information. Listing 3.1 clearly demonstrates how simple the reflection facilities are. To reinforce a recurring theme, we do not know in which language `Object` was written, but this fact is of no consequence. You could also write the sample program in any CLR language and retrieve and display the same information.

Listing 3.2 extends Listing 3.1 by displaying more metadata, but this time about the `String` class. This code reveals its constructors and the name of the parameters.

Listing 3.2 *Use of the* `Type` *object for the* `String` *class*

```
using System;
using System.Reflection;

namespace StringSampleExtended
{
  class Sample
  {
    static void Main(string[] args)
    {
      Type t = Type.GetType("System.String");
      Console.WriteLine(t.FullName);
      Console.WriteLine(t.AssemblyQualifiedName);
      Console.WriteLine("GUID: " + t.GUID);
      Console.WriteLine("IsAbstract: " + t.IsAbstract);
      Console.WriteLine("IsClass: " + t.IsClass);
      Console.WriteLine("IsInterface: " + t.IsInterface);
      Console.WriteLine("IsSealed: " + t.IsSealed);
      ConstructorInfo[] constructorArray =
                     t.GetConstructors();
      Console.WriteLine("Constructors: " +
                     constructorArray.Length);
      foreach(ConstructorInfo c in constructorArray)
      {
        Console.WriteLine("\t{0}", c);
        ParameterInfo[] parameterArray = c.GetParameters();
        foreach(ParameterInfo p in parameterArray )
          Console.WriteLine("\t\t{0}", p.Name);
      }
    }
  }
}
```

The basic structure of Listing 3.2 is the same as that for Listing 3.1, the example using the `Object` class. The first really different line of code is the one that uses the `String`'s `Type` object to retrieve an array of `ConstructorInfo` objects. The number of constructors, represented by the length of the array, is written to the console. Next, the program loops through the array of `ConstructorInfo` objects using the C# `foreach` looping construct. The first line inside the loop implicitly uses the `ToString` method on each `ConstructorInfo` object to output a string representing itself on the console. Then, for every constructor, the program retrieves an array of `ParameterInfo` objects. It uses the `ParameterInfo` object's `Name` property to display its name.

Listing 3.2 produces the following output:

```
System.String
System.String, mscorlib, Version=1.0.3300.0,
Culture=neutral, PublicKeyToken=b77a5c561934e089
GUID: 296afbff-1b0b-3ff5-9d6c-4e7e599f8b57
IsAbstract: False
IsClass: True
IsInterface: False
IsSealed: True
Constructors: 8
        Void .ctor(Char*)
                value
        Void .ctor(Char*, Int32, Int32)
                value
                startIndex
                length
        Void .ctor(SByte*)
                value
        Void .ctor(SByte*, Int32, Int32)
                value
                startIndex
                length
        Void .ctor(SByte*, Int32, Int32,
                System.Text.Encoding)
                value
                startIndex
                length
                enc
```

continues

```
Void .ctor(Char[], Int32, Int32)
        value
        startIndex
        length
Void .ctor(Char[])
        value
Void .ctor(Char, Int32)
        c
        count
```

Note that String resides in the same assembly as Object—namely, mscorlib—and that String is a sealed class—that is, you cannot create subtypes of String. All instance constructors share the same name, .ctor. Although the output from Listing 3.2 does not include one, the single class constructor is called .cctor. A type can have only one constructor because the constructor for the class is automatically called at runtime and no provision has been made for developers to supply an argument list to that call. As a consequence, you cannot overload the class constructor signature.

Listings 3.1 and 3.2 demonstrate only a fraction of the functionality available with the reflection facilities for ascertaining metadata on a type.

Example: Use of Type as an Abstract Type

If, as mentioned previously, Type is an abstract type, then exactly what type of object is returned when you invoke the GetType method? The simple answer is found by invoking the GetType method on the Type object returned by GetType. Listing 3.3 does exactly that for the String's Type object.

Listing 3.3 Invoking the GetType method on the Type object returned by GetType

```
using System;

namespace GetTypeGetType
{
  class Sample
  {
    static void Main(string[] args)
    {
      Type t = Type.GetType("System.String");
```

```
        t = t.GetType();.
        Console.WriteLine(t.FullName);
        Console.WriteLine(t.AssemblyQualifiedName);
        Console.WriteLine("Base Type: " + t.BaseType);
        Console.WriteLine("Attributes: " + t.Attributes);
        Console.WriteLine("Module: " + t.Module);
    }
  }
}
```

Listing 3.3 produces the following output:

```
System.RuntimeType
System.RuntimeType, mscorlib, Version=1.0.3300.0,
Culture=neutral, PublicKeyToken=b77a5c561934e089
Base Type: System.Type
Attributes: AutoLayout, AnsiClass, NotPublic, Sealed,
Serializable, BeforeFieldInit
Module: CommonLanguageRuntimeLibrary
```

This output demonstrates some other aspects of the CLR, such as versioning and public keys, which are covered later in this book.

Metadata Tools and Extensions

A Tool for Reading Metadata

At this point, you are probably thinking that a generic tool for reading and displaying metadata would be a simple and easy application to write and very useful when working with CLR types. In fact, writing such a tool is great first application for familiarizing yourself with the CLR and its concepts. The SDK also supplies such a tool, called the Intermediate Language Disassembler (ILDASM); a tutorial for using ILDASM appears in the SDK as well. Although this book generally avoids using tools that hide the facilities of the CLR, ILDASM is such a wonderful aid when you are starting with the CLR that you are strongly advised to examine types with it. Invoking ILDASM on `mscorlib` and selecting the `Object` class would display the information shown in Figure 3.2.

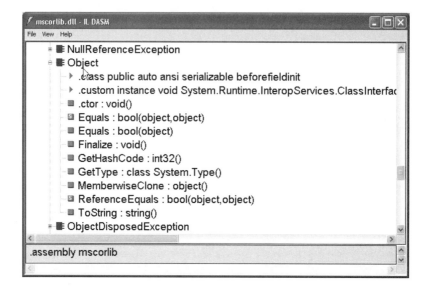

Figure 3.2 *Invoking ILDASM on* `mscorlib` *and selecting the* `Object` *class*

Metadata Extensibility

A number of extensions to IDLs provide more semantic information about the interfaces they describe. Some extensions have involved expansion of IDLs and specific IDL compilers with new keywords. This tactic adds the extra semantic information but effectively reduces the extensions to a proprietary language, making sharing of the IDL files produced in this way difficult. Other extensions have added structured comments to IDL files; these comments are ignored by standard IDL compilers but "processed" by extended compilers. Still other extensions have added specific objects or interfaces that describe or provide access to semantic information. Each approach offers certain advantages, and all of them highlight the need to add semantic information.

Custom Attributes

The CLR's metadata facility is extensible via *custom attributes*. Custom attributes provide a simple and easy means for developers to annotate a type or its members. A custom attribute is essentially a class; an instance of an attribute class is attached to a type or its members and persisted in the metadata for that type. The .NET Framework makes extensive use of custom attributes, as you will see in examples later in this chapter.

Custom attributes share some similarities with the IDL extensions described previously:

- As with structured comments, the addition of an attribute does not make the type unusable from a compiler that does not understand the attribute. In general, compilers that do not understand the custom attribute will ignore it. Naturally, this characteristic is both an advantage and a disadvantage; if the compiler does not understand the attribute, then the semantic information it conveys may be lost.
- Because attributes are classes, it is possible to access instances of these classes at runtime to retrieve information. This ability is similar to that offered by IDL extensions that use interfaces to generate information that can be retrieved at runtime. One limitation of custom attributes is the fact that they do not generate code that is automatically called by the CLR at runtime.

For example, it would be useful if you could use custom attributes to indicate that a parameter of an integral type should contain a value between two user-specified limits. Although you can use an attribute to do so, you cannot instruct the runtime environment to automatically test for this condition. Instead, programs must look for custom attributes and process them as they see fit. Currently, a number of researchers are looking at ways of using custom attributes to provide facilities such as preconditions and postconditions.

While custom attributes classes are not required to inherit from the class `System.Attribute`, it is recommended that they do so. CLS-compliant custom attributes *must* inherit from this type. As `System.Attribute` does not have to be the base class for all attributes, methods such as `GetCustomAttributes` return arrays of `Object`s rather than arrays of `Attribute`s.

Listing 3.4 demonstrates the definition and use of custom attributes. The user-defined attribute stores the name of the author of the type or member to which it is attached. After the initial `using` directives, we see the use of an attribute, `AttributeUsage`. It describes the user-defined attribute class that follows. `AttributeUsage` states that the following attribute class can be applied to all possible targets, including types and members; that multiple instances of this attribute can be applied to a target; and that subtypes and methods inherit these custom attributes.

Listing 3.4 *Using custom attributes*

```
using System;
using System.Reflection;

[AttributeUsage(AttributeTargets.All,
    AllowMultiple = true,
    Inherited = true)]
public class AuthorAttribute: Attribute
{
  private string FamilyName;
  private string GivenName;
  public AuthorAttribute(string FamilyName)
  {
    this.FamilyName = FamilyName;
  }
  public override String ToString()
  {
    return String.Format("Author: {0} {1}",
                         Family, Given);
  }
  public string Family
  {
    get
    {
      return FamilyName;
    }
    set
    {
      FamilyName = value;
    }
  }
  public string Given
  {
    get
    {
      return GivenName;
    }
    set
```

```
        {
            GivenName = value;
        }
    }
}

[Author("Watkins", Given = "Damien")]
[Author("Abrams")]
public class AttributeSample
{
    [Author("Hammond", Given = "Mark")]
    public static void Main()
    {
        Type t = typeof(AttributeSample);
        object[] attributes = t.GetCustomAttributes(true);
        Console.WriteLine("Custom Attributes are: ");
        foreach(Object o in attributes)
        {
            System.Console.WriteLine("\t{0}", o);
        }
    }
}
```

The first class defined in Listing 3.4, `AuthorAttribute`, is a user-defined custom attribute. This fact is implied by its inheritance specification, in which it inherits from the `Attribute` class. The new class contains two fields, `String`s that represent the author's family and given names. It contains two methods and a constructor that specifies that at least the family name must be supplied. The class also overrides the `ToString` method it inherits from `Object`. From the class's definition, you may wonder how the `FirstName` member is ever assigned a value. The member can be accessed in a manner similar to a named parameter in languages that support this concept. An example of this type of usage is shown later in the file.

The next class defined in Listing 3.4 is a C# class called `AttributeSample`. Its definition is preceded by two custom attributes of type `Author`, the program's user-defined custom attribute class. These attributes annotate the class `AttributeSample` and, in effect, indicate that two authors were responsible for writing this class. The first custom attribute uses the name of the member `FirstName` to assign a value to that member. The `Main` method in the `AttributeSample` class is also annotated with a single instance of the user-defined attribute class, this time designating the author of this method. The `Main` method in the `AttributeSample` class uses the `GetCustomAttributes` method to access an array of custom attributes for this class and then displays them on the screen. It produces the following output:

```
Custom Attributes are:
        Author: Abrams
        Author: Watkins Damien
```

The custom attribute for the author of the `Main` method is not shown, as the program gets only the attributes for the class. Extending the program to get the attributes for the method is a simple matter. Also, note that even though one method in the class is annotated, the other methods do not have to be.

If you open the executable program with ILDASM (see Figure 3.3), you can see the user-defined attribute class. In addition, you can see how instances of this class are persisted in the metadata.

Standard Attributes

Although you can define your own attributes, the Framework Class Library provides a number of predefined standard attributes, including those shown in Figure 3.4. All the types that inherit from `System.Attribute` in Figure 3.4 end with the suffix `Attribute`—for example, `WebMethod-Attribute`. For brevity, the word "Attribute" is omitted in the figure. Likewise, as you saw in Listing 3.4, the C# compiler permits developers to omit the `Attribute` suffix in source code.

Listing 3.5 demonstrates the use of one of the standard attributes, `ObsoleteAttribute`. The "Obsolete" part of the name indicates that a program element, such as a type or method, should no longer be used. For example, one method may be superceded by another method in a subsequent version of a type. In this situation, the developer may continue to provide both methods to avoid breaking clients using the original method but *document* to clients that they should use the newer method. To do so, the developer

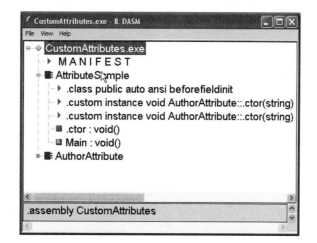

Figure 3.3 *Reviewing the custom attributes created in Listing 3.4*

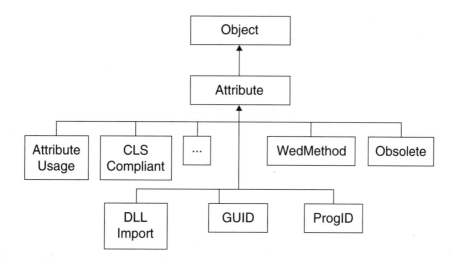

Figure 3.4 *Selected standard attributes predefined by the BCL*

can apply the Obsolete attribute to the method. Then every time a client is compiled that uses the original method, a warning or an error is raised. In Listing 3.5, OldMethod has been superceded by NewMethod. In this case, using OldMethod is not really an error, so only a warning is generated if a client calls this method.

Listing 3.5 *Using a standard attribute:* `ObsoleteAttribute`

```
using System;

namespace Sample
{
  public class TestClass
  {
    [Obsolete("Use NewMethod instead of OldMethod")]
    public static void OldMethod()
    {
      Console.WriteLine("Hi World");
    }
    public static void NewMethod()
    {
      Console.WriteLine("Hello World");
    }
  }
}
```

The following Visual Basic code uses the `Obsolete` method:

```
Imports System
Module MyModule
  Sub Main()
    Sample.TestClass.OldMethod()
  End Sub
End Module
```

Compiling the Visual Basic program generates the following output:

```
Microsoft (R) Visual Basic .NET Compiler version 7.00.9466
for Microsoft (R) .NET Framework version 1.00.3705.209
Copyright (C) Microsoft Corporation 1987-2001. All rights
reserved.

C:\Project7\Demos\Obsolete\Obsolete.vb(4) : warning BC40000:
'Public Shared Overloads Sub OldMethod()' is obsolete:
'Use NewMthod instead of OldMethod'

    Sample.TestClass.OldMethod()
    ~~~~~~~~~~~~~~~~~~~~~~~~~~~
```

Listing 3.6 demonstrates the use of another standard attribute, DllImportAttribute. In this program, the developer wants to access the ASCII version of the MessageBox method found in user32.dll. The DllImportAttribute annotates a method's prototype—in this example, MessageBoxA—by stating that the method body can be found in user32.dll so no definition of the method is provided in the Sample class. Any call to this method will result in the marshaling of parameters, if required, and then the invocation of the MessageBoxA method.

Listing 3.6 *Using a standard attribute:* DllImportAttribute

```
using System;
using System.Runtime.InteropServices;

class Sample
{
   [DllImport("user32.dll")]
   public static extern int
      MessageBoxA(int p, string m, string h, int t);
   public static int Main()
   {
      return MessageBoxA(0, "Hello World!",
                      "DLLImport Sample", 0);
   }
}
```

Executing the program given in Listing 3.6 produces the dialog box shown in Figure 3.5.

Figure 3.5 *Output of Listing 3.6*

Dynamic Discovery of Types

The dynamic discovery and instantiation of types is becoming increasingly important in modern software architectures. Why? Traditionally, programming languages and systems held to the notion that as much as possible should be known at compile time. It is true that the more information is available to the compiler, the potentially more type-safe and efficient the executable code could be. But it is also true that this approach leads to platform-specific code that is very difficult to migrate and execute on different systems. With the recent widespread use of distributed systems, such as the Internet, more dynamic facilities have become a necessity. In addition, today's programs must frequently deal with types that are developed after the original program was developed. As an example, consider programs such as the ActiveX Test Container, which is capable of interacting with COM controls created by many developers.

Both CORBA and COM provide facilities for dynamic type discovery, instantiation, and invocation, including the Dynamic Invocation Interface (DII) and `IDispatch`. The .NET Framework provides dynamic type discovery through its reflection facilities. In addition, it enables developers to create both local and remote objects at runtime. That is, the `Activator` class provides the functionality to dynamically create an instance of a class. The `Activator` class, which is a subtype of `Object`, has four methods:

- `CreateComInstanceFrom`: Creates an instance of a COM object and returns a handle to that object.
- `CreateInstance`: Creates an instance of an object and returns a reference to that object.
- `CreateInstanceFrom`: Creates an instance of an object and returns a handle to that object, as opposed to returning a reference to that object.
- `GetObject`: Creates a proxy object to an already running, well-known remote object. Methods then invoked on the proxy object will be forwarded to the remote instance.

Two of the `CreateInstance` methods—the ones ending in `From`—deal with creating types when the metadata describing the types is located in another application domain. Application domains are covered in Chapter 4, so explaining the reasons behind the use of these methods is a little premature at this point. For now, simply consider an application domain to be a subprocess. If types are passed between multiple application domains, then each application domain may need to know about a large number of different types. As an alternative, application domains can pass handles to objects; in such a case, only when an object is extracted from its handle is the metadata required to be loaded into that specific application domain.

The `CreateInstance` method, of which several variations exist, is the principal method for dynamically creating instances of a type. In this method, one parameter identifies the type of the object to be created. This type is specified by using either a `Type` object or a string that represents the type's name. When a string is used to specify the type's name, it may be necessary to pass the name of the assembly containing the type as well. Variations of the `CreateInstance` methods may take the following parameters:

- Constructor arguments—an array of objects used as the argument list to the constructor call
- Binding information—for selecting among multiple candidates
- Culture information
- Security requirements

Listing 3.7 demonstrates how to create a dynamic object of type `String`. This example is greatly simplified, as both the name of the type and the method to be invoked are specified in the source code. This program creates an instance of a string after creating an array of characters to be passed to the constructor. Next, it retrieves the `MethodInfo` object for the `Insert` method that takes an integer and a string as parameters. Finally, it invokes this method and writes the result to console.

Listing 3.7 *Creating a dynamic* `String` *object*

```
using System;
using System.Reflection;

namespace DynamicInstantiation
{
  class Sample
  {
    static void Main(string[] args)
    {
      Type t = Type.GetType("System.String");
      Object[] argumentArray = new Object[1];
      Char [] charArray =
              new Char[]{'H', 'e', 'l', 'l', 'o'};
      argumentArray[0] = charArray;
      Object dynamicObject =
              Activator.CreateInstance(t, argumentArray);
      Type[] typeOfParameters = new Type[2];
      typeOfParameters [0] = Type.GetType("System.Int32");
      typeOfParameters [1] = Type.GetType("System.String");
      MethodInfo methodName =
                  t.GetMethod("Insert",typeOfParameters );
      argumentArray  = new Object[2];
      argumentArray [0] = 5;
      argumentArray [1] = " World!";
      Console.WriteLine("Invoking this method: " +
                          methodName);
      Console.WriteLine(methodName.Invoke(dynamicObject,
                                          argumentArray));
    }
  }
}
```

Executing Listing 3.7 produces the following output:

```
Invoking this method: System.String Insert(Int32,
System.String)
Hello World!
```

Assemblies and Manifests

Packaging a component so that other programs can use it presents a number of challenges. Traditionally, a COM component is packaged in a dynamically linked library. When client programs seek to access a component, the operating system loads the component's DLL into the client's address space. The client can then utilize the functionality of the component. Although this system offers benefits, such as code reuse and efficiency, it creates a number of problems as well. For instance, the loading of DLLs is normally based on the name of the DLL. With versioning of the components, the name of the DLL does not necessarily change but the version of the component does. Thus, clients may get incompatible versions of the DLL loaded at different times, as DLLs are often replaced during software upgrades. This introduction of incompatible upgrades of component DLLs is often referred to as *DLL hell*.

To address these issues, the CLR packages types in an *assembly*. To use a simple analogy, an assembly could be described as a super-DLL. That is, an assembly remains the executable housing for a component, but it also provides facilities such as version information and type resolution (which traditional DLLs do not). Assemblies are covered in more detail in Chapter 5, on building applications, but a simple overview is provided here because they are such a fundamental building block in the CLR.

From a client's viewpoint, an assembly is a collection of publicly available types and resources that developers use in their programming. From a developer's viewpoint, it is a collection of files that form a functional unit. These files can contain types and resources that are either publicly available to other assemblies or an internal implementation detail. In other words, an assembly represents a means of grouping related types. It is also the unit of deployment and versioning, as all types within an assembly are part of the same version.

Figure 3.6 shows the logical elements of a simple assembly, called Assembly A in the diagram. An assembly comprises one or more modules, one of which has a manifest. It is the addition of a manifest to a module that creates the assembly. The manifest contains information about the assembly, such as its name, its version information, and the names of all modules and files that form the assembly. A module is a file that contains CLR metadata. Also shown in Figure 3.6 is a non-CLR file, called File A here. Because it is not a module, this file would not contain any CLR metadata but it might hold resources used by the assembly's type, such as bitmaps.

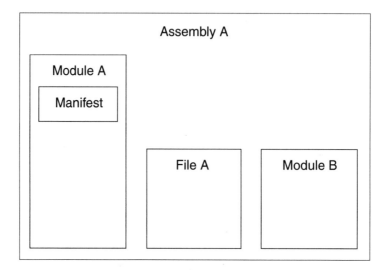

Figure 3.6 *A simple assembly*

Like .NET types, assemblies are self-describing. Information about an assembly appears in its manifest. A manifest contains the following data:

- Name, originator, and version information
- Configuration and culture information
- A list of types and their locations in the assembly

An assembly always has a simple name, but it may also have a strong name. A strong name utilizes public and private keys to ensure the security of the assembly; no one can produce an assembly with the same strong name without knowing the keys for the publisher that produced the assembly. If a strong name is provided, the manifest will contain a public key token that is based on the public key for the publisher as well as information identifying the hashing algorithm used.

The version number consists of four parts:

- Major version
- Minor version
- Build number
- Revision number

The version number can be used to differentiate between versions of the assembly. Thus, two assemblies with the same name and publisher will be considered different if they vary in terms of their version numbers. The execution engine permits the loading of different versions of assemblies into an executing program.

To help clarify the information contained in an assembly's manifest, Listing 3.8 demonstrates how developers access aspects of an assembly. This program uses the assembly mscorlib, which contains the Object and String classes along with other types, and displays information about the assembly, such as its full name, version, and location. Next, the program displays the modules and files that make up the assembly.

Listing 3.8 *Using an assembly*

```
using System;
using System.Reflection;
using System.IO;

namespace AssemblyInformation
{
  class Sample
  {
    static int Main(string[] args)
    {
      Type t= Type.GetType("System.String");
      Assembly a = Assembly.GetAssembly(t);
      AssemblyName an = a.GetName(false);
      Console.WriteLine("AssemblyName: {0}", an.Name);
      Console.WriteLine("FullName: {0}", an.FullName);
      Console.WriteLine("Codebase: {0}", an.CodeBase);
      Console.WriteLine("Version: {0}", an.Version);
      Console.WriteLine("Location: {0}", a.Location);
      Module[] modules = a.GetModules();
      Console.WriteLine("Module Name(s):");
      foreach(Module m in modules)
      {
        Console.WriteLine("\t FullName: {0}",
                          m.FullyQualifiedName);
        Console.WriteLine("\t ScopeName: {0}",
                          m.ScopeName);
        Type[] types = m.GetTypes();
        Console.WriteLine("Module Types:");
        foreach(Type tn in types)
```

continues

```
                Console.WriteLine("\t\t {0}", tn);
        }
        FileStream[] files = a.GetFiles(true);
        Console.WriteLine("File Name(s):");
        foreach(FileStream f in files)
        {
          Console.WriteLine("\t {0}", f.Name);
        }
        String[] rn = a.GetManifestResourceNames();
        Console.WriteLine("Resource Name(s):");
        foreach(String s in rn)
        {
          Console.WriteLine("\t {0}", s);
        }
        return 0;
      }
    }
  }
```

The program first retrieves the `String` class's `Type` object and then uses this `Type` object to access its assembly information. It displays information about the assembly, such as its name, code base, version, and location on disk. The program iterates through each module, displaying module identification information as well as types from the module. Finally, it iterates through the files contained within the assembly and then through all resources.

Although the output generated by Listing 3.8 on your system may vary from that shown below because of differences in versions of the CLR, the structure of the output will remain the same. The number of types displayed is enormous, so the following output has been edited; ellipses (…) indicate parts of the output where editing has occurred.

```
AssemblyName: mscorlib
FullName: mscorlib, Version=1.0.3300.0, Culture=neutral,
  PublicKeyToken=b77a5c561934e089
Codebase: file:///c:/windows/microsoft.net/framework/
  v1.0.3705/mscorlib.dll
Version: 1.0.3300.0
Location:
c:\windows\microsoft.net\framework\v1.0.3705\mscorlib.dll
```

```
Module Name(s):
    FullName:
c:\windows\microsoft.net\framework\v1.0.3705\mscorlib.dll
    ScopeName: CommonLanguageRuntimeLibrary
Module Types:
    System.Object
    System.ICloneable
    System.Collections.IEnumerable
    System.Collections.ICollection
    System.Collections.IList
    System.Array
    ...
File Name(s):
    c:\windows\microsoft.net\framework\v1.0.3705\mscorlib.dll
    c:\windows\microsoft.net\framework\v1.0.3705\prc.nlp
    c:\windows\microsoft.net\framework\v1.0.3705\prcp.nlp
    c:\windows\microsoft.net\framework\v1.0.3705\ksc.nlp
    c:\windows\microsoft.net\framework\v1.0.3705\ctype.nlp
    c:\windows\microsoft.net\framework\v1.0.3705\xjis.nlp
    c:\windows\microsoft.net\framework\v1.0.3705\bopomofo.nlp
    c:\windows\microsoft.net\framework\v1.0.3705\culture.nlp
    c:\windows\microsoft.net\framework\v1.0.3705\region.nlp
    c:\windows\microsoft.net\framework\v1.0.3705\sortkey.nlp
    c:\windows\microsoft.net\framework\v1.0.3705\charinfo.nlp
    c:\windows\microsoft.net\framework\v1.0.3705\big5.nlp
    c:\windows\microsoft.net\framework\v1.0.3705\sorttbls.nlp
    c:\windows\microsoft.net\framework\v1.0.3705\l_intl.nlp
    c:\windows\microsoft.net\framework\v1.0.3705\l_except.nlp
Resource Name(s):
    mscorlib.resources
    prc.nlp
    prcp.nlp
    ksc.nlp
    ctype.nlp
    xjis.nlp
    bopomofo.nlp
    culture.nlp
    region.nlp
    sortkey.nlp
    charinfo.nlp
    big5.nlp
    sorttbls.nlp
    l_intl.nlp
    l_except.nlp
      ...
```

Chapter 4, on the execution system, discusses assemblies and execution system functioning in more detail. Also, Chapter 6, on application deployment, provides more information about the creation of assemblies.

Meta-Programming

The ability to dynamically create new types at runtime is known as meta-programming. The CLR provides this capability through `Reflection.Emit`. Creating dynamic types is a fundamental facility in the remoting services. For example, COM and CORBA can produce code for proxy objects at IDL compile time. This code is then linked with the client and server programs. With the CLR's remoting services, the runtime environment dynamically creates proxy objects whenever the need arises. This

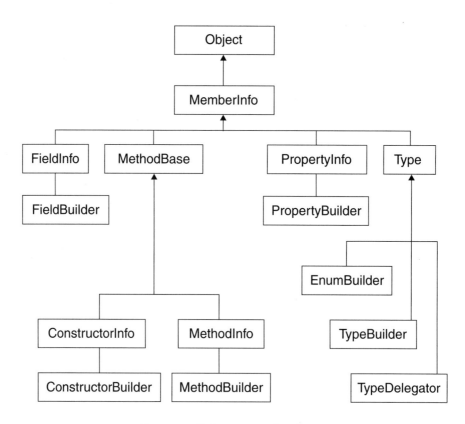

Figure 3.7 *Meta-programming classes*

approach eliminates the problem of locating and loading the DLL that contains the proxy code at runtime.

Figure 3.7 shows some of the classes involved in providing meta-programming facilities. The diagram is similar to Figure 3.1, which depicts the reflection class hierarchy. The `Builder` classes provide the functionality needed to create a new type or member at runtime.

Listing 3.9 demonstrates how to dynamically create a new type and then persist it to disk. It loads the assembly from disk, creates an instance of the new type, and calls a method on the new type. As types are located in modules and modules are located within assemblies, it follows that the creation of a new type requires the creation of a module and an assembly.

Listing 3.9 *Using meta-programming*

```
using System.Reflection.Emit;
using System.Threading;

public class DynamicType
{
  private static void CreateMethodBody(MethodBuilder m)
  {
    ILGenerator il = m.GetILGenerator();
    il.EmitWriteLine("Hello World! from a new type");
    il.Emit(OpCodes.Ret);
  }
  public static int Main(String[] args)
  {
    AssemblyName an = new AssemblyName();
    an.Name = "MyAssembly";
    AssemblyBuilder ab =
            Thread.GetDomain().DefineDynamicAssembly(an,
                      AssemblyBuilderAccess.RunAndSave);
    ModuleBuilder mb = ab.DefineDynamicModule("MyModule",
                              "MyAssembly.dll", true);
    TypeBuilder tb = mb.DefineType ("Sample.NewType",
                              TypeAttributes.Public);
    MethodBuilder m = tb.DefineMethod("MyMethod",
                              MethodAttributes.Public,
                              null, null);
    CreateMethodBody(m);
```

continues

```
      tb.CreateType();
      ab.Save("MyAssembly.dll");
      Type t = Type.GetType("Sample.NewType,MyAssembly",
                            true);
      Object o = Activator.CreateInstance(t);
      MethodInfo myMethod = t.GetMethod("MyMethod");
      myMethod.Invoke(o,null);
      myMethod = t.GetMethod("ToString");
      Console.WriteLine(myMethod.Invoke(o,null));
      return 0;
   }
}
```

Listing 3.9 produces the following output:

```
Hello World! from a new type
Sample.NewType
```

Of course, running this program creates an assembly in the current directory. You can use ILDASM to display its contents, just to show it is a valid CLR file (see Figure 3.8).

Also using ILDASM, you can show the emitted IL for `MyMethod` (see Figure 3.9).

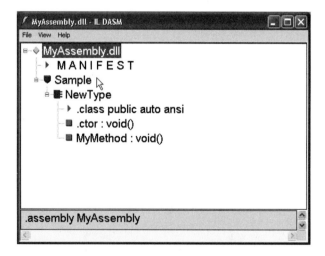

Figure 3.8 *Output of Listing 3.9: an assembly in the current directory*

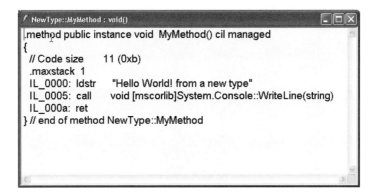

Figure 3.9 *IL for* `MyMethod`

Meta-programming is somewhat beyond the scope of this book, so it will not be covered in detail here. This short introduction should whet your appetite to learn more, however.

Metadata File Format

This section provides a brief description of the logical layout of metadata in files. It provides very superficial coverage of this topic, as this subject is generally considered to be an advanced topic and is beyond the scope of this book.

The creation of metadata follows one of two paths: using an unmanaged API or using a managed API. Unmanaged APIs could be considered a lower–level path; they do not provide much support to ensure that the structures produced are consistent. In contrast, managed APIs form a higher-level path. They were used earlier in this chapter to create a dynamic type.

Logically, a CLR file looks like Figure 3.10. It follows the standard Windows Portable Executable (PE) file layout. The metadata, seen in the middle of the figure, is stored in either tables or heaps. A table can be considered an array of structures that uses indexes to identify each new record, whereas a heap is essentially a sequence of bytes. The reason for the difference is that some aspects of metadata—for example, the version

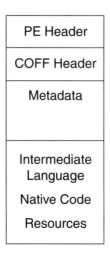

Figure 3.10 *A CLR file*

number of an assembly—are regular and can be stored in tables. The name of an assembly, however, is a string and therefore can be of varying length. In such a case, it is better to store the name in a heap and provide an address that indicates the start of the string.

Metadata tokens are used to identify metadata. A metadata token is four bytes in size. The most significant byte represents the type of metadata element referred to by the token and, therefore, identifies the metadata structure holding the definition. The remaining three bytes serve as indexes into that structure used to locate the metadata. A quick examination of corhdr.h would reveal the following:

```
typedef ULONG32 mdToken;
...
typedef mdToken mdModule;
typedef mdToken mdTypeRef;
typedef mdToken mdTypeDef;
typedef mdToken mdFieldDef;
...
```

From the first line, you can see that metadata tokens are type-defined to be 32-bit unsigned values. Two types of tokens exist: definitions, such as mdTypeDef, and references, such as mdTypeRef. A definition defines the type, indicating that the type lives within this assembly. A reference refers to a type in another assembly.

Listing 3.10 uses a mixture of both Managed and Unmanaged C++ to access the raw metadata tables within a PE file. Note that this program is very poorly written, as it includes little or no error checking and very some terse variable names. This approach keeps the example simple, but it is definitely not good coding practice.

Listing 3.10 *Accessing metadata tables within a PE file*

```
#using <mscorlib.dll>
#include <cor.h>
using namespace System;

void PrintTypeDefProperties(IMetaDataImport *imdi,
                             mdTypeDef token)
{
  const ULONG maxNameSize = 1024;
  WCHAR lTypeName[maxNameSize];
  ULONG actualNameSize = 0;
  DWORD flags = 0;
  mdToken extends;
  imdi->GetTypeDefProps (token, lTypeName, maxNameSize,
                          &actualNameSize, &flags,
                          &extends);
  String *s = lTypeName;
  Console::WriteLine(s);
}

int main()
{
  CoInitialize(0);
  IMetaDataDispenser *imdd = 0;
  IMetaDataImport *imdi = 0;
  IMetaDataAssemblyImport *imdai = 0;
  HRESULT hr =
          CoCreateInstance(CLSID_CorMetaDataDispenser,
                            NULL, CLSCTX_INPROC_SERVER,
                            IID_IMetaDataDispenser,
                            (void**)&imdd);
  unsigned short pModuleFilename [] =
          L"C:\\WINDOWS\\...\\v1.0.3705\\mscorlib.dll";
```

continues

```
    HRESULT h = imdd->OpenScope(pModuleFilename, 0,
                                IID_IMetaDataImport,
                                (IUnknown **)&imdi);
    h = imdd->OpenScope(pModuleFilename, 0,
      IID_IMetaDataAssemblyImport, (IUnknown **)&imdai);
    HCORENUM enr = 0;
    const arraySize = 256;
    mdTypeDef lTypeDefTokens[arraySize];
    ULONG count = 0;
    h = imdi->EnumTypeDefs (&enr, lTypeDefTokens, arraySize,
                           &count);
    for (ULONG i = 0; i != count; ++i)
    {
        PrintTypeDefProperties(imdi, lTypeDefTokens[i]);
    }
    imdi->CloseEnum (enr);
    imdd->Release();
    imdi->Release();
    imdai->Release();
    CoUninitialize();
    return 0;
}
```

Executing the program in Listing 3.10 produces the following output:

```
System.Object
System.ICloneable
System.Collections.IEnumerable
System.Collections.ICollection
System.Collections.IList
System.Array
SorterObjectArray
...
System.Collections.Hashtable
bucket
KeyCollection
ValueCollection
SyncHashtable
System.Collections.IDictionaryEnumerator
HashtableEnumerator
System.Collections.Queue
SynchronizedQueue
QueueEnumerator
```

COM Interop

Interoperability between different architectures is a major issue facing programmers. The CORBA specification includes the Interworking Specification, which deals with interoperability between COM and CORBA. An RMI-to-IIOP bridge links Java and CORBA.

The CLR uses COM Interop to provide a gateway between components in the CLR and COM worlds. In essence, COM Interop works on metadata. Because both COM and the CLR describe their types with metadata, tools can read the metadata description of one type in one architecture and produce an appropriate metadata description for the other architecture. Tools can also automatically generate proxy objects; these proxy objects may be located in the client's and server's processes. They provide a local representation of the component by using the same execution semantics expected by their environment. For example, if a CLR component is accessing a COM component, it does not want to deal with issues such as interface navigation (`QueryInterface`) and memory management (`AddRef` and `Release`). Instead, the proxy object will handle interface navigation and lifetime issues for the COM component.

A few tools provide the interoperability functionality:

- Type Library Importer (`tlbimp.exe`) takes a type library and provides an assembly with metadata for the components.
- Type Library Exporter (`tlbexp.exe`) generates a type library description for a CLR assembly.
- Register Assembly (`regasm.exe`) provides Registry entries for an assembly so that COM components can find and activate objects.

The following program gives a short example of the COM Interop facilities at work. Listing 3.11 shows the IDL for a COM component. `HelloATL` is a small COM component[3] that displays a message box on the screen along with user-supplied text.

---

[3] This application was originally written by Don Box.

Listing 3.11 Using COM Interop: `HelloATL`

```
// helloatl.idl
import "oaidl.idl";
[
    object, uuid(FFA03426-9E54-11D0-BF81-0060975E6A6A),
    dual, helpstring("IHelloATL Interface"),
    pointer_default(unique)
]
interface IHelloATL : IDispatch
{
    HRESULT Hello([in] BSTR bstr);
}
[
    uuid(FFA03419-9E54-11D0-BF81-0060975E6A6A),
    version(1.0), helpstring("HelloATL 1.0 Type Library")
]
library HELLOATLLib
{
    importlib("stdole32.tlb");
    [
        uuid(FFA03427-9E54-11D0-BF81-0060975E6A6A),
        helpstring("HelloATL Class")
    ]
    coclass HelloATL
    {
        [default] interface IHelloATL;
    };
};
```

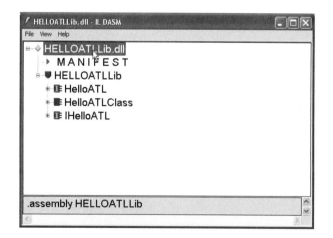

Figure 3.11 *Output of Listing 3.11*

Compiling this IDL file and then running the resultant type library through the type library importer produces a CLR file. When opened in ILDASM, it produces the information shown in Figure 3.11.

The type library importer has created two CLR interfaces and a CLR class. A small program is then written that uses the CLR metadata, as shown in Listing 3.12. Remember that these CLR types are merely proxies for the COM component; the COM component still does all the work.

Listing 3.12 Using the CLR metadata created by Listing 3.11

```
using System;
using System.Reflection;
using HELLOATLLib;

public class COMInterop
{
    public static int Main(String[] args)
    {
        HelloATL h = new HelloATL();
        Type t = h.GetType();
        Console.WriteLine(t.FullName);
        Console.WriteLine(t.AssemblyQualifiedName);
        Console.WriteLine(t.BaseType);
        MethodInfo[] ma = t.GetMethods();
        foreach(MethodInfo m in ma)
            Console.WriteLine(m);
        h.Hello("Hello World from COM/ATL");
        return 0;
    }
}
```

Running the program produces the following output:

```
HELLOATLLib.HelloATL
HELLOATLLib.HelloATL, HELLOATLLib, Version=1.0.0.0,
Culture=neutral, PublicKeyToken=null
System.__ComObject
Void Hello(System.String)
System.Runtime.Remoting.ObjRef CreateObjRef(System.Type)
System.Object InitializeLifetimeService()
System.Object GetLifetimeService()
Int32 GetHashCode()
```

continues

```
Boolean Equals(System.Object)
System.String ToString()
System.Type GetType()
```

It also produces the message box shown in Figure 3.12.

Figure 3.12 *Output of Listing 3.12*

Summary

This chapter introduced the facilities provided by the CLR's metadata system. Much of the basic functionality described here exists in other component architectures, albeit with some differences. A major difference between the CLR and COM/CORBA relates to the fact that the CLR does not use IDL to generate metadata. In this respect, the CLR more closely resembles SmallTalk and Java.

One predominant design consideration with component architectures is the move toward more dynamic and distributed systems. The CLR provides great support for both of these requirements; facilities such as automatic generation of proxy objects at runtime from their metadata and versioning and cultural attributes on assemblies address them at length. Chapter 6 discusses assemblies in more depth.

■ 4 ■

The Execution System

A S NOTED EARLIER, the CLR consists of three subsystems: the type and metadata systems (covered in Chapters 2 and 3, respectively) and the execution system (the focus of this chapter). The execution system is primarily responsible for the controlled execution of programs that contain managed code. For example, one responsibility of the execution system, and possibly the most immediately obvious, is the just-in-time (JIT) compilation of Common Intermediate Language/Intermediate Language (CIL/IL) to native code for the current execution platform. However, the execution system accomplishes much more than just JIT compilation; for example, it ensures that executing code meets the system's security requirements.

Many important requirements affect the design of the execution system. A primary design goal for the execution system was that it not be tied to any specific hardware or software platform. Therefore, the execution model makes no assumptions about the hardware architecture or operating system services available to it. This flexibility makes porting the CLR to other execution environments—such as the Pocket PC, BSD UNIX, and mobile telephones—a simpler task.

This chapter describes how the CLR executes programs. It discusses the concepts related to execution, such as the CIL, JIT compilation, application domains, and security. The term "application domain" is probably new to most readers. In earlier chapters, you saw how assemblies are similar to

DLLs but more powerful, thanks to concepts such as versioning and culture information. Just as assemblies build on and extend the concepts associated with DLLs, so application domains build on and extend the concept of a process. Application domains can be thought of as subprocesses within a process. They provide the same facilities as traditional processes, such as memory isolation. In general, however, a process is a heavy operating system entity; application domains provide logical processes at a much lower cost.

This chapter begins with an overview of the execution system, comparing it to other component models. Next comes an overview of the CIL, its structure, and its execution model. The concepts and use of application domains are then introduced. The chapter concludes with an overview of the security system, which highlights how it is integrated into the execution system.

The Execution System Versus Other Component Models

The type and metadata systems share many similarities in the component architectures mentioned so far in this book. In general, because .NET was created after the development of the other architectures, it provides some evolutionary enhancements to their type and metadata systems. For example, COM, CORBA, and .NET all provide a set of primitive built-in types and allow developers to define their own value types and interface types. An evolutionary difference between .NET and these other component architectures is that the former supports the notion of classes that are available across languages for inheritance. The metadata systems also share many underlying concepts; for example, an evolutionary difference is developers' ability to extend the metadata system with custom attributes in a standardized manner. Nevertheless, the execution system arguably provides the most substantial differences between the different architectures.

COM is largely tied to the Windows family of operating systems. Although some attempts have been made to port COM to other operating systems, many facilities and services continue to be implemented in a very Windows-specific manner. For example, the Single Threaded Apartment (STA) model, which uses a message queue to serialize messages to

STA-bound components, does not lend itself naturally to implementation on other platforms. Other concepts, such as the Registry, while not strictly incompatible with other operating systems, inherently lead to complications when trying to provide a seamless means to move components from one platform to another.

CORBA provides platform independence in a somewhat different manner. The OMG initially standardized the IDL, IDL-to-language mappings, and communication protocol—General Inter-ORB Protocol (GIOP) and Internet Inter-ORB Protocol (IIOP)—but left the execution environment as mainly an implementation detail. This choice allows IDL compilers to emit code, such as proxy objects and base classes, that are specific to a target language and a platform. A large amount of effort has recently gone into providing more interoperability within the CORBA execution environment, as evidenced by the replacement of the Basic Object Adapter (BOA) with the Portable Object Adapter (POA).

Effectively, many of the issues that COM and CORBA face relate to the generation of proxy objects and implementation code at IDL compile time. In the CORBA world, this often means, for example, that for every language and platform that wants to access a remote object, an IDL compiler is run to produce language- and platform-specific code for clients to bind against.

A variation on these execution models is the notion of a standard execution environment, such as those provided by virtual machines that have been in use since the 1960s and that became extremely popular in the 1990s with the introduction of the Java Virtual Machine (JVM). The initial reservation in adopting these execution environments focused on their poor performance at a time when their main advantages, such as code mobility, were not a high priority. Clearly, as hardware has increased in power and decreased in price and the use of distributed systems has grown, the balance has tilted in these environments' favor. The CLR favors supporting an abstract execution environment, one that is independent of a specific hardware platform. A clear difference between the CLR's execution environment and traditional virtual machines, however, is the fact that the CLR execution system was never designed to be interpreted. The CLR performs JIT compilation, or possibly compilation at install time, to maximize runtime performance. In fact, one can argue that this JIT compilation actually provides the most optimized code, as critical aspects of the execution environment—such as system memory, available disk space, and the exact version of the CPU—become known only at deployment or runtime.

Intermediate Language

Compilers that target the CLR translate their source code into CIL and metadata. CIL is often described as an object-oriented assembly language for an abstract stack-based machine. What exactly does this description mean? CIL instructions resemble an assembly language; they include instructions to *load* values onto an execution stack, sometimes referred to as *push* instructions; instructions to *store* values from the stack into memory locations, sometimes referred to as *pop* instructions; and instructions to invoke method calls. This assembly language is not specific to any hardware architecture. For example, it makes no assumptions about the number of registers or their size in its instruction set. Rather, the instructions execute on a pseudo-machine architecture—hence the term *abstract machine*. Because IL is machine independent, it can be moved from machine to machine; translation from IL to native code can be accomplished at any stage up to execution of the code.

IL is said to be object-oriented because it includes a number of instructions specifically designed to support object-oriented concepts. These instructions include the following:

- `box` and `unbox` move value types from the stack and into corresponding reference types allocated on the managed heap.
- `callvirt` provides a dynamically dispatched method call where the runtime type of the object on which the call is invoked determines the actual method called. This is a form of polymorphism, one of the cornerstones of object-oriented programming.
- `newobj` allocates a new object on the managed heap.

Example: Generating Intermediate Language

This section uses a simple C# program to describe the IL produced by compiling a source file. The program consists of two functions, which add the values of two integers and write the result to the console window. Although this example is not the definitive guide to IL , it does demonstrate most of the basic concepts.

The C# program in Listing 4.1 provides two static methods:

- `Main`, the program's entry point, calls the `Add` method and passes two integer values to it.
- `Add` takes two integer arguments and returns the sum of its two arguments.

Listing 4.1 *C# program used for generating IL*

```
using System;

namespace SampleIL
{
  class EntryPoint
  {
    private static int Add(int a, int b)
    {
      return a + b;
    }
    static void Main(string[] args)
    {
      int a = 40;
      int b = 2;
      int c = Add(a, b);
      Console.WriteLine("Total is: {0}", c);
    }
  }
}
```

This trivial program is next compiled to produce an executable file containing IL. If you used a tool such as ILDASM to examine the generated executable, the IL for the `Main` method would look something like the following:

```
.method private hidebysig static void  Main(string[] args)
cil managed
{
  .entrypoint
  // Code size       30 (0x1e)
```

continues

```
    .maxstack  2
    .locals init ([0] int32 a,
             [1] int32 b,
             [2] int32 c)
  IL_0000:  ldc.i4.s   40
  IL_0002:  stloc.0
  IL_0003:  ldc.i4.2
  IL_0004:  stloc.1
  IL_0005:  ldloc.0
  IL_0006:  ldloc.1
  IL_0007:  call       int32 SampleIL.EntryPoint::Add(int32,
                                                      int32)
  IL_000c:  stloc.2
  IL_000d:  ldstr      "Total is: {0}"
  IL_0012:  ldloc.2
  IL_0013:  box        [mscorlib]System.Int32
  IL_0018:  call       void
              [mscorlib]System.Console::WriteLine(string,
                                                  object)
  IL_001d:  ret
} // end of method EntryPoint::Main
```

The method header, which consists of the first line of the output, specifies the contract of the method. A simple explanation of the keywords in the header follows:

- .method specifies that this is a method.
- private specifies that this method has private accessibility.
- hidebysig specifies that this method hides other methods with the same name and signature, as is characteristic of the semantics of a language such as C#. Methods can hide methods by name only (hidebyname), the semantics for programming languages such as C.
- static specifies that this is a static (type) method.
- void specifies that this method does not return a value.
- Main is the name of the method. The name Main is not special; that is, any method can serve as the entry point for a program. The .entrypoint annotation within the method body identifies the method as the program's entry point.

- (String[] args) specifies the parameter list that is passed to this function. In this case, the parameter list consists of an array of strings that represent the command-line arguments given to the program.
- cil states that this method's body is written in CIL.
- managed states that this method is managed—that is, executed under the control of the execution engine.

Next comes the method's body, designated by the matching curly braces ({}). The .maxstack value indicates the maximum depth of the stack at any point during program execution. This value is used by the verification algorithm when it allocates data structures to ensure that methods do not underflow/overflow the stack. This technique is often used to circumvent security requirements.

The .locals directive defines storage locations for the three integer variables: a, b, and c. All local variables for a method are declared at the beginning of a method even if their declaration in the source file occurs at some point during the method. Local variables can be accessed by their locations within the local variable array. Thus, the number in square brackets, such as [0], provides the index into the local variable array containing the variable's storage location. This technique of using an index also allows two variables to share the same index and, therefore, the same location, similar to a *union* in some programming languages.

In the IL generated from Listing 4.1, the first instruction loads the constant 40 onto the stack (ldc.i4.s 40); the second IL instruction then stores this value into the location of variable a. Here you could read the store instruction as "store into local variable array at index 0 the value on the top of the stack" (stloc.0). A similar instruction sequence is then executed for the value 2, which is stored into variable b. Next, the values of a and b are loaded onto the stack. Once again, they are referred to by their indexes—0 and 1, respectively (ldloc.0 and ldloc.1).

A simple method call comes next. Because the method being called is located within the same class, the method signature is not decorated with information needed by the runtime environment to locate the method if it was located in another assembly. (We will see an example of a more decorated call shortly.) The call instruction includes more information than you might at first expect. The `call` keyword is followed by the return type of the method. Next comes the scoped name of the method, which specifies the `Add` method found in the `SampleIL.EntryPoint` class. Finally, the signature describes the types of the arguments passed to the method.

Executing this method call has a number of effects. The values stored on the stack, which are copies of the values of the local variables `a` and `b`, are popped during the method call. In this way, the size of the stack is reduced by 2 when the method returns. Pushed onto the stack by the method is its return value, which is of type `int`. This move increases the stack size by 1. Thus, the net effect of the call on the stack is that the stack size is decreased by 1, with the return value appearing on the stack immediately after the call instruction is executed. Executing the store instruction after the method call, therefore, stores the value on the top of the stack into the local variable `c`. The store instruction also pops the top of the stack, reducing its size by 1.

The `ldstr` instruction is an example of an IL-supplied instruction intended to support one of the built-in reference types, `System.String`. It allocates a string object in the managed heap and returns a reference to it on the top of the stack. Next, the value in `c` is loaded onto the stack. Recall that `c` is of type `int32`, a value type. Here it demonstrates the use of a box instruction, which takes the value on the stack and stores it into an object on the managed heap. In effect, this instruction reduces the stack size by 1 when it pops the actual argument off but then adds a value back onto the stack—namely, the return value of the method call. The net result is that stack effectively remains constant, but swaps a value type for a reference type.

The following `call` instruction uses a more decorated format than the previous example. The specified signature informs us that the call goes to the `System.Console::WriteLine` method found in the assembly `mscorlib`. This method takes two references from the stack: a reference to a string and a reference to an object. The method does not return anything, but the program produces the following output:

```
Total is: 42
```

At this point, you may be wondering why the stack size is so important. In general, developers do not need to worry about controlling the stack, because the compilers and execution system will regulate its growth correctly. However, to prevent errors, a number of rules govern the use of the stack. For example, when a method returns, the stack size delta (the change in the stack size) must be equal to the number of values returned from the function, which may be zero if the function is void, minus the number of arguments passed to the function. Most of these stack-related rules are designed to prevent malicious code from exploiting erroneous conditions that can arise if stack underflow or overflow occurs. These requirements often become important when verifying CIL to ensure that it is type-safe. (The topic of verification is covered shortly.)

While also not complicated, a quick look at the Add method highlights some other informative points:

```
.method private hidebysig static int32  Add(int32 a,
                                             int32 b) cil
managed
{
  // Code size       8 (0x8)
  .maxstack  2
  .locals ([0] int32 CS$00000003$00000000)
  IL_0000:  ldarg.0
  IL_0001:  ldarg.1
  IL_0002:  add
  IL_0003:  stloc.0
  IL_0004:  br.s        IL_0006
  IL_0006:  ldloc.0
  IL_0007:  ret
} // end of method EntryPoint::Add
```

Arguments, like local variables, are accessed as elements in a local variable array, so the instruction to load arguments resembles the instruction to load a local variable. The Add method uses the "load value from argument array index 0" (ldarg.0) instruction to load the value of a. It works similarly for b. Note that the add instruction does not specify the types of the values to be added, unlike some other execution environments. Instead, the stack is strongly typed. The execution system knows what types have been loaded onto the stack and, therefore, what type of addition operation is required—in this case, the addition of two integers. The only local variable created in the method, which was not defined by the source code, holds the return value.

At first glance, CIL may not appear to be extremely well optimized. For example, the unconditional branch from `IL 0004` to the next instruction is nonsense. This lack of optimization occurs for two reasons in most of the sample code given in this book. First, the code shown is often compiled to be unoptimized but simple to debug, as this approach provides a closer match between the source code and the IL. Second, and most importantly, most of the optimization happens at JIT compilation. This delay offers a significant advantage: An increase in the performance of the JIT complier benefits all languages targeting the CLR.

Note that the example class also contains a constructor for an instance of type `SampleIL.EntryPoint`. The IL for this method follows:

```
.method public hidebysig specialname rtspecialname
        instance void  .ctor() cil managed
{
  // Code size       7 (0x7)
  .maxstack  8
  IL_0000:  ldarg.0
  IL_0001:  call instance void
              [mscorlib]System.Object::.ctor()
  IL_0006:  ret
} // end of method EntryPoint::.ctor
```

As far as IL is concerned, the interesting part is the way that the `this` pointer (argument 0) is stored on the stack and then the base class constructor is invoked. When an optimizing JIT compiler compiles this method, it will probably be eliminated as both this method and the only method it calls do no work.

Verification of Intermediate Language

As programs have become more dynamic and distributed, hosts, such as operating systems and browsers, have been asked more often to execute remote, downloaded, or mobile code. This execution can be quite problematic. Some programs, known as viruses, are intended to cause mischief when executed within unsuspecting hosts. Traditionally, execution environments have offered only a simplistic approach to dealing with this scenario—specifically, either the code is allowed to executed or it is not. An improvement over this scenario limits the execution environment provided to download code. For example, the "sandbox" provided by the Java Virtual Machine allows code to be downloaded and executed but restricts the interaction that the code can have with local resources and the distributed systems with which the code can communicate. Central to the notion of safe execution of mobile code within the .NET Framework is the concept of *type safety*.

Executing un-type-safe CIL, whether the code was accidentally or intentionally created, can produce erroneous or destructive behavior within the execution system. This behavior may manifest itself as errors in the operation of the system or even as permanent loss of sensitive data. To prevent this kind of situation, an assembly undergoes a pre-execution inspection to see whether it will act in a type-safe manner. Just because IL can be proved to be type-safe, however, does not mean that executing the code may not have destructive effects. For example, a method called `FormatDisk` should, as its name suggests, format a disk, thereby removing all data from it. While an administrator might legitimately call this method, ordinary users should not have access to it. The security system, which is a component of the execution system, is responsible for preventing CIL from calling methods that it does not have permission to call.

Verifying an assembly for type safety involves two tasks:

- Checking the assembly itself—that is, checking the assembly manifest
- Checking the types the assembly contains

Checking an Assembly

Verifying assembly metadata is vital. In fact, the entire verification process is based on the integrity of an assembly's metadata. Assembly metadata is verified either when an assembly is load into a cache—for example, the global assembly cache (GAC)—or when it is read from disk if it has not been inserted into a cache. The GAC is a central storage location for assemblies that are used by a number of programs; the download cache holds assemblies downloaded from other locations, such as the Internet.

Metadata verification involves such requirements as examining metadata tokens to confirm that they index correctly into the tables they access and that indexes into string tables do not point at strings that exceed the size of the buffers that should hold them, thus eliminating buffer overflow.

Once the assembly manifest has been verified, the types with the assembly can be checked.

Checking Types

All types in the CLR specify the contracts that they will implement, and this information is persisted as metadata along with the CIL. For example, when a type specifies that it inherits from another class or interface, thereby indicating that it will implement a number of methods, this specification creates a contract. A contract may also be related to visibility. For example, types may be declared as public (exported from their assembly) or private.

CIL can be described as type-safe or not type-safe. Type safety is a property of code that ensures that the code accesses types only in accordance with their contracts. Type safety also includes requirements other than just accessing types correctly, such as prohibition of stack underflow/overflow, correct use of the exception-handling facilities, and object initialization.

The CLR's type-safety verification algorithm can be described as conservative. That is, CIL that passes verification is deemed type-safe but some type-safe CIL may not pass verification. Verification represents a fundamental building block in the security system, although it is currently performed only on managed code. Unmanaged code executed by the CLR must be fully trusted, as the CLR cannot verify it.

Classification of CIL Verification Status

To understand verification, it is important to understand how CIL can be classified. CIL can be categorized in one of four ways: as illegal, legal, type-safe, or verifiable:[1]

---

[1]　The following definitions are more informative than normative. More precise versions can be found in other documentation, such as the ECMA specification.

- Illegal CIL is CIL for which the JIT compiler cannot produce a native representation. For example, CIL containing an invalid operation code cannot be translated into native code. Likewise, a jump instruction whose target is the address of an operand rather than an opcode constitutes illegal CIL.
- Legal CIL is all CIL that satisfies the CIL grammar and, therefore, can be represented in native code. Note that this classification includes CIL that uses non-type-safe forms of pointer arithmetic to gain access to members of a type, for example.
- Type-safe CIL interacts with types only through their publicly exposed contracts. CIL that attempts to access a private member of a type from another type would not be considered type-safe, for example.
- Verifiable CIL is type-safe CIL that can be proved to be type-safe by a verification algorithm. As noted earlier, the conservative nature of the verification algorithm means that some type-safe CIL may not pass verification. Of course, verifiable CIL is also type-safe and legal but not illegal.

The verification process occurs during the JIT compilation and proceeds intermittently within this phase; thus verification and JIT compilation do not execute as two separate processes. If a sequence of unverifiable CIL is found within an assembly, the security system checks whether the assembly can skip verification. If the assembly was loaded from a local disk, for example, under the default settings of the security model avoiding verification is possible. If the assembly can skip verification, then the CIL is translated into native code. If the assembly cannot skip verification, then the offending CIL is replaced with a stub that throws an exception if the method is called. At runtime, any call to this code will produce an exception. A commonly asked question is, "Why not check whether an assembly needs verification before verification begins?" In general, verification, as it is performed during the JIT compilation, is often faster than checking whether the assembly can skip verification.[2] Verification and the elimination of un-type-safe code is the first part of security on the CLR.

---

[2] The decision to skip verification is actually smarter than the process described here. For example, results of previous verification attempts can be cached to provide a quick lookup scenario.

Starting a CLR Program

An executable CLR program contains at least three components:

- The user-defined assembly with an entry point
- The execution system, found in either `mscorsvr.dll` or `mscorwks.dll`
- The basic type system, found in `mscorlib.dll`

Whenever a CLR program starts, the runtime environment must start, too. One of the first instructions within any CLR executable achieves this task by calling either `_CorExeMain` or `_CorDllMain`, both of which are found in `mscoree.dll`. As its name suggests, `mscoree.dll` is the initial part of the execution engine. If an executable serves as a program's entry point, then `_CorExeMain` is called; if it does not, then `_CorDllMain` is called. Naturally, `mscoree.dll` is an unmanaged executable, as it needs to interact with a number of low-level system APIs.

The code in `mscoree.dll` decides which version of the runtime environment to load. This environment is housed in a file named `mscorsvr.dll` (the version for servers) or `mscorwks.dll` (the version for workstations). Multiprocessor server machines normally have the server version loaded; all other configurations activate the workstation version.

An executing CLR program also needs access to the types defined in other assemblies. Because all CLR programs need access to the definition of `System.Object`, `mscorlib.dll` is loaded as well.

COR Debugger

Like ILDASM, the Common Language Runtime debugger (`cordbg`) is a useful tool supplied with the SDK.[3] It is helpful to use `cordbg` to demonstrate aspects of the execution system. This section provides a quick start

---

[3]   As the name suggests, this tool dates back to the time when the .NET Framework was known as the Com Object Runtime (COR).

with `cordbg` but does not offer a complete tutorial on its use; instead, it simply provides sufficient information to help a developer get started with this tool.

To start `cordbg` on a CLR executable program, type the command `cordbg` and the name of the program you wish to debug. For example:

```
cordbg SampleIL.exe
```

A useful exercise is to configue `cordbg` to display *load* events. Load events occur whenever the CLR loads new application domains, assemblies, modules, or types. Most `cordbg` commands can be abbreviated, with only sufficient characters to avoid ambiguity being required. The following command turns on the reporting of many load events, with most commands having been entered in a shortened format:

```
(cordbg) mod App 1
AppDomain and Assembly load events are displayed
(cordbg) mod cla 1
Class load events are displayed
(cordbg) mod mod 1
Module load events are displayed
```

After entering these commands, you can quit `cordbg` and then restart it on an executable. You should gain an appreciation for the work done by the runtime environment when you see how many classes are loaded. Following is the extremely abbreviated output generated by `cordbg` when executing the sample program that adds two integers. At this stage, readers are not expected to understand all of the output shown here, but concepts such as loading and unloading of the class `System.Object` from the assembly `mscorlib.dll` should be meaningful, for example. The output also demonstrates the use of application domains, which are described shortly, and modules, which are described in Chapter 5.

```
Microsoft (R) Common Language Runtime Test Debugger Shell
Version 1.0.3705.0
Copyright (C) Microsoft Corporation 1998-2001.
All rights reserved.
```

continues

```
(cordbg) Process 380/0x17c created.
Appdomain #1, DefaultDomain -- Created
Assembly 0x000964dc, c:\windows\...\mscorlib.dll -- Loaded
   in appdomain #1, DefaultDomain
Module 0x00093094, c:\...\v1.0.3705\mscorlib.dll -- Loaded
   in assembly 0x000964dc, c:\windows\...\mscorlib.dll
   in appdomain #1, DefaultDomain
Loaded class: System.Object
Loaded class: System.ICloneable
Loaded class: System.Collections.IEnumerable
Loaded class: System.Collections.ICollection
Loaded class: System.Collections.IList
...
Loaded class: System.ArgumentException
Loaded class: System.ArgumentOutOfRangeException
Loaded class: System.IO.Path
Assembly 0x0009f724, C:\...\SampleIL.exe -- Loaded
   in appdomain #1, SampleIL
Module 0x0009f7c4, C:\...\SampleIL\SampleIL.exe -- Loaded
   in assembly 0x0009f724, C:\...\SampleIL.exe
   in appdomain #1, SampleIL
Loaded class: SampleIL.EntryPoint
Loaded class: System.Int32
Loaded class: System.Console
...
Total is: 42
Loaded class: System.EventHandler
[thread 0x434] Thread created.
Unloaded class: SampleIL.EntryPoint
Module 0x0009f7c4, C:\Project7\...\SampleIL.exe -- Unloaded
   in assembly 0x0009f724, C:\...\SampleIL\SampleIL.exe
   in appdomain #1, SampleIL.exe
Assembly 0x0009f724, C:\...\SampleIL.exe -- Unloaded
Unloaded class: System.Object
Unloaded class: System.ICloneable
Unloaded class: System.Collections.IEnumerable
Unloaded class: System.Collections.ICollection
Unloaded class: System.Collections.IList
Unloaded class: System.Array
Unloaded class: System.IComparable
Unloaded class: System.IConvertible
Unloaded class: System.String
...
Module 0x00093094, c:\...\v1.0.3705\mscorlib.dll -- Unloaded
   in assembly 0x000964dc, c:\...\mscorlib.dll
```

```
    in appdomain #1, SampleIL.exe
  Assembly 0x000964dc, c:\windows\...\mscorlib.dll -- Unloaded
  Appdomain #1, SampleIL.exe -- Exited
  [thread 0x178] Thread exited.
  Process exited.
```

The line `Total is: 42` shown in the output is the string written to the console during execution of the program.

Typing `help` at the `cordbg` prompt will cause a few pages of information about `cordbg` commands to be displayed on the screen. Throughout the rest of this chapter, `cordbg` is used to highlight some aspects of the runtime nature of the execution system. Of course, some developers may prefer to use the graphical debugger supplied as part of Visual Studio rather than `cordbg`.

Application Domains

Application domains have previously been described as subprocesses within a process. Processes are the unit of fault tolerance within an operating system. If one process behaves erroneously, such as by trying to access the memory of another process's address space, then the operating system will terminate the erroneous process but leave all other processes unaffected. However, processes are often expensive in terms of resource usage, because the operating system must continually monitor processes. By comparison, a number of application domains can exist with a single process, yet require no extra overhead from the operating system. Instead, the execution system manages the application domains. Compared with using multiple processes, application domains offer even more advantages. With application domains, threads that switch from one application domain to another do not incur the same costs as if they switched from one process to another. It is also possible to remove an application domain from a process without adversely affecting the process or the other application domains within that same process, just as you can remove an errant process from memory without affecting other processes.

An assembly is always loaded into an application domain—normally, the application domain that requested it. Assemblies can be domain-neutral, meaning that the code within an assembly is shared between all application domains. For example, `mscorlib` is always loaded as a domain-neutral assembly. This approach resembles the shared use of a DLL between processes. Sometimes assemblies must be loaded as domain-specific—if, for example, they will receive different permissions depending on their use. References to data from assemblies in other application domains naturally cross application domain boundaries and are subject to constraints. For example, an object cannot directly access data in an object in another application domain; instead, either a copy of the object will be placed in the client's application domain or a proxy object will provide the necessary access.

Figure 4.1 depicts a simplified view of an executing CLR application. A process may contain one or more application domains; in the figure, it has two. Each application domain may contain one or more assemblies. Each assembly may contain one or more modules.

Effectively, threads remain independent of application domains. Thus, threads can cross from one application domain to another, and an application domain can have more than one thread. Developers rarely interact

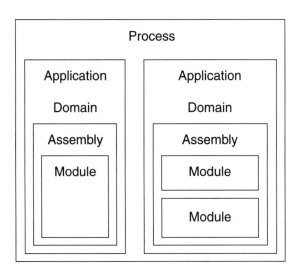

Figure 4.1 *An executing CLR application*

directly with application domains, although such interaction is possible if the need for it arises. The Base Framework includes an `AppDomain` class that developers can use to manipulate application domains. Application domains are covered in more detail in Chapter 5.

If `cordbg` was started on the IL-generation program given in Listing 4.1, then typing the `ap` command at the `cordbg` prompt would display the application domains. The following output has been edited for brevity:

```
(cordbg) ap
1) * AppDomainName = <SampleIL.exe>
        DebugStatus: <Debugger Attached >
        ID: 1
        Assembly Name :
            C:\Project7\Demos\SampleIL\SampleIL.exe
            Module Name :
                C:\Project7\Demos\SampleIL\SampleIL.exe
        Assembly Name :
            c:\...\framework\v1.0.3705\mscorlib.dll
            Module Name :
                c:\...\framework\v1.0.3705\mscorlib.dll
```

This output shows one application domain, SampleIL.exe, with two assemblies loaded—namely, `SampleIL.exe` and `mscorlib.dll`. Each assembly has one module—`SampleIL.exe` and `mscorlib.dll`, respectively.

Memory Management

The CLR provides automatic memory management. Essentially, this means that when developers create a value (i.e., an instance of any type), the CLR is responsible for allocating and freeing the memory in which that value is stored. Value types and reference types have their memory allocated and freed via different mechanisms, however.

Value Types Versus Reference Types
Value types are normally allocated on the program's stack. Whenever a parameter or a local variable is needed, such as when a method is called, memory for the value is allocated on the stack. This memory remains available until the method returns; the stack is then unwound and the

memory is automatically reclaimed. This model of allocating and freeing stack-based memory for parameters and local variables is very common in programming languages, being used by C, C++, and Java, for example. The mechanism is also simple to implement, because growing and freeing stack memory is as simple as adjusting a stack pointer during program execution. The major limitation with this approach is the fact that the lifetimes of values remain tied to the method invocation that creates them; when the method returns, the memory allocated for the values is reclaimed.

Reference types often have lifetimes that are not related to the methods that create them, so their allocation and freeing are a bit more complicated. Objects, which are values of `Object types`, are allocated on a heap. The lifetime of an object may differ from that specified by the method that allocates it. From this viewpoint, object allocation in the CLR resembles heap allocation in C or C++. In those programming languages, however, the allocated memory is reclaimed when `free` or `delete` is manually called on the memory. This mechanism requires the programmer to explicitly reclaim memory, which leads to two major issues:

- Memory can be reclaimed while references still refer to an object. As long as no attempt is made to access the object, this situation does not normally cause any problems. By contrast, using a reference to access an object after its memory has been reclaimed may lead to undefined behavior from the program.
- Programs may forget to free memory allocated for objects even when they are no longer being used. In this situation, programs may exhaust their available memory and fail.

Whenever an object is allocated in the CLR, the runtime environment takes charge of tracking all references to that object. It guarantees that while an object has a reference to it (i.e., while it is still reachable), its memory will not be reclaimed. It also guarantees that once an object becomes unreachable, its memory will be reclaimed if available memory becomes scarce. This scenario provides for a good compromise between safety, performance, and memory usage. Programmers need not manage memory manually, which makes writing programs simpler, and memory is reclaimed as needed, thereby avoiding the overhead of reclaiming it unnecessarily. The problem with this scenario is that programs cannot be sure when, or even if, objects will have their memory reclaimed and, therefore, their destructors executed.

Garbage Collection

The algorithm for the garbage collector is extremely specialized, but the simplistic model described here should provide developers with a basic understanding of its operation.

The managed heap is a large area of memory in which the CLR sequentially allocates objects. As each object is allocated, it is placed in the heap just after the last object allocated on the heap. Because each object can be of a different size, the CLR adds the size of the new object to its starting location; this position indicates where the next object will be allocated. The CLR returns a reference to the object, and the program continues executing. When the next object is allocated, the CLR repeats the allocation algorithm.

At some point during program execution, the CLR may start reclaiming the memory allocated for unreachable objects. This situation may be triggered, for example, by the program calling `GC.Collect()` or by the runtime noticing that most of the available memory in the heap has been allocated. When such an event occurs, the garbage collector starts by assuming that all objects on the heap are unreachable; an object is considered "unreachable" when no references point to it. The garbage collector knows where primary object references can be stored—for example, as local variables and parameters—so it first locates all of these primary references and marks all objects referenced by them as "reachable." As an object is found to be reachable, its members are inspected for references to other objects, with each object that the current object refers to also being marked as reachable.[4]

---

[4] This book calls the second type of references "secondary references," which is purely our own terminology. The reason for distinguishing between primary and secondary references is that two objects may share a cycle where they each refer to each other—that is, they may have secondary references to each other. If neither of these objects has a primary reference, then clearly the objects can be removed without causing any problems.

After it has identified all reachable objects, the garbage collector examines all unreachable objects to see whether their finalization methods should be executed. If so, then a reference to the object is added to the list of objects requiring finalization. The object then becomes reachable again and, therefore, is not available for deletion until its finalization method executes. In general, although finalization methods sound appealing, they can create a number of problems. For example, these methods are never guaranteed to run, the order in which objects are finalized is not specified, and the use of finalization methods keeps objects in memory longer than necessary. Also, a finalization method may cause an object to be resurrected by creating a reference to the object that the garbage collector will see during its next operation. The interactions and possibilities seem endless.[5]

At this point, the garbage collector deletes all unreachable objects by moving the reachable objects into a sequential array of memory, along the way overwriting any unreachable objects. This compaction minimizes memory usage as well as eliminates unused objects. To ensure that all object references remain valid, the garbage collector must update these references. After garbage collection, object references might point to another location in the garbage collected heap but they will still point to the same object.

The garbage collection algorithm described here is greatly simplified, but some optimizations can be applied to increase its efficiency. For instance, objects may be placed in generations, where a "generation" represents a garbage collection cycle. An object that has not been through a cycle is part of generation 0. After each cycle, each object's generation increases by one. Thus, objects in each generation are compacted together, and the generations are arranged from highest to lowest throughout the managed heap. Long-lived objects, such as those that persist for the entire life of the program, will be moved to one end of the managed heap and basically stay there. As a consequence, references to those objects will rarely need to be changed. As a performance optimization, garbage collection might work on only specific generations. The assumption here is that long-lived objects (i.e., those in higher generations) are more likely to persist and

---

[5]   A detailed discussion of the semantics of finalization is beyond the scope of this book. Refer to the SDK documentation for a more detailed specification.

do not need to be subjected to testing for garbage collection as often as newly allocated objects.

Example: Generation-Based Garbage Collection

Listing 4.2 demonstrates how the generation-based garbage collection works. The program first displays the maximum number of generations for the system (three, ranging from generation 0 to generation 2, inclusive). Next, it allocates a new object and calls GC.Collect which takes a single parameter that specifies the number of generations to be processed. As this parameter is also the maximum number of generations supported by the system, objects in all generations are checked. This checking moves the only object allocated by the program (p1) up by one generation. The allocation/aging cycle is repeated three more times. Eventually, the first object reaches generation 2 and cannot be aged anymore.

Listing 4.2 *Generation-based garbage collection*

```
using System;
using System.Runtime.InteropServices;

public class GCSample
{
  public static int Main()
  {
    Console.WriteLine(
        "Maximum Generations = {0}",
         GC.MaxGeneration);
    Object p1 = new Object();
    Console.WriteLine(
        "p1: {0}\n", GC.GetGeneration(p1));
    GC.Collect();
    Console.WriteLine(
        "p1: {0}\n", GC.GetGeneration(p1));
    Object p2 = new Object();
    GC.Collect(0);
    Console.WriteLine(
        "p1: {0}", GC.GetGeneration(p1));
    Console.WriteLine(
        "p2: {0}\n", GC.GetGeneration(p2));
    GC.Collect(1);
    Console.WriteLine(
        "p1: {0}", GC.GetGeneration(p1));
```

continues

```
        Console.WriteLine(
            "p2: {0}\n", GC.GetGeneration(p2));
        return 0;
    }
}
```

Listing 4.2 produces the following output:

```
Maximum Generations = 2
p1: 0

p1: 1

p1: 1
p2: 1

p1: 2
p2: 2
```

Security

The CLR's security system provides two different security models: role-based security and evidence-based security. The role-based security system is based on the concepts of identity and roles, which represent the same abstractions that *users* and *groups* do in traditional operating system security. The evidence-based security system is based on the code (rather than the user executing the code) and is designed to provide security for mobile and downloaded code. This section discusses both security models, although more space is devoted to evidenced-based security because this model of security is newer to most developers.

In general, the following discussion and samples are based on the default settings for the security system within the CLR. Almost every aspect of the security system can be configured by administrators, but this reconfiguration of the security settings and their subsequent effects are well beyond the scope of this book.

Role-Based Security

As noted earlier, role-based security utilizes the concepts of identities and roles, which are similar to the notions of users and groups in many current operating systems. Two core abstractions in role-based security are the Identity and the Principal. An Identity represents the user on whose behalf the code is executing; it could be a logical user as defined by the application or developer, rather than the user as seen by the operating system. A Principal represents the abstraction of a user and the roles in which he or she belongs. Classes representing a user's Identity implement the `IIdentity` interface. A generic class providing a default implementation of this interface within the Framework Class Library is `GenericIdentity`. Classes representing Principals implement the `IPrincipal` interface. A generic class providing a default implementation of this interface within the FCL is `GenericPrincipal`.

At runtime, each thread has one and only one current Principal object associated with it. Code may, of course, access and change this object, subject to security requirements. Each Principal has one and one only Identity object. Logically, the runtime structure of the objects resembles Figure 4.2.

Listing 4.3 demonstrates how developers can use the generic classes. This program demonstrates how to set and test for different identities and

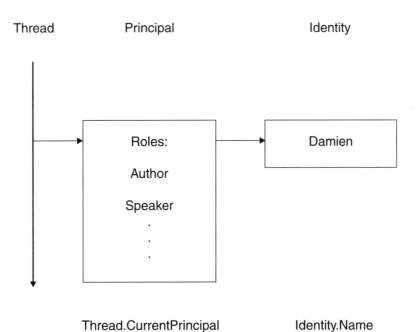

Figure 4.2 *Runtime structure under role-based security*

roles. In this case, the developer supplies the security model, the name "Damien"; the roles "Author" and "Speaker" are not tied to any user or roles that the operating system may support.

Listing 4.3 *Generic classes under role-based security*

```csharp
using System;
using System.Threading;
using System.Security;
using System.Security.Principal;

namespace RoleBasedSecurity
{
  class Sample
  {
    static void Main(string[] args)
    {
      String [] roles = {"Author", "Speaker"};
      GenericIdentity i = new GenericIdentity("Damien");
      GenericPrincipal g = new GenericPrincipal(i, roles);
      Thread.CurrentPrincipal = g;
      if(Thread.CurrentPrincipal.Identity.Name == "Damien")
        Console.WriteLine("Hello Damien");
      if(Thread.CurrentPrincipal.IsInRole("Author"))
        Console.WriteLine("Hello Author");
      if(Thread.CurrentPrincipal.IsInRole("Publisher"))
        Console.WriteLine("Hello Publisher");
    }
  }
}
```

Listing 4.3 produces the following output:

```
Hello Damien
Hello Author
```

You can also use the Windows security model. In this situation, users and roles are tied to those on the hosting machine, so the developer may need to create accounts on the hosting system. Listing 4.4 uses the local machine's user accounts. This program demonstrates how to limit access to methods based on the user's identity. The example also includes some "syntactic sugar": The BCL's PrincipalPermissionAttribute effectively encapsulates the calls to methods such as `IsInRole` to allow developers to use a simplified syntax.

Listing 4.4 *Role-based Windows security*

```
using System;
using System.Security.Permissions;
using System.Security.Principal;

namespace RoleBased
{
  class Sample
  {
    [PrincipalPermissionAttribute(SecurityAction.Demand,
                   Name=@"PROJECT42\Damien Watkins")]
    public static void UserDemandDamien()
    {
      Console.WriteLine("Hello Damien!");
    }
    [PrincipalPermissionAttribute(SecurityAction.Demand,
                   Name=@"PROJECT42\Dean Thompson")]
    public static void UserDemandDean()
    {
    Console.WriteLine("Hello Dean!");
    }
    static void Main(string[] args)
    {
      AppDomain.CurrentDomain.SetPrincipalPolicy(
                   PrincipalPolicy.WindowsPrincipal);
      try
      {
        UserDemandDamien();
        UserDemandDean();
      }
      catch(Exception)
      {
        Console.WriteLine("Exception thrown");
      }
    }
  }
}
```

The `PrincipalPermissionAtribute` ensures that a runtime check occurs each time the program calls the methods `UserDemandDamien` and

`UserDemandDean`. Naturally, the program can be executed by Dean or Damien or someone else, so the security check should fail on at least one of the two method calls, if not both. The first line of `Main` sets the Principal policy to that employed by Windows, the operating system on which this example was executed. Listing 4.4 produces the following output when executed by the user "PROJECT42\Damien Watkins":

```
Hello Damien!
Exception thrown
```

Evidence-Based Security

Essentially, evidence-based security assigns permissions to assemblies based on evidence. It uses the location from which executable code is obtained as a primary factor in determining which resources the code should be able to access. Whenever an assembly is loaded into the CLR for execution, the hosting environment attaches a number of pieces of evidence to the assembly. The security system in the CLR must then map this evidence into a set of permissions, which will determine the code's access to a number of resources.

Permissions

Permissions represent authorization to perform operations, many of which require access to a resource. In general, an operation may involve accessing resources such as files, the Registry, the network, the user interface, or the execution environment. An example of a permission that does not involve a tangible resource is the ability to skip verification. The fundamental abstraction of a permission is the `IPermission` interface.

A *permission grant* represents the authority to perform an action that has been granted to an assembly based on the evidence presented to the security system when it was loaded. A *permission demand* triggers a security check to see whether a specific permission has been granted; if the demand fails, then an exception is raised.

The class `System.Security.PermissionSet` represents a collection of permissions. Methods on this class include `Intersect` and `Union`, which take another `PermissionSet` as a parameter and provide a `Permission-`

Set that is either the union or intersection of all permissions in both sets. With these facilities, the security system can work with permissions sets and not have to understand the semantics of each individual type of permission. This flexibility allows developers to extend the permission hierarchy without modifying any of the security engine's functionality.

Evidence

Whenever an assembly is loaded into the CLR, the hosting environment presents the security system with evidence related to it. A number of types of evidence exist:

- Zone: The same concept as zones used in Internet Explorer.
- URL: A specific URL or file location that identifies a specific resource, such as http://www.aw.com/catalog/academic/product/1,4096,0201770180,00.html.
- Hash: The hash value of an assembly generated with algorithms such as SHA1.
- Strong name: The use of digital signing with hashing.
- Site: The site from which the code came. A URL is more specific than the notion of a site; for example, www.aw.com is a site.
- Application directory: The directory from which the code is loaded.
- Publisher certificate: The use of digital signatures, such as Authenticode.

As noted above, the concept of zones is similar to that used in Internet Explorer. A zone may be any of the following (note that the default permissions are listed here):

- The My Computer zone (see the output from Listing 4.5 later in this section) is for executables run from the local hard disk; these programs often receive the most powerful permission sets.
- The Local Intranet zone represents executables run from a local intranet. These programs are less trusted than code from the local hard disk so, for example, they cannot access the Registry.

- The Internet zone represents code executed from the Internet. It has limited resources available during execution.
- The Trusted Sites zone includes a specified list of trusted sites. By default, this kind of zone executes with the same capabilities as the Internet zone.
- The Untrusted Sites zone includes a specified list of untrusted sites. Applications from these sites cannot be executed.

Administrators may reconfigure the permissions listed above as they see fit. For example, it is not immediately obvious why both an Internet zone and a Trusted Sites zone exist, given that they receive the same permission sets. In this case, the distinction makes sense only if administrators actually do reconfigure the settings.

Both strong names and publisher certificates constitute assembly-based evidence; in other words, they are carried within the assembly. The hosting environment provides all other evidence.

Example: Passing Evidence to the CLR Security System

Listing 4.5 provides a simple example of the evidence passed to the CLR security system when an assembly is loaded. In this case, `mscorlib` is the loaded assembly; it contains many of the CLR types, such as `Object` and `String`.

Listing 4.5 *Evidence-based security*

```
using System;
using System.Collections;
using System.Reflection;
using System.Security.Policy;

namespace AssemblyEvidence
{
  class EntryPoint
  {
    static void Main(string[] args)
    {
      Type t = typeof(System.String);
      Assembly a = Assembly.GetAssembly(t);
      Evidence e = a.Evidence;
```

```
      IEnumerator i = e.GetEnumerator();
      while(i.MoveNext())
        Console.WriteLine(i.Current);
    }
  }
}
```

The output from Listing 4.5 shows the evidence passed to the security system; it has been edited for brevity. The security system takes this evidence and produces a permission set for the assembly.

```
<System.Security.Policy.Zone version="1">
   <Zone>MyComputer</Zone>
</System.Security.Policy.Zone>

<System.Security.Policy.Url version="1">
   <Url>file://C:/windows/microsoft.net/framework/
   v1.0.3705/mscorlib.dll</Url>
</System.Security.Policy.Url>

<StrongName version="1"
            Key="0000000000000000004000000000000000"
            Name="mscorlib"
            Version="1.0.3300.0"/>

<System.Security.Policy.Hash version="1">
   <RawData>4D5A90000030000000400000FFFF0000B800000000000
   00040000000000
      . . .
      000000000000000000000000000000000000000000000000000
   </RawData>
</System.Security.Policy.Hash>
```

As an aside, many aspects of the security system, as well as many parts of the .NET Framework, use eXtended Markup Language (XML) as a fundamental means of describing data. Developers using the CLR are strongly advised to explore its design and use.

Policy Manager

The Policy Manager in the CLR performs a number of functions by using the evidence supplied to it. Essentially, the Policy Manager takes this evidence and produces a set of permissions. As shown in Figure 4.3, it includes four policy levels:

- Enterprise
- Machine
- User
- Application Domain

Each level normally produces a permission set based on the evidence. These permission sets are then "intersected" to generate the permission set for the entire assembly. As a consequence, all levels must allow a permission before it can enter the assembly's granted permission set. For example, if the Enterprise policy level does not grant a permission, regardless of

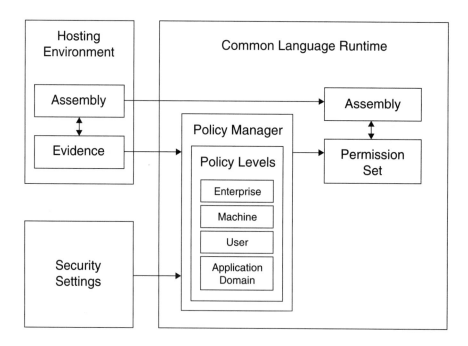

Figure 4.3 *Role of the Policy Manager under the CLR*

what the other levels specify, that permission will not be granted. Sometimes, however, a policy may direct the security system to not evaluate lower policy levels. This flexibility provides a means to allow a higher policy level, such as the Enterprise policy level, to effectively override subordinate levels.

Each policy level within the security system has a similar architecture. Each level consists of three parts:

- A tree of code groups
- A set of named permissions
- A list of policy assemblies

Code Groups

A code group consists of a conditional expression and a permission set. If an assembly satisfies the conditional expression, then it is granted the permission set. The set of code groups for each policy level is arranged into a tree structure. Every time a conditional expression evaluates to true, the permission set is granted and the traversal of that branch continues. Whenever a condition evaluates to false, the permission set is not granted and that branch is not examined further. As an example, consider the tree of code groups shown in Figure 4.4.

Assume you have an assembly with the following evidence: It came from `www.project42.net` and, because it came from the JJJLK product group, it has a strong name of JJJLK.

The code group tree traversal may proceed as follows:

1. The root node has a condition of All Code that is satisfied by any code. The permission set for All Code is granted to the assembly; it is called "Nothing" and effectively grants code no permissions.
2. The next code group checked is the one requiring that the code be loaded from My Computer. This condition fails, so the permission set is not granted and no subordinate nodes of this condition are checked.
3. We return to the last successfully granted code group, All Code, and continue checking its subordinate nodes. The next code group could

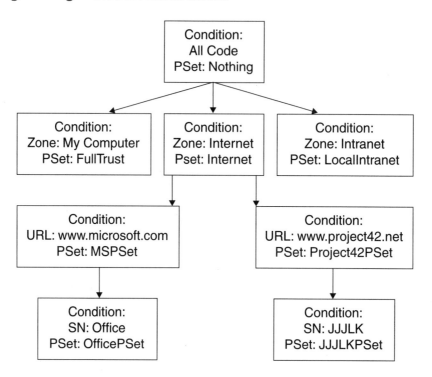

Figure 4.4 *A tree of code groups*

be Zone: Internet. As the code in this example was downloaded from the Internet, this condition is satisfied. The permission set, possibly called "Internet," is granted.

4. Continuing with the next subordinate code group in the same branch, this code group has a condition of Url: stating that the code came from `www.microsoft.com`. This condition fails as the code came from `www.project42.net`.

5. We return to the Zone: Internet code group, look for other nodes beneath it, and find a node for URL: www.project42.net. As this condition is satisfied, the "Project42PSet" permission set is granted.

6. We find a node for Strong Name: JJJLK. As this condition is satisfied, the "JJJLK" permission set is granted.

7. As no code groups remain below this level, we return to last code group that a condition matched and that has subordinate code groups and continue.

Eventually, the conditions satisfied and the granted permission sets would include the following:

- Condition: All Code; permission set: Nothing
- Condition: Zone: Internet; permission set: Internet
- Condition: URL: www.project42; permission set: Project42PSet
- Condition: Strong Name: JJJLK; permission set: JJJLKPSet

Inspection of the policy level code group is fairly simple. It is stored as XML in a well-known location. For example, the Enterprise policy is found at a location such as the following:

```
C:\WINDOWS\Microsoft.NET\Framework\v1.0.3705\CONFIG\enter-
prisesec.config
```

It looks like the following, again edited for brevity:

```
<?xml version="1.0" encoding="utf-8" ?>
<configuration>
 <mscorlib>
  <security>
   <policy>
    <PolicyLevel version="1">
     <SecurityClasses>
      <SecurityClass Name="StrongNameMembershipCondition"
       Description=
        "System.Policy.StrongNameMembershipCondition,
        mscorlib, Version=1.0.3300.0, Culture=neutral,
        PublicKeyToken=b77a5c561934e089"/>
       ...
     </SecurityClasses>
     <NamedPermissionSets>
      <PermissionSet class="NamedPermissionSet"
       version="1" Unrestricted="true" Name="FullTrust"
       Description="Allows full access to all resources"/>
      <PermissionSet class="NamedPermissionSet"
       version="1" Name="LocalIntranet"
```

continues

```
              Description="Default rights...local intranet">
              <IPermission class="EnvironmentPermission"
               version="1" Read="USERNAME"/>
              <IPermission class="FileDialogPermission"
               version="1" Unrestricted="true"/>
               ...
           <CodeGroup class="UnionCodeGroup" version="1"
            PermissionSetName="FullTrust" Name="All_Code"
            Description="Code ... of the code group tree.">
           <IMembershipCondition class="AllMembershipCondition"
            version="1"/>
           </CodeGroup>
           ...
           <FullTrustAssemblies>
            <IMembershipCondition
             class="StrongNameMembershipCondition"
             version="1"
             PublicKeyBlob="00000000000000000400000000000000"
             Name="mscorlib.resources"
             AssemblyVersion="1.0.3300.0"/>
            <IMembershipCondition
             class="StrongNameMembershipCondition"
             version="1"
             PublicKeyBlob="00000000000000000400000000000000"
             Name="System"
             AssemblyVersion="1.0.3300.0"/>
           </FullTrustAssemblies>
          </PolicyLevel>
        </policy>
      </security>
    </mscorlib>
  </configuration>
```

Administrators can edit the XML directly to modify the default policy. In addition, a Microsoft Management Console snap-in provides a visual interface for changing these settings.

Named Permission Sets

A policy level contains a list of named permission sets; the code groups may assign these sets to code that satisfy various code group conditions. Examples of predefined permission sets include the following:

- FullTrust: Allows unrestricted access to system resources
- SkipVerification: Allows an assembly to skip verification
- Execution: Allows code to execute
- Nothing: No permissions; not granting the permission to execute effectively stops code from running

Policy Assemblies

During security evaluation, other assemblies may need to be loaded for use in the policy evaluation process. Such assemblies may, for example, contain user-defined permission classes. Of course, if these assemblies also need to be evaluated and they refer to other assemblies, a circular dependency could result. To avoid this problem, each assembly contains a list of trusted assemblies that it needs for policy evaluation. This list of required assemblies is naturally referred to as the list of "policy assemblies."

Examining Policy Levels and Permission Sets

Listing 4.6 displays the policy levels and permission set for an application. The application is a C# program run from the local disk, so it receives a fairly powerful permission set.

Listing 4.6 Examining the policy levels and permission set for a C# program

```
using System;
using System.Collections;
using System.Security;
using System.Security.Policy;

namespace SecurityResolver
{
  class Sample
  {
    static void Main(string[] args)
    {
```

continues

```
       IEnumerator i = SecurityManager.PolicyHierarchy();
       while(i.MoveNext())
       {
       PolicyLevel p = (PolicyLevel) i.Current;
       Console.WriteLine(p.Label);
       IEnumerator np =
                  p.NamedPermissionSets.GetEnumerator();
       while (np.MoveNext())
       {
         NamedPermissionSet pset =
                         (NamedPermissionSet)np.Current;
         Console.WriteLine(
       "\tPSet: \n\t\t Name: {0} \n\t\t Description {1}",
                            pset.Name, pset.Description);
       }
      }
     }
   }
}
```

The output of the program is shown below. It has been edited for brevity.

```
Enterprise
  PSet:
    Name: FullTrust
    Description: Allows full access to all resources
    ...
  PSet:
    Name: LocalIntranet
    Description: Default rights given to applications
                on your local intranet
    ...
Machine
    ...
  PSet:
    Name: Nothing
    Description: Denies all resources, including the right
to execute
    ...
User
  ...
```

```
   Name: SkipVerification
   Description: Grants right to bypass the verification
 PSet:
   Name: Execution
   Description: Permits execution
 ...
```

Stack Walks

A stack walk is an essential, but expensive, part of the security system. The following description is a logical model of how stack walks and the security system work within the CLR.

A new *activation record* is put on the stack every time a method is called. This record contains the parameters passed to the method (if any), the address to return to when this function completes, and any local variables. As a program executes, the stack grows and shrinks as functions are called. At certain stages during execution, the thread may seek to access a system resource, such as the file system. Before allowing this access, the security system may *demand* a stack walk to verify that all functions in the call chain have permission to access the system resource. At this stage, each activation record will be checked to confirm that callers do indeed have the required permission.

At any stage during its execution, a function may wish to check the permissions of all its callers before it accesses a system resource. To do so, it may demand a security check for a specific permission. This demand triggers a stack walk, which has one of two results:

- The function continues if all callers have the permission granted.
- An exception is thrown if the callers do not have the required permission.

Figure 4.5 depicts this process.

Functions may choose to modify the stack walk using any of several mechanisms. First, one function may vouch for the functions that called it by *asserting* a specific permission. If a stack walk looks for the asserted permission, and this function's activation record is checked for the permission,

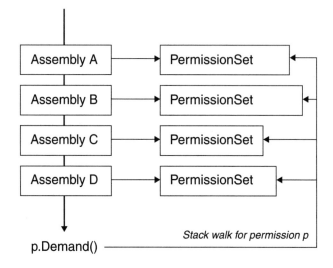

Figure 4.5 *A stack walk for permission*

then if the function has the asserted permission the check will succeed and the stack walk will terminate. The Assert model does have an interesting semantic, however. You do not need to have a permission to assert it. In such a case, the assertion will succeed when it is called but an exception will be thrown at runtime if a stack walk discovers that the function did not have the permission it asserted.

A second way to modify the stack walk is for a function to *deny* permissions. This situation may occur when a function knows that it should not be able to assess a resource. *PermitOnly* provides similar functionality to the denial in that it causes a stack walk to fail. Whereas the Deny operation specifies a set of permissions that would cause the stack walk to fail, however, PermitOnly specifies the set of permissions required to continue the stack walk.

Note that a stack frame can have only one Deny, one PermitOnly, and one Assert in effect at any time. For example, if developers need to assert a number of permissions, they should create a PermissionSet to represent that set and perform a single Assert operation. Some methods remove the current PermissionSet setting for a single stack walk modifier, allowing another permission set to be registered—for example, RevertPermitOnly and RevertAll.

Listing 4.7 demonstrates many of the aspects of code-based security, such as the asserting, demanding, and denying of specific permissions.

Listing 4.7 *Asserting, demanding, and denying permissions*

```
using System;
using System.Security;
using System.Security.Permissions;

namespace PermissionDemand
{
    class EntryPoint
    {
        static void Main(string[] args)
        {
            String f = @"c:\System Volume Information";
            FileIOPermission p =
                new FileIOPermission(
                    FileIOPermissionAccess.Write, f);
            p.Demand();
            p.Deny();
            p.Demand();
            CheckDeny(p);
            p.Assert();
            CheckDeny(p);
        }
        static void CheckDeny(FileIOPermission p)
        {
            try
            {
                p.Demand();
            }
            catch(SecurityException)
            {
                Console.WriteLine("Demand failed");
            }
        }
    }
}
```

Listing 4.7 produces the following output, which appears very counterintuitive at first:

```
Demand failed
Demand failed
```

The first call to `Demand` succeeds, even though the program attempts to access a restricted system directory. This result occurs because the CLR security system is not tied to the operating system's security system. Therefore, although the operating system will prohibit access to the system directory should the program seek it, the CLR security system will not fail the `Demand` call because the code has full trust, which includes file access as far as the CLR's security system is concerned.

The next call to `Demand`, which occurs immediately after the `Deny` call, also succeeds. The demanding function's activation record is not checked when a `Demand` call is made—only its callers. Therefore, although the function has denied access, this fact is not detected by the `Demand` call. The call to `CheckDeny` and the subsequent call to `Demand` do fail, however. The `Deny` call in the previous method is checked, as it appears in a caller's stack frame.

Next, the program returns to `Main` and makes a call to `Assert`. Here the function has asserted a permission that was denied in this stack frame. When the program enters `CheckDeny`, the call to `Demand` again raises an exception. But why? A `Deny` overrides an `Assert`, because the `Deny` permission set is always checked before the `Assert` permission set is examined.

Declarative and Imperative Style

The CLR allows developers to express security constraints in two styles: declarative and imperative. Expressing security constraints in the *declarative style* means using the attribute syntax. These annotations are persisted in the metadata for the type, effectively becoming baked into the assembly at compile time. The following is an example of declarative-style security from Listing 4.4:

```
[PrincipalPermissionAttribute(SecurityAction.Demand,
                    Name=@" PROJECT42\Damien Watkins ")]
```

Expressing security requirements in the *imperative style* entails creating instances of `Permission` objects at runtime and invoking methods on them. The following is an example of imperative-style security from Listing 4.7:

```
FileIOPermission p = new FileIOPermission(
                    FileIOPermissionAccess.Write, f);
p.Demand();
```

There are a few reasons for choosing one style over the other. For instance, all security requirements can be expressed using the declarative style; the same is not true for the imperative style. However, the declarative style requires that all security constraints be expressed at compile time; the imperative style is more flexible because it allows constraints to be expressed at runtime.

A side effect of persisting declarative security requirements in the metadata is that you can use tools to extract this metadata information and then provide functionality based on this fact. For example, a tool may display a list of the declarative security attributes set on an assembly. This feature is not available with imperative security. Developers need to be aware and fluent with both styles.

Summary

This chapter described the execution system and its major functions, providing example programs that demonstrate how developers can interact with the execution system. In summary, the execution system provides facilities such as the following:

- Class loading
- Just-in-time compilation and verification
- Memory management and garbage collection
- Security

The execution system may be the source of the biggest difference between the CLR and other component models such as COM and CORBA. COM offers little support for ensuring the type safety of components, accomplishes life-cycle management through developer-controlled reference counting, and supports security as only an afterthought. CORBA provides little in the way of a standardized execution system; under this model, programs execute in the environment offered by the language in which they are written. While this simplicity is helpful for developing distributed systems, it hinders the construction of component-based systems. Facilities such as CORBA's object-by-value will prove difficult to implement for languages that do not supply a common execution environment.

■ 5 ■

Building Applications

So far, most of the examples in this book have focused on simple, single-file .NET applications. In the real world, of course, applications tend to be much larger, consisting of many discrete files. These files will include both program files that contain code (both managed and unmanaged), and non–code-related files, such as data, message, or icon files. To complicate matters even further, many modern applications draw resources from many disparate locations—portions of the application may come from one server, while other portions come from another server. From the user's point of view, these discrete portions all combine at runtime to form the final application.

These concepts should be familiar to anyone experienced in creating applications using traditional techniques. The traditional model for building Windows applications is to compile multiple source code files into discrete object files, and then to link them together into a package such as a dynamically linked library (DLL) or an executable. The complete application can then be considered a grouping of these executables, DLLs, and files. This is particularly true when using COM or other component models. Individual components are built and distributed as a DLL, and the final application is generally a collection of such components, plus "glue"—that is, the executable that combines them into a usable application.

The traditional model of packaging applications works reasonably well, but has a number of shortcomings that .NET attempts to overcome. Notably, when working with distributed applications or applications deployed via the Internet, a number of problems can surface that should be well known to any experienced developer:

Version Conflicts. As later versions of particular components are released, conflicts can arise with other applications that use the same component. For example, Application A and Application B may both use the Widget component. After the installation of both applications, a new version of Application A may be released that uses a later version of the Widget component. Under this scenario, Application B might fail when the new version of Application A is installed on a machine as the new Widget component is not 100% compatible with Application B. This situation is commonly referred to as "DLL hell."

Trojan Horse Components. A malicious (or well-intentioned but misguided) person may attempt to replace the Widget component with a completely different component that merely shares the same base name. Much as in the version conflict problem, this new component may (or may not) work well with some applications, but may cause others to fail. Debugging such failures in the field can prove very difficult.

Locale Information. Traditionally, managing locale-related or cultural differences has fallen to the application author. Although string tables and other such techniques are commonly used, the operating system and application loading process offer no real support for this task, which can make deployment painful for multiple versions of an application differing only in terms of its locale or culture.

The fundamental .NET concept for solving all of these problems is the assembly. This chapter defines and discusses the .NET assembly and demonstrates how assemblies solve these problems. In addition, it describes how to build and deploy assemblies to take advantage of the facilities offered by .NET. The final section delves further into the concept of an application domain and examines how programmers can programmatically utilize this concept.

Existing Technologies to Solve Application-Related Problems

The problems associated with deploying different versions of an application have existed for a number of years, and various systems have been implemented to overcome these problems. These solutions include the use of "well-known" locations to store globally accessible code, the use of user-configurable search paths to modify the way in which the names of executables are resolved at runtime, and the use of symbolic names which add a level of indirection during name resolution.

Well-Known Locations

Most operating systems provide one or more "well-known" directories that may hold publicly accessible executable files. Administrators can install an application or components into one of these well-known directories to make them potentially available to all users on a system.

For example, UNIX operating systems often have directories named `bin` for just this purpose. Normally these directories hold many executable files that are fundamental to running different applications, including the operating system itself. A UNIX operating system may support a number of well-known directories, such as `/bin`, `/usr/bin` and `/usr/local/bin`. Individual users can also create a directory off their home directories, again often named `bin`, and insert programs that they wish to execute into this directory. In most cases, these programs remain private to individual users.

In the Windows operating systems, the `System32` directory is another example of a well-known directory.

Search Paths

Many operating systems allow the user to define a `PATH` variable that contains a list of directories. The operating system uses this list of directories when searching for executables on behalf of a user, by sequentially looking in each directory in the PATH variable until it finds the named program. The search stops when the file name is first found, without taking any other context or any other installed versions into account. Thus the order of the directories in the PATH variable can be critical. For instance, the desired file may exist on the system but not be used if the directory is located later on the PATH variable's list than another file with the same name.

Recent versions of Microsoft Windows support a concept called "side-by-side component sharing" that uses a variation on search paths to implement multiple versions of the same component. This technique simply searches the application's directory for matching components before checking the well-known system location. Although this approach goes some way toward solving the problem, it relies on vendors to modify their applications to support this technique, and it does not cover every scenario where components need to be shared.

Symbolic Names

Most operating systems allow users to create symbolic names (or links) to files. A symbolic link is another name that refers to the same file. It may be located in any directory and may have any valid file name. For example, a meaningful symbolic name, such as `MyEditor`, might refer to a file such as `ed_eng_12_3`.

This concept can also be extended to directories. For example, the X11 windowing system, also known as X Windows, which is commonly found on Linux installations, uses symbolic names to point to the specific installation version. In the following directory listing, the `/usr/lib` directory has a directory named `X11`, which is actually a symbolic link to the `/usr/X11R6` directory:

```
[skip@localhost lib]$ ls -l X11
lrwxrwxrwx    1 root ...          16 Apr 19  2001 X11 ->
../X11R6/lib/X11
[skip@localhost lib]$
```

Applications can simply refer to `/usr/lib/X11` without having any knowledge of the specific version installed on the machine.

Versioning-Related Technologies

A combination of the concepts of well-known directories, PATH variables, and symbolic links provides a solution to problems related to versioning. Suppose that version 1 of a program called `Editor` is installed on a system in a subdirectory called `Editor1`. The system administrator may install a symbolic link called `Editor` in a well-known directory that points to the `Editor` executable in the directory `Editor1`. Users then include the well-known directory in their individual PATH variables, so that when a user types `Editor` and presses the return key the `Editor` program executes.

What happens when the vendor releases the next version of `Editor`? The system administrator might install the new `Editor` program in an `Editor2` subdirectory. Changing the symbolic link so that it no longer points to the `Editor` executable in directory `Editor1` but rather points to the version in `Editor2` upgrades all users on the system without any intervention on their behalf. A limitation with this approach, however, is that it upgrades all users at the same time; users who wish to continue using version 1 of the `Editor` program must now take explicit actions to access the previous version (but at least they can do so).

Now if a user wishes to use the beta version of `Editor3`, then he or she can install the beta version in one of the user's own directories, such as a local `bin` directory. If the user changes the PATH variable to look in the local directory before looking in the global directories, then the beta version will be loaded when the user types `Editor` at the prompt. A limitation here is that changing the PATH variable affects lookup of all executable programs.

Does the use of these schemes solve all versioning problems? While they do provide an amount of useful functionality, some problems persist. First, configuring a system involves a number of processes and people, from system administrators to users. Second, these strategies function well in a fairly static system; systems that incorporate the dynamic downloading of executable code do not fit well into this model.

Windows Registry

The Windows Registry provides some of the abilities described previously. It is a well-known location where the operating system and applications can go to resolve a call for executable code. One of the elements in the Registry that COM uses is program IDs; they provide some of the benefits of symbolic names, where each program ID can be translated into an executable file on disk. An example of a program ID is `Excel.Application.10`, where 10 is the version number. Over a period of time, the location of the code referenced by a program ID can change without the need for clients to take any action.

Use of the Registry has a number of limitations. First, only one Registry exists; users cannot add their own private registry. Second, the Registry is fairly complicated when compared to a directory structure. Indeed, inserting an executable into a well-known directory is much simpler than adding entries to the Windows Registry.

The major limitation of the Registry, however, is that the information contained in it and the executable files to which it refers remain separate. Therefore, whenever an executable file that requires information to be inserted in the Registry is moved to a new machine, the installation scripts must update the Registry. Maintaining consistency between the Registry and the actual files on disk can be an arduous task. One goal of any deployment system should be improved simplicity in copying a file to a location and making it available for subsequent use without any additional overhead.

Assemblies

An assembly is a collection of modules and resources that are part of the same version of an application and are deployed together; thus these items are considered to make up a single unit. The term *resource* refers to anything (other than code) used by an assembly. Resources can include graphical resources (such as icons, bitmap images, and so forth) or anything else that a program uses to perform its job (such as text or binary files). Simple assemblies often consist of just one file (a .NET module), whereas more complex assemblies may include numerous files (both modules and resources).

Exactly one file in the assembly (generally a .DLL file) contains an assembly manifest that fully describes the assembly. This manifest contains its own metadata, which includes version, culture, and originator information, as well as references to and checksums of the items in the assembly. The existence of an assembly manifest is what turns a module into an assembly. Sometimes this manifest is attached to a module in an assembly; at other times a special, empty module is created solely to hold the manifest for the assembly. The assembly manifest references all other modules in the assembly, plus any other resources required by the assembly.

Example: A Simple Assembly

To explain the assembly concepts, this chapter includes a progressive example that demonstrates the development of an `AboutBox` component as an assembly. The shared `AboutBox` component in this assembly can be reused by any number of applications. As the example progresses, it highlights the use of embedded and linked resources, different versions of assemblies living side by side in the .NET environment, and several other key concepts.

The code for this example has been split up among many directories, with each directory containing a fully functional code segment. The full source code for each example is not shown in this book, but rather only the relevant changes required to demonstrate the concepts under discussion. Each code segment does indicate the directory containing the complete source code for that particular stage of the assembly.

The example assembly makes use of a base class `AboutBoxBase` (implemented in `AboutBoxBase.cs`), which provides much of the GUI logic needed for the dialog. As development of the example progresses, new subclasses are created from this base class, but the base class itself is never modified. As the purpose of this example is to demonstrate assembly concepts, this base class is not shown, but it can be found with the example code segments. The base class expects the programmer to provide a single overridden method, `GetAboutText()`, to return the text for the dialog.

The assembly example also uses a client program called `UseAboutBox.exe`. As with `AboutBoxBase.cs`, the source code in `UseAboutBox.cs` does not change during the development of the progressive example. For each version of the example, the client application is simply recompiled, referencing the specific version of `AboutBox` code it uses.

Version 1 of `AboutBox`

The first version of the `AboutBox` example uses a hard-coded string in the text of the dialog. Listing 5.1 provides the code for this version. As you can see, this trivial example defines a single namespace (AboutBoxSample), a single class (AboutBox) that derives from the base class (AboutBoxBase), and one method (GetAboutText()) that returns the hard-coded string. This file is found in the AboutBoxSample directory of the samples.

Listing 5.1 AboutBox: *Version 1*

```
namespace AboutBoxSample
{
  public class AboutBox : AboutBoxBase
    {
        public override string GetAboutText()
        {
            return "Simple AboutBox";
        }
    }
}
```

Building the Assembly with nmake and makefile

As this chapter progresses, the instructions for building the examples become more complex and more vulnerable to errors. For this reason, the assembly example uses the Microsoft nmake utility, and makefile files are provided with each code sample.

nmake is Microsoft's version of the UNIX make tool, and a version is included with the .NET platform SDK. nmake processes a makefile, which indicates how to build each target (often an output file) and lists dependencies between files involved in the build process. For example, a makefile might indicate that the target AboutBox.dll depends on AboutBox.cs (meaning that any changes to AboutBox.cs should cause AboutBox.dll to be rebuilt) and that a specific command can be used to create AboutBox.dll.

The makefile for version 1 of the assembly example follows. Although a complete discussion of nmake and makefile is beyond the scope of this book, a quick description of these tools should help you to understand the intention behind their use. The first line in the following code indicates that to build the first target in the makefile, all, you need to build two other targets, AboutBox.dll and UseAboutBox.exe. The next two lines indicate that AboutBox.dll should be rebuilt whenever AboutBox.cs or

`..\AboutBoxBase.cs` changes; to build this DLL, the C# (`csc`) command specified in the makefile should be executed. Next, the code indicates that `UseAboutBox.exe` depends on `UseAboutBox.cs` from the parent directory, and the C# command line is given. Finally, the code identifies a target called `clean`; like the target `all`, it does not identify an output file but rather indicates how to clean up after building so that only the source files remain.

```
all: AboutBox.dll UseAboutBox.exe

AboutBox.dll:  AboutBox.cs ..\AboutBoxBase.cs
  csc /t:library AboutBox.cs ..\AboutBoxBase.cs

UseAboutBox.exe: ..\UseAboutBox.cs
  csc /t:winexe /r:AboutBox.dll /out:UseAboutBox.exe \
     ..\UseAboutBox.cs

clean:
    -del *.exe
    -del *.dll
```

To build this sample, simply change to the sample directory, and execute `nmake`. You should see a number of commands executed as each target is built, and a directory listing should include `AboutBox.dll` and `UseAboutBox.exe`.

After building this example, you can execute it by running `UseAboutBox.exe`, and selecting About from the Help menu. See Figure 5.1

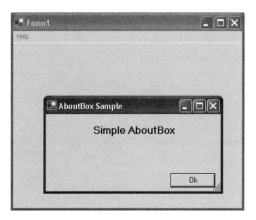

Figure 5.1 *First version of* `UseAboutBox.exe` *in action*

Functioning of the `makefile`

You may be wondering: What exactly does the `makefile` instruct the C# compiler to do?

The command line used to build version 1 of the assembly (from the `makefile`) follows:

```
csc /t:library AboutBox.cs ..\AboutBoxBase.cs
```

The code passes two source file names: the source file for version 1 of the assembly and the base class that is shared among all versions of the assembly. The `/t:library` option directs C# to build an assembly from the two source files. When C# creates an assembly, it places the assembly manifest in the single output file created by the compiler; thus a single `About-Box.dll` is created that contains both the module with the compiled code and the assembly manifest.

Figure 5.2 shows this simple assembly. It includes a single assembly (`AboutBox`), which consists of a single file (`AboutBox.dll`). This file contains both the module code and the assembly manifest.

`UseAboutBox.exe` is the example application that uses this assembly. The following command line is used to build this application:

```
csc /t:winexe /r:AboutBox.dll /out:UseAboutBox.exe \
    ..\UseAboutBox.cs
```

Note that only one source file is used to build this application, `..\Use-AboutBox.cs`. As this code is reused for all subsequent versions of the assembly, it resides in the parent directory.

Version 1 of the assembly also passes three options to the compiler:

- `/t:winexe` instructs C# to create a GUI executable (rather than a library, module, or console executable).
- `/r:AboutBox.dll` informs C# that the code references types defined in the `AboutBox.dll` assembly file. The compiler will load this DLL to resolve type references during the compilation step, and it will also embed information about this assembly in the final executable. When the executable is run, the .NET runtime environment will locate the reference to the assembly and load it accordingly.

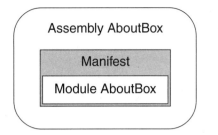

Figure 5.2 *Construction of version 1 of the assembly*

- `/out:UseAboutBox.exe` specifies to the compiler the file name to create for the final executable.

Embedded and Linked Resources

.NET allows arbitrary resources to be bundled within the assembly. Such resources might include image or icon files, as well as text files containing error or other messages—but ultimately any file can be used as a resource. Assemblies can either directly embed these resources or provide a link to external resources.

Embedding a resource takes a copy of the named file and physically places it in the assembly file. Once the assembly has been built, the external file is no longer needed. At runtime, a request to access the file will be satisfied by the copy of the file included in the assembly.

As you have probably guessed, *linking a resource* simply embeds the file name of the resource as part of the assembly. This approach makes the file become an integral part of the assembly, and the file must subsequently be distributed as part of the assembly.

A number of reasons exist for favoring embedding over linking or linking over embedding. In some cases, linking to the original file allows you to modify the external file without rebuilding the entire assembly (but see the discussion later in this chapter on strong names and public assemblies for information on situations in which this technique does not work). Embedding a resource simplifies the deployment of an assembly, as fewer files make up the assembly; on the other hand, embedding the same resource in a number of files increases disk usage.

Example: A .NET Assembly with Embedded Resources

To demonstrate these concepts, let's extend the example assembly to use an external resource. Instead of hard-coding the `AboutBox` string as was done in version 1, let's use a `message.txt` file to hold the string.

The example must be modified in several ways to work with an embedded or linked file:

- Create the resource file—`message.txt` for this example.
- Modify the `makefile` to embed or link the resource.
- Modify the code to open the linked resource and read its contents.

The complete code for this version of the assembly is found in the `AboutBoxEmbed` directory.

The `message.txt` file consists of single line:

```
Embedded Application
```

If all goes according to plan, the modified code will display this text in a dialog.

The C# compiler used to generate the assembly supports two relevant command-line options: `/resource:` to embed a resource and `/linkresource:` to link to an external resource. This version of the assembly demonstrates embedding a resource, so the `makefile` uses the `/resource:` option.

The complete command (from the `makefile`) for building the assembly follows:

```
csc /t:library /resource:message.txt AboutBox.cs \
    ..\AboutBoxBase.cs
```

The C# code will reference the embedded resource, so it will take advantage of the `System.Reflection.Assembly.GetManifestResource-Stream()` function. This function returns a `System.IO.Stream` object, which is wrapped in a `System.IO.StreamReader` object to read the contents as a simple string. Listing 5.2 shows the modified code.

Listing 5.2 AboutBox: *Version 2*

```
using System.Reflection;
using System.IO;

namespace AboutBoxSample
{
    public class AboutBox : AboutBoxBase
    {
        public override string GetAboutText()
        {
            // Get the about box text from the
            // embedded text file.
            Assembly ass = Assembly.GetExecutingAssembly();
            Stream stream =
                ass.GetManifestResourceStream("message.txt");
            StreamReader reader = new StreamReader(stream);

            return reader.ReadToEnd();
        }
    }
}
```

You build and run this version in the same way as version 1 of the assembly. Note the text in the dialog matches that in the message.txt file (Figure 5.3).

Embedding the resource in the assembly takes a copy of the message.txt file rather than referencing the copy on disk. If you rename or remove the message.txt file, the application will still run correctly. Changing the text in the file has no effect on the text in the application.

In this scenario, the file message.txt is technically not part of the assembly. Rather, the contents of message.txt are copied into the assembly and can be referenced by the assembly, but the file itself is not part of the

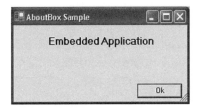

Figure 5.3 *Second version of* UseAboutBox.exe *in action*

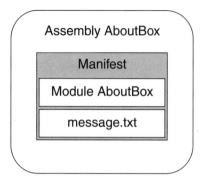

Figure 5.4 *Construction of assembly with embedded resource*

assembly. This relationship is shown in Figure 5.4, where the module and the contents of the `message.txt` file both appear inside the single assembly file that holds the assembly manifest.

Example: A .NET Assembly with Linked Resources

To link to a resource instead of embedding it, you simply modify the C# command line in the `makefile` to use the `/linkresource:` option. The new `makefile` can be found with this chapter's samples, but the new command line appears here:

```
csc /t:library /linkresource:message.txt AboutBox.cs \
    ..\AboutBoxBase.cs
```

The `message.txt` file now has the following text:

```
Linked Application
```

The C# source file remains unchanged. Again, you can build and test the new example, and confirm that the `AboutBox` message matches that expected from the new `message.txt`.

To prove that .NET has truly linked the resource (rather than embedded it), let's attempt to rename or remove the `message.txt` file. In this case, the application should not run. `AssemblyBuilder.GetManifestResourceStream()` will return `null`, causing the application to fail. Similarly, if you attempt to copy only the assembly DLL to a new directory, without also copying all referenced modules and files, the assembly should fail to work.

Figure 5.5 shows the result of executing the program with the `message.txt` file removed.

If you change the text in the file, the application as it stands will continue to run and will display the new text. However, as discussed later in this chapter, you may need to sign the assembly so that it can be effectively deployed for use. Once the assembly is signed, you cannot modify the text file, as .NET will detect the tampering.

When you link to external resources, these resources become full-fledged members of the assembly, and the assembly manifest refers to the file by name. Figure 5.6 shows this relationship. Here the assembly

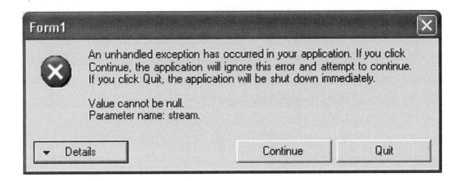

Figure 5.5 *Result of executing the assembly program without the message file*

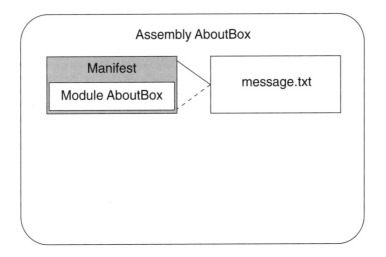

Figure 5.6 *Construction of assembly with linked resource*

manifest remains in the same file as the module, but the assembly manifest also refers to the `message.txt` file, as shown by the solid line. The module contains an indirect reference to `message.txt` via a call to `GetManifestResourceStream()`, as shown by the dashed line.

The Assembly Linker

The .NET Framework SDK comes with a useful tool called the Assembly Linker (`al.exe`). This tool can take any number of modules and files, and link them together into a single assembly. Although the C# compiler can perform many of the same functions as the Assembly Linker, the Assembly Linker is useful in mixed-language or non-C# environments.

Unlike the traditional "object file linkers" with which many developers are familiar from their C and C++ experiences, the Assembly Linker does not actually create a single new file with each module or resource embedded inside it. Instead, it creates a new .NET module that contains an assembly manifest referencing all of the modules for the assembly. Like the C# compiler, the Assembly Linker allows resources to be either embedded or linked. Any .NET modules that are part of the assembly can only be linked, however—there is no equivalent embedding option for modules.

Let's continue the evolution of the example assembly by using the Assembly Linker tool for the next assembly. The C# compiler is still used to create a .NET module from the C# source file, but it will not put an assembly manifest in the newly created module.

The C# source code remains exactly the same for this version of the assembly, but both `makefile` and `message.txt` are modified. The complete source code appears in the `AboutBoxLinkedAL` subdirectory.

The following commands are now used to build the assembly:

```
csc /t:module AboutBox.cs ..\AboutBoxBase.cs
al /linkresource:message.txt /out:AboutBox.dll \
    \AboutBox.netmodule
```

The `makefile` passes `/t:module` to the C# compiler to request that the compiler create a module rather than an assembly. By default, C# adds an extension of `.netmodule` to the modules it creates, yielding

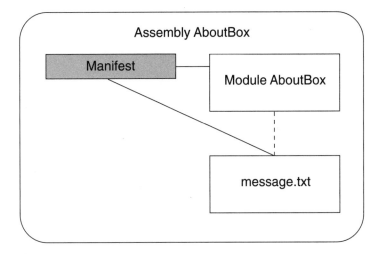

Figure 5.7 *Assembly Linker–constructed assembly with linked resource*

`AboutBox.netmodule`. The Assembly Linker is then invoked, with a request to create the assembly as `AboutBox.dll`, link to the module `AboutBox.netmodule`, and link to the resource `message.txt`.

Let's build and execute this version of the assembly. It should produce the exact same behavior as did the previous incarnation of the assembly; only the tools used to build it have changed. To demonstrate that the module is actually linked to the assembly rather than embedded inside it, simply remove the file `AboutBox.netmodule`, and the assembly `About-Box.dll` will fail to load.

Figure 5.7 depicts the assembly created with this version. The file `AboutBox.dll` contains the assembly manifest, but nothing else of significance to this discussion. The module and resource files are included as part of the assembly by virtue of the reference in the assembly manifest to the two files, as shown by the solid lines. The implied relationship between the module and the text file is shown by the dashed line.

Public and Private Assemblies

An assembly can be either private (available only to the application that uses it) or public (available to all applications resident on the machine). To this point, all of the examples in this chapter have used private assemblies: They are simply shipped with the application program and stored in the application directory or one of its subdirectories. The application program generally refers only to the file name of the assembly and ships this assembly with the application.

The concept of a public assembly is probably familiar to traditional Windows programmers in the form of the `system32` directory. Programs often install or upgrade critical DLLs in this directory, leading to obvious version conflicts and inevitable problems known as "DLL hell."

To support public assemblies, .NET manages a repository of assemblies, and runtime assembly resolution facilities perform all versioning, locale, and security management. In this way, applications can specify exactly which version (and possibly culture) assembly they wish to use; .NET will ensure that this exact version will always be used, even after the installation of new versions of the assembly. To support these features, .NET imposes some additional requirements on public assemblies (that is, assemblies found in the global repository), the main one being that the assembly must have a *strong name* (as discussed later in this section).

Before considering these public assemblies in depth, it is worth noting that in some circumstances you should try to avoid creating public assemblies that are stored in the repository. By keeping your assemblies private to your application's directory, you can install your application very simply—that is, by copying the files to a subdirectory on another computer and executing it, assuming certain security settings are compatible. With public assemblies, you will probably need to create an installation program that correctly installs your public assembly, allows for its uninstallation, and so forth. Use public assemblies only when you need explicit sharing of assemblies.

Strong Names

A strong name, which is also known as an assembly identity, consists of the assembly name, version and culture information, and a public key.[1] It is generated using a public/private key pair, ensuring that the strong name

---

[1] An optional Authenticode signature can be added, but it is not part of the strong name.

remains cryptographically secure. The strong name is stored in the assembly manifest, which itself contains the names and hashes of all files referenced in the assembly. Thus, the entire assembly is identified and secured by the assembly strong name.

The purpose of the strong name is to ensure that the assembly is what the application thinks it is. The original developer of the assembly uses a public and private key pair to create a digital signature, which is stored inside the assembly itself. .NET can then use the public key to confirm that the assembly is exactly as provided by the developer; using this technique, it can be certain that each bit in each file in the assembly is exactly what the developer signed the assembly with.

Although this strategy guarantees the *authenticity* of the assembly, it does not address any *trust* issues. An optional Authenticode signature allows the user to determine whether the assembly has been signed by a trusted individual, possibly to allow some kind of trusted access to the computer on which it runs. This chapter does not discuss Authenticode signatures in any detail.

In a nutshell, a strong name allows .NET to provide the exact assembly the application desires, with absolute certainty. As such, it can bring about the death of DLL hell!

Assembly Caches

In version 1 of .NET, the assembly repository consists of two assembly caches managed by the system: the global assembly cache (GAC) and the download cache. Both caches are very similar in operation and purpose; both allow applications to share assemblies with absolute safety. They differ only in the way they are populated and managed.

Global Assembly Cache

The GAC is a systemwide cache of signed assemblies. Assemblies are placed into the GAC, and their identities (i.e., strong names) are registered with the system. Any application needing such an assembly can then access it from this cache. The GAC manages different versions and locations of assemblies and, by utilizing strong names, the application can be assured that the bits of the assembly used when building the application are the exact same bits used when the user runs the application.

Assemblies are generally placed in the GAC in one of two ways: by installation programs or manually using one of the GAC management tools provided with .NET. In general, application installers will increment a reference count for the assembly, thereby allowing the system to uninstall the assembly from the GAC as the last application is uninstalled.

Only fully signed assemblies can be placed in the cache. Because assemblies without strong names do not come with any identifying information about their originator or version, no guarantees can be made to applications about the integrity of such an assembly. Furthermore, assemblies added to the GAC can reference only other strongly named assemblies in the GAC. If a strongly named assembly itself references another assembly by a simple name, then that other assembly (and therefore the original strongly named assembly) becomes vulnerable to all the DLL conflict problems that strong names are designed to avoid. Optionally, signed assemblies can include an Authenticode signature that verifies the author's identity. Authenticode signatures are not required for an assembly to be installed into the GAC.

Download Cache

The download cache is intended specifically to hold "slow" content—that is, any content hosted on a slow resource. For example, if an assembly is referenced from a Web page, a floppy disk, network, or CD resource, it will be stored in the download cache and be used for the application referencing it. Unlike with the GAC, content in the download cache always refers to the original location and may need to be refetched at any time. In contrast, once an assembly is installed in the GAC, the cache never implicitly drops it; consequently, the cache does not need to remember the original location from which the assembly was installed.

The download cache also stores each assembly on behalf of each individual application that references it. This strategy prevents conflicts arising from any other applications' attempts to use this same assembly.

Managing the Caches

The GAC can be managed either via installation programs, a GUI interface, or command-line tools. Of these techniques, only using installation programs is officially supported by .NET; these programs will always use reference counting and ensure that the lifetime of these assemblies is managed correctly. Using command-line tools or a GUI interface means that the assemblies will be installed without reference counting and can, therefore, be removed only explicitly (presumably by the same GUI interface or command-line tool). See the documentation for your installer tool for information on how assemblies are stored in the GAC.

During application development, however, the GUI and command-line tools are often your friends. On the GUI side of the world, Windows Explorer has an extension that allows you to use standard GUI operations on the cache. Opening the `%windir%\assemblies` directory using Windows Explorer, you will see a list containing the relevant strong name information, such as the assembly name and version (see Figure 5.8).

As you can see in Figure 5.8, Windows Explorer shows much of the information used by the assemblies' strong names; the versions and public keys are shown (but none of the visible assemblies have a culture identifier specified). In addition, Figure 5.8 shows how multiple assemblies with the same name can be contained in the GAC—for example, multiple versions of Microsoft's `CalcR` reside on this machine. There is also an example of a precompiled assembly in Figure 5.8, called `CustomMarshalers`. Later

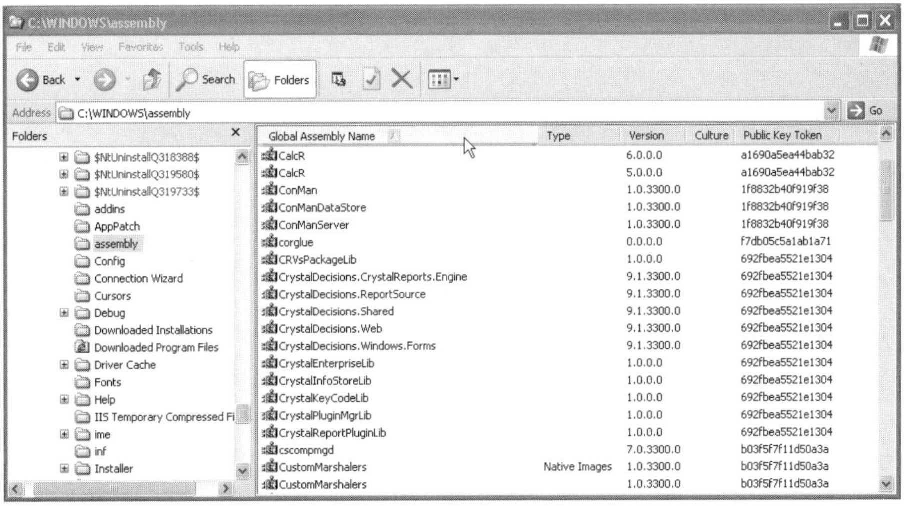

Figure 5.8 *Global assembly cache as shown by Windows Explorer*

sections in this chapter dig a little deeper into this directory structure and look at the actual files found inside the cache.

As you would expect with a Windows Explorer extension, you can delete files from the cache or add them by using drag-and-drop or the standard cut-copy-paste Clipboard operations. A Microsoft Management Console (MMC) snap-in allows you to manage the GAC along with a host of other .NET options, which you can start by executing `mscorcfg.msc`.

For developing and building applications, the .NET Framework SDK provides a command-line tool that provides management capabilities for the GAC. This tool, called `gacutil`, allows you to install files into the GAC, dump the contents of the GAC, and add references to assemblies. It is particularly useful for developers who may need to install their built assemblies directly into the GAC for testing; indeed, the rest of the examples in this chapter will use this tool to install public assemblies into the GAC.

Example: Creating and Using Public Assemblies

Let's extend the progressive example to work as a public assembly. This step involves creating a strong name for the assembly and installing it into the GAC.

To create a strong name for the assembly, you must create a public and private key pair in a file, and then pass the name of this key file to the Assembly Linker. The Assembly Linker will then create a strong name for the assembly, allowing you to use `gacutil` to install the assembly in the GAC.

This modification requires changes only to the `makefile`. No changes to the C# sources are needed, but these items can be found in the `AboutBox-GAC` directory containing this chapter's examples. The significant changes to the `makefile` from the previous versions are as follows:

- The strong name utility (`sn.exe`) is used to generate the key pair into `..\AboutBox.key`. This key pair file is generated only once, and is used by later code in this chapter.
- The key pair file is passed to the Assembly Linker via the `/keyfile:` parameter. In addition, the version portion of the strong name is filled with 1.0.0.0; later, you will see how side-by-side versioning works when this value is incremented.

- The `gacutil` utility is used to install the assembly into the GAC.
- When building the "clean" target, the key pair file is removed and the assembly is uninstalled from the GAC.

Listing 5.3 shows these changes.

Listing 5.3 *Revised* `AboutBox` makefile

```
all: AboutBox.dll UseAboutBox.exe

..\AboutBox.key:
    sn -k ..\AboutBox.key

AboutBox.dll: AboutBox.cs message.txt ..\AboutBox.key
    csc /t:module AboutBox.cs ..\AboutBoxBase.cs
    al /v:1.0.0.0 /keyfile:..\AboutBox.key \
        /link:message.txt /out:AboutBox.dll \
        AboutBox.netmodule
    gacutil /i AboutBox.dll

UseAboutBox.exe: AboutBox.dll ..\UseAboutBox.cs
    csc /t:winexe /r:AboutBox.dll /out:UseAboutBox.exe \
        ..\UseAboutBox.cs

clean:
    -gacutil /u AboutBox,Version=1.0.0.0
    -del *.exe
    -del *.netmodule
    -del *.dll
    -del ..\AboutBox.key
```

Even though this assembly has been built and installed into the GAC, it must still exist locally so that you can build the application that relies on the assembly. You must pass the name of the assembly on the command line of the application so that all references to the assembly can be correctly resolved.

To demonstrate that the correct assembly is used, the `message.txt` file is altered to contain only a single line:

```
Public Assembly
```

Now you can again build and test the new program. In the About Box dialog, the text matches the content of the new `message.txt` file.

To prove that this assembly is indeed public, you can run the executable in a directory *without* the built assembly. If you copy the resulting Use-AboutBox.exe to another directory and attempt to execute it, you will find that it works correctly, as expected. If you had tried this step with any of the earlier programs, their use of private assemblies would have caused them to fail.

Strong Names and Security

Using this public assembly, let's check out some of the security offered by strong names. To demonstrate how the .NET use of strong names prevents a modified assembly from being used in place of the original assembly, a file will be modified and an attempt made to install it in the GAC. To try this, change the message.txt file and then attempt to reinsert the assembly in the GAC using the following command:

```
gacutil /i AboutBox.dll
```

The gacutil utility responds with the following message:

```
Microsoft (R) .NET Global Assembly Cache Utility.  Version
1.0.3617.0
Copyright (C) Microsoft Corporation 1998-2001. All rights
reserved.

Failure adding assembly to the cache: One or more modules
were streamed in which did not match those specified by the
manifest.  Invalid file hash in the manifest?
```

Thus, once an assembly has been signed, it cannot be modified in any way. Applications can therefore rest assured that the version they have is exactly what the original developer provided.

Note that modifying message.txt prevented reinstallation in this example, as the text file is linked (rather than embedded) in the assembly; thus message.txt is part of the assembly. If you had embedded the file in the assembly, you could freely modify the text file, as its contents would have already been embedded in the main assembly DLL.

If you are so inclined, you can get your hands very dirty and experiment directly with the GAC to see what happens if you modify the `message.txt` file *after* installing the assembly.

■ **WARNING**

The following exercise is not supported and would be severely frowned upon by Microsoft. It is not guaranteed to work in future versions, and it may harm dolphins or cause your house or office to spontaneously explode. Use at your own risk.

Ensure that you have administrator privileges for the machine you are using, and perform the following steps:

1. Switch to the GAC directory.
2. Recursively search for any files called message.txt in the tree.
3. Edit and save the file.
4. Rerun this example's application.

Following is a command-prompt session that performs these steps:

```
C:\WINDOWS\Assembly\GAC> dir message.txt /s
...
Directory of
C:\WINDOWS\Assembly\GAC\AboutBox\1.0.0.0__a0df1539bc79861c

24/01/2002  02:58p                    19 message.txt
            1 File(s)                  19 bytes
...
C:\WINDOWS\Assembly\GAC> notepad
AboutBox\1.0.0.0__a0df1539bc79861c\message.txt
```

If you now execute the application, you do indeed see the new text in the dialog. By default, .NET does not attempt to verify the contents of an assembly each time it is loaded from the GAC, but only at GAC installation time. It stores the GAC under the Windows directory for exactly that reason; once a file appears in the GAC, .NET relies on Windows' built-in security to keep it safe (hence the requirement for administrator privileges). This approach allows .NET to avoid the time-consuming strong name validation for each assembly load.

Delayed Signing of Assemblies

In the interests of securing private keys, .NET supports the concept of delayed signing of assemblies. With delayed signing, the assembly creation step sets up the output file with all the structures needed to be a signed assembly, but the actual signing of the assembly takes place in a later, separate step.

The key advantage of this concept is that the private key used to sign your assemblies need not be distributed to all developers or installed on your build machines. Rather, the actual signing step can occur on a separate secure machine that need not have all the development tools required to build the application.

The Assembly Linker (`al.exe`) tool supports a `/delaysign` option that is used when the assembly is first created. The strong name tool (`sn.exe`) is then used to finalize the signed assembly.

Assembly Versioning

.NET versioning occurs at the assembly level. As discussed previously, a version number forms part of the assembly strong name, so it therefore constitutes part of the assembly identity. As different versions of the same assembly have different strong names (and therefore different identities), .NET considers them to be completely different assemblies. Note that although Windows executable files contain a version information resource (which can be viewed in Windows Explorer by viewing the properties of the file), this resource remains completely discrete from the .NET version information; thus .NET ignores the Win32 version information.

When you build your own assemblies, .NET records the complete strong names of all assemblies referenced by them. This practice allows the .NET runtime environment to know exactly which version of an assembly is required, and it can apply its versioning policy to determine which assembly to provide. The default .NET versioning policy states that applications use the same assembly version with which they were built and tested.

Example: Building a Second Version of an Assembly

Let's extend the progressive example by building a "version 2" of the assembly and installing it into the GAC. If all goes well:

- After installing the assembly into the GAC, you should see two `AboutBox` assemblies, each with a different version number.
- The earlier example code that uses version 1 should continue to use version 1 of the assembly (that is, the new version of the assembly will not automatically be used for applications that reference the old version).
- The new program should use version 2 of the assembly.

As you might guess, the changes to the code are minimal. You simply change the version number in the `al` command line and change the message text in the `message.txt` file. The files for the example appear in the `AboutBoxGACV2` directory, but the new `makefile` has the following `al` command line:

```
al /v:2.0.0.0 /keyfile:..\AboutBox.key /link:message.txt \
   /out:AboutBox.dll AboutBox.netmodule
```

The `message.txt` file has the following content:

```
Second Public Assembly
```

You build the example in the same way, by executing `nmake`. After building, you can check that two `AboutBox` assemblies appear in the cache. The `gacutil` tool supports a `/l` option to list the contents of the GAC, so executing `gacutil /l AboutBox` should show the entries:

```
C:\>gacutil /l AboutBox
Microsoft (R) .NET Global Assembly Cache Utility.  Version
1.0.3617.0
```

continued

```
Copyright (C) Microsoft Corporation 1998-2001. All rights
reserved.

The Global Assembly Cache contains the following
assemblies:
        AboutBox, Version=1.0.0.0, Culture=neutral,
                PublicKeyToken=...
        AboutBox, Version=2.0.0.0, Culture=neutral,
                PublicKeyToken=...

The cache of ngen files contains the following entries:

Number of items = 2
```

Both versions of the assembly are listed here. You can also use the Windows Explorer extension to see them.

When this sample code is executed, the new text is displayed in the About Box dialog. Executing the original code shows that it still uses version 1 of the assembly, as shown by the text displayed in that application. Thus .NET supports two versions of the same assembly, providing the correct assembly for each application.

.NET allows this version discrimination to happen per assembly, rather than just per application. Thus a single application can indirectly use two versions of the same assembly. This duality is more common than you might think—your application might use `ObjectA` and `ObjectB` for different purposes, even though both use a common assembly for their implementation. If a vendor creates a new `ObjectB` (with a new version of the common assembly) but `ObjectA` remains the same, then your application will indirectly require two different versions of the common assembly. This results in side-by-side assemblies, which .NET supports in the same way it supports different assemblies across different applications.

Example: Binding to a Different Version of an Assembly

.NET uses configuration files to apply different versioning policies. Configuration files, which are discussed in more detail in Chapter 6, allow you to specify different assembly bindings per assembly, per application, or systemwide.

Let's bind the code in the progressive example to a different assembly version by using an application configuration file. Application configuration files are the simplest to create and set up. As implied by their name, each file applies to a single application.

An application configuration file appears in the same directory as the application, and has the same name as the application but a .config suffix. Note that the original file extension is maintained; thus, for the example application, the application configuration file is named UseAboutBox.exe.config.

As discussed in more detail in Chapter 6, all configuration files are XML text files. The .NET documentation for configuration files lists all element and attribute names recognized by .NET, and the one that is of interest here is the dependentAssembly element. Listing 5.4 shows the relevant configuration file.

Listing 5.4 *Configuration file for assembly binding*

```
<configuration>
    <runtime>
        <assemblyBinding
          xmlns="urn:schemas-microsoft-com:asm.v1">
          <dependentAssembly>
            <assemblyIdentity name="AboutBox"
              publicKeyToken="a0df1539bc79861c"/>
            <bindingRedirect oldVersion="1.0.0.0"
                             newVersion="2.0.0.0"/>
          </dependentAssembly>
        </assemblyBinding>
    </runtime>
</configuration>
```

The dependentAssembly element contains the name and public key token of the assembly to which rebinding occurs. If necessary, you could also specify the assembly culture here. In the bindingRedirect element, you specify the oldVersion (that is, the version requested by the application) and the newVersion (that is, the new version provided to replace the old version).

In Listing 5.4, the file specifies that version 2.0.0.0 be used instead of version 1.0.0.0. For this reason, it makes sense to run the version 1 assembly with this configuration file; the second example is set up to use version 2.

To test the configuration file, simply place the application (`UseAbout-Box.exe`) and the configuration file (`UseAboutBox.exe.config`) in the same directory and execute the application. Displaying the About Box dialog confirms that the application uses version 2 of the assembly. You can further confirm this fact by removing version 1 from the GAC and checking whether the application still runs correctly.

Although the demonstration program here has used an application configuration file, it would clearly generate a lot of work if each and every application using a common assembly required such a configuration file. To eliminate this problem, .NET allows you to specify such bindings in a systemwide configuration file—more on that later.

Obviously, if you rebind one assembly to another, you must ensure that both assemblies are compatible. If they are not, your application will likely fail due to these differences as well as your direction to .NET to allow these versions to be interchanged. Use rebinding at your own risk, and even then only under the advice of the original assembly's author or publisher.

Internationalization and Localization

Often you may need to provide localized versions of your application or component, so that it can be used effectively in environments where U.S. English is not the primary language. You have probably already seen similar requirements with existing projects; the requirement to provide local versions of applications is certainly not unique to .NET.

Definitions

Deploying a component for other locales involves two steps: internationalization and localization.

Internationalization (also known as i18n, because there are 18 letters between the initial *i* and final *n* in the word "internationalization") enables a program to work effectively in all supported locales. Traditionally, it entails two steps:

- Converting the application to use Unicode or other "non-ASCII" string technology. Fortunately, you can usually avoid this step in .NET;

all .NET strings are implemented using Unicode, so they are automatically capable of storing all characters supported by .NET.

- Replacing all embedded strings with string resources. You should be able to change the culture used by an application without changing the application source code. Suppose your application has code similar to the following:

```
MsgBox("Can not open the file")
```

You must change this code so that the specific text in the message box can be translated without changing the source code itself. This modification generally involves some sort of string resource concept—messages are given IDs (often numeric), and the source code refers to these messages by their IDs. The ID-to-string mapping is maintained elsewhere and can be localized independently of the application source code.

.NET applications must perform this chore just like any other application framework. To accomplish this task, a common and very simple practice is to use string literals in your source code that do not translate into localizable applications.

Localization (also known as l10n, for same reasons that internationalization is called i18n) is the process of actually translating your application. Unlike the internationalization step, localization must be performed once for every translated version of the application. Often the developers of the application do not perform this step, but rather the experts in the culture of the translation take care of localization.

Existing Technologies: Separation of Code and User Interfaces

The problem of providing localized versions of an application predates .NET, so not surprisingly a number of strategies have evolved over time to solve it. Obviously, programmers want to minimize the effort required to create localized applications, both during initial development of the application and during ongoing maintenance and localization throughout the application's life.

A time-honored technique for dealing with this requirement is to separate the code (that is, the application logic) from any user interface (that is, anything displayed to or collected from the user). Traditional Windows developers have had a number of tools at their disposal to assist in the development of such applications. Windows allows resources (dialog or menu definitions, text strings, or any binary resource) to be embedded directly inside executable and DLL files, and this approach remains the most popular technique for localization. Typically, an application vendor will provide a DLL or executable file with the application code containing the resources for the application's primary language (generally U.S. English). The vendor will then create separate DLL files containing resources for each supported language (that is, for each localization).

.NET Localization Concepts

The building blocks for localization in .NET are assemblies and cultures. This chapter has already discussed assemblies, but when applications are localized, it is common practice to split resources from the main code and build them into separate culture-specific assemblies (known in .NET as "satellite assemblies").

The class library provides some helper classes for locating resources from these localized assemblies. If you structure your resources correctly, .NET will search for the "best" resource for the given culture. If it cannot locate a resource specific to that culture, it will use the default (or culture-neutral) resource.

Cultures

A *culture* is defined as the user's language, and optionally the user's location. Cultures are identified by culture tags of the format `primary[-secondary]`, where the `primary` tag is the language code and the optional `secondary` tag is the country/region code. The language codes are defined in ISO 639, "Codes for the Representation of Names of Languages"; the country/region codes are defined in ISO 3166, "Codes for the Representation of Names of Countries." Valid codes include "en" (specifying a primary language tag of English and no secondary tag) and "en-AU" (specifying English plus a secondary country/region code of Australia).

If the end user's culture is known, an application can take advantage of a large set of user preferences—for example, date formatting, day and month names, currency symbols, and so forth. Furthermore, the application can determine the most appropriate resources for that user.

For many of the culture-specific preferences, .NET will provide high-level functions that allow you to ignore the intricacies of these preferences. For example, if you need to display a date to the user, you should never build your own date format. While it may be tempting to write code similar to

```
Console.WriteLine("Today is {0}/{1}/{2}", dt.Month,
                  dt.Day, dt.Year);
```

this code works correctly only in the United States. You should always attempt to locate a function that does culture-aware formatting, such as the following:

```
Console.WriteLine("Today is {0:d}", dt.ToString("d"));
```

This code will automatically apply the appropriate separators and day-month-year ordering for the user's culture.

To assist you in utilizing your own localized resources, .NET defines the concept of a *satellite assembly* and provides the `ResourceSet` and `ResourceManager` classes to automatically provide the most culturally appropriate resources for an application. A satellite assembly contains only resources for a specific culture; as noted earlier, it is created during the localization process. Each supported culture generally has its own satellite assembly, supplementing the primary, or parent, assembly. The `Resource-Set` and `ResourceManager` classes, along with some file and directory naming conventions for these satellite assemblies, automatically provide the most culturally appropriate resources for the application.

Resource Fallback Process

.NET provides some naming and directory structure conventions that the resource fallback process uses to provide this cultural sensitivity. File naming conventions apply to satellite assemblies: For the parent assembly

`MyApp.dll`, for example, satellite assemblies for this assembly are named `MyApp.resources.dll`. Directory naming conventions apply to each culture-specific version of the satellite assembly—that is, the directory containing each `MyApp.resources.dll` file.

The resource fallback process aims to always provide *some* resource, even if it cannot find an exact match for the requested culture. For most applications, a default (or neutral) set of resources (most often English resources) is built into the primary assembly. If the search of satellite assemblies for a culture-specific version of a resource fails, this culture-neutral resource is generally better than no resource at all!

The process of locating a resource involves the following steps:

- Search the GAC for the exact satellite assembly. If the named assembly exists in the cache with the exact culture specified and the resource exists in the assembly, use this resource. Otherwise, the search continues.
- Search the directory of the currently executing assembly for a directory with the same name and culture as the specified culture. If the named assembly exists in this directory and the resource exists, use this resource. Otherwise, the search continues.
- Search the GAC again for the "parent culture" of the specified culture. If a resource is found, use it. The "parent culture" is the fallback culture for the specified culture. For example, if the specified culture is "fr-CA" (for French–Canada), the parent culture is "fr," meaning region-independent French. There may be many parents—although any culture can have only one parent, this parent may itself have a parent, and so on.
- Search the directory of the currently executing assembly again, this time for the parent culture. If the resource is found, use it. Otherwise, the search continues.
- Repeat Steps 3 and 4, using the next parent culture if one exists.
- If no other resource is available, use the default resource. If no default resource is available, throw an exception.

Example: A Localized Application

Let's demonstrate these concepts with a simple, contrived example. This example is kept as small as possible to maintain a focus on the key internationalization concepts rather than the details of the application itself. The simple application loads two strings (one to say "Hello" and one to say "Goodbye") and prints them to the console. It supports a command-line option to specify the culture to use for the strings.

The C# code that implements this application is quite simple, as shown in Listing 5.5. The .NET class library hides the complexities of locating the correct satellite assembly. UseCulture.cs shows the source code.

Listing 5.5 A simple localized application

```
using System;
using System.Reflection;
using System.Resources;
using System.Globalization;

class UseLocale
{
  public static void Main(string [] args)
  {
    string value;
    // First set up the default culture.
    CultureInfo ci = null;
    // If a command-line argument has been given,
    // assume it is a culture name.
    if (args.Length>0)
    {
      ci = new CultureInfo(args[0]);
      Console.WriteLine("(using culture {0})", ci);
    }
    // Create the resource manager that does
    // all the hard work.
    ResourceManager rm = new ResourceManager("strings",
                    Assembly.GetExecutingAssembly());
    // Load the specific string for the culture.
    value = rm.GetString("hello", ci);
    Console.WriteLine(value);
    value = rm.GetString("goodbye", ci);
    Console.WriteLine(value);
```

continued

```
        }
}
```

The program in Listing 5.5 supports specification of a culture on the command line. If no command-line option is given, then culture-neutral resources are used (because the `CultureInfo` variable remains `null`). Next, the code creates a resource manager for the resources identified by the name `strings`. It then loads two string values, using the keys `hello` and `goodbye`, respectively.

This is all well and good, but it implies the existence of a resource named `string` that contains the keys `hello` and `goodbye`. Let's see how they are defined.

Defining Resources

The .NET Framework comes with a tool called the Resource Generator (`resgen.exe`), which takes a text file and creates a resource file suitable for use with the `ResourceManager` class. This module is then linked or embedded into the assembly. As discussed previously, the culture-neutral resources are provided in the primary (or parent) assembly, and a satellite assembly is created for each supported culture.

The format of the text file is quite simple. All lines beginning with the semicolon symbol (`;`) are considered comments. Every other line follows the format `key=value`, where `key` is used by the source code to extract the text, and `value` is the string returned.

The text file for the culture-neutral strings is shown in `strings.txt` (see Listing 5.6). Listing 5.6 includes a few comment lines, followed by trivial definitions for `hello` and `goodbye`. As you can see from the C# code in Listing 5.5, these definitions act as the keys used in the source code.

Listing 5.6 `strings.txt` *holding culture-neutral string resources*

```
; Sample strings for the localization example.
; Define 2 strings: hello and goodbye.
; The other culture-specific string files may override one
; or both of these strings.

hello=Hello
goodbye=Goodbye
```

Building the Assembly

As with the other examples in this chapter, let's use a `makefile` to build the assembly. The complete `makefile` is included with the example source code, but Listing 5.7 shows the relevant entries for the primary assembly.

Listing 5.7 `makefile` *portion that builds the primary assembly*

```
UseCulture.exe: UseCulture.cs strings.resources
    csc /resource:strings.resources UseCulture.cs

strings.resources: strings.txt
    resgen strings.txt strings.resources
```

The code in Listing 5.7 results in a single assembly, `UseCulture.exe`, that is built from a single source file and that has one embedded file.

The first block indicates that building `UseCulture.exe` depends on `UseCulture.cs` (the source code) and `strings.resources` (a file containing the compiled string resources). The C# compiler is invoked, and the string resources are embedded in the assembly.

The second block indicates how `strings.resources` is built. It depends on `strings.txt` (the message definition file) and invokes the Resource Generator tool to generate the compiled file. In this example, it is important that the resource name be `strings.resources`, as `strings` is the name passed to the `ResourceManager` class that locates the resources. Executing `resgen.exe` with no argument will print usage options for the tool.

Defining a Satellite Assembly

To complete the example, you must define a satellite assembly for at least one culture. As two of the authors of this book are Australian, we decided that it is appropriate to support our own unique culture—the `en-AU` culture—in our own application.

As described in the "Resource Fallback Process" section, the simplest way of achieving this result is first to create a subdirectory with the name of the supported culture, and then to place a satellite assembly in that directory. That is exactly the approach followed here.

As this satellite assembly contains only resources, no C# code is required. All that is needed is a localized `strings.txt` file. Listing 5.8 shows the Australian version of `strings.txt`.

Listing 5.8 `en-AU\strings.txt` *holding localized string resources*

```
; Sample strings for the localization example.
; Australian English version - override only hello.
hello=G'Day
```

In Listing 5.8, only the `hello` string is overridden. If all goes according to plan, the culture-neutral version of `goodbye` should still be used for this culture.

To build the satellite assembly, the `makefile` contains the entries shown in Listing 5.9.

Listing 5.9 `makefile` *portion that builds the satellite assembly*

```
en-AU/UseCulture.resources.dll: en-AU/strings.txt
    resgen en-AU/strings.txt en-AU/strings.en-AU.resources
    al /embed:en-AU/strings.en-AU.resources \
        /culture:en-AU/out:en-AU/UseCulture.resources.dll
```

As you can see, the target to be built is an assembly named `UseCulture.resources.dll` in the `en-AU` directory. As mentioned previously, both the name of the file and the directory are critical for this example to work. To create the assembly itself, you must perform two discrete steps:

1. Compile the string resources.
2. Create the assembly itself.

Let's use the Resource Generator tool to create the module, and then the Assembly Linker tool to create the final assembly. Note that the module name is `strings.en-AU.resources`; once again, this name is critical to ensure that the `ResourceManager` can locate the resource.

At this point, running `nmake` should produce the `UseCulture.exe` and `en-AU\UseCulture.resources.dll` assemblies. You can then run the example code to ensure that it works as expected.

First, let's execute the application with no command-line arguments, which should cause the application to use the culture-neutral resources:

```
C:\> UseCulture.exe
Hello
Goodbye
```

To test the Australian culture, pass en-AU on the command line:

```
C:\> UseCulture.exe en-AU
(using culture en-AU)
G'Day
Goodbye
```

You can specify any valid culture, even if no direct support for that culture is available. For example, specifying fr-CA for Canadian French will still result in the culture-neutral resource being used:

```
C:\> UseCulture.exe fr-CA
(using culture fr-CA)
Hello
Goodbye
```

If you specify an invalid culture string, the program will throw an exception. Obviously, a robust application should catch this exception and insist that the user specify a valid culture string.

Note that in the general case, using the null CultureInfo is not the most appropriate behavior, as it will always use culture-neutral resources regardless of the user's current culture settings. If you change the line of code from

```
        CultureInfo ci = null;
```

to

```
        CultureInfo ci = CultureInfo.CurrentCulture;
```

the current culture will be used in preference to the neutral culture. (The example program used null simply for purposes of demonstration.)

Onward: Application Domains

This point concludes the overview on creating assemblies. This section has shown how use of assemblies and assembly caches attempts to solve many of the issues associated with versioning of applications. The next section returns to the concept of application domains, which were introduced in Chapter 4. Assemblies and application domains are tied together in a simple way: At runtime, assemblies are always loaded into application domains. Now that you have a better understanding of assemblies, it should be easier to see their relationship to application domains.

Application Domains

Application Domains Versus Processes

Chapter 4 briefly introduced the concept of an *application domain.* Traditionally, operating systems have allowed multiple processes to apparently execute simultaneously in memory.[2] An operating system monitors each process and isolates the address space of each application, thereby preventing a process from accessing any other process's memory. If a process does attempt to access memory outside of its address space, then the operating system will terminate the erroneous process to safeguard the integrity of the other processes, including the operating system itself. This idea of process isolation is fundamental to any modern operating system. Unfortunately, processes often require a large amount of system resources to create, monitor, and terminate; this is unfortunate when a number of short-lived processes are sometimes required to perform a task.

Application domains provide an alternative to processes in the Common Language Runtime. An application domain is similar to the concept of a process, in that each application domain remains protected from other application domains reading or writing directly into it. An application domain is much less expensive to create than a separate process, however. Application domains also share one other useful trait: They are the smallest

---

[2] Of course, on a single-processor machine, really only one process can execute at any time. With the use of time slicing and other techniques, however, one can create the illusion of the simultaneous execution of multiple processes.

units of an executing .NET program that can be released (unloaded) from memory. Clearly, if a long-lived process must load and use a large number of external binary files, such as assemblies, it needs some means to unload these files when they are no longer needed; otherwise, it will eventually exhaust the supply of available memory.

Use of Application Domains

As an example of the use of application domains, consider a server process, such as a Web server. Web servers should have a long lifetime; generally they should start when an operating system loads and stop only when the operating system shuts down. Web servers often need to run many external scripts and programs created by developers to satisfy the requests they receive from external clients, such as browsers. Naturally, the developers of the Web servers want the execution of these external programs to be both fast and reliable. "Fast" would require that a server not create large numbers of short-lived processes to generate the needed data; "reliable" means that a server requires memory isolation from the external programs. In the past, processes such as Web servers have often sacrificed reliability for performance and allowed external programs to execute with their own address spaces. As a consequence, Web servers have tended to terminate unexpectedly. This is exactly the situation addressed by application domains.

In general, application domains are of greatest importance to developers of long-lived servers and not necessarily of interest to developers of other types of applications. For this reason, full coverage of application domains is really beyond the scope of an introductory text such as this book. For completeness, a small amount of coverage is provided here.

Example: Retrieving Current Application Domain Information

The program in Listing 5.10 offers a simple example of how to retrieve information about the current application domain from within a program. Whenever the CLR starts a program, it creates a default application domain, which is, not surprisingly, referred to as the default domain. Listing 5.10 shows how many of the concepts that are associated with a process are also relevant to an application domain, such as the application's base directory and search path.

Listing 5.10 *Retrieving information about the current application domain*

```
using System;
public class Start
{
  public static int Main()
  {
    AppDomain d = AppDomain.CurrentDomain;
    Console.WriteLine("Friendly name: {0}",
                      d.FriendlyName);
    Console.WriteLine("Base Directory: {0}",
                      d.BaseDirectory);
    Console.WriteLine("Relative Search Path: {0}",
                      d.RelativeSearchPath);
    return 0;
  }
}
```

Listing 5.10 generates the following output:

```
Friendly name: AppDomainInfo.exe
Base Directory: C:\Project7\Demos\AppDomainInfo\
Relative Search Path:
```

Example: Creating and Manipulating Application Domains

The next example shows how a developer can create and manipulate an application domain. Listing 5.11 creates a second application domain, giving it the friendly name of MyDomain. When creating an application domain, you can readily change its security and configuration settings. Here, the base directory for the application domain is changed to cause the application domain to initially look in this directory for assemblies it needs to load. The MyDomain application domain also has another search directory added to its path. Finally, both the original and the new application domains are instructed to execute the program in Listing 5.10, which displays information about the current application domain.

Listing 5.11 *Creating and manipulating application domains*

```
using System;
using System.Security.Policy;
public class Start
{
  public static int Main()
```

```
{
  AppDomain c = AppDomain.CurrentDomain;
  AppDomainSetup s = new AppDomainSetup();
  // using a 'verbatim' string (prefixed by '@') allows us
  // to avoid doubling backslashes.
  s.ApplicationBase = @"C:\Project7\Demos";
  s.PrivateBinPath = @"C:\Windows";
  AppDomain d = AppDomain.CreateDomain("MyDomain",
                                       null, s);
  Console.WriteLine("Starting App Domain c");
  c.ExecuteAssembly("AppDomainInfo.exe");
  Console.WriteLine("Starting App Domain d");
  d.ExecuteAssembly("AppDomainInfo.exe");
  return 0;
  }
}
```

As expected, the output shows the differences in the configuration settings that have been applied to the two application domains:

```
Starting App Domain c
Friendly name: AppDomain.exe
Base Directory: C:\Project7\Demos\AppDomainExecute\
Relative Search Path:
Starting App Domain d
Friendly name: MyDomain
Base Directory: C:\Project7\Demos
Relative Search Path: C:\Windows
```

Example: Loading Assemblies into Application Domains

The final application domain example shows how developers can load individual assemblies into different application domains, then create objects in those domains and call methods on the objects. In Listing 5.12, a helper function, PrintAssemblies, is used to display the assemblies loaded with an application domain.

Listing 5.12 Loading an assembly into an application domain

```
using System;
using System.Reflection;
using System.Runtime.Remoting;
using System.Threading;
```

continues

```
public class AppDomainSample
{
  private static void PrintAssemblies(AppDomain ad)
  {
    Assembly[] aa = ad.GetAssemblies();
    foreach(Assembly a in  aa)
      Console.WriteLine(a);
  }
  public static int Main(String[] args)
  {
    AppDomain ad1 = AppDomain.CreateDomain("Domain1");
    AppDomain ad2 = AppDomain.CreateDomain("Domain2");
    ad1.Load("first");
    ad2.Load("second");
    PrintAssemblies(ad1);
    PrintAssemblies(ad2);
    ObjectHandle oh1 = ad1.CreateInstance(
                          "first", "ObjectType1");
    ObjectHandle oh2 = ad2.CreateInstance(
                          "second", "ObjectType2");
    Object o1 = (Object) oh1.Unwrap();
    Object o2 = (Object) oh2.Unwrap();
    Console.WriteLine(o1);
    Console.WriteLine(o2);
    AppDomain.Unload(ad1);
    AppDomain.Unload(ad2);
    Console.WriteLine(
      "Application Domains unloaded before process ends");
    return 0;
  }
}
```

Main first creates two application domains: ad1 and ad2. Next, it loads
a different assembly into each domain: first.dll and second.dll. Each
assembly contains the definition of an object type that inherits directly from
MarshalByRefObject: ObjectType1 in first.dll and ObjectType2 in
second.dll. The program then displays the assemblies in each application
domain, showing that mscorlib is available to both and that each assembly contains one other assembly, either first.dll or second.dll.

Next, the program creates objects of each type in the different application domains. Because the objects are created in different application
domains than the application domain that called CreateInstance, the
program returns ObjectHandles. The ObjectHandle class allows a handle

to an object to be passed between different application domains without requiring that its metadata be passed with it. When an `ObjectHandle` is unwrapped in an application domain, its metadata is introduced into that application domain only—not in those application domains through which it has merely passed. After the objects are unwrapped, they are converted to strings and written to the console. The implementation of the `ToString` method that is called will write out the type of the object and its application domain, as shown in the program's output.

The application domains are unloaded before a message is written to the console. Finally, the program terminates.

The following output from `cordbg` shows the sequence of application domain creation and exiting, along with the program's output. The output has been abbreviated for space reasons.

```
Microsoft (R) Common Language Runtime Test Debugger Shell
Version 1.0.3705.0
Copyright (C) Microsoft Corporation 1998-2001.
All rights reserved.

(cordbg) Process 1472/0x5c0 created.
Appdomain #1, DefaultDomain -- Created
Assembly 0x00097024, c:\windows\...\mscorlib.dll -- Loaded
   in appdomain #1, DefaultDomain
...
Appdomain #2, Domain2 -- Created
...
Appdomain #3, Domain3 -- Created
...
Assembly 0x00109904, c:\project7\...\first.dll -- Loaded
   in appdomain #2, Domain1
...
Assembly 0x0010d824, c:\...\second.dll -- Loaded
  in appdomain #3, Domain2
...

=====AppDomains.exe=====
mscorlib, Version=1.0.3300.0, Culture=neutral,
PublicKeyToken=b77a5c561934e089
AppDomains, Version=0.0.0.0, Culture=neutral,
PublicKeyToken=null
first, Version=0.0.0.0, Culture=neutral,
```

continues

```
 PublicKeyToken=null
 second, Version=0.0.0.0, Culture=neutral,
 PublicKeyToken=null

 =====Domain1=====
 mscorlib, Version=1.0.3300.0, Culture=neutral,
 PublicKeyToken=b77a5c561934e089
 first, Version=0.0.0.0, Culture=neutral,
 PublicKeyToken=null
 =====Domain2=====
 mscorlib, Version=1.0.3300.0, Culture=neutral,
 PublicKeyToken=b77a5c561934e089
 second, Version=0.0.0.0, Culture=neutral,
 PublicKeyToken=null
 . . .
 ObjectType1 in Domain1
 ObjectType2 in Domain2
 . . .
 Appdomain #2, Domain1 -- Exited
 . . .
 Appdomain #3, Domain2 -- Exited
 Application Domains unloaded before process ends
 Unloaded class: AppDomainSample
 . . .
 Assembly 0x00097024, c:\...\mscorlib.dll -- Unloaded
 Appdomain #1, AppDomains.exe -- Exited
 [thread 0x7bc] Thread exited.
 Process exited.
 (cordbg)
```

Summary

This chapter began to look at the larger picture—namely, building applications for distribution. It discussed the concept of .NET assemblies, including what they are and how to use them. You can use private assemblies when you do not need to share your code among different applications. The process of building and installing a private assembly is simple: Just copy the files along with the application. If you do need to share your code among many applications, you can create a public assembly and store it in the global assembly cache. The GAC provides storage and management of all public assemblies, preventing naming or version conflicts in a reliable and predictable manner.

A combination of several techniques is often best for solving the problem of assembly management. The GAC provides a well-known location into which you can load shared executables. It also provides a form of symbolic naming, wherein subdirectories, which are identified by version information, contain the different versions of the executable. The CLR takes care of resolving version information, without forcing users to create their own symbolic names to avoid version conflicts. Finally, the use of local private assemblies provides a means of resolving assembly lookup locally with resorting to the GAC.

6

Deploying Applications

C HAPTER 5 DISCUSSED how to build and package applications.
Building and packaging an application is only half of the story, however; you must get your application onto the target computer before it will be of any use to anyone. This chapter examines the various options available to deploy and configure applications on other machines.

In the trivial case, deploying an application can be as simple as copying a single executable file into a directory. In the real world, however, an application often needs to use one or more shared components, needs to be configured for its deployment environment, and should come with a simple technique for removing the application from the computer.

Furthermore, applications may wish to target a number of .NET-supported platforms, including Win32, Windows CE, and BSD, and conceivably any other platform should any non-Microsoft implementations of .NET become available. This chapter covers these topics.

Configuration Files

There has always been a need to configure applications for the specific machines on which they run. This need arises because of a number of factors, including differing security requirements, differing levels of functionality provided in different environments, and differing capabilities provided by the machines on which the applications execute.

Text-Based Configuration Files

UNIX and Windows 3.x have traditionally solved the issue of configuration using text files. Often these files follow a specific format and are stored in system directories, such as `\Windows\System` or `/etc`. When applications start up, they read these files to configure themselves. For example, the process `syslogd`, which logs system messages into files, uses the `syslog.conf` file to see which message should be redirected to which files. Lines in the `syslog.conf` file have a specific layout.

Another example on UNIX systems involves a process called `inetd` that listens for incoming network connections on multiple ports. When a connection is requested, `inetd` will start the appropriate server, if one is available and not already running, and pass the connection to that server. To accommodate different configurations, `inetd` reads its configuration information from a text file, usually called `inetd.conf`. An interesting point about `inetd` is that dynamic configuration is achieved by editing the configuration file and then sending a `signal` to the process. On receipt of the `signal`, the process will reread the configuration file and thus be updated with the new settings. The configuration file often has the following format:[1]

```
ftp       stream  tcp  nowait  root  /etc/ftpd    ftp
telnet    stream  tcp  nowait  root  /etc/telnetd telnetd
bootp     dgram   tcp  wait    root  /etc/bootp   bootp -f
```

The use of text-based configuration files offers a number of advantages. Such files are generally easy to read and can be easily edited by numerous programs. Of course, binary configuration files have some additional drawbacks as well. When using the Registry to store configuration information, for example, the programmer needs to understand a complex hierarchical structure. Also, the developer must use tools such as `regedit` to open and access Registry entries. Finally, because all programs share the Registry, if

---

[1]   Nemeth, E., Snyder, G., Seebass, S., and Hein, T. (1995). *UNIX System Administration Handbook,* 2nd ed., Prentice-Hall.

the Registry becomes corrupted then many programs may exhibit faulty behavior.

Unfortunately, although text files are easy to read and modify, they do not readily describe their structure—that is, what each *column* means. Normally, comments are inserted in the file to describe the structure. A more self-describing structure would be beneficial.

CLR Configuration Files

CLR configuration files are XML files that allow an application (or many applications, or even .NET itself) to use a different configuration without recompiling. Thus your application's configuration may change according to the configuration of the machine on which the application is deployed. As these files are written in XML, the elements provide a more self-describing quality than traditional text-based files such as those used in UNIX.

Configuration files were mentioned in Chapter 5 during the discussion of how to bind to a different version of an assembly than that used when building an application. Ideally, configuration files should do a lot more than version binding for single applications—and, in fact, they do.

.NET supports several different configuration files: one that applies at the machine level, one that applies at the application level, ones that relate directly to security, and so forth. Individual applications can use the `System.Configuration` class library to use and extend these configuration files for their own purposes.

Configuration File Format

As XML files, configuration files consist of tagged XML elements, each containing zero or more attributes. Chapter 5 included the following example:

```
<configuration>
  <runtime>
    <assemblyBinding
      xmlns="urn:schemas-microsoft-com:asm.v1">
```

continues

```
<dependentAssembly>
    <assemblyIdentity name="AboutBox"
        publicKeyToken="a0df1539bc79861c"/>
    <bindingRedirect oldVersion="1.0.0.0"
        newVersion="2.0.0.0"/>
</dependentAssembly>
            </assemblyBinding>
        </runtime>
    </configuration>
```

Here the top-level `configuration` element consists of a single subelement `runtime`, which consists of a single subelement `assemblyBinding`, which consists of a single subelement `dependentAssembly`, which is where the action finally starts! `DependentAssembly` has two subelements (`assemblyIdentity` and `bindingRedirect`), with each subelement having two properties.

Configuration File Schema

The root element of configuration files is always the `configuration` element. The valid subelements of the configuration element, which are detailed in the .NET documentation, include elements such as `runtime`, `startup`, `network`, and so forth.

This section offers a brief description of the top-level elements supported by .NET, but makes no attempt to demonstrate or document all of the supported elements. In version 1 of .NET, the following elements are supported under the top-level `configuration` element:

- `startup`

  Configuration options that affect how the process is created. Currently, the only option available is `requiredRuntime`, which allows an application to specify the version of the .NET runtime environment that should be used.

- `runtime`

  Configuration options that change the runtime behavior of the .NET system, most notably the assembly loading and garbage collection subsystems. Assembly policies can dictate version binding policies, the directories to be searched (including debugging support), the code base (download location) for referenced assemblies, and more. The concurrency of garbage collection can also be changed to control the threading semantics of object destructors.

- `system.runtime.remoting`
Configuration options that allow you to fine-tune how .NET manages remote objects. A huge array of options allows you to specify timeouts and lease times for remote sessions, and to dictate how objects implement and use SOAP services. These options also include debugging techniques for remote objects.

- `system.net`
Configuration options that dictate how network resources are used and authenticated. You can specify how many connections an application can open on a specific server and how authentication with that server is achieved. Proxy server settings are also specified in the `defaultProxy` element.

- `cryptographySettings`
Advanced options that allow you to customize the encryption providers used by the system.

- `system.diagnostics`
Configuration options that can prove useful when debugging .NET applications. You can configure how .NET reacts to an application assertion or redirect application debugging messages to various locations to enhance debugging. Some options control exactly which debug settings and verbosity levels are used by the application.

- `system.web`
Configuration options for ASP.NET.

Note that not all configuration options are supported in all configuration files. Certain options make sense only in the context of a single application or for the entire machine, whereas others could be used in either machine or application files depending on the specific site requirements.

Machine Configuration Files

One machine configuration file per computer applies to an entire computer: `machine.config`. It is found in the `\{Windows Directory}\`

`Microsoft.NET\Framework\{Framework Version Installation Direc-tory}\Config` directory.

Application Configuration Files

An application configuration file is found in the same directory as the application executable; it carries the name of the executable file with ".config" appended to it. In Chapter 5, for example, the application `UseAboutBox.exe` had an application configuration file named `UseAboutBox.exe.config`.

Security Configuration Files

.NET permits configuration of security settings via configuration files. Because security settings are so vitally important and complex to set up, it is strongly recommended that you use the .NET Framework Configuration Tool to maintain these files. .NET defines Enterprise Policy, Machine Policy, and User Policy configuration files. The Enterprise and Machine Policy files are named `enterprisesec.config` and `security.config`, respectively, and are found in the `\{Windows Directory}\Microsoft.NET\Frame-work\{Framework Version Installation_Directory}\Config` directory. The User Policy file is also named `security.config` but is found in the user profile directory tree (the exact location depends on the particular operating system).

ASP Configuration Files

ASP.NET supports configuration files named `web.config` and provides its own hierarchical namespace (based on the file system) for these files. Thus, an ASP.NET Web site may have a large number of `web.config` files, each tailoring the settings for that specific part of the site. See the ASP.NET documentation for more information.

Custom Configuration Sections

Applications can store their own configuration data in the machine or application configuration files. The configuration file schema allows custom configuration sections to be defined, then permits the section itself with the configuration data to appear. The definition of a section includes the name of the .NET class that is responsible for parsing the data contained within the section, and the configuration data include anything allowed by the definition.

To see how this definition works, let's look at an example from the default `machine.configuration` file. Listing 6.1 shows the entries.

Listing 6.1 *Default* `machine.configuration` *file*

```
<?xml version="1.0" encoding="UTF-8"?>
<configuration>
 <configSections>
  <sectionGroup name="system.web">
    <section name="httpHandlers"
      type="System...HttpHandlersSectionHandler..."
      />
  </sectionGroup>
 </configSections>
 <system.web>
  <httpHandlers>
    <add verb="*" path="trace.axd" type="..." />
  </httpHandlers>
 </system.web>
</configuration>
```

The first `sectionGroup` element defines a namespace called `system.web`. This group supports a section named `httpHandlers`; this section is parsed and extracted by the .NET type `System.Web.Configuration.HttpHandlersSectionHandler`.

After the `</configSections>` element, the code creates the previously defined `system.web` group and defines the `httpHandlers` section. The subentries here depend on what is allowed by the `System.Web.Configuration.HttpHandlersSectionHandler` implementation.

The .NET class library provides a few general-purpose configuration handlers designed for reuse by applications, including the `System.Configuration.SingleTagSectionHandler` and `System.Configuration.NameValueSectionHandler` classes. Both allow you to define fairly arbitrary string data.

Let's demonstrate custom configuration data very simply by using application configuration files. The example application is named `ReadCustomData.exe`, so the application configuration file is called

`ReadCustomData.exe.config`. Simply create this file with the contents shown in Listing 6.2.

Listing 6.2 *Application configuration file:* `ReadCustomData.exe.config`

```
<configuration>
 <configSections>
  <section name="customSection"
    type="System.Configuration.SingleTagSectionHandler"
  />
 </configSections>
<customSection setting1="some value"
               setting2="value two"
               setting3="third value" />
</configuration>
```

The `SingleTagSectionHandler` section allows you to place arbitrary keys and values into a single tag. At runtime, the application uses the `System.Configuration.ConfigurationSettings` class to fetch the data, which in turn causes .NET to call the `SingleTabSectionHandler` class to deserialize the data. Reading the documentation reveals that `SingleTagSectionHandler` returns the data via an `IDictionary`, so you can cast the object accordingly.

Listing 6.3 shows the code to fetch the data in `ReadCustomData.cs`.

Listing 6.3 *Fetching data, version 1:* `ReadCustomData.cs`

```
using System;
using System.Collections;
using System.Configuration;

namespace Samples
{
  class Demo
  {
    public static void Main()
    {
      IDictionary sampleTable = (IDictionary)
        ConfigurationSettings.GetConfig("customSection");
      Console.WriteLine(
        "First is: {0}, second is: {1}, third is: {2}",
        sampleTable["setting1"],
        sampleTable["setting2"],
```

```
                    sampleTable["setting3"]);
        }
      }
    }
```

You can build and run this example as follows:

```
First is: some value, second is: value two, third is: third
value
```

In addition to `SingleTagSectionHandler`, another useful option parser class is available: `System.Configuration.NameValueSectionHandler`. Using this handler, your configuration options can support discrete elements per configuration value. For example, `ReadCustomData2.exe.config` (see Listing 6.4) shows an alternative representation for the example data.

Listing 6.4 *Representing data:* `ReadCustomData.exe.config`

```
<configuration>
 <configSections>
  <section name="customNamedSection"
    type="System.Configuration.NameValueSectionHandler" />
 </configSections>
 <customNamedSection>
   <add key="setting1" value="some value" />
   <add key="setting2" value="value two" />
   <add key="setting3" value="third value" />
 </customNamedSection>
</configuration>
```

The code to read these data is very similar to the version given in Listing 6.3. `NameValueSectionHandler` sections are returned at runtime as a `System.Collections.Specialized.NameValueCollection`, as shown in `ReadCustomData2.cs` (see Listing 6.5).

Listing 6.5 *Fetching data, version 2:* `ReadCustomData.cs`

```
using System;
using System.Collections.Specialized;
using System.Configuration;
```

continues

```
namespace Samples
{
  class Demo
  {
    public static void Main()
    {
      NameValueCollection sampleTable =
        (NameValueCollection)
        ConfigurationSettings.GetConfig(
        "customNamedSection");
      Console.WriteLine(
        "First is: {0}, second is: {1}, third is: {2}",
        sampleTable["setting1"],
        sampleTable["setting2"],
        sampleTable["setting3"]);
    }
  }
}
```

Note that the custom section does not include any information about the application that needs the data. If you store the custom configuration data in your application configuration file, no problem arises—by definition, all settings in this file remain local to your application. However, if you store the data in the machine configuration file, then the settings are shared among all applications. Thus, in the preceding example, any application could fetch the settings simply by referring to customNamedSection. If another .NET application expects to find configuration data under this key, a conflict would result.

Which Configuration Files to Use?

In many cases, you may have a choice as to which configuration file to use for a particular setting. In both the version binding and custom configuration examples described here and in Chapter 5, you could place the information in either an application configuration file or the machine configuration file.

In many cases, it is clear that the configuration setting you want to change is local to a single application; the custom data example in the preceding section demonstrates this scenario. In many cases, however, you may want to modify a setting that is either global to all applications or used by a component that is itself shared among many applications, so that its configuration data are also shared among applications.

Unfortunately, no easy answer to this dilemma exists. .NET provides only a very global machine configuration file or a very local application configuration file. To help you determine the best course of action, this section briefly discusses some of the advantages and disadvantages of each scheme.

If you store your settings in the application configuration file, deployment of your application remains simple: An `xcopy` of your application is all that is required. Because the application configuration file appears in the same directory as your application, it, too, is copied to the new computer.

Another key advantage of application configuration files is that they tend to be far smaller than machine configuration files, thereby allowing you to readily see all relevant settings required by your application. If the same settings were stored in the machine configuration file, they might get lost in the noise.

The only advantage that machine configuration files offers over application configuration files is sometimes also the killer advantage: They apply to multiple applications. In some cases, options cannot practically be stored in application configuration files because they apply to too many applications for this approach to be feasible. In this case, the machine configuration file is the only reasonable alternative.

Downloading Web Content

In many cases, you may want to deploy your application remotely via the Web. You can use Internet Explorer to download and run .NET applications, simply by creating HTML that describes which assemblies to download, where each assembly is located, and what custom configuration settings apply to the application.

As you might expect, Internet Explorer leverages many of the concepts used by the .NET Framework—particularly the use of assemblies and application configuration files. Deploying an application via Internet Explorer can be as simple as building your application and uploading it to your Web server of choice! The executable can then be referenced via a standard URL, and Internet Explorer will detect the fact that it is a .NET application and respond appropriately.

Let's demonstrate this approach with a simple example: a trivial "Hello World" application that creates a message box. To demonstrate that the assembly truly is considered remote, the message box displays the `code base` of the assembly—that is, the location from which the assembly was downloaded. Listing 6.6 shows the source code, which is located in `RemoteHelloWorld.cs`.

Listing 6.6 `RemoteHelloWorld.cs` *source code*

```
using System.Reflection;
using System.Windows.Forms;

class Demo
{
  public static void Main()
  {
    Assembly ass = Assembly.GetExecutingAssembly();
    string msg = "Hello, my codebase is " + ass.CodeBase;
    MessageBox.Show(msg);
  }
}
```

Let's build this application using the C# compiler, and then build a standard Windows application, resulting in `RemoteHelloWorld.exe`. The next step is to upload this file to some Web server. Any Web server will do; nothing here replies in ASP or ASP.NET. This approach assumes that you can use FTP or some other facility for transferring this file from your development machine to the Web server.

With the application in place, you need simply reference the executable from Internet Explorer. The simplest way to do so is to type the complete URL to the file in the Internet Explorer address bar.[2] If all goes according

---

2 The security system's configuration on your machine could prohibit the downloaded code from executing. To resolve this issue, you may need to either allow code downloaded from the Internet to execute or make the site you reference trusted and ensure that code from trusted sites can execute. In this chapter, we assume that such settings have been specified.

to plan, Internet Explorer should automatically download and execute the
.NET code.

As shown in Figure 6.1, .NET knows the location from which the application was loaded and has set the `CodeBase` property of the assembly
appropriately.

This example also demonstrates how the .NET security system works.
You probably noticed that, unlike with other executable files that you reference on the Web, Internet Explorer did not ask your permission to download and run the file. As the file is a .NET application, Internet Explorer
defers to .NET for security settings, including exactly which tasks remote
applications are allowed to perform. The example application is quite
benign: It references the `CodeBase` property of a user-defined assembly
and displays a message box. The default .NET security configuration normally permits these operations, so the application downloads and runs
without incident. If you experienced trouble executing the application, you
might find that your local security policies are tighter than the default and

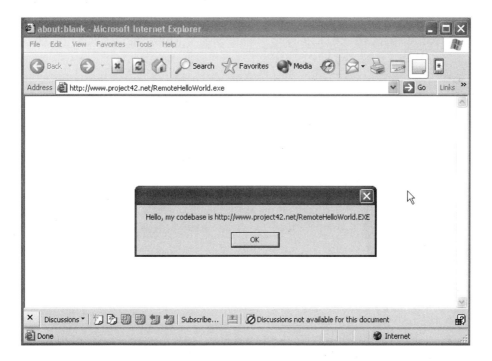

Figure 6.1 *Remote application running under Internet Explorer*

so prevent the application from running, in which case you will generally receive a security exception message. Indeed, if you modify the application to do anything more sophisticated (such as opening a file on the local computer), you will find that .NET will halt the operation.

Referencing Assemblies with the `codeBase` Element

Configuration files also allow you to specify an alternative code base for your assemblies—that is, a location that .NET will search for your assembly. This option allows you to override the default .NET assembly search algorithm so your application can automatically download referenced assemblies from any location that you choose.

To achieve this goal, you can add a `codeBase` element to any of the .NET supported configuration files. In this way, you can provide this behavior for only a single application by using the application configuration file or for the entire machine by using the machine configuration file. The `codeBase` element specifies the identity of the assembly as well as the URL from which the assembly can be downloaded. If the referenced assembly has a strong name (see Chapter 5), then the URL can be any valid URL. If the referenced assembly is a private assembly (that is, the assembly has no strong name), then the URL must be a path relative to, and a child of, the application's directory.

For complete details on the `codeBase` element, consult the .NET documentation. This section provides a short example that demonstrates downloading content. As in some of the previous examples, two assemblies are created here: the assembly to be downloaded from a remote Web server and an application that uses this assembly.

The remote assembly is quite trivial—just a single method that displays a message box. As in the previous example, the program displays the `code-Base` property of the assembly to prove it really comes from the remote location. Listing 6.7 shows the source code, which is located in `Remote-Assembly.cs`.

Listing 6.7 Source code for `RemoteAssembly\RemoteAssembly.cs`

```
using System.Reflection;
using System.Windows.Forms;

public class Demo
```

```
{
  public static void DisplayCodeBase()
  {
    Assembly ass = Assembly.GetExecutingAssembly();
    string msg = "Hello, my codebase is " + ass.CodeBase;
    MessageBox.Show(msg);
  }
}
```

As mentioned earlier, any assembly downloaded from a remote code base must have a strong name. Chapter 5 described ways to give strong names to assemblies, and the same pattern is followed here: Create a key with the strong name utility (sn.exe) and create the final assembly with the Assembly Linker tool (al.exe). These commands are shown in the makefile (see Listing 6.8).

Listing 6.8 *Contents of* RemoteAssembly\makefile

```
all: RemoteAssembly.dll

RemoteAssembly.key:
    sn -k RemoteAssembly.key

RemoteAssembly.dll: RemoteAssembly.cs RemoteAssembly.key
    csc /t:module RemoteAssembly.cs
    al /v:1.0.0.0 /keyfile:RemoteAssembly.key \
        /out:RemoteAssembly.dll RemoteAssembly.netmodule

clean:
    -del *.netmodule
    -del *.dll
```

To build this assembly, simply execute nmake in the example directory.

The next step is to transfer this assembly to the remote Web server. As you will recall from Chapter 5, this process creates an assembly consisting of two files: RemoteAssembly.dll is the module containing the assembly manifest, and RemoteAssembly.netmodule is a module referenced by the main assembly module. You must transfer these two files to your Web server using whatever technique you prefer.

Finally, you can create the application that downloads and uses this assembly. This application is truly trivial: It simply calls the static method defined in the remote assembly. Listing 6.9 shows the source code, which is located in `UseRemoteAssembly.cs`.

Listing 6.9 *Source code for* `UseRemoteAssembly\UseRemoteAssembly.cs`

```
class UseRemoteAssembly
{
  public static void Main()
  {
    Demo.DisplayCodeBase();
  }
}
```

To build the application, let's use a `makefile`, which is shown in Listing 6.10. Note that you must reference the remote assembly to successfully build the application. Referencing external assemblies at build time is discussed in Chapter 5.

Listing 6.10 *Contents of* `RemoteAssembly\makefile`

```
all: UseRemoteAssembly.exe

UseRemoteAssembly.exe: UseRemoteAssembly.cs
    csc UseRemoteAssembly.cs \
        /reference:..\RemoteAssembly\RemoteAssembly.dll

clean:
    -del *.exe
```

If you attempt to execute the application as it stands, it fails with an error message similar to the following:

```
Unhandled Exception: System.IO.FileNotFoundException:
File or assembly name RemoteAssembly, or one of its
dependencies, was not found.
```

As expected, .NET cannot find the `RemoteAssembly` assembly. Depending on the .NET configuration, debugging information may also be printed that shows where .NET searched for the assemblies. Note that the global assembly cache (GAC) is always used in preference to any locations specified in the configuration files; if a matching assembly is found in the GAC, it is always used.

Next, you can create the application configuration file that specifies the location from which this assembly can be downloaded. Much like in the version binding example in Chapter 5, the `codeBase` element is a child of the `assemblyIdentity` element, which specifies the assembly name and public key token. Listing 6.11 shows the complete application configuration file, which is found in `UseRemoteAssembly.exe.config`.

Listing 6.11 `UseRemoteAssembly.exe.config` *application configuration file*

```
<configuration>
  <runtime>
    <assemblyBinding
      xmlns="urn:schemas-microsoftcom:asm.v1">
      <dependentAssembly>
        <assemblyIdentity
            name="RemoteAssembly"
            publicKeyToken="c15b091d4324f090"
            culture=""/>
        <codeBase
            version="1.0.0.0"
            href=
            "http://www.project42.net/RemoteAssembly.dll"/>
      </dependentAssembly>
    </assemblyBinding>
  </runtime>
</configuration>
```

The configuration file shows the public key token of the remote assembly (extracted by executing `sn -T RemoteAssembly.dll`) and the URL from which this assembly can be downloaded. The configuration file also assumes that you previously uploaded the two remote assembly files to `http://www.project42.net/`; obviously, you will need to modify this URL to specify your own location.

Once this configuration file is in place, you can execute the application without incident. Figure 6.2 shows this application in action and confirms that the code base for the assembly is, indeed, on the HTTP server specified.

Figure 6.2 *Application using the remote assembly*

The Download Cache Revisited

As discussed briefly in Chapter 5, a download cache controls all content downloaded from the Web. It is responsible for downloading the appropriate assemblies and keeping them isolated from other assemblies that may be downloaded by other users or applications. This isolation is critical when you consider that assemblies downloaded from the Web need not be signed (recall the first `RemoteHelloWorld` example in this chapter) and, therefore, do not have strong names. This can lead to the situation in which two different applications use `MyApp.exe` as the name of the assembly, but are completely unrelated files. .NET must ensure that each application has its own discrete copy of `MyApp.exe`.

The `gacutil` tool (as described in Chapter 5) supports a `/ldl` option that lists the contents of the download cache. You can use this tool to verify that the assembly created by the example code is, indeed, present in the download cache, as shown in Listing 6.12.

Listing 6.12 Using `gacutil` *to list the contents of the download cache*

```
Microsoft (R) .NET Global Assembly Cache Utility.   Version
1.0.3705.0
Copyright (C) Microsoft Corporation 1998-2001. All rights
reserved.


The cache of downloaded files contains the following
entries:
        RemoteAssembly, Version=1.0.0.0, Culture=neutral,
           PublicKeyToken=c15b091d4324f090, Custom=null
        RemoteHelloWorld, Version=0.0.0.0, Culture=neutral,
           PublicKeyToken=null, Custom=null

Number of items = 2
```

The machine running Listing 6.12 has two entries: `RemoteAssembly` has a strong name, while `RemoteHelloWorld` does not.

Web Controls

Another popular way to create and deploy applications using .NET is to embed Web controls in an ASP.NET Web page. Web controls, also known as ASP.NET server controls, are special in that they combine server-side and client-side functionality into a single control. When ASP.NET is asked to render a page containing such a control, it generates some extra HTML or JScript for the client that delivers local events to the server. This approach allows your control to be hosted in an ASP.NET page executing at the server, but to handle events just as if the control resided locally on the client.

ASP.NET routes these events using standard HTML and ECMAScript (JScript). It does not use Internet Explorer's DHTML extensions, which means that the code should work in all modern browsers.

For an overview of how this system works, let's consider a simple example. To create a simple control, you just create a class deriving from `System.Web.UI.Control` and implement the `INamingContainer` interface. One method that you can override is `CreateChildControls`, which gives you the opportunity to create your own controls or other HTML elements to build your control.

The code fragment in Listing 6.13 shows such a class. It defines the class `MyControl` and implements the `CreateChildControls` method, which creates two additional buttons and a label as children. Clicking on either of the two buttons changes the text in the label.

Listing 6.13 *C# code fragment a defining Web control*

```
using System;
using System.Web;
using System.Web.UI;
using System.Web.UI.WebControls;

namespace Project42
{
  public class MyControl : Control,
                           INamingContainer
  {
```

continues

```
      private Button firstButton = new Button();
      private Button secondButton = new Button();
      private Label outputLabel = new Label();
      protected override void CreateChildControls()
      {
        firstButton.Text = "Hello";
        firstButton.Click +=
               new EventHandler(this.FirstButtonClick);
        this.Controls.Add(firstButton);
        secondButton.Text = "Goodbye";
        secondButton.Click +=
               new EventHandler(this.SecondButtonClick);
        this.Controls.Add(secondButton);
        outputLabel.Text="Press a button!";
        this.Controls.Add(outputLabel);
      }
      private void FirstButtonClick(object sender,
                                     System.EventArgs e)
      {
         outputLabel.Text = "Hello";
      }
      private void SecondButtonClick(object sender,
                                     System.EventArgs e)
      {
         outputLabel.Text = "Goodbye";
      }
    }
}
```

Before an ASP.NET Web page can use a control, it must be compiled and stored in a *well-known* place: a directory called `bin` that is located in a directory off the parent directory holding the ASP.NET Web page that will access the control. The following `makefile` compiles the control's source code and stores the resulting DLL in the `bin` directory:

```
all: MyWebControl.dll

MyWebControl.dll: MyWebControl.cs
   csc /t:library /out:..\bin\MyWebControl.dll \
       /debug MyWebControl.cs

clean:
   del *.dll
```

To display this control on a Web page, an ASP.NET (.aspx) file will be created that references the control. This ASP.NET page must contain an @Register directive to indicate where to find the custom control. This control is then added to the HTML body, which includes runat=server directives to indicate that all event processing happens on the server side. Such an ASP.NET page is shown in Listing 6.14.

Listing 6.14 *ASP.NET page using a custom Web control*

```
<%@ Register TagPrefix="MyWebControl"
    Namespace="Project42"
    Assembly="MyWebControl" %>
<html>
    <body>
        <form method="POST" action="TestControl.aspx"
          runat=server>
          <MyWebControl:MyControl id="MyControl"
            runat=server/>
        </form>
    </body>
</html>
```

The ASP.NET Web page must be located on an ASP.NET-enabled Web server. If you were to merely open the page with a browser on a local hard disk, then the control would not display correctly. After the files are installed on a Web site, Figure 6.3 shows the output generated when accessing the page.

As mentioned earlier, ASP.NET performs its control magic by generating some extra HTML for the client. To see this magic in operation, you can view the page in your favorite Web browser. For the ASP.NET page in Listing 6.14, ASP.NET will generate the page for the client as shown in Listing 6.15.

Listing 6.15 *HTML generated for an ASP page*

```
<html>
  <body>
    <form name="_ctl0" method="POST"
          action="MyWebControl.aspx" id="_ctl0">
    <input type="hidden" name="__VIEWSTATE"
           value="dDwxNzI1ODgyMzE0Ozs+IFybHNgVDzLdmHT2..."
    />
```

continues

```
    <input type="submit" name="MyControl:_ctl0"
           value="Hello" />
    <input type="submit" name="MyControl:_ctl1"
           value="Goodbye" />
    <span>Press a button!</span>
  </form>
</body>
</html>
```

The HTML generated in this way should work on any browser. It defines a standard HTML form with three controls. One control is a special hidden control used by the ASP.NET server to maintain the correct state between the server and the client. The other two controls are the children controls added in the C# code given in Listing 6.13. The buttons created by the HTML will produce a standard POST event to the nominated page whenever the user presses one of them. The ASP.NET server will respond to this event by generating the appropriate Click event for the control.

For more information on Web controls, consult the ASP.NET documentation or another ASP.NET reference.

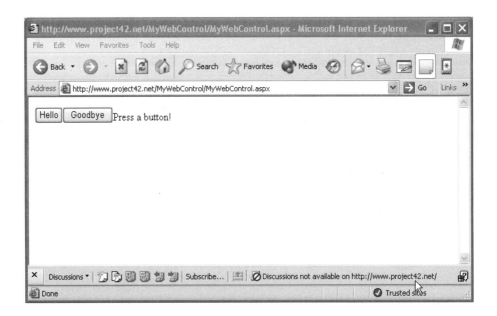

Figure 6.3 *Output generated when accessing the ASP.NET Web page*

Installing Applications

Once you have built your application, you must install it on the computer on which it is to run. Of course, "installing an application" can mean different things to different applications. In general, you can use any of three different techniques for installing your application:

- Copying files to the computer
- Downloading files to the computer
- Traditional installation programs that install files on to the computer

In some cases, an application may take advantage of more than one technique.

Copying Files to the Computer

Simple applications can be installed by copying the application files to the computer and running the application. Applications that use no external assemblies or only private assemblies are examples of such applications. All private assemblies and application configuration files exist either in the application directory or one of its subdirectories, meaning that everything needed for the application can be copied with one simple operation.

Apart from the obvious drawback—namely, that you cannot install public assemblies into the GAC—the other major problem with this approach is that many applications require some Windows integration features, such as Start menu icons or an Uninstall option available to the user. While you may be able to use batch files or other specialized scripts to overcome some of these limitations, a professional installation program will quickly demonstrate its superiority. Thus, while copying files can prove useful in some limited scenarios, this technique will rarely fulfill the needs of commercial applications.

Downloading Files to the Computer

This chapter has already discussed a few ways that applications can be completely or partially hosted on the Internet, and then downloaded as required.

The first scenario depicted an application being downloaded and executed by Internet Explorer. One option for this sort of deployment is to create a Web page that contains a link to the .NET-created executable, with users then being directed to that Web page. .NET will manage the download and security verification of the application and execute it (albeit possibly with reduced permissions, depending on the site configuration).

Another scenario discussed earlier in this chapter is to install the main application on the local machine, then reference other dependent assemblies via a `codeBase` element in a .NET configuration file. Referenced assemblies will be downloaded as necessary using the application configuration file to locate each assembly. This scenario works particularly well when the application always uses the same assemblies. For example, consider a word processor configuration that specifies a remote spell-checker assembly. This assembly would be downloaded only when the spell checker was actually started, rather than when the application starts.

Using this approach for deploying applications is associated with several drawbacks. One disadvantage is that the security settings for remote assemblies could restrict the functionality of the application. In general, .NET severely restricts access to assemblies downloaded from the Internet, so you might have to develop a custom security configuration for these assemblies.

Another problem with this approach is that the downloaded assemblies are typically stored in the download cache. Depending on the configuration and resources of the machine, the assembly may later be removed from the cache, and re-downloaded when the application is next run, making the application appear quite slow. Storing these assemblies as either private assemblies or public assemblies in the GAC prevents this problem.

Using Traditional Installation Programs

Traditional installation programs are used to install most complex or commercial applications, if for no better reason than "first impressions": A single program can be executed to install your application, complete with wizards, flashy graphics, and a professional interface. More practical reasons for using installation programs include the ability to modify the Start menu, to provide Uninstall and Rollback capabilities, and to allow complete customization of the installation options.

For whatever reasons, most companies find themselves investigating dedicated installation packages for their applications. Companies such as InstallShield and Wise produce well-regarded offerings, and a number of highly capable, free installers have appeared recently. Most of these packages provide some kind of graphical user interface to define the installation options and any dialogs or wizard pages displayed by the installer. They generally combine the application files into a single, compressed executable file ready to be installed by users.

In an effort to increase the reliability of its operating system and better manage the installation of applications, and particularly any shared files installed by applications, Microsoft recently introduced the Microsoft Windows Installer. This operating system service manages the installation of applications, which is driven by an installer script that defines the installation properties and options. The Windows Installer manages all versioning and features such as Uninstall, Rollback, or Install on Demand, so that poorly written installation programs cannot destroy the system. It is built into all versions of Windows later than Windows 2000; it is available as a stand-alone component for Windows 95 and Windows 98.

The script used by the Windows Installer is fully documented and can be created in a number of ways. Most commercial vendors have released or are releasing versions of their installation programs that create Windows Installer packages rather than the stand-alone executable files they previously created. Such programs allow you to leverage these vendors' user interfaces so as to quickly and simply build installations for your users.

Microsoft has released version 2.0 of the Windows Installer containing features specific to .NET, such as the ability to install public assemblies in the GAC. Most commercial installation programs have already released .NET-aware versions of their products, which you can use immediately to deploy your .NET applications.

Installing the .NET Framework

In many cases, for your applications to run correctly, you will need to ensure that the .NET Framework is correctly installed on your target PCs. Although .NET will ship with all future Microsoft operating systems, at time of writing no operating systems came with a default .NET installation.

To assist you with this dilemma, Microsoft provides a redistributable version of the .NET Framework, which currently weighs in at around 20MB (it can be downloaded from `http://www.microsoft.com/net`). The better installation programs will automatically manage the task of confirming the .NET Framework's presence. If your program does not, then you must make your own arrangements for ensuring that the .NET Framework is installed on each PC that needs to run your application.

Using the CLI on Non-Windows Platforms

Of course, your CLI-based applications may not necessarily be targeted at computers running the Windows operating system; you may want to deploy them on non-Windows operating systems, too. Nothing in the design of the CLI ties it exclusively to either the Windows operating system or Intel processors. This section highlights this platform portability; specifically, it considers the Compact Framework, a version of the CLI for handheld devices such as Pocket PCs that use a variety of processors, and the Shared Source version of the CLI (SSCLI), which runs on operating systems such as Windows XP and BSD UNIX.

In general, this book has discussed the CLR, CLI, and .NET Framework as though only one implementation existed—the implementation provided in the .NET Framework SDK. In truth, Microsoft provides several implementations of the CLR, and potentially other developers might write more. At this point, it is important to reiterate that the CLR and CLI are ECMA standards, of which numerous implementations are possible, in the same way that different vendors provide numerous implementations of the CORBA standard.

The ECMA CLI Standards

Before delving into the issues involved in porting the CLI to other platforms, it is important to understand how the ECMA standards define the CLI and assist in the porting process.

Profiles and Libraries

The ECMA CLI standard specifies a number of *profiles*; each profile essentially defines a set of functionality, as implemented by a group of libraries. Implementations of the CLI on various platforms specify which profiles—that is, which set of libraries—they support. Initially, there are two profiles of interest: the Kernel profile and the Compact Framework profile.

The Kernel profile is the base profile that is supported by all implementations of the CLI. It consists of the Runtime Infrastructure Library (RIL) and the Base Class Library (BCL). The RIL provides fundamental types and facilities such as those needed by compilers that target the CLI and those needed to load and execute types. The BCL provides basic types and services, such as strings, custom attributes, security, and collections.

The Compact Framework profile is a profile designed for mobile devices. It includes the Kernel profile as well as the Networking library, the Reflection library, and the XML library.

Figure 6.4 illustrates the relationship between these profiles and libraries.

Some other libraries, such as the floating-point library, are not part of any specific profile but can be supported by various implementations of the

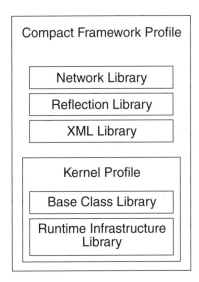

Figure 6.4 *Relationship between profiles and libraries in the CLI*

CLI. A complete discussion of the ECMA standard is beyond the scope of this book, but interested readers are advised that the specifications are available online at the ECMA Web site or at mirror sites.

Platform Adaptation Layer

An issue that arises with porting any software architecture, such as the CLR, to different platforms is the variation in interfaces and services exposed by the underlying operating system. To reduce this mismatch, the CLR uses a Platform Adaptation Layer (PAL). The PAL provides an application program interface (API) to the CLR; this API interacts with the underlying operating system's API to translate calls from the CLR into calls on the operating system. As a result, the PAL provides a consistent API to the CLR on any platform. When the CLR is ported to another platform, much of the work therefore remains confined to retargeting the PAL source code at the different operating system.

The interface provided by the PAL to the CLR is similar to the Win32 API. As such, on platforms such as Windows-based platforms, the PAL is fairly simple; that is, the interface expected by the CLR and the API provided by the operating system are a very close match. On other operating systems, such as BSD UNIX, the PAL may be quite complicated. For example, if the windowing or threading model provided by the operating system differs significantly from the one expected by the CLR (or possibly is not even provided at all), then the PAL may need to either provide this functionality, such as threading, or offer complex translations to map one windowing system to another.

Figure 6.5 illustrates the relationships among the CLR, PAL, and the operating system.

Compact Framework

The Compact Framework is, naturally, an implementation of the Compact Framework profile; as such, it targets mobile devices, such as the Pocket PC. These devices are often referred to as *resource constrained*, reflecting the fact they traditionally have had significantly more limited capabilities, such as memory and screen size, than their desktop counterparts. For this reason, the functionality provided by the Compact Framework is a subset of

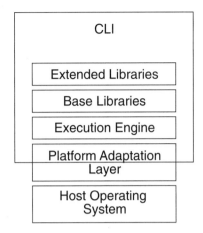

Figure 6.5 *Relationships among the CLI, PAL, and operating system*

the desktop CLI. The Compact Framework profile provides functionality such as the Windows Forms library, XML, and ADO.NET.

Given that the Compact Framework provides a subset of the functionality provided by the .NET Framework, developers familiar with the desktop CLI need learn no more concepts or libraries if they wish to target the Compact Framework. At worst, developers who are familiar with the desktop CLI need to know only which libraries are *not* available on the Compact Framework.

What types of functionality are currently not available in the Compact Framework? While developers can call COM components, COM components cannot be authored within this framework. Likewise, no support is provided for `Reflection.Emit` or the Remoting services. Also, facilities such as JIT compilation at installation time, which is otherwise provided by `ngen`, is not available under the Compact Framework.

Smart Device Extensions

A version of the Compact Framework implementation, called the *Smart Device Extensions* (SDE), is currently available in beta form. The SDE makes the development of programs that target the Compact Framework much simpler. By integrating the SDE into Visual Studio, developers can produce applications that run on mobile devices but use the abilities of Visual Studio to do so. For example, services such as the Forms Designer, remote debugging, and device emulation simplify development of Compact Framework applications under Visual Studio. When a programmer is developing applications for the Compact Framework, Visual Studio automatically filters the developer's views, removing components and facilities that are not available under the Compact Framework (see Figure 6.6).

If the application depicted in Figure 6.6 is compiled, downloaded to a Pocket PC, and executed, it produces the output shown in Figure 6.7.

Shared Source Common Language Infrastructure

The SSCLI is an implementation of the CLI that runs on both Windows XP and BSD UNIX. It includes both C# and ECMA script compilers and is

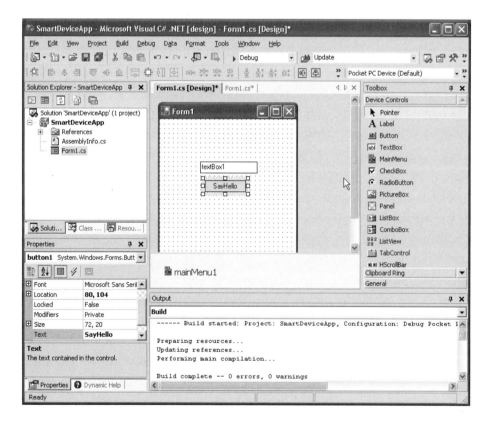

Figure 6.6 *Designing an application with Smart Device Extensions*

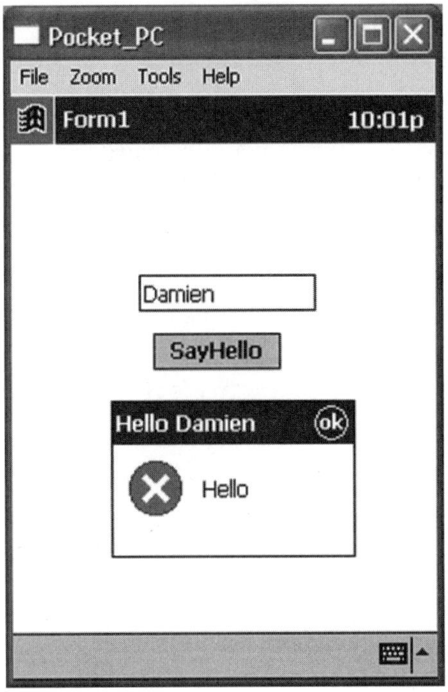

Figure 6.7 *Output produced by an SDE-generated application*

available for noncommercial use. Potential users are strongly urged to read the SSCLI license before installing the source code to ensure that the license meets their needs. A major goal of the SSCLI is to promote experimentation by developers on a real version of the CLI, and it is anticipated that researchers and universities will make extensive use of the SSCLI. The source code has been designed and documented to facilitate porting to other platforms (porting the SSCLI to another platform is left as an exercise for the reader).

The SSCLI is distributed as source code and compiled after installation on a machine. The current source code tree consists of approximately 12MB; this download is a single compressed file. When expanded, the SSCLI includes almost 2 million lines of source code and nearly 6000 individual source files; the majority of this code (roughly 1.1 million lines) is written in C/C++. In addition, the SSCLI include some 600,000 lines of C#, some CIL code, and some processor-specific assembly code. The distribution contains an assembler, disassembler, linker, and debugger.

Be forewarned: There are a number of simplifications in and omissions from the SSCLI as compared with the commercial version of the .NET Framework. Some of these decisions were made for technical reasons—for example, COM Interoperability mechanisms are not provided because COM is not available on platforms other than Windows. Windows Forms, the library that wraps the Windows GUI components, is also not supported. In addition, because the SSCLI is an implementation of the CLI, it does not provide an implementation of all of the libraries built on top of the CLI, such as ASP.NET.

To make the SSCLI more approachable for developers and to increase its chances of adoption by universities in the teaching setting (and to differentiate it from the commercially available product), the SSCLI contains some components that are less complicated than their commercial counterparts. For example, its garbage collector is a much simpler and less optimized component than the commercial product. Similarly, the class library that ships with the SSCLI is a subset of the class library available with the .NET Framework.

The following program output was generated by running one of the previous sample applications (Listing 4.5) under the Windows SSCLI execution engine. No recompilation or modification of any sort was required.

```
C:\Project7\Demos\AssemblyEvidence>c:\sscli\build\v1.x86fst
chk.rotor\clix.exe AssemblyEvidence.exe
<System.Security.Policy.Zone version="1">
  <Zone>MyComputer</Zone>
</System.Security.Policy.Zone>

<System.Security.Policy.Url version="1">
<Url>file://C:/sscli/build/v1.x86fstchk.rotor/mscorlib.dll
</Url>
</System.Security.Policy.Url>

<StrongName version="1"
          Key="00000000000000000400000000000000"
          Name="mscorlib"
          Version="1.0.3300.0"/>
```

Summary

Chapters 5 and 6 tackled two of the more difficult areas of modern program development—packaging and deploying applications and components for distributed systems. This chapter concentrated on strategies for deploying applications on target machines. It discussed options for moving an application onto a target machine, including the very simple approach of downloading an application to a Web browser for execution.

CLI configuration files can be used to modify program execution without requiring the recompilation of the application. The CLI can use these files, for example, to modify assembly version binding. Likewise, applications can use configuration files to perform application-specific configuration options. Configuration files are written in XML, which makes them easier to read and simpler to edit than working in the Registry.

The CLI architecture also addresses the issue of platform portability. Two types of platform portability were discussed in this chapter: the Compact Framework and the Smart Devices Extensions, which target small mobile devices, and the SSCLI, which targets non-Windows platforms such as BSD UNIX.

■ 7 ■

The Framework Class Library

T HE FRAMEWORK CLASS Library provides a cohesive set of managed types that provides the developer's view of the .NET Framework. This group of libraries serves as the runtime type libraries for many of the languages that target the Common Language Runtime. As such, the libraries must satisfy a diverse set of needs unique to the individual languages while still supporting interoperability across languages. The Framework Class Library is integral to the .NET Framework security model in that it provides encapsulation of privileged operations (such as access to the file system) in a restricted way so that code that comes from a *semi-trusted* [1] source can access the resource in a controlled manner. The libraries also provide a high level of abstraction for building applications; they are designed to help developers be more productive.

Figure 7.1 provides an architectural diagram of the .NET Framework libraries. At the lowest level is the Base Framework, also known as the Base Class Library (BCL), which exposes fundamental system services. Built on top of the BCL are the XML and data support services, which are used ubiquitously in applications that target the framework to access data in XML format or from a database. At the top are the primary application

---

[1] Traditionally code has either been *trusted*, and thereby permitted to execute, or not. Semi-trusted code is allowed to execute but the execution environment may be both restricted and monitored to prevent code from damaging resources.

models offered by the framework: ASP.NET, shown in the `System.Web` namespace, and Windows Forms, shown in the `System.Windows.Forms` and `System.Drawing` namespaces. ASP.NET provides both Web Forms (HTML-based functionality for thin clients, such as browsers) and Web Services (XML-based functionality for other applications).

This chapter first discusses how the Framework Class Library relates to similar technologies. Next, it looks at the design goals and guidelines that underpin the library. Newly developed libraries that follow these goals and guidelines will present an interface that is consistent with that associated with the Framework Class Library. Finally, the chapter takes a high-level look at many of the top-level namespaces in the library, providing simple example applications to demonstrate the use of the libraries.

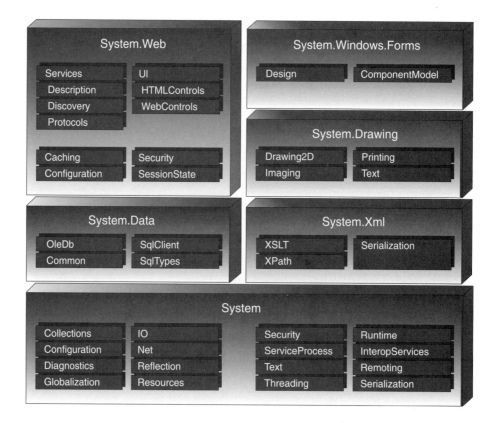

Figure 7.1 *The .NET Framework libraries*

A Historical Perspective

The idea of a runtime library is certainly not a new one to the computing industry. The .NET Framework is built on an extensive history of programming systems, but it provides a unique blend of features and some evolutionary developments that extend traditional computing concepts. This section cannot hope to provide a complete list of the programming systems that form the historical basis for the .NET Framework, nor can it fully explore the list of contributions from each system. Rather, by comparing and contrasting the various language systems, it seeks to highlight the key features of the .NET Framework.

C/C++

With the introduction of the C programming language in 1972, the notion of a standard library that ported to different computing architectures emerged as a popular concept. For example, the C library includes standard I/O functions (in the `stdio` header and library file) that define how to handle input and output to files and the console. The .NET Framework provides a similar set of functions that often work in a similar way, but has an object-oriented design that provides a higher level of abstraction. The framework defines an inheritance hierarchy to represent streams (including a concrete class to represent random access to a file), whereas the C standard library represents a file with an integer file handle.

The C language's successor, C++, offers similar concepts to the BCL in its `iostream` library.

SmallTalk

Around the same time that the C programming language was introduced, SmallTalk popularized the notion of a unified type system wherein every type in the system has a single base type from which all types are derived. This unification adds elegance to the SmallTalk library. Any item can be stored or accessed via this common base type. For example, any type can be stored in a collection directly without the use of intermediate wrapping. Unfortunately, this unification comes at a price to performance, because it turns all types into reference types. Doing even simple integer arithmetic can generate a large amount of transient memory usage on the heap that needs to be managed. (Such transient memory is often called *garbage*.)

The .NET Framework also supports this notion of a unified type system, but does so in such a way that primitive types are allocated on a stack (as in C/C++) when used specifically and allocated on a managed heap when they are used generically (as in SmallTalk). This approach allows the .NET Framework to achieve the same level of elegance as the SmallTalk library without necessarily incurring the performance penalty associated with it. Naturally, a trade-off is required with the CLR's type system: Moving data between the stack and the heap could degrade performance in some cases.

LISP

As early as 1959, LISP popularized the use of automatic memory management (garbage collection), which avoids many of the programming problems that frequently crop up in C/C++ programs. This automatic memory management feature allows the standard library in LISP to follow more of a functional programming model in which it is common to create temporary objects to cleanly express an operation. The Framework Class Library also benefits from a garbage collection system, which adds a functional programming flavor to a basically object-oriented system.

C++

The Base Framework has an object-oriented design that was popularized by SmallTalk, Eiffel, and C++ in the late 1980s and early 1990s. Object-oriented design allows functionality to be encapsulated as classes and operations on those classes. Libraries can then leverage this functionality to produce rich inheritance hierarchies that enable meaningful reuse of code. In contrast, because C++ retains many low-level operations of the C language, such as pointer manipulation, unsafe casts, and so forth, it is extremely difficult to use C++ to write applications that need to run in semi-trusted environments (such as code downloaded from the Internet or user code running in a SQL or Web server).

Java

Targeted to respond to the increasing use of the Internet, around 1995 Java became one of the first languages to introduce the idea of semi-trusted execution. Java is an object-oriented language that provides a substantial class library. It enables applications downloaded from the Internet to run in a "sand-box" where they can access only a small amount of system resources (screen real estate, network access, and file system access). Libraries control these resources, employing permissions to protect them. The .NET Framework uses a similar mechanism to protect resources. It brings forward many ideas from C++ that Java does not, however. For example, user-defined, stack-allocated primitive types (structures) and operator overloading allow extension of the base type system; users can add their own base types that fit right into the system. Enumerations allow for much cleaner, self-documenting API design. Also unlike Java, the .NET Framework offers built-in support for component design such as properties and events.

Support for Multiple Programming Languages

In the past, many attempts have been made to build systems that support multiple programming languages. Most notably, COM provided support for early-bound languages such as C and C++ as well as late-bound languages such Visual Basic and Script. It accomplished this goal by requiring each type to support different interfaces for the various languages. That is, COM types need to support custom interfaces for C/C++ as well as `IDispatch` for Visual Basic and Scripting languages. This split in the model meant that some functionality was exposed to only some developers but not to others, because library developers had to do extra work to target each group. On the other hand, CORBA objects do not know, or care, if their clients use early or late binding when invoking methods. This is also the situation for the CLR.

Unlike COM, the .NET Framework defines the Common Language Specification (CLS). As a result, no matter which language developers use, they have equal access to the framework. Developers building libraries are not forced to target each language explicitly. If they adhere to the set of features described in the CLS, their library will automatically be accessible to many languages. This approach ensures a consistent availability of features regardless of the programming language employed.

Goals of the .NET Framework

The .NET Framework was designed with four main goals in mind:

- Unify programming models.
- Be factored and extensible.
- Integrate with Web standards and practices.
- Make development simpler.

Unify Programming Models

The .NET Framework unifies various programming models. In the early 1990s, it was common to develop against flat, C-style APIs—that is, APIs that used few object-oriented concepts. The user interface (UI) handled Windows messages via a function pointer to a global function (`WinProc`) that contained a large and cumbersome switch statement. While this approach worked, it was not particularly productive or easy. Over time, various programming models created on top of the Windows API have emerged to address these problems.

In the early 1990s, productivity tools such as Visual Basic, Delphi, and PowerBuilder introduced the rapid application development (RAD) paradigm. Visual Basic, for example, introduced a level of abstraction over the Win32 APIs. The common programming model with this language is to instantiate a form, drag components onto the form, double-click on components, and write event handlers for them. This model simplifies the process of building a common line of business applications, but it is not extensible; using a component that is not specifically wrapped for Visual Basic is not possible. Under this view, the system is a black box, and it is not possible to "see into it" or extend it.

With the popularity of C++ in the 1990s came a series of more object-oriented approaches to programming models, such as the Microsoft Foundation Classes (MFC). The key concept underlying these programming models is subtyping. You subtype from an existing monolithic, object-oriented framework and extend the functionality to match the functionality required in your application. While this model does offer more power and expressiveness, it does not really match the ease or productivity of the RAD-style composition model.

The growth of the Web in 1990s led to the emergence of server-side Hypertext Markup Language (HTML) generation in application models such as Application Server Pages (ASP) and Java Server Pages (JSP). This model promotes writing stateless code to generate the UI in the form of HTML, Dynamic HTML (DHTML), and script that is rendered on the client. It rarely takes advantage of good development or design tools and, as mentioned earlier, suffers from interleaving of code and the UI.

One problem with the current state of development is that the developer's choice of a programming model often also dictates the choice of a programming language and the libraries that can be used (and vice versa). Skilled MFC developers cannot easily write code in ASP, for example, because their skills do not translate into the different paradigm. Likewise, if developers are familiar with a RAD model, little of that knowledge transfers to a C/C++-style API.

The models also provide inconsistent functionality. Each offers slightly different solutions to a number of problems that are actually common to all of the models. For example, file I/O, string formatting, security, and threading are exposed in different ways in each model. As a consequence, knowing how they work in one context does not help the developer understand how to work with them in another context.

The .NET Framework was designed to unify these disparate programming models. Its core concepts are applicable regardless of which application model is being built. For instance, Web developers are right at home with ASP.NET and can easily move to building a "smart" client part of their application with the same set of underlying technologies. Likewise, traditional Visual Basic developers of business applications can leverage the skills they already know to create Web-based applications. The choice of programming language no longer dictates the range of options available. Instead, the .NET Framework allows developers to choose the combination of programming language and application architecture that best solves the problem at hand.

Be Factored and Extensible

The .NET Framework is not a closed system. It is factored (that is, broken down into distinct, meaningful units) and extensible, thereby enabling a high degree of customization and specialization. Almost any class that exists in the framework is available for extension using inheritance. Unlike in COM, you actually extend the class itself—not a wrapper around some external functionality.

The extensibility of the .NET Framework also supports plug-and-play components and subsystems. For example, the ASP.NET system offers a pluggable model where users can add their own extensions to the underlying system. Developers can plug in their own user authentication modules by inheriting from the base classes provided by the framework, then provide customized functionality in the descendant class that overrides the standard functionality.

Object-oriented design concepts permeate the Framework Class Library. Because the runtime environment supports multiple languages at its core, cross-language inheritance is not merely possible but mandatory. It does not matter which language the developer uses to extend the framework, write components, or implement applications. Common functionality is exposed as base classes with shared and specialized members. Shared utility methods are exposed as nonvirtual members that allow for meaningful reuse of code. Defined points of specialization are exposed as virtual methods but given meaningful default implementations so that subtypes have to specialize only in desired areas. Many of the libraries in the .NET Framework expose system resources such as windows handles (`HWnds`) and file handles. In such cases, the underlying resource is exposed to provide a "back door" for the case in which one particular feature is *not* exposed in the encapsulation. Tailoring the operation becomes possible even if the library does not expose that functionality.

Integrate with Web Standards and Practices

Web standards and practices are deeply integrated into the .NET Framework. HTML, XML, and SOAP are at its foundation. By adhering to these standards, the .NET Framework provides a transition path from traditional client-server applications (which are not Internet-ready) into loosely coupled, stateless applications (which are Internet-ready).

The platform addresses some of the key problems with Web application development today. With ASP and JSP, developers writing the code that runs the Web site and designers creating the look and feel of the Web site must share the same source file. That is, presentation and business logic are combined in HTML, resulting in a source of potential conflict between developers and designers. The .NET Framework addresses this problem by allowing the application code and the HTML to be maintained as separate entities.

XML is a core concept in the .NET Framework. In addition to offering a Document Object Model (DOM)-level XML reader and writer that comply with the World Wide Web Consortium's (W3C) standards, the .NET Framework supports a higher-level way to read and write XML called XML serialization. XML serialization allows programmers to interact with XML as a set of objects, elements, and attributes represented as properties. The common data format through the .NET Framework is XML. The configuration store, object serialization, and security policy settings are all stored in XML formats. SOAP is the standard for machine-to-machine communications. Likewise, XML is the foundation for Web Services, the model for programmatically accessing Web-based resources.

The .NET Framework offers a well-defined asynchronous execution pattern and a high-performance thread pool implementation. Web Services, network connections, file I/O, and method calls through asynchronous delegate invocations support this pattern fully. In addition, the ASP.NET application model, including Web Services, offers support for a stateless programming model. Such a model enables the developer to scale out Web-based applications from one machine to a large Web farm of machines without changing the applications.

Make Development Simpler

The Framework Class Library was designed to facilitate the process of building applications. It enables developers to more easily write full-featured applications by "up-leveling" the platform—that is, by increasing the level of abstraction. The library design focuses on the developer or, more accurately, on the tasks the developer is trying to accomplish rather than inherent limitations of the underlying technology.

For example, in Win32, certain window properties cannot be set after a window is created, whereas other properties can be changed at any time.

Presumably, this inconsistency is a by-product of how the Windows operating system itself is implemented. However, the developer need not be limited by this implementation detail. The .NET Framework's encapsulation of this API (in Windows Forms) is designed around what the developer needs to do rather than the implementation detail. In Windows Forms, you can set any property at any time. The Framework Class Library does the work "under the covers" to re-create the window handles as needed, but the developer never needs to know about these details.

The .NET Framework can be expressive in its design because it takes advantage of the rich support of the underlying execution engine. It expresses functionality on types using three different constructs: properties, events, and methods. Each construct denotes its own set of information and usage patterns to the developer:

- *Properties* express a logical backing store. Developers understand that they can treat these elements just like data members (fields) in terms of their performance characteristics and semantics.
- *Events* indicate that the developer can register a method to be called back when an event occurs.
- *Methods* express operations of a type. For example, a value type indicates to the developer that it will behave very much like the `int` or `double` type in a particular programming language. It will be passed by value and, by default, allocated on the stack. Similarly, developers understand that types that subtype `System.Attribute` should be used as custom metadata annotations in a declarative way. Enumerations are a special kind of value type used to represent named integral constants (such as the days of the week).

Design Guidelines

Becoming familiar with the design guidelines of the .NET Framework libraries will help you in using the framework and creating your own classes.

A well-designed managed class library is:

- *Consistent:* Similar design patterns are implemented across libraries.
- *Predictable:* Functionality is easily discoverable. There is typically only one way to perform a specified task.
- *Secure:* The library is callable from semi-trusted code.
- *Multilingual:* Functionality is accessible to many different programming languages.

For several reasons, you are strongly advised to treat these guidelines as prescriptive when building your own library. Developer productivity can be demonstrably hampered by inconsistent design. Development tools and add-ins will turn some of these guidelines into de facto rules, thereby reducing the value of nonconforming components. These nonconforming components may work, but will not function to their full potential.

Even so, in some instances good library design dictates that you should break these rules. In such cases, you should provide solid justification for your decision.

This section primarily focuses on creating libraries that are consistent and predictable. Chapter 4 focuses on security issues for libraries. The CLR makes it very easy to write multilanguage libraries by adhering to the Common Language Specification (CLS); see Chapter 2 for more information on the CLS.

Naming Guidelines

One of the most important elements of predictability and discoverability in a managed class library is the use of a consistent naming pattern. One goal with consistent naming is to avoid many common user questions once these conventions are understood and widely used.

Naming guidelines focus on three issues:

- Casing: using the correct capitalization style
- Mechanics: using the correct nouns for class names, verbs for method names, and so forth
- Word choice: using terms consistently across libraries

This section focuses primarily on casing guidelines. For more information on mechanics and word choice, see the .NET Framework Design Guidelines.

The .NET Framework uses two primary casing styles: one popularized by the Pascal language and one that is reminiscent of a hump on a camel.

- Pascal casing: This convention capitalizes the first character of each word. Example: **B**ack**C**olor.
- Camel casing: This convention capitalizes the first character of each word except the first word. Example: **b**ack**C**olor.

All types of identifiers (such as type names and member names) should use Pascal casing except for protected instance fields (which generally should not be used, because properties are almost always a better choice) and parameter and local variables that should use camel casing.

Keep in mind the following best practices for naming:

- Do not use names that require case sensitivity, as components must be fully usable in both case-sensitive and case-insensitive languages. Because case-insensitive languages cannot distinguish between two names within the same context that differ only by case, components must avoid this situation.
- Do not use Hungarian notation[2] for parameter or variable names. Instead, use descriptive parameter names based on a parameter's or variable's meaning or semantics, rather than its type.
- Do not use abbreviations in identifiers (including parameter names), if possible. If you must use abbreviations, then follow the casing rules for that type of identifier for any abbreviation consisting of more than two characters, even if it is not the standard abbreviation. (Use all uppercase for abbreviations consisting of two or fewer characters). Example: namespace `System.Web.UI`.

---

[2]   Hungarian notation (HN) is a naming convention invented by Charles Simonyi. Hungarian notation names identifiers with a lowercase prefix to identify the class or usage of the variable. Examples: `m_nSize`, `hwndParent`, and `lpszFile`.

- Do not specify the same name for namespaces and classes. For example, do not use `Debug` for a namespace name and have a class named `Debug`. Also, avoid using identifiers that conflict with common keywords in other languages such as `Alias` and `Select`.

Member Usage

Having a well-designed library involves more than simply using the correct naming conventions. You must know how and when to use the different kinds of members on a type to express specific concepts. The library designer uses members to communicate such information to the developers using the particular library. For example, a designer might choose to use a property rather than a method to express the length of a collection because the semantics of a property most closely fit the need at hand.

Properties Versus Methods

A library developer often faces the choice of when to use a method to represent functionality and when to use a property for this purpose. The underlying technology is flexible enough to allow any operation to be expressed as a property or a method. There are clear motivations to maintain two distinct concepts, however. Because of language syntax and consistent use in the .NET Framework, developers have come to think of properties as being synonymous with fields. They do not think of a field as being able to perform some operation; rather, a field simply holds information. This statement does not mean that the implementation of the property must simply return a field; complex cache schemes and event notifications are common within property accessors. Methods, on the other hand, are reserved for operations; they are active things that perform some operation on the state of the world. Here are some guidelines on the use of properties versus methods:

- **Do** use a property if the member has a logical backing store.
- **Do** use a method:
  - If the operation is a conversion (such as `Object.ToString()`).
  - If the operation is expensive (orders of magnitude slower than a field set would be).

- If the get accessor has an observable side effect.
- If calling the member twice in succession produces different results.
- If the order of execution is important.
- If the member is static but returns a mutable value.
- If the member must return an array.

Properties that return arrays can be very misleading. Usually, it is necessary to return a copy of the internal array to ensure that the user cannot change the internal state. This requirement, coupled with the fact that a user could easily assume the member is an indexed property, leads to inefficient code such as the following:

```
EmployeeList l = FillList();
for (int i = 0; i < l.Length; i++)
{
    if (l.All[i]== x){...}
}
```

In the preceding code, each call to the `All` property creates a copy of the array—$n + 1$ copies for this loop. Had the library designer used a method instead of a property, this line of code would look like the following:

```
if (l.GetAll()[i]== x){...}
```

This code more obviously indicates when the user is doing the wrong thing.

Use of Indexed Properties

In the same way that properties represent logical backing stores, indexed properties represent logical arrays. They are often referred to as "indexers" because in their most common usage they overload the indexer operator ("[]" in C#, for example). In C#, you define a default indexed property in the following way:

```
public object this[int index]
{
}
```

The usage of such a property is very natural:

```
Object o = l[42];
```

Following are best practices for using indexed properties:

- **Do** use only one named indexed property per class and make it the default indexed property for that class. (The C# language enforces this practice automatically.)
- **Do not** use nondefault indexed properties. (The C# language enforces this practice automatically.)
- **Do** use the name "Item" for indexed properties unless there is an obviously better name (for example, a `Chars` property on `String`). (The C# language enforces this practice automatically.)
- **Do** use indexed properties when the logical backing store is an array.
- **Do not** mix indexed properties and overloaded methods.

Use of Methods

Guidelines for good use of methods can be summarized as follows:

- **Do** default to having nonvirtual methods when possible.
- **Do** use overloading only when providing different methods that do semantically the same thing.
- **Do** favor overloading rather than default arguments (default arguments do not version well and are not allowed in the CLS).
- **Do** use default values correctly.
- **Do not** use "reserved" parameters. If more data are needed in the next version, you can add more overloading.
- **Do** use overloading for variable numbers of parameters.

Let's look at several of these guidelines in more detail.

Virtual Versus Nonvirtual Methods   Virtual methods are points of specialization in your library and, as such, they must be carefully defined. Users can subtype your type and customize the implementation of any virtual method to do almost anything. For this reason, you must exercise caution whenever you call a virtual method in your library. Users will expect you to continue to call the virtual methods in the same way as you version your framework. Decide explicitly when to use virtual methods, and document clearly the contract of that member (for example, when you are guaranteed to call it).

Overloading   Many languages do not provide a way for developers to select exactly which overload is called. In such a case, all methods with the same name should do the same thing, so it doesn't really matter which method is called. A good example involves `String.Append()`, which has overloads that take `Int32`, `Object`, `Double`, and other types of arguments. Of course, all of these overloads do the same thing—append the string version of the argument to a new string and return it.

Another example of this problem involves `String.IndexOf()`. The beta release of the .NET Framework included overloads of `IndexOf()` that took a string and returned the index of the start of that substring in the string as well as an overload of `IndexOf()` that took a char array and returned the index of the first occurrence of any element in the array. This was a poor design, as these methods did semantically different things. The COBOL language clearly highlighted this issue. COBOL offers a subtle conversion from a string to a `char` array that prevented the COBOL user from being able to select which method was called. The Beta2 version of the .NET Framework fixed this problem by including an `IndexOfAny` method for the `char` array overload.

Default Values   In a family of overloaded methods, the complex method should use parameter names that indicate a change from the default state assumed in the simple method. For instance, in the example below, the first method assumes that the lookup will not be case sensitive. In the second method, the name "`ignoreCase`" is used rather than "`caseSensitive`" because the former indicates how we are changing from the default behavior.

```
1: MethodInfo Type.GetMethod (String name);
                            //ignoreCase = false
2: MethodInfo Type.GetMethod (String name,
                            boolean ignoreCase);
```

It is very common to use a zeroed state for the default value (such as 0, 0.0, false, or "").

Variable Numbers of Parameters Where it is appropriate to have variable numbers of parameters to a method, use the convention of declaring N methods with increasing numbers of parameters and provide a method that takes an array of values for numbers greater than N. For most cases, $N = 3$ or $N = 4$ is appropriate. Make only the most complete overload virtual (if extensibility is needed) and define the other operations in terms of it. Listing 7.1 illustrates this point.

Listing 7.1 *Using variable numbers of parameters*

```
public class Foo
{
  public void Bar(string a)
  {
    Bar (a, 0, false);
  }

  public void Bar(string a, int b)
  {
    Bar (a, b, false);
  }

  public void Bar(string a, int b, false c)
  {
    // core implementation here
  }

}
```

Use of Types

Types are the unit of encapsulation in the runtime environment. As described in Chapter 2, two basic kinds of types exist:

- Object types (*classes*) are by far the most common kind of types used. Classes can be abstract (subclasses must provide an implementation) and sealed (no subclasses are allowed).
- Value types describe values that are represented as sequences of bits.

Enumerations (enums) are special kinds of value types that serve as named constants. An interface type is a partial description of a value, potentially supported by many object types.

Classes Versus Interfaces   From a versioning perspective, interfaces are less flexible than classes are. With a class, you can ship version 1 of the application and then decide to add another method in version 2. As long as the method is not abstract (i.e., as long as you provide a default implementation of the method), any existing derived classes will continue to function with no changes.

- **Do** favor using classes over any other type.
- **Do** use interfaces:
    - If you have concrete examples where several unrelated classes want to support the protocol.
    - If these classes already have established base classes (i.e., some are UI controls, some are Web services).
    - If aggregation is not appropriate or practical.

Use of Value Types   The .NET Framework has an extensible primitive type system. Value types are the mechanisms it offers to create your own types that behave like, and are as efficient as, the built-in primitive types such as `Int32` and `Double`. You should use value types only to represent values that behave like primitive types—that is, types that have value (copy) semantics by default. When you pass a value of a value type to a method, you expect to pass a copy of the value (pass by value), you expect assignments to copy the value, and you expect the method to return a copy.

Use value types for types that meet any of the following criteria:

- The types act like primitive types.
- Value semantics are desirable.
- The instance size is less than 16 bytes (with anything larger, the copying may become expensive).
- The types are immutable (they offer no way to change the state of an instance).

Use of Enumerations Enumerations are the mechanism that the .NET Framework uses to support named constants. Enumerations are a much better way to represent named constant values than the traditional methods such as #define or public static constants, because the latter mechanisms do not offer compile-time type checking. Consider an API such as the following:

```
public static FileStream Open (string name, int mode)
```

You have no idea what values to pass for mode, and you have no choice except to look up this information in the documentation (if it is documented at all!). If you use an enumeration to represent the mode, then the API becomes more self-documenting, as in the following case:

```
public static FileStream Open (string name, FileMode mode)
```

You can even build tools to automatically show the possible options for the enumeration.

Be aware that the .NET Framework supports C-style enumerations, so the compiler and runtime environment do not perform any type checking to ensure that the value passed into the enumeration is actually defined on the enumeration. For this reason, you must check all enumeration values to confirm that they are in the expected range. Listing 7.2 illustrates a common pattern for making sure enum values are defined.

Listing 7.2 Checking enum values

```
public static FileStream Open (string name, FileMode mode)
{
  switch (mode)
  {
    case FileMode.Append:
      //do Append
      break;
    case FileMode.Create:
      //do Create
      break;
    //etc...
    default:
```

continues

```
                    throw new ArgumentException("not a valid FileMode");
            }
            //create new FileStream and return it
```

Namespaces

With some perspective on the design goals and guidelines of the .NET Framework, let's now look at the functionality offered by many of the Framework Class Library's namespaces. Throughout this section, simple applications are provided to demonstrate the use of the libraries.

System

The `System` namespace is the root namespace; it offers common functionality that is needed by a wide variety of application types. It includes common base classes, types, and utility classes that will be required in nearly any application. Although you have encountered many of the common base classes earlier in this book, a short overview of them is provided here for completeness:

- `System.Object` is the ultimate base class for all types in the system. It defines the base set of services that any type in the system is able to provide. Not surprisingly, `Object` provides default implementations for all of these services.
- `System.ValueType` is a reference type that serves as the base class for all value types. It customizes the implementations of the virtual methods on `Object` so that they are more appropriate for value types.
- `System.Enum`, a reference type that derives from `System.ValueType`, is the base class for all enumerations in the system. It further customizes the virtual methods from `System.ValueType` so that they deal with exactly one integral field of instance data. `System.Enum` also offers utility methods for formatting and parsing enumeration values.
- `System.Exception` is the ultimate base class for all exceptions in the system.

- All custom attributes derive from the `System.Attribute` base class, which contains utility methods for reading custom attributes off of reflection elements. (Reflection is discussed in detail in Chapter 3.)

Table 7.1 summarizes the base data types that are found in the `System` namespace. These types are so commonly used that languages typically use keywords as aliases for them. The `System` namespace classes represent those types and provide formatting and parsing, comparing, and coercion support for them.

Other classes provide services including supervision of managed and unmanaged applications, mathematics, remote and local program invocation, data type conversion, and application environment management.

Listing 7.3 demonstrates the use of some of the common base data types. This command-line tool returns the date plus or minus *n* days from today. The first thing it does is set up a try/catch block—a lazy way to validate parameters. If any error occurs, the program displays a message indicating that the problem probably arose because invalid values were passed on the command line. If there is no argument, the program prints today's date. If there is an argument, it is parsed with `Convert.ToInt32` and a `TimeSpan` representing that many days is created. This `TimeSpan` is then added to today's date and displayed to the user.

Listing 7.3 *Using base data types*

```
using System;
public class Today
{
  const string Usage = "Usage: Today [[+/-]offset]";
  static void Main(string[] args)
  {
  try
    {
      if (args.Length == 0)
      {
        Console.WriteLine ("{0:dddd, MMMM dd, yyyy}",
                           DateTime.Now);
        return;
      }
      if (args.Length == 1)
```

continues

```
        {
            int offset = Convert.ToInt32(args[0]);
            TimeSpan t = new TimeSpan (offset,0,0,0);
            Console.WriteLine ("{0:dddd, MMMM dd, yyyy}",
                                    DateTime.Now+t);
            return;
        }
        Console.WriteLine (Usage);
    }
    catch (Exception )
    {
        Console.WriteLine (Usage);
    }
  }
}
```

Listing 7.3 produces output like the following:

```
C:\Project7\Demos\Today>Today.exe
Tuesday, July 23, 2002

C:\Project7\Demos\Today>Today.exe +6
Monday, July 29, 2002

C:\Project7\Demos\Today>Today.exe -100
Sunday, April 14, 2002
```

System.Collections

The System.Collections namespace contains classes and interfaces for in-memory data storage and manipulation. It provides three main types.

The first set of types in the System.Collections namespace consists of concrete implementations of commonly used collection classes such as ArrayList (a dynamic array), Hashtable, Stack, and Queue. Application developers use these classes as a convenient way to store and retrieve in-memory data.

The second set of types in this namespace is a set of interfaces to define a formal contract between developers who are creating new collections and developers who are consuming collections. For example, the IEnumerable interface defines the contract for collections that can offer sequential access via an enumerator. The ASP.NET application model supports the data

TABLE 7.1 .NET Framework Built-in Value Types

Category	Class Name	Description	Visual Basic Data Type	C# Data Type	Managed Extensions for C++ Data Type
Integer	Byte	An 8-bit unsigned integer	Byte	byte	char
	SByte	An 8-bit signed integer; not CLS compliant	SByte No built-in type	sbyte	signed char
	Int16	A 16-bit signed integer	Short	short	short
	Int32	A 32-bit signed integer	Integer	int	int or long
	Int64	A 64-bit signed integer	Long	long	__int64
	UInt16	A 16-bit unsigned integer; not CLS compliant	UInt16 No built-in type	ushort	unsigned short
	UInt32	A 32-bit unsigned integer; not CLS compliant	UInt32 No built-in type	uint	unsigned int or unsigned long
	UInt64	A 64-bit unsigned integer; not CLS compliant	UInt64 No built-in type	ulong	unsigned __int64

continues

TABLE 7.1 *continued*

Category	Class Name	Description	Visual Basic Data Type	C# Data Type	Managed Extensions for C++ Data Type
Floating point	Single	A single-precision (32-bit) floating-point number	Single	float	float
	Double	A double-precision (64-bit) floating-point number	Double	double	double
Logical	Boolean	A Boolean value (true or false)	Boolean	bool	bool
Other	Char	A Unicode (16-bit) character	Char	char	__wchar_t
	Decimal	A 96-bit decimal value	Decimal	decimal	Decimal
	IntPtr	A signed integer—that is, a 32-bit value on a 32-bit platform and a 64-bit value on a 64-bit platform	IntPtr No built-in type	IntPtr No built-in type	IntPtr No built-in type
	UIntPtr	A native-sized unsigned integer; not CLS compliant	UIntPtr No built-in type	UIntPtr No built-in type	UIntPtr No built-in type

binding of controls to data sources that honor the IEnumerable contract; thus any new collection that implements this interface can automatically be bound as data in the ASP.NET model.

The third set of types in the System.Collections namespace supports the creation of strongly typed collections. The CollectionBase class offers data storage that is convenient for developers who are creating their own strongly typed collections. Library developers, for example, frequently want to do something such as expose an EmployeeCollection that has its Add and Remove methods typed to take an Employee instance. By implementing the EmployeeCollection to derive from CollectionBase, the developer avoids much of the tedious work involved in rewriting the collection from scratch.

Listing 7.4 illustrates how to use some of the basic collections. In this program, three different collection classes are used: ArrayList, Stack, and an array of Strings. The method PrintItems can display the contents of all three collections, however, as it accesses each collection via a shared interface, ICollection.

Listing 7.4 *Using collections*

```
using System;
using System.Collections;

namespace Samples
{
  public class Collections2
  {
    static void Main(string[] args)
    {
      Console.WriteLine("From an ArrayList");
      ArrayList l = new ArrayList ();
      l.Add ("Damien");
      l.Add ("Mark");
      l.Add ("Brad");
      PrintItems (l);

      Console.WriteLine("From a stack");
      Stack s = new Stack();
      s.Push(4.5);
      s.Push(12.3);
```

continues

```
            s.Push(66.2);
            PrintItems (s);

            Console.WriteLine("From an array");
            PrintItems (new string[] {"monkey","cat","dog"});
        }

        static void PrintItems (ICollection c)
        {
            int ct=0;
            foreach (object o in c)
            {
                Console.WriteLine ("\t{1}:{0}", o,ct++);
            }
        }
    }
}
```

Listing 7.4 would produce the following output:[3]

```
From an ArrayList
        0:Damien
        1:Mark
        2:Brad
From a stack
        0:66.2
        1:12.3
        2:4.5
From an array
        0:monkey
        1:cat
        2:dog
```

System.Data

The System.Data namespace is the home for the ADO.NET programming model. Over the last few years, it has become clear that classic ADO does not address key requirements for building scalable server-side applications. System.Data was designed specifically for the Web, with scalability, statelessness, and XML considerations in mind.

---

[3] This example in no way implies that Damien resembles a 66-year-old monkey, Mark a 12-year-old cat, or Brad a 4-year-old dog!

If you already work with ADO, many of the concepts underlying ADO.NET will look familiar, such as the `Connection` and `Command` objects. ADO.NET also introduces some new objects and types, including `DataSet`, `DataReader`, and `DataAdapter`.

The `DataSet` class points to an important distinction between ADO.NET and other data architectures, in that it offers a disconnected view of the data as separate and distinct from any data stores. As a consequence, a `DataSet` functions as a stand-alone entity. You can think of a `DataSet` as an always disconnected *recordset* that knows nothing about the source or destination of the data it contains. Inside a `DataSet`, much like in a database, you can find tables, columns, relationships, constraints, views, and so forth.

The `DataSet` class offers built-in support for XML. It allows you to read in data as XML and populate a database or, as in Listing 7.5, read data from a database and output it into XML.

Listing 7.5 *Using the* `DataSet` *class to read data from a database and output XML*

```
using System;
using System.Data;
using System.Xml;
using System.Data.SqlClient;

namespace Samples
{
  public class DataSetSample
  {
    static void Main(string[] args)
    {
      SqlConnection myConn = new SqlConnection(
          "server=...;database=...;uid=...;password=...");
      SqlDataAdapter da = new SqlDataAdapter(
                  "select * from customers", myConn);
      DataSet ds = new DataSet();
      da.Fill(ds, "Customers");
      ds.WriteXml("Customers.xml");
    }
  }
}
```

Listing 7.5 produces the following output:

```
mydata.xml contains:
<?xml version="1.0" standalone="yes"?>
<NewDataSet>
  <Employees>
    <CustomerID>ALFKI</CustomerID>
    <CompanyName>Alfreds Futterkiste</CompanyName>
    <ContactName>Maria Anders</ContactName>
    <ContactTitle>Sales Representative</ContactTitle>
    <Address>Obere Str. 57</Address>
    <City>Berlin</City>
    <PostalCode>12209</PostalCode>
    <Country>Germany</Country>
    <Phone>030-0074321</Phone>
    <Fax>030-0076545</Fax>
  </Employees>
  <Employees>
    ...
  </Employees>
</NewDataSet>
```

System.Globalization

The `System.Globalization` namespace contains classes that define culture-related information, including the language, country/region, calendars in use, sort order for strings, and format patterns for dates, currency, and numbers.

The .NET Framework introduces a new distinction to the globalization world. The concept that was previously referred to as "locale" has been split into two separate types that allow much more flexibility: who you are (culture) and where you are (region). The locale is represented as two different types in the .NET world: `CultureInfo` and `RegionInfo`. `CultureInfo` gives information about the user's culture, such as what language is spoken, how numbers should be formatted, and which calendar is used. The `RegionInfo` class gives information about where a person physically is, what currency symbol is used, and whether the metric system is employed.

Listing 7.6 demonstrates how to print out the date in different cultures. By default, the date is printed in the current UI culture: `Thread.CurrentCulture`. However, it is customizable as shown in the example.

Listing 7.6 *Printing culture-based dates*

```
using System;
using System.Globalization;

namespace Samples
{
  public class GlobalizationExample
  {
    static void Main(string[] args)
    {
      CultureInfo c = new CultureInfo("en-US");
      string s = string.Format (c,"{0,-25}: {1:D}",
                             c.DisplayName, DateTime.Now);
      Console.WriteLine(s);
      c = new CultureInfo("fr-CA");
      s = string.Format (c,"{0,-25}: {1:D}",
                             c.DisplayName,DateTime.Now);
      Console.WriteLine(s);
      c = new CultureInfo("de-AT");
      s = string.Format (c,"{0,-25}: {1:D}",
                             c.DisplayName,DateTime.Now);
      Console.WriteLine(s);
    }
  }
}
```

Listing 7.6 produces output like the following:

```
English (United States)  : Tuesday, July 23, 2002
French (Canada)          : 23 juillet, 2002
German (Austria)         : Dienstag, 23. Juli 2002
```

System.Resources

Creating resources can help you develop robust, culture-aware programs without having to recompile your application just because the resources have changed. Resources are an application-building feature that allows you to place culture-specific data inside satellite data files (called resource files), rather than directly in the main application. The main assembly does not strongly bind to these satellite data files, which offers you the flexibility of deploying them in different phases. When building your application, you can identify culture-specific aspects such as user-visible strings and graphics, and then put these characteristics in a different resource file for each culture where your application may be used. At runtime, the appropriate set of resources will be loaded based on the user's culture settings. The setting used is the `CurrentUICulture` for the main thread of execution, which the user can set programmatically.

The `ResourceManager` class provides the user with the ability to access and control resources stored in the main assembly or in resource satellite assemblies. Use the `ResourceManager.GetObject` and `ResourceManager.GetString` methods to retrieve culture-specific objects and strings.

Listing 7.7 creates a resource manager bound to the localizable resource file associated with this assembly. In the body of the program, the code pulls the string with the key "Hello" out of the resource file that is the best match for the current culture.

Listing 7.7 *Creating a resource manager and matching resources and cultures*

```
using System;
using System.Reflection;
using System.Globalization;
using System.Resources;

namespace Sample
{
  class ResourcesClass
  {
    static ResourceManager rm =
        new ResourceManager("strings",
                  Assembly.GetExecutingAssembly());
    static void Main(string[] args)
    {
      CultureInfo ci = CultureInfo.CurrentUICulture;
      Console.Write ("In '{0}': ", ci.DisplayName);
      Console.WriteLine (rm.GetString ("Hello",ci));
      ci = new CultureInfo("en-NZ");
      Console.Write ("In '{0}': ", ci.DisplayName);
      Console.WriteLine (rm.GetString ("Hello",ci));
    }
  }
}
```

```
strings.txt

Hello="Hello"

En-NZ\ strings.en-nz.txt

Hello="Hello from the land of the long white cloud"

Makefile:

all: Resources.cs
    resgen strings.txt
    csc /debug /res:strings.resources Resources.cs
    cd en-NZ
    resgen strings.En-NZ.txt
    al /embed:strings.en-NZ.resources /culture:en-NZ \
       /out:resources.resources.dll
    cd ..
```

Listing 7.7 produces output like the following:

```
In 'English (United States)': "Hello"
In 'English (New Zealand)': "Hello from the land of the long
white cloud"
```

System.IO

The System.IO namespace contains the infrastructure pieces you need to work with input/output (I/O). It includes a model for working with streams of bytes, higher-level readers and writers that consume those bytes, interesting implementations of streams such as FileStream and MemoryStream, and a set of utility classes for working with files and directories.

System.Stream is the base class for all streams in the system. It provides a model for byte-level access to a backing store, which can be a file on disk, memory, network, or another stream. Implementations of the stream class can support reading, writing, and/or seeking. Predicates (CanSeek, CanRead, CanWrite) on the stream class advertise this support to consumers. In addition, the System.Stream class provides a model for both synchronous and asynchronous access to the backing store—functionality important for the loosely coupled, disconnected world of the Internet.

The .NET Framework offers stream implementations for backing stores such as the file system, the network, and memory; it also provides streams for composition such as a buffering stream and an encrypting stream. As is the pattern throughout the framework, the stream classes are designed to provide sensible default behavior so that the developer does not have to implement a large amount of boilerplate code. For example, the FileStream class is buffered by default, eliminating the need to wrap it in a BufferedStream. Although this feature makes for a less purely object-oriented model, it does enhance developer productivity.

The Reader and Writer classes are adapters that consume streams so as to provide higher-level views of the data. For example, the TextReader and TextWriter classes associate a stream of bytes with an encoding to present a textual view of the data. Although streams allow you only to read bytes, a TextReader will consume a stream and allow you to read strings of data from the stream.

Listing 7.8 outputs text to the console from a variety of sources. Because these sources share the same stream model, the code remains fairly simple.

Listing 7.8 Outputting text from a variety of sources that share a stream model

```
namespace Samples
{
  using System;
  using System.IO;
  public class EntryPoint
  {
    static void Main(string[] args)
    {
      Console.WriteLine ("File from Disk");
      PrintText (new FileStream (
                      "hello.txt",FileMode.Open));

      Console.WriteLine ("From memory");
      byte[] ba = new byte []
         {0x48,0x65,0x6c,0x6c,0x6f,0x20,
          0x57,0x6f,0x72,0x6c,0x64,0x21,00};
      PrintText (new MemoryStream(ba));
    }
    static void PrintText (Stream s)
    {
      TextReader r = new StreamReader (s);
```

```
      string str;
      int ct = 0;
      while ((str = r.ReadLine()) != null)
      {
        Console.WriteLine ("{0:00}: {1}",ct++,str);
      }
    }
  }
}
```

Listing 7.8 produces the following output:

```
File from Disk
00: Hello from the file...
01: Hope you enjoy the book!
From memory
00: Hello World!
```

System.Net

The classes in the `System.Net` namespace support the creation of applications that use Internet protocols to send and receive data. Using a layered approach, the .NET classes enable applications to access the network with varying levels of control, depending on the needs of the application. The spectrum covered by these levels includes nearly every scenario on the Internet today—from fine-grained control over sockets to a generic request/response model. Furthermore, the model can be extended so that it will continue to work with an application as the Internet evolves.

Listing 7.9 reads some HTML from an Internet site and displays it to the console. First, it creates a `WebRequest` to the URL being accessed. This activity is merely setup work, as the result does not actually hit the network. When the program is ready to make the request, it does so synchronously (i.e., the program blocks until the entire request returns from the Web). You might find it interesting to use the asynchronous `Begin` and `End` methods on `WebResponse`, instead. Finally, the program receives the raw HTML from the server and prints it to the console. Listing 7.9 uses C#'s `using` construct to ensure that the request is closed when the program is finished with it.

Listing 7.9 *Sending data to and receiving data from the Internet*

```
using System;
using System.Net;
using System.IO;
using System.Text;

namespace Samples
{
  class NetSample
  {
    static void Main(string[] args)
    {
      WebRequest wReq = WebRequest.Create(
                          "http://www.GotDotNet.com");
      WebResponse wResp = wReq.GetResponse();
      using (StreamReader sr = new StreamReader(
              wResp.GetResponseStream(), Encoding.ASCII))
      {
        string line = null;
        while ((line = sr.ReadLine()) != null)
        {
          Console.WriteLine(line);
        }
      }
      Console.ReadLine();
    }
  }
}
```

Listing 7.9 produces the following output:

```
<TITLE>Welcome to the GotDotNet Home Page!</TITLE>
<HTML>
  <HEAD>
    <!- Nav control will supply title below ->
    <TITLE>
    </TITLE>
    <link rel="stylesheet" type="text/css"
      href="/includes/gotdotnet_stylenew.css">
  </HEAD>
  <BODY background="/images/expando.gif"
      TOPMARGIN="0" LEFTMARGIN="0"
      MARGINHEIGHT="0" MARGINWIDTH="0">
```

```
       . . .
     </BODY>
     </HTML>
```

System.Reflection

As discussed in Chapter 3, metadata is a core concept for the .NET Framework's functionality. The `System.Reflection` namespace provides ways to read that information and emit it in a logical programming model. The reading portion of reflection APIs is used primarily in two scenarios: browsing and late-bound invocation.

Browsing Support

The browsing support is rooted on the `System.Type` class. The `Type` class represents the metadata for a class: the class's name, its visibility, the members that it defines, and so forth. `System.Type` instances are obtained from three places:

- The nonvirtual `GetType` method
- The `typeof()` operator
- Fully qualified string names

You can call the nonvirtual `GetType` method on any object type. For every object, this method returns its type. For example:

```
string s = "hello";
Type t = s.GetType ();
Console.WriteLine (t.FullName);
```

The output from the program would look like this:

```
System.String
```

The `typeof()` operator is found in many languages. Given a valid reference to a type, this method returns the `Type` instance. For example:

```
Type t = typeof(string[]);
Console.WriteLine(t.FullName);
```

The output from the program would look like this:

```
System.String[]
```

Finally, returning to the roots of the late-bound nature of reflection, you can access the type object from a fully qualified string name of the type. Commonly, the `Type.GetType()` static method is used to provide this information. For example:

```
Type t = Type.GetType ("System.Int32, mscorlib");
Console.WriteLine (t.FullName);
```

The output from the program would look like this:

```
System.Int32
```

Notice that the arguments include both the full name ("`System.Int32`") and the assembly where that type is defined ("`mscorlib`"). Both pieces of information are required because namespaces are not unique in the .NET world; uniqueness is relative to the assembly boundary.

Once you have the type, you can find out other information, such as all the members of the class. As an example, Listing 7.10 prints out all the members of a type.

Listing 7.10 *Printing the members of a type*
```
using System;
using System.Reflection;

namespace Samples
{
  class ReflectionSample
  {
    public static void PrintType (Type t)
    {
      Console.WriteLine (t);
      foreach (MemberInfo m in t.GetMembers())
      {
        if (m is ConstructorInfo)
        {
          Console.WriteLine ("Constructor: {0}", m);
```

```
      }
      else if (m is MethodInfo)
      {
        Console.WriteLine ("Method: {0}", m);
      }
      else if (m is PropertyInfo)
      {
        Console.WriteLine ("Property: {0}", m);
      }
      else if (m is EventInfo)
      {
        Console.WriteLine ("Event: {0}", m);
      }
    }
  }
  static void Main(string[] args)
  {
    PrintType(typeof(string));
    PrintType(typeof(object));
  }
 }
}
```

Listing 7.10 produces the following output:

```
System.String
Method: System.String ToString(System.IFormatProvider)
Method: System.TypeCode GetTypeCode()
Method: System.Object Clone()
Method: Int32 CompareTo(System.Object)
Method: Int32 GetHashCode()
Method: Boolean Equals(System.Object)
Method: System.String ToString()
Method: System.String Join(System.String, System.String[])
Method: System.String Join(System.String, System.String[],
Int32, Int32)
Method: Boolean Equals(System.String)
Method: Boolean Equals(System.String, System.String)
Method: Boolean op_Equality(System.String, System.String)
Method: Boolean op_Inequality(System.String, System.String)
Method: Char get_Chars(Int32)
...
Method: System.String Intern(System.String)
```

continues

```
Method: System.String IsInterned(System.String)
Method: System.CharEnumerator GetEnumerator()
Method: System.Type GetType()
Constructor: Void .ctor(Char*)
Constructor: Void .ctor(Char*, Int32, Int32)
Constructor: Void .ctor(SByte*)
Constructor: Void .ctor(SByte*, Int32, Int32)
Constructor: Void .ctor(SByte*, Int32, Int32,
System.Text.Encoding)
Constructor: Void .ctor(Char[], Int32, Int32)
Constructor: Void .ctor(Char[])
Constructor: Void .ctor(Char, Int32)
Property: Char Chars [Int32]
Property: Int32 Length
System.Object
Method: Int32 GetHashCode()
Method: Boolean Equals(System.Object)
Method: System.String ToString()
Method: Boolean Equals(System.Object, System.Object)
Method: Boolean ReferenceEquals(System.Object,
System.Object)
Method: System.Type GetType()
Constructor: Void .ctor()
```

Invocation Support

The invocation support available through the reflection feature allows for late-bound invocation of code. It is an important consideration in script scenarios or other instances where you know only at runtime which methods to call. There are two main entry points for dynamic invocation:

- `Type.InvokeMember()`
- The `Invoke` method applied off the various subclasses of `MemberInfo`

You use the `Invoke` member when you have little context for the type of member being called. As an example, consider the following Visual Basic code:[4]

---

[4] Strict type checking must be turned off for this code to work in VB.NET. Put the command `Option Strict Off` at the top of your program to test for this condition.

```
Dim x as Object
x = new Foo()
Console.WriteLine (x.Bar)
```

Because x is statically typed to be an `Object`, the compiler can't look up exactly what `Bar` is and emit the specific call at compile time. Instead, it must emit a late-bound call. Ah, but to what? To the member `Bar` on the instance x. From the syntax, it appears that `Bar` may be a field, property, or zero-argument method. Ultimately, the `Type.InvokeMember` function is called for this kind of construct.

To handle this problem, Listing 7.11 first creates an instance of the target class. It then invokes the `Bar` member via `Type`'s `InvokeMember` method. It specifies to search for members of that name that are public and either static or instance. Based on the syntax (it is on the right-hand side), the instance must be a property getter, a field get, or a method call, so the code lists those choices. It turns out to be a property getter. Because that fact isn't known at the call site, however, the code must pass all the alternatives. No custom binding is specified and no parameters are passed, so those values can be null. As a result, the `Bar` property on `Foo` is called and returns "Hello"; the code then displays that result to the console.

Listing 7.11 *Using late-bound invocation*

```
using System;
using System.Reflection;

namespace Samples
{
  public class Foo
  {
    public string Bar
    {
      get
      {
        return "Hello";
      }
    }
  }
  class ReflectionSample
  {
    static void Main(string[] args)
```

continues

```
      {
        object t = new Foo();
        object res = typeof(Foo).InvokeMember("Bar",
                         BindingFlags.Public |
                         BindingFlags.Instance |
                         BindingFlags.Static |
                         BindingFlags.GetProperty |
                         BindingFlags.GetField |
                         BindingFlags.InvokeMethod,
                         null, t, null);
        Console.WriteLine(res);
      }
    }
}
```

Listing 7.11 produces the following output:

```
Hello
```

Invocation off the various subclasses of `MemberInfo` works in a very similar way, except that it is much more efficient because the member resolution (which member to call) has already taken place. Listing 7.12 demonstrates this technique.

Listing 7.12 *Using invocation off subclasses*

```
using System;
using System.Reflection;

namespace Samples
{
  public class Foo
  {
    public string Bar
    {
      get
      {
        return "Hello";
      }
    }
    public string GetName (int empId)
    {
      switch (empId)
```

```
      {
        case 0: return "Judy";
        case 1: return "Frank";
        case 2: return "Tamara";
        case 3: return "Lisa";
        case 4: return "Cam";
        case 5: return "Emma";
        default: return "unknown";
      }
    }
    class ReflectionSample
    {
      static void Main(string[] args)
      {
        object t = new Foo();
        MethodInfo m = typeof (Foo).GetMethod ("GetName");
        object res = m.Invoke (t, new object[] {1});
        Console.WriteLine (res);
      }
    }
  }
}
```

Listing 7.12 produces the following output:

```
Frank
```

Reflection Emit

Reflection Emit is used to dynamically emit new types at runtime. It is primarily targeted at compiler authors and higher-end tools that need to emit executable code on the fly. A classic example of a tool that uses Reflection Emit is the .NET Framework regular expression engine. It has a mode where the regular expression passed by the user is compiled into an assembly, allowing you to achieve the speed of JIT-compiled code at execution time. Of course, you must pay a start-up penalty to "compile" the regular expression, but that cost is amortized away for a sufficiently large number of uses of the resulting regular expression.

In the example in Listing 7.13, the goal is to create an assembly, execute a method on it while the assembly remains in memory, and then write it out to disk.

Listing 7.13 Using Reflection Emit

```
using System;
using System.Reflection;
using System.Reflection.Emit;
using System.Threading;

namespace Samples
{
  public class DynamicType
  {
    public static int Main(string[] args)
    {
      string g = "out";
      AssemblyName asmname = new AssemblyName();
      asmname.Name = g;
      AssemblyBuilder asmbuild =
        Thread.GetDomain().DefineDynamicAssembly(asmname,
                        AssemblyBuilderAccess.RunAndSave);
      ModuleBuilder mod = asmbuild.DefineDynamicModule(
                        "Mod1", asmname.Name + ".exe" );
      TypeBuilder tb = mod.DefineType("Class1");
      MethodBuilder mb1 = tb.DefineMethod("Main",
                        MethodAttributes.Public |
                        MethodAttributes.Static,
                null,new Type[]{typeof(System.String[])} );
      ILGenerator ilg1 = mb1.GetILGenerator();
      ilg1.Emit(OpCodes.Ldstr, "Hello World");
      ilg1.Emit(OpCodes.Call,
              typeof( System.Console ).GetMethod("WriteLine",
              new Type[]{typeof(String)}));
      ilg1.Emit(OpCodes.Ret);
      Type t = tb.CreateType();

      //Invoke the Main method just for fun
      t.GetMethod("Main").Invoke(
      null,new object[] {new string[]{}});

      //Now emit it to disk
      asmbuild.SetEntryPoint( mb1 );
      asmbuild.Save( asmname.Name + ".exe" );
      Console.WriteLine ("assembly written: {0}",
                asmname.Name + ".exe");
      return 0;
    }
  }
}
```

First, the program sets up the name of the assembly; then, it creates the assembly within the context of the current application domain. It specifies that this assembly should run from memory and be saved. If you didn't want to save the assembly, Reflection Emit would optimize it differently for in memory-only access.

Next, the code defines a module within the new assembly. Many .NET languages perform this task transparently for developers; at the lowest levels of the runtime environment, you as the developer have to handle this bit of housekeeping yourself.

The next step is to define a type within the new assembly, as with the name "Class1". A main method is then created: It is public, is static, and takes an array of strings.

Now you are ready to start writing IL. To get an idea of what IL instructions do, you can use the ILDASM tool to look at code written with a higher-level language. You also may need to reference the IL instruction set specification in the SDK documentation. The instructions in Listing 7.13 are simple: Load a `const` string on the stack, and then invoke the `WriteLine()` method off the console. You must be exact here and specify the `WriteLine` overload that takes a string.

After the instructions are executed, the code creates the type, which "bakes" the type at runtime. This `Type` object is now as good as any other type, whether built-in or user-defined. You can do anything with it that you can do with any type, including late-bound invocation and browsing. Just to prove the point, the code in Listing 7.13 invokes the main method and writes the assembly to an executable file on disk. Before writing the assembly out, it sets the entry point explicitly to be the main method.

Listing 7.13 produces the following output:

```
Hello
assembly written: out.exe
```

Figure 7.2 shows the result of running the ILDASM tool over the assembly created in Listing 7.13. Figure 7.3 shows the IL code emitted for the method created in Listing 7.13 when viewed with ILDASM. Notice the correlation between the three "emit" statements in Listing 7.13 and the IL code displayed.

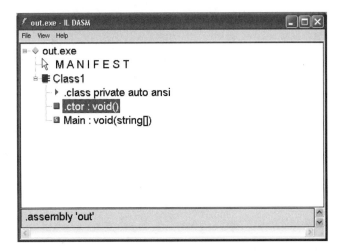

Figure 7.2 *ILDASM tool running over the user-defined assembly*

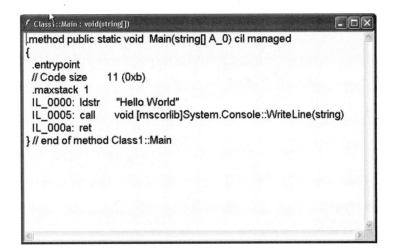

Figure 7.3 *IL code produced by Listing 7.13*

System.Security

The System.Security namespace contains the infrastructure for working with a permissions-based security system—specifically, code access security. A permissions-based system protects resources (such as the user's file system or network) by checking whether the caller is granted a particular permission (or set of permissions) represented by classes that implement IPermission. A user could have the permission because he or she has taken on a particular role (role-based security), such as "user" or "administrator." Alternatively, in the case of code access security, the user might be granted the permission because of evidence from the actual code that is executing on the stack. This evidence includes where the code is running from (a local machine is more highly trusted than one on the Internet) and who published the code (an administrator could choose to trust code from Microsoft more highly than that from FlyByNight.com). This system can be extended by the user. For example, when you create libraries that access some resource, you can create your own permission that can be administratively granted to code based on evidence.

Listing 7.14 shows part of the code from the implementation of the FileStream class. First, it gets the fully qualified path name to canonicalize the path. Next, it creates a new FileIOPermission with the appropriate flags. Then, it calls the Demand method. If the demand operation fails, the code throws a SecurityException; otherwise, execution continues and Win32 is called to read the file (not shown).

Listing 7.14 *Using code access security*

```
public FileStream(string fileName)
{
    string fullPath = Directory.GetFullPathInternal(fileName);
    new FileIOPermission(FileIOPermissionAccess.Read,
                        fullPath).Demand();
    //[… read the specified file at behest of caller(s) …]
}
```

System.Text

The System.Text namespace contains classes representing ASCII, Unicode, UTF-7, and UTF-8 character encodings; abstract base classes for converting blocks of characters to and from blocks of bytes; and a helper class that manipulates and formats String objects without creating intermediate instances of String.

Listing 7.15 demonstrates the conversion of a Unicode string into a byte array in a given code page encoding. This kind of transformation is useful for dealing with legacy data formats that predate the Unicode standard now used through the .NET Framework. By working with the encoding abstraction, you can write a single routine that works for a wide range of encodings.

Listing 7.15 *Converting blocks of characters to and from blocks of bytes*

```
using System;
using System.IO;
using System.Globalization;
using System.Text;

namespace Samples
{
  public class Encoding_UnicodeToCodePage
  {
    public static void Main()
    {
      // Simple ASCII characters
      PrintCodePageBytes("Hello, World!",1252);
      PrintCodePageBytes("Hello, World!",932);

      // Japanese characters
      PrintCodePageBytes(
              "\u307b,\u308b,\u305a,\u3042,\u306d",1252);
      PrintCodePageBytes(
              "\u307b,\u308b,\u305a,\u3042,\u306d",932);

      // GB18030
      PrintCodePageBytes("\u00A4",54936);
    }
    public static void PrintCodePageBytes(string str,
                                          int codePage)
    {
      Encoding targetEncoding;
      byte[] encodedChars;

      // Get the requested encoding
      targetEncoding = Encoding.GetEncoding(codePage);

      // Get the byte representation
      encodedChars = targetEncoding.GetBytes(str);
```

```
        // Print the bytes
        Console.WriteLine (
            "Byte representation of '{0}' in CodePage '{1}':",
            str,codePage);
        for (int i = 0; i < encodedChars.Length; i++)
          Console.WriteLine("Byte {0}: {1}",
                              i,encodedChars[i]);
      }
    }
  }
```

Listing 7.15 produces the following output:

```
Byte representation of 'Hello, World!' in CodePage '1252':
Byte 0: 72
Byte 1: 101
...
Byte 12: 33
Byte representation of 'Hello, World!' in CodePage '932':
Byte 0: 72
...
Byte 12: 33
Byte representation of '?,?,?,?,?' in CodePage '1252':
Byte 0: 63
...
Byte 8: 63
Byte representation of '?,?,?,?,?' in CodePage '932':
Byte 0: 130
...
Byte 13: 203
Byte representation of '?' in CodePage '54936':
Byte 0: 161
Byte 1: 232
```

Within the System.Text namespace, the System.Text.RegularExpressions namespace contains classes that provide access to the .NET Framework regular expression engine. Regular expressions allow for easy parsing and matching of strings to a specific pattern. Using the objects available in the RegularExpressions namespace, you can compare a string with a given pattern, replace a string pattern with another string, or retrieve only portions of a formatted string.

One of the most impressive things about this support is that you can compile the regular expressions into in-memory IL using the Reflection Emit functionality described earlier. This facility allows regular expressions to be executed at the same speed as native code, although it does take some overhead to set them up. For this reason, you should use this option only when working with regular expressions that are frequently used and rarely change.

Consider the simplest case, in which regular expressions are used to compare strings with a particular pattern. You might allow only strings in a particular length range, especially when accepting passwords. Listing 7.16 demonstrates the process of creating a regular expression (Regex) and testing whether a string matches the specified pattern with the IsMatch method.

Listing 7.16 *Using regular expressions to search for string patterns*

```
using System;
using System.Text.RegularExpressions;

namespace Samples
{
  class RegExExample
  {
    static void Main(string[] args)
    {
      Regex emailregex =
              new Regex("(?<user>[^@]+)@(?<host>.+)");
      bool ismatch = emailregex.IsMatch(args[0]);
      string not = "";
      if (!ismatch) not="not ";
      Console.WriteLine(
              "'{0}' is {1}in e-mail address format",
              args[0],not);
    }
  }
}
```

Listing 7.16 produces the following output:

```
C:\> isEmail darb@smarba.com
'darb@flybynight.com' is in e-mail address format
C:\> isEmail Eat.At.Eds
'Eat.At.Eds' is not in e-mail address format
```

Regular expressions are often useful when you are trying to retrieve small portions of text from a large document or result set, or when you are filtering a stream. The `MatchCollection` object contains all valid `Match` objects for a given regular expression after a successful match occurs. Listing 7.17 demonstrates this use of regular expressions.

Listing 7.17 Using regular expressions to retrieve strings

```
using System;
using System.Text.RegularExpressions;

namespace Samples
{
  class RegExExample
  {
    static void Main(string[] args)
    {
      Regex digitregex = new Regex("(?<number>\\d+)");
      string s = "the8bl5ind1mou5se8ra8nin3side";
      MatchCollection ms = digitregex.Matches(s);
      foreach (Match m in ms)
      {
        Console.WriteLine ("'{0}' matches", m.Value);
      }
    }
  }
}
```

Listing 7.17 produces the following output:

```
'8' matches
'5' matches
'1' matches
'5' matches
'8' matches
'8' matches
'3' matches
```

Functions from the regular expressions library can often minimize the time needed to generate your own string replacement functions. By specifying a pattern of strings to be replaced, you do not have to search for every possible variation of a string. Once you have created a `Regex` object that matches every possible string to be replaced, you can use the `Replace` method to generate a result. For example, you can pass in the source string and the replacement string, and the `Replace` method will return the results as a `String` (see Listing 7.18).

Listing 7.18 *Using regular expressions to replace strings*

```
using System;
using System.Text.RegularExpressions;

namespace Samples
{
  class RegExExample
  {
    static void Main(string[] args)
    {
      Regex digitregex = new Regex("(?<digit>[0-9])");
      string before =
      "Here is so4848me te88xt with emb4493edded numbers.";
      string after = digitregex.Replace(before, "");
      Console.WriteLine (after);
    }
  }
}
```

Listing 7.18 produces the following output:

```
Here is some text with embedded numbers.
```

System.Threading

The .NET Framework provides a rich set of functionality to support multithreaded programming. Functionality in the `System.Threading` namespace allows you to write programs that perform more than one task at the same time. The `Thread` class represents a task, an isolated flow of execution in a program. By default, when you program starts, it receives a single thread of execution. To create an additional thread, you create a new `Thread` object and pass it a pointer to a method in your class via the `ThreadStartDelegate`. Listing 7.19 creates a new thread on the `Run` method.

Listing 7.19 *Creating a new thread*

```csharp
using System;
using System.Threading;

namespace Samples
{
  class ThreadSample
  {
    static void Run()
    {
      Console.WriteLine(
          "This is the secondary thread running.");
    }
    static void Main()
    {
      Console.WriteLine(
          "This is the primary thread running.");
      Thread t = new Thread(new ThreadStart(Run));
      t.Start();
      t.Join();
      Console.WriteLine(
          "The secondary thread has terminated.");
    }
  }
}
```

Listing 7.19 produces the following output:

```
This is the primary thread running.
This is the secondary thread running.
The secondary thread has terminated.
```

Be careful when dealing with multithreaded code, as each thread has access to the same state and the various threads' reads and writes to it can be interleaved.

System.Runtime.InteropServices

The InteropServices namespace contains functionality to allow .NET objects to access unmanaged code and unmanaged code to call into .NET objects. The two primary features in this namespace are Platform Invocation Services (PInvoke), which allows managed code to call unmanaged functions that are implemented in a DLL, and COM Interoperability (COM Interop), which allows COM objects to be accessed from .NET objects, and vice versa. COM+ services, such as transactions and object pooling, are exposed directly in the .NET Framework via the `System.EnterpriseServices` namespace, which is outside the scope of this book.

PInvoke

PInvoke takes care of finding and invoking the correct function, as well as marshaling its managed arguments to and from their unmanaged counterparts (such as integers, strings, arrays, and structures). PInvoke is intended primarily to allow managed code to call existing unmanaged code, typically written in C. A good example is the several thousand functions that constitute the Win32 API.

Listing 7.20 demonstrates calling the Win32 API `CreateFontIndirect` from managed code. In the `Win32API` class, a PInvoke stub is added that points to the `CreateFontIndirect` entry point in `gdi32.dll`. The code then specifies how the string should be marshaled at runtime as well as how the `lplf` parameter should be marshaled. Next, a `LOGFONT` class is created on the managed side that exactly mirrors the unmanaged version. The runtime environment lays it out sequentially and a specific size is given for the `lfFaceName` string. After this setup work is complete, you can call the `CreateFontIndirect` method just like any other method.

Listing 7.20 *Calling a Win32 API from managed code*

```
using System;
using System.Runtime.InteropServices;

class Win32API
{
    [DllImport("gdi32.dll", CharSet=CharSet.Auto)]
    public static extern int CreateFontIndirect(
        [In, MarshalAs(UnmanagedType.LPStruct)]
        LOGFONT lplf   // characteristics
    );
    public static void Main()
    {
        LOGFONT lf = new LOGFONT();
        lf.lfHeight = 9;
        lf.lfFaceName = "Arial";
```

```
        int i = CreateFontIndirect(lf);
        Console.WriteLine("{0:X}", i);
    }
}

[StructLayout(LayoutKind.Sequential)]
public class LOGFONT
{
    public const int LF_FACESIZE = 32;
    public int lfHeight;
    public int lfWidth;
    public int lfEscapement;
    public int lfOrientation;
    public int lfWeight;
    public byte lfItalic;
    public byte lfUnderline;
    public byte lfStrikeOut;
    public byte lfCharSet;
    public byte lfOutPrecision;
    public byte lfClipPrecision;
    public byte lfQuality;
    public byte lfPitchAndFamily;
    [MarshalAs(UnmanagedType.ByValTStr,
        SizeConst=LF_FACESIZE)]
    public string lfFaceName;
}
```

Listing 7.20 produces the following output:

```
C0A0996
```

COM Interop

In many ways, interoperating with COM is more seamless than interoperating with PInvoke. COM already has many of the basic constructs, such as objects, classes, methods, and properties. The CLR offers bidirectional COM interoperability.

You can readily use COM objects from managed code. The Type Library Importer (Tlbimp.exe) is a command-line tool that converts the coclasses and interfaces contained in a COM type library to metadata. It creates an assembly and namespace for the type information automatically. After the metadata of a class becomes available, managed clients can create instances of the COM type and call its methods, just as if it were a .NET instance. The Type Library Importer converts an entire type library to metadata at once, but it cannot generate type information for a subset of the types defined in a type library.

To generate an assembly from a type library, use the following command to produce the dx7vb.dll assembly in the DxVBLib namespace:

```
c:\>tlbimp dx7vb.dll
```

Adding the /out: switch, as shown below, produces an assembly with an altered name—in this case, DirectXWrapper. Altering the COM Interop assembly name can help distinguish it from the original COM DLL.

```
c:\>tlbimp dxvb7.dll /out: DirectXWrapper.dll
```

Similarly, you can expose any .NET object to COM. Of course, only those constructs that COM already recognizes can be exposed; thus static methods and parameterized constructors are not exposed, for example. For this reason and because of some version issues, the .NET library designer must decide at development time whether user-defined objects should be exposed to COM. If so, the designer can apply the ComVisible() attribute to these types. Types without this attribute are not exposed to COM. The Type Library Exporter (Tlbexp.exe) is a command-line tool that converts the classes and interfaces contained in an assembly to a COM type library. Once the type information of the class becomes available, COM clients can create an instance of the .NET class and call its methods, just as if it were a COM object. Tlbexp.exe converts an entire assembly at one time.

The following command generates a type library with the same name as the assembly found in myTest.dll:

```
tlbexp myTest.dll
```

The following command generates a type library with the name clipper.tlb:

```
tlbexp myTest.dll /out:clipper.tlb
```

System.Windows.Forms

Windows Forms is a framework for building "smart" client applications. Applications within this framework can be written in any language that supports the CLR. Windows Forms offers a programming model for developing Windows applications that combines the simplicity of the Visual Basic 6 programming model with the full power and flexibility of the CLR and the .NET Framework.

To illustrate some basic concepts of Windows Forms, let's look at a very simple application that keeps track of "to do" items. It leverages the extensive set of common controls that Windows Forms offers to perform the heavy lifting and the richness of the framework to handle some of the details. The application allows you to add items to your list and check them off when they are done (see Figure 7.4). It uses System.Xml to preserve the state of the application data when you start up and shut down the application, so no items ever fall off your list. Listing 7.21 provides the code for this example.

Figure 7.4 *Simple application using Windows Forms*

Listing 7.21 *Using Windows Forms*

```
using System;
using System.Xml;
using System.IO;
using System.Drawing;
using System.Collections;
using System.ComponentModel;
using System.Windows.Forms;
using System.Data;


namespace WinFormsExample
{
  public class Form1 : System.Windows.Forms.Form
  {
    private System.Windows.Forms.Button button1;
    private System.Windows.Forms.CheckedListBox
              checkedListBox1;
    private System.Windows.Forms.TextBox textBox1;
    private System.ComponentModel.Container components =
                                             null;

    public Form1()
    {
      InitializeComponent();
    }
    protected override void Dispose( bool disposing )
    {
      using (StreamWriter s = new StreamWriter("todo.xml"))
      {
        XmlTextWriter t = new XmlTextWriter (s);
        t.WriteStartElement("items");
        for (int i = 0; i < checkedListBox1.Items.Count;
                                             i++)
        {
          t.WriteStartElement ("Item");
          t.WriteAttributeString ("Name",
          checkedListBox1.Items[i].ToString());
          t.WriteAttributeString("State",
              checkedListBox1.GetItemCheckState(i).
                  ToString());
          t.WriteEndElement();
        }
        t.WriteEndElement();
      }
```

```
  if( disposing )
  {
    if (components != null)
    {
      components.Dispose();
    }
  }
  base.Dispose( disposing );
}
#region Windows Form Designer generated code
private void InitializeComponent()
{
  this.button1 = new System.Windows.Forms.Button();
  this.checkedListBox1 =
      new System.Windows.Forms.CheckedListBox();
  this.textBox1 = new System.Windows.Forms.TextBox();
  this.SuspendLayout();
  // button1
  this.button1.Location =
      new System.Drawing.Point(176, 24);
  this.button1.Name = "button1";
  this.button1.TabIndex = 0;
  this.button1.Text = "&Add";
  this.button1.Click +=
      new System.EventHandler(this.button1_Click);
  // checkedListBox1
  this.checkedListBox1.Location =
      new System.Drawing.Point(24, 56);
  this.checkedListBox1.Name = "checkedListBox1";
  this.checkedListBox1.Size =
      new System.Drawing.Size(224, 154);
  this.checkedListBox1.TabIndex = 1;

  // textBox1
  this.textBox1.Location =
      new System.Drawing.Point(24, 24);
  this.textBox1.Name = "textBox1";
  this.textBox1.Size =
      new System.Drawing.Size(144, 20);
  this.textBox1.TabIndex = 2;
  this.textBox1.Text = "";
  // Form1
  this.AutoScaleBaseSize =
      new System.Drawing.Size(5, 13);
  this.ClientSize = new System.Drawing.Size(292, 273);
```

continues

```
    this.Controls.AddRange(
        new System.Windows.Forms.Control[] {
            this.textBox1,
            this.checkedListBox1, this.button1});
    this.Name = "Form1";
    this.Text = "ToDo List";
    this.Load +=
        new System.EventHandler(this.Form1_Load);
    this.ResumeLayout(false);
}
#endregion
[STAThread]
static void Main()
{
    Application.Run(new Form1());
}
private void Form1_Load(object sender,
                        System.EventArgs e)
{
    if (File.Exists ("todo.xml"))
    {
        using (StreamReader s =
                        new StreamReader("todo.xml"))
        {
            XmlTextReader t = new XmlTextReader (s);
            int ct = 0;
            while(t.Read())
            {
                string n = t.GetAttribute ("Name");
                if (n != null)
                {
                    this.checkedListBox1.Items.Add(n);
                    CheckState v = (CheckState)Enum.Parse(
                                    typeof(CheckState),
                                    t.GetAttribute("State"));
                    this.checkedListBox1.SetItemCheckState (
                                                        ct,v);
                    ct++;
                }
            }
        }
    }
}
private void button1_Click(object sender,
                        System.EventArgs e)
```

```
        {
            this.checkedListBox1.Items.Add(this.textBox1.Text);
            textBox1.Text = String.Empty;
        }
    }
}
```

To load the form, the program calls the `Form_Load` method. This method reads the data file from disk and populates the checked list box.

The program calls the `Dispose` method when the application is shut down; it gives you a chance to do any necessary cleanup before the application exits. The `disposing` parameter is true if this method was explicitly called or false if it was called as part of the garbage collection operation that cleans up the object before it is collected. In either case, the current state is saved.

System.Web

The `System.Web` namespace encapsulates the functionality of ASP.NET, a server-side programming model whereby the UI is generated on the server and pushed down to clients. The UI is commonly written in HTML, but it can also follow an XML, WAP, or other format. This model enables lower-level clients to access your application with just an HTML 3.2 browser.

The `System.Web` namespace consists of two main parts:

- Web Application services: Infrastructure dealing with security, configuration, or caching
- Web Forms: A user interface model that uses the same drag-and-drop application development paradigm that Windows Forms and Visual Basic 6 use, but creates server-side applications that push HTML (or other content) to the client

In keeping with the history of ASP, you build ASP.NET applications by creating pages that contain HTML markup and embedded script that executes on the server.

Figure 7.5 depicts a very trivial ASP.NET page. When this page is requested for the first time, ASP.NET parses it (see Listing 7.22). The script

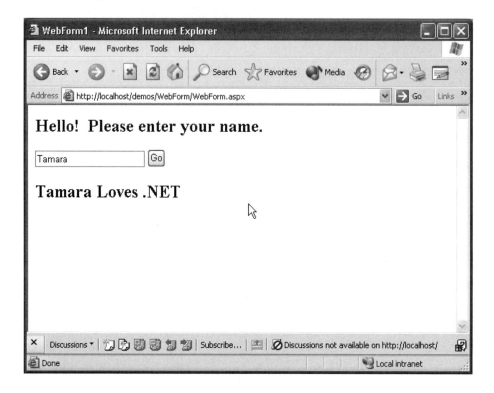

Figure 7.5 *An ASP.NET page*

code is written to a file and compiled into a managed assembly. As ASP.NET is building the response (in this case, in HTML), it calls out to the library when it needs to perform some action. In this example, the action is to process a button click. When the processing on the server is complete, the server sends an HTML response back to the client. Notice that the compilation and loading of the code needs to happen only on the first hit.

Listing 7.22 *Using ASP.NET*

```
<%@ Page language="c#" %>
<HTML>
  <HEAD>
    <title>WebForm1</title>
  </HEAD>
  <script language="C#" runat=server>
    void Button1_Click(Object sender, EventArgs e)
    {
      this.Label1.Text = String.Format(
```

```
          "<h2> {0} Loves .NET </h2>",
          this.TextBox1.Text);
      }
    </script>
    <body>
      <form id="Form1" method="post" runat="server">
        <H2>Hello!  Please enter your name.</H2>
        <P>
          <asp:TextBox id="TextBox1" runat="server">
          </asp:TextBox>
          <asp:Button id="Button1" OnClick="Button1_Click"
                      runat="server" Text="Go">
          </asp:Button>
        </P>
        <P>
          <asp:Label id="Label1" runat="server">
          </asp:Label>
        </P>
      </form>
    </body>
  </HTML>
```

To run the program in Listing 7.22, copy the code to a file called `WebForm1.aspx` and put it in a directory that has been mapped to a `VRoot` (for example, something under `Inetpub\wwwroot\`).

System.Web.Services

Web Forms is a great way to build Web applications with which a user interacts, but it does not address the problem of communicating programmatically via the Web. On many occasions, developers want to build applications that pull data from and post data to a Web site. Today, the only way to do so is to "screen scrap" or to use proprietary protocols. With screen scrapping, a developer makes an HTTP request and gets back HTML. Instead of displaying this HTML to the user, the application sniffs out and uses only the desired parts. Unfortunately, this approach is extremely error prone: Make one small change to the site, and the clients are broken. Also, content owners often don't appreciate this repackaging of their data. The alternative is not particularly attractive, either: Custom protocols are not easily usable by different vendors and are often blocked by firewalls.

What is needed is an open standard for programmatically communicating across the Internet. Enter SOAP. SOAP offers a way to package information in the well-known XML format and send it via HTTP across the Internet. It is supported across a wide range of computing environments by many vendors, including IBM and Microsoft.

The `System.Web.Services` namespace allows you to build SOAP-based Web services and conveniently access them. This functionality turns XML requests into .NET classes and instances, giving developers a well-understood way to interact with them. It can also turn .NET instances into standard XML that can be read by consumers on any platform.

Creation of a Web Service

To define a Web service, you write a .NET class and decorate it with the `System.Web.Services.WebMethodAttribute`. This attribute tells the .NET Framework to expose this method on the network as a Web service. Listing 7.23 gives an example of this process. To run this program, place the code in a file called `Grades.asmx` in a `Vroot` (typically off `Intnet\wwwroot\`).

Listing 7.23 *Defining a Web service*

```
<%@ WebService Language="csharp" Class="Grades" %>
using System;
using System.Collections;
using System.Web.Services;

public class Grades
{
  private Hashtable table;
  public Grades()
  {
    //Really should pull this out of a database
    table = new Hashtable();
    table.Add ("Steve",new int [] {100,12,99,98});
    table.Add ("Ken",new int [] {98,79,52,88});
    table.Add ("Dawn",new int [] {87,86,95,98});
    table.Add ("Dusty",new int [] {100,100,99,98});
    table.Add ("Jill",new int [] {53,100,100,100});
    table.Add ("Ed",new int [] {97,83,71,77});
    table.Add ("Jeff",new int [] {99,88,70,100});
  }
```

```
[WebMethod]
public double GetAverage (string studentName)
{
  ICollection grades = (ICollection)table[studentName];
  if (grades == null) return 0.0;
  int sum = 0;
  foreach (int i in grades)
  {
    sum+=i;
  }
  return sum/grades.Count;
}
}
```

The first line tells the ASP.NET infrastructure information such as the language in which the Web service is written and the class to expose. Each time a request comes in, the program creates the grades class and runs its constructor. The code then marshals the arguments passed in from XML into .NET types and invokes the method. Next, it marshals the return value from a .NET type into XML format. To test a Web service, simply navigate to the asmx page in your browser, where you will see a form that allows you to test each of these services.

Use of a Web Service

After creating a Web service with .NET, you may wonder how to use one. Listing 7.24 gives a very simple program to consume the GetAverage Web service defined in Listing 7.23. The command-line program takes the name of the student as an argument and returns his or her average grade. Notice how the .NET Framework automatically handles all the complexity involved in marshalling the arguments to XML format and back again.

Listing 7.24 Consuming a Web service

```
using System;

public class Client
{
  public static void Main (string [] args)
  {
    Grades g = new Grades();
```

continues

```
        double d = g.GetAverage (args[0]);
        Console.WriteLine (d);
    }
}
```

This code creates an instance of the proxy class for the `Grades` Web service, then invokes the `GetAverage` Web service by passing in the name given at the command line. This process is where a Web request and response occur, so in some cases it might be better to use the asynchronous methods also available on the proxy class. The code then prints out the results.

The `Grades` class is automatically created by the WSDL tool that ships with the .NET Framework SDK. This tool takes an XML scheme that describes a service (WSDL) and creates a client proxy for the service. To create the `Grades` class, you simply run the WSDL tool and compile the code:

```
all:     client

client:  GetAverage.cs
    wsdl http://localhost/Demos/WebService/Grades.asmx
    csc GetAverage.cs Grades.cs
```

Of course, the Visual Studio.NET tool makes it very simple to produce and consume Web services. The command-line tools are shown here simply for explanatory purposes.

System.Xml

If you have not heard of XML yet, you must be living under a rock! This meta-markup language provides a format for describing structured data, thereby supporting the creation of a new generation of Web-based data viewing and manipulation applications. XML, which is the universal language for data on the Web, gives developers the power to deliver structured data from a wide variety of applications to the desktop for local computation and presentation.

Although XML support is spread across the entire .NET Framework, the `System.Xml` namespace provides key XML processing functionality. This namespace contains a comprehensive set of XML classes for parsing, validation, and manipulation of XML data using readers, writers, and World

Wide Web Consortium (W3C) DOM-compliant components. It also covers XML Path Language (XPath) queries and eXtensible Stylesheet Language Transformations (XSLT).

The main classes in the XML namespace are as follows:

- The `XmlTextReader` class provides fast, noncached, forward-only, read access to XML data.
- The `XmlNodeReader` class provides an `XmlReader` over the given DOM node subtree.
- The `XmlValidatingReader` class provides DTD, XDR, and XSD schema validation.
- The `XmlTextWriter` class provides a fast, forward-only way of generating XML.
- The `XmlDocument` class implements the W3C DOM Level 1 Core and the Core DOM Level 2.
- The `XmlDataDocument` class provides an implementation of an `XmlDocument` that can be associated with a `DataSet`. You can view and manipulate structured XML simultaneously through the `DataSet`'s relational representation or the `XmlDataDocument`'s tree representation.
- The `XPathDocument` class provides a very high-performance, read-only cache for XML document processing for XSLT.
- The `XPathNavigator` class provides a W3C XPath 1.0 data model over a store with a cursor-style model for navigation.
- The `XslTransform` class is a W3C XSLT 1.0-compliant XSLT processor for transforming XML documents.
- The `XmlSchema` object model classes provide a navigable set of classes that directly reflect the W3C XSD specification. They provide the ability to programmatically create an XSD schema.
- The `XmlSchemaCollection` class provides a library of XDR and XSD schemas. These schemas, which are cached in memory, provide fast, parse-time validation for the `XmlValidatingReader`.

Listing 7.25 demonstrates the functionality in the `System.XML` namespace by opening an XML document containing information about a number

of book titles and then processing the document to produce text output
describing those titles.

Listing 7.25 *Processing an XML document using* `System.XML`-*based functionality*

```
using System;
using System.Xml;
using System.Xml.Serialization;
using System.IO;

class EntryPoint
{
  static void Main(string[] args)
  {
    XmlTextReader r = new XmlTextReader ("books.xml");
    {
      while (r.Read())
      {
        switch (r.NodeType)
        {
          case XmlNodeType.Text:
            Console.WriteLine (r.Value);
            break;
          case XmlNodeType.Element:
            if (r.Name == "book")
            {
              Console.WriteLine ("————————-");
              string genre = r["genre"];
              string pub = r["publicationdate"];
              string isbn = r["ISBN"];
              Console.WriteLine ("{0} {1} {2}",
                                  genre,pub,isbn);
            }
            break;
        }
      }
    }
  }
}
```

Listing 7.25 produces the following output:

```
——————— --
autobiography 1981 1-861003-11-0
The Autobiography of Benjamin Franklin
```

```
Benjamin
Franklin
8.99
_____--

novel 1967 0-201-63361-2
The Confidence Man
Herman
Melville
11.99
_____--

philosophy 1991 1-861001-57-6
The Gorgias
Sidas
Plato
9.99
```

Looking Back and Looking Ahead

The .NET Framework covers a broad set of functionality (this chapter didn't even look at all of it!). Even so, the framework has great room for growth.

The first release of the .NET Framework focuses on putting the right infrastructure in place for building applications on the server and on the client. It removes the drudgery from the software development and maintenance process in several ways:

- By reducing the "glue code" that developers have to write in many of today's systems
- By making designing for customization and extensibility possible (the framework is not a black box)
- By building in from the ground up standards and best practices from the Web
- By offering a unified programming model that decouples the developer's choice of language from the choice of application model

This broad, consistent, secure library of functionality is sure to form a kernel of application development for years to come.

Of course, there is certainly more work to do. Far too many real-world applications must resort to COM Interop or PInvoke to gain necessary access to platform features. The ability to drop down to native code is an important back door, but developers forced out that door lose many of the core benefits of the .NET Framework: Development becomes more tedious (more of the glue code returns), installation affects more elements and becomes more complicated, and semi-trusted execution is not possible. Both more depth and more breadth are required in the framework. For the areas already exposed in the .NET Framework, more of the underlying features need to be exposed (Windows XP theme support in Windows Forms, for example). However, most of the work needed in the framework will focus on extending its scope. The framework needs to be broad enough that nearly every application requires functionality from only the framework or a similar third-party library. Along those lines, multimedia support is an obvious omission in the current version of the .NET Framework.

Summary

This chapter described the programming surface of the .NET Framework: the Framework Class Library. This library contains a very rich set of functionality accessible to the application developer in the form of types and methods. Much of the feel of writing applications for the .NET Framework comes from interactions with this library and its functionality.

This chapter first described the history that led up to the development of the Framework Class Library. It then highlighted some of the important guidelines and patterns that were used in the design and implementation of the library. Next, it gave a high-level overview of the major sections of the library. Finally, it peered into the future, suggesting where the library is likely to be extended.

■ APPENDIX A ■

Visual Basic .NET

Paul Vick

THE BASIC LANGUAGE has been a member of Microsoft's language products from the very beginning—indeed, the first product produced by Microsoft was a BASIC interpreter for the Altair written by Bill Gates and Paul Allen. Every major platform produced by Microsoft has had a companion BASIC product, from BASIC-A and GW-BASIC for DOS through Visual Basic for the Windows platforms. As such, it is no surprise that one of the first languages to be ported to the .NET platform would be BASIC.

The move from Windows to .NET, though, was in many ways a much bigger and more difficult step for BASIC than the move from DOS to Windows. The sheer magnitude and complexity of the .NET platform meant that a number of new concepts had to be integrated into the language. Previous versions of Visual Basic were intimately tied to the specifics of the Win32 APIs and its Common Object Model (COM). Although .NET is built on top of Win32 and COM, .NET nonetheless revises or replaces many of the concepts of the underlying platform. And finally, because the .NET platform was designed as an inherently multilingual platform, more consideration had to be given to interoperating with other languages than had been given in the past.

This appendix discusses a number of the major issues that the Visual Basic .NET team dealt with when designing the latest revision of the language. A full discussion of all the changes between Visual Basic 6.0 and Visual Basic .NET is well beyond the space allowed here—it could easily fill a book in its own right. However, the issues discussed are intended to give an idea of the kinds of problems and solutions that a language author might encounter when adapting an established language to the .NET platform. There is also some discussion at the end of the chapter of language changes made that were not directly related to the move to the .NET platform. These will mostly be of interest to Visual Basic developers who are familiar with previous versions of the language.

Type System Additions

The .NET type system is considerably richer than the COM type system and so required a number of concepts to be added to the Visual Basic language. The most important was inheritance, but overloading, namespaces, and name hiding were also significant changes.

Classes

A *class* in previous versions of Visual Basic is equivalent to a COM *coclass*, which is a collection of supported interfaces. A coclass does not have a distinct identity—when creating a coclass, the creator requests one of the interfaces that the coclass implements. It is then possible to request other supported interfaces by requesting the `IUnknown` interface of the instance. However, in general it is not possible to know what coclass you have in hand given a particular interface pointer.

Previous versions of Visual Basic simplify this situation slightly through the concept of default interfaces. When a class is defined in these versions of Visual Basic, a hidden interface is created that contains all the public members defined in the class. The class then implements that default interface. Because COM lacks the concept of a class as a thing in and of itself, data members of classes have to be exposed as property methods. For example, given the following class definition in Visual Basic 6.0 (`class1.cls`),

```
Public Value As Integer

Public Sub PrintValue()
    ...
End Sub

Public Function CalculateValue() As Integer
    ...
End Function
```

the following would have been generated:

- An interface named `_class1` that contained four members: a property get method for `Value`, a property let method for `Value`, a method `PrintValue`, and a method `CalculateValue`
- A coclass `class1` that implemented `_class1`

In contrast to COM, the .NET type system invests identity in classes rather than interfaces. A class in .NET is a first-class object with its own identity and storage managed by the runtime environment. Classes can implement interfaces, but a reference—even to an interface—always refers to a particular instance of a class, never just an interface on its own. There are many benefits to this scheme (not the least of which is that data members do not have to be expressed as properties), but it does make interoperability between versions of Visual Basic a little more difficult.

As a side note, one incompatibility between COM and .NET that is unavoidable is that the unit of identity changes between the two platforms. For example, given a class `class1` that implements an interface `interface1`, Listing A.1 will produce two different answers on COM and on .NET.

Listing A.1 `module1.bas` **(VB6)**

```
Sub Main()
    Dim c As Class1
    Set c = New Class1        ' VB6 syntax used
```

continues

```
        Dim i As Interface1
        Set i = c                    ' VB6 syntax used
        Debug.Print TypeName(i)      ' VB6 syntax used
    End Sub
```

Under COM, the name printed out will be "interface1," because that is the unit of identity (i.e., there is no true concept of "class1"). Under .NET, however, the name printed out will be "class1," because the thing that holds identity is the class, not the interface. No matter what interface a class is cast to, the .NET runtime environment still knows what class the instance is.

The question then becomes how the COM concepts should be mapped to the .NET concepts when attempting to access a COM object from .NET. The simplest answer would be to map a COM coclass to a .NET class and a COM interface to a .NET interface. However, in this case, the tricks that Visual Basic 6.0 played become troublesome in .NET. The problem is that because the unit of identity in COM was the interface, that is what is used when calling methods. So, given a coclass `class1`, a method taking a `class1` would actually be expressed as taking the default interface, `_class1`. This was fine in Visual Basic 6.0, because the compiler hid the distinction. But because both classes and interfaces are first-class types in Visual Basic .NET, this means using COM objects would require a lot of casting if strict type checking (new in Visual Basic .NET) is used. Consider Listings A.2 and A.3.

Listing A.2 `Class1.cls` *(VB6)*

```
Private Value As Integer

Public Function CreateNewInstance() As Class1
    CreateNewInstance = New Class1()
End Sub
```

Listing A.3 `test.vb` *(VBNET)*

```
Option Strict On

Module Test
    Sub Main()
```

```
        Dim x As Class1 = New Class1()
        Dim y As Class1 = CType(x.CreateNewInstance(), _
                                Class1)
    End Sub
End Module
```

In Listing A.3, the return value of `CreateNewInstance` has to be explicitly cast to the interface `_Class1` because strict type checking requires that a cast from an interface to a class that supports the interface be explicit (as the instance might be of some other class type).

To avoid forcing the distinction between interfaces and classes on users as soon as they attempt to upgrade code (because it is likely that code will use COM objects such as ADO), the language slightly modified its rules to make this situation more straightforward. Instead of the simple mapping, the .NET runtime environment changes the name of the default interface to the name of the coclass, and appends "Class" onto the end of the name of the coclass. Thus a coclass `class1` with a default interface `_class1` would be mapped to a class `class1Class` and an interface `class1`.

The result is that a user creating an instance of a COM class will actually appear to be instantiating an instance of the default interface. Under the covers, the compiler then maps this to an instantiation of the coclass. Now the variable is correctly typed, however, and will not require any casts to be assigned to by an API or passed to another API.

Inheritance

Adding inheritance to the Visual Basic .NET language was a relatively straightforward operation. The main set of decisions that had to be made dealt with how explicit to make the various inheritance concepts and what terms to use to refer to them. Because Visual Basic is a language that has a long history that does not include inheritance, we felt it was best to make the most conservative choices in regard to defaults. We also felt that it would be better to choose more descriptive (and more verbose) keywords rather than using C++-style keywords.

Table A.1 lists the keywords defined by the Visual Basic .NET language and their C# equivalents. It is worth noting that to both make a method virtual and override it requires explicit keywords on the part of the developer.

TABLE A.1 Visual Basic .NET and C# Keywords

VB .NET Keyword	C# Keyword
Overridable	virtual
NotOverridable	final
Overrides	overrides
MustOverride	abstract (on a method)
MustInherit	abstract (on a class)
NotInheritable	sealed

When implementing inheritance, we had to choose what kind of name hiding would be done across the inheritance chain. A robust name hiding scheme was seen as critical to avoiding many of the versioning issues that Visual Basic had with COM. In particular, it was important to be able to "drop in" a new version of a Base Class Library that contained new methods and have code compiled against it still continue to work. The canonical example of this situation would be ASP.NET—it is desirable to be able to upgrade ASP.NET without requiring all the Web pages on a Web site be recoded.

For simplicity, the default name hiding semantic we initially chose was *hide by name*. In other words, a member defined with a particular name would hide all members by that name in the base classes. The Shadows keyword was added to the language, but purely for developer awareness— all members were implicitly marked *shadow by name*, and omitting Shadows only caused a warning, rather than an error, to be emitted.

This choice, however, presented a problem with overloading, which we were also adding to the language. Given a hide by name semantic, it is not possible for a method to be overloaded across a base class and a derived class, because the derived class members hide the base class members by the same name. At this point it would have been possible to decide that overloading across inheritance was not allowed and be done with it, but this seemed to be a shame. A more desirable outcome would be to allow developers to explicitly state that they wished to overload a method in a base class rather than hide it. To this end, we added the `Overloads` keyword. The `Overloads` keyword specifies that a member has a *hide by name and signature* semantic associated with it rather than a hide by name semantic. As a result, a method will only hide a method with the same name and exact signature, allowing overloading across the inheritance hierarchy (see Listing A.4).

Listing A.4 `test.vb` *(VB.NET)*

```
Class Base
    Public Sub A(ByVal x As Integer)
        . . .
    End Sub

    Public Sub B(ByVal x As Integer)
        . . .
    End Sub
End Class

Class Derived
    Inherits Base

    Public Shadows Sub A(ByVal y As Double)
        . . .
    End Sub

    Public Overloads Sub B(ByVal y As Double)
        . . .
    End Sub

    Public Sub C()
        A(10)              ' Calls Derived.A
        B(10)              ' Calls Base.B
    End Sub
End Class
```

Given that a method could now have one of two separate name-hiding semantics associated with it, the question arose as to which should be the default. We initially chose hide by name as the default, but would it make more sense to choose hide by name and signature as the default? Ultimately, we decided that it did not make more sense because of the implications for overload resolution. Because overload resolution chooses among all the methods in the inheritance hierarchy with the same name (see the "Overloading" section for more details), a method marked as `Overloads` was vulnerable to changes in the base class.

To explain in more detail, imagine this situation: A base class vendor, Acme, produces a class called `Base`. Another company, MegaCorp, buys Acme's base class `Base` and derives a class `Derived` from it. The class `Derived` contains a set of methods `Foo` that are marked `Overloads`. Mega-Corp then builds an end-user application that uses `Derived` and calls method `Foo`. After some period of time, Acme releases an upgrade to class `Base`, adding a method called `Foo` to the class. MegaCorp purchases the new base class, installs it, and rebuilds `Derived` and the end-user application. The problem is that because `Derived.Foo` was marked as `Overloads`, the method `Base.Foo` will now be incorporated into the overload resolution for method `Foo`. If there was an unlucky choice of types for the overloads of `Foo`, it's possible that the end-user application will silently start calling `Base.Foo`, even though that method may do something radically different than `Derived.Foo` does!

The only way to completely solve this issue would be to choose a method of overload resolution similar to the one that C# uses, as discussed in the next section. Barring that, choosing `Shadows` as the default name-hiding semantic for methods seemed the safest choice. There is still some danger in using `Overloads`, but the risk can be assumed explicitly by the developer when he or she adds the keyword.

Overloading

Because overloading is a fundamental part of the .NET runtime environment, it was necessary to add it to the Visual Basic .NET language. Visual Basic already had a similar kind of mechanism in optional parameters, but in most cases overloading is a more robust way of accomplishing the same goals. This is especially true given that the values of optional parameters are compiled into the caller rather than staying under the control of the method being called.

As mentioned in the "Inheritance" section, the primary question that had to be answered regarding overloading was how overloading would interact with inheritance. We chose what we thought was the simplest answer to the question, figuring that it would be the most straightforward and understandable: When doing overload resolution on a method, we consider all the methods by the particular name in the inheritance hierarchy at once. This means that the most specific overload is always guaranteed to be chosen.

The downside of this is that, as previously discussed, it creates fragility in a derived class in the face of base class changes. An alternative method was considered that was closer to C#'s method of overload resolution: Consider all the methods overloaded on a name one class at a time, starting with the most derived class and moving to the most base class. This would have solved the fragility issue, but we felt that for Visual Basic programmers the results would be non-intuitive in a number of cases because a less specific overload in a derived class might be chosen over a more specific overload in a base class. Given this possibility, we felt the trade-off was worth it.

One other interesting thing to note about overload resolution in Visual Basic .NET is the way that arguments typed as `Object` are treated. Although Visual Basic .NET is a strongly typed language, it has a number of features that allow it to be used in a typeless way. The typeless ability of the language comes in handy when doing rapid prototyping or dealing with script-like scenarios. However, overload resolution against arguments typed purely as `Object`, given a straightforward set of resolution rules, will most likely fail. Because `Object` is the root type of the type system, a conversion from `Object` to any other type will be a narrowing conversion and the compiler will be unable to determine a most specific argument from the various choices.

To enable typeless calls to overloaded methods, another rule was added to the Visual Basic .NET overload resolution rules: If overload resolution fails solely because of arguments typed as `Object`, the resolution of the call is deferred until runtime. In other words, the call is implicitly turned into a late-bound call (assuming strict semantics are not being used). The late-bound method invocation code has the ability to perform overload resolution at runtime, allowing the resolution to be done on the actual type of the parameter at runtime.

Namespaces

Visual Basic already had an extremely rudimentary concept of a namespace: In previous versions, the name of the project functioned as a namespace for everything declared within it. This allowed for multiple projects to have something named `Class1` yet still reference one another. For .NET, the concept just had to be extended to arbitrarily complex namespace schemes. We felt that most users would not want to see `Namespace` statements in their source code, so we still retained some of the original concept of a project-wide namespace. Essentially, every project can define a namespace that all declarations in the project are implicitly wrapped in. This allows users to define their own namespace hierarchies if they wish, but by default each project gets its own namespace.

Type System Modifications

In addition to the extensions to the Visual Basic type system, a number of modifications to the existing type system were necessitated by the move to the .NET platform. For the most part, they were required because many of the .NET types that corresponded to COM types (such as arrays and variants) utilized different underlying storage.

Arrays

Arrays on the .NET platform are much more sophisticated than Safearrays are in COM. There are two principal differences that caused changes from Visual Basic 6.0.

The first difference is that all arrays in .NET encode their rank within their type. Because COM Safearrays did not encode their rank as an attribute of an array instance within the array type, code from previous versions of Visual Basic that declare arrays cannot be ported unchanged. In most cases, however, this is not a serious problem—most variables are assigned only an array of one particular rank, and the common case is that the rank of the array can be inferred easily from the code around it. See, for example, Listings A.5 and A.6.

Listing A.5 `module1.bas` *(VB6)*

```
Sub Main()
    Dim x() As Integer

    ReDim x(10, 10)
    x(1, 1) = 10
End Sub
```

Listing A.6 `test.vb` *(VB.NET)*

```
Module Test
    Sub Main()
        Dim x(,) As Integer    ' 2-dimensional array

        ReDim x(10, 10)
        x(1, 1) = 10
    End Sub
End Module
```

This difference in array types can cause problems, however, when trying to interoperate with COM methods. In that case, it is impossible to know what rank array a COM method expects because there is no way to inspect the API's code. Currently, the .NET platform treats all COM array parameters as one-dimensional arrays of the specified type. This takes care of the most common situations, but is not perfect. At this point, there is no simple way to specify the rank of an array parameter of an imported COM method.

The other difference between Safearrays and .NET arrays is more problematic. A Safearray type can contain a set of bounds for each dimension of the array, but those bounds are not considered to be part of the actual type, just like the rank of the array is not considered to be part of the type. In .NET, however, the lower bounds of each dimension of the array are allowed to be (but not required to be) considered to be part of the type itself. So while there is, for example, a one-dimensional `Integer` array type that can have any lower bound for its one dimension, there are also one-dimensional `Integer` array types whose one dimension has a fixed lower bound of zero, of one, of two, and so on. While any array of the particular rank and type can be assigned to the first kind of array type (i.e., the one without any fixed lower bounds), only an array that has matching lower bounds can be assigned to the other kinds of array types (i.e., a one-dimensional Integer array with a lower bound of 5 cannot be assigned to a variable of type one-dimensional Integer array with a lower bound of 6).

Overall, this whole question would be academic if not for one fact: The Common Language Specification (CLS) decrees that all CLS-compliant languages must be able to use array types that have fixed lower bounds of zero. This is because languages such as C# and C++ do not allow the lower bounds of their arrays to be anything but zero. They could, conceivably, still use the array types that do not fix the lower bounds to represent an array that has a fixed lower bound of zero, but to do so would mean that several code optimizations based on knowing the lower bound of each dimension of an array would be lost. This was unacceptable to the designers of those languages.

A simple solution to this problem would be to say that Visual Basic .NET should use the array types that do not fix the lower bounds and just throw exceptions if you tried to pass one with nonzero lower bounds to a CLS-compliant method. The problem is that array types can make up part of the signatures of methods. So, when overriding a method defined in C# that takes an array, the signature of the Visual Basic method has to match completely, including the fact that the array type has a fixed lower bound of zero. The result is that if Visual Basic .NET wishes to have nonzero-lower-bound arrays in the language, it must distinguish between array types that can have nonzero lower bounds and array types that have their lower bounds fixed at zero.

After much deliberation, it was decided that having two separate types of arrays in the language would be too confusing for most users. In many cases, it would be unclear as to which type should be used when declaring a method. Even worse, when errors occurred, it would be difficult to concisely explain exactly what was wrong. However, the removal of nonzero-lower-bound arrays is a significant issue for many users who routinely declared arrays with lower bounds other than zero. More consideration will be given to this problem in the future versions.

Variant and `Object` Types

Previous versions of Visual Basic could be used in a typeless way because of the variant data type. A variant was a structure that contained a union of all the different types that could be contained in a COM variable: `Integer`, `Double`, `BSTR`, `IDispatch`, and so on. This allowed a variant to contain any value that another variable could contain. As a result, if you declared all variables to be of type variant (implicitly or explicitly), Visual Basic became a typeless language. A number of helper routines in COM also allowed converting a variant from one type of value to another.

This same scheme could not be straightforwardly used in .NET because the runtime environment does not allow reference types to be unioned together with other types in a structure. The .NET runtime manages references to values on the heap and tracks them for garbage collection purposes. To allow an `Integer` to be unioned with a reference type in a structure would mean that the runtime environment would not be able to reliably know whether a particular instance of the structure contained a reference or an `Integer` in the field. This would cause safety and security issues and make garbage collection impossible. It would have been possible for the .NET runtime environment to instead expose a variant type that it natively understood—that is, the runtime environment would ensure that the "type" field of the variant structure was always consistent with the "value" field. However, this was not ideal because of the existence of the .NET `Object` type.

The .NET runtime type system was designed as a single-root type system. What this means it that every type in the type system ultimately derives from `Object`. For reference types, this is no different than COM—in COM, every coclass implemented the `IUnknown` interface, which was equivalent to the `Object` type in Visual Basic 6.0. For value types (i.e., structures and primitive types), though, this is a big change. It is accomplished by something of a trick. Each value type can exist in one of two forms: its *boxed* form or its *unboxed* form. An unboxed value type is just a regular value type—it exists on the stack, in an array, or within another type and has no identity in and of itself. Unboxed value types are not managed by the .NET runtime environment because they are always part of something else. A boxed value type is the tricky part. When a value type is boxed, a copy of the value is made on the system heap and a reference to the heap location is returned. From this point on, the boxed value type can be treated just as if it was a reference type. Essentially, a value type is boxed when it is cast to `Object` and unboxed when it is cast from `Object`.

The problem may be becoming clearer at this point. Because every type in the .NET type system can be cast to `Object`, an `Object` is functionally equivalent to a variant. It is worth noting that even though `Object` and variant are functionally equivalent, they are two very different types. Assigning a value to a variant variable only copies the value into the variant itself, no matter how many values are assigned to the variable. Assigning a value to an `Object` variable allocates space on the heap and then copies the value into that space. Each time you assign a new value to the `Object` variable, an allocation occurs on the heap. Thus, there is more overhead when using `Object` than when using variant.

Ultimately, we had a choice to make: We could keep variant and live with the confusion over whether to use `Object` or variant when a "universal" type was needed, or we could just use `Object` exclusively and suffer some performance penalty. After much analysis, we determined that in most cases the performance of `Object` would not appreciably affect applications. Additionally, we were concerned that even within Microsoft itself the teams designing various parts of the .NET Framework would not be able to decide between using variant and `Object` consistently. It became clear that using `Object` exclusively was the best option.

A side effect of this decision relates to how `ByRef` parameters of type `Object` behave. The COM variant type can not only store a value, but also store a pointer to a value. This means that when a method in Visual Basic 6.0 calls a method declared with a `ByRef` variant parameter, the argument passes a pointer to itself, allowing the called method to modify the original argument storage. Because of the complexity that would have been involved in allowing it, the .NET runtime environment does not allow arbitrary pointers to storage to be passed around unless the code is declared to be "unsafe." Visual Basic .NET does not support writing unsafe code, so there was no simple way to simulate the `ByRef` variant behavior on the .NET run time.

There is a way to simulate the `ByRef` variant behavior on .NET in a safe way by using the `RefAny` type, but this type had some significant limitations and greatly complicated the implementation of the language. A simpler mechanism that we ultimately settled on was passing values to `ByRef Object` parameters (the .NET equivalent to `ByRef` variant parameters) using copy-in/copy-out semantics rather than true reference semantics. Thus, instead of passing a pointer to the storage of the argument, a temporary `Object` variable is allocated, the argument copied into it, and a pointer to the temporary variable passed to the method. Then, when the method returns, the value in the `Object` variable is cast back to the argument type and assigned back to the argument source. This means that changes to the parameter will not be reflected in the original argument location until the method returns. In practice, this distinction should not be often noticed.

As an example, consider Listing A.7.

Listing A.7 `test.vb` *(VB.NET)*

```
Module Test
    Public g As Integer = 10

    Function ChangeValue(ByRef o As Object)
        o = 20
        Console.WriteLine(g & " " & o)
    End Function

    Sub Main
        ChangeValue(g)
    End Sub
```

Listing A.7 will print "10 20" because it is equivalent to Listing A.8.

Listing A.8 `test.vb` *(VB.NET)*

```
Module Test
    Public g As Integer = 10

    Function ChangeValue(ByRef o As Object)
        o = 20
        Console.WriteLine(g & " " & o)
    End Function
```

continues

```
Sub Main()
      Dim Temp As Object

      Temp = g
      ChangeValue(Temp)
      g = Temp
   End Sub
```

Structures

Structures, also called *user-defined types* in Visual Basic 6.0, were renamed and had their functionality significantly expanded in Visual Basic .NET. The name was changed both because the functionality was expanded and because the keyword `Type` conflicts with the type name `System.Type`. `System.Type` is the fundamental type in reflection (the .NET system of runtime type inspection), so keeping the keyword `Type` would have meant that writing code that utilizes reflection would require frequent use of bracketing.

In Visual Basic .NET, structures are just user-defined value types. As there is no distinction made in terms of functionality between value types and reference types (just a distinction in terms of storage and lifetime), structures can now have methods, events, properties, and so on, and their data members can now have accessibility modifiers placed on them. The choice between a class and a structure boils down more to storage considerations and value versus reference semantics than to functionality.

Date, Currency, and Decimal Types

There were a few other data type changes that are worth noting. First, COM has both a `Currency` type and a `Decimal` type. Because `Decimal` has a greater range and precision than `Currency` (i.e., it can store all the values `Currency` can), we decided to replace the `Currency` type with the `Decimal` type.

The other change was more subtle. In COM, a `Date` variable is stored using a double-precision floating-point number. The number to the left of the decimal point represents the number of days since December 30, 1899. The number to the right of the decimal point represents the number of seconds since midnight. This is a simplified description of the actual representation, but should give the general idea. Because the `Date` data type is represented as a floating-point number, the data type has the same limitations in terms of range and exactness that the underlying data type does.

The .NET `DateTime` class, in contrast, is stored using a signed 64-bit integer number representing the number of milliseconds since midnight, January 1, 1 A.D. This is a more precise representation and can represent a greater range of dates. It has a dual impact on the Visual Basic language, however. First, it means that `Double` values can no longer implicitly be converted to and from `Date` values. Second, transferring dates from COM to .NET, and vice versa, involves a translation. By and large, this is mostly a question of whether the .NET date will fit into the range of the COM date, but there is one special situation that can cause problems.

In previous versions of Visual Basic, there was no way to express just a time value (i.e., a time of day not tied to a particular day). To work around this, Visual Basic would treat the time of day on the first day representable (December 30, 1899) as just a time value. In other words, printing the date constant `#12/30/1899 1:43PM#` would just output `1:43 PM`. December 30, 1899, is also the *zero day* for the COM `Date` type—in other words, a `Date` variable that has no value assigned to it will by default represent midnight, December 30, 1899.

To preserve this behavior, Visual Basic .NET treats the zero day of the `DateTime` type (January 1, 1 A.D.) as the "time only" date. In the case of code migrated from previous versions of Visual Basic, this preserves the semantics of the code. However, it does mean that interoperation with COM is slightly more complicated. Basically, any time during the zero date of `DateTime` is translated to the same time on the zero date of COM `Date`, even though the two dates are different. Although this can cause some slightly anomalous results, by and large it produces the "expected" behavior.

Platform Changes

Above and beyond the changes to the type system in Visual Basic .NET, there were also a number of changes required by the underlying structure of the .NET runtime environment itself.

Deterministic Finalization and Garbage Collection

The .NET platform was built from the ground up to be a garbage-collected system. That is to say, the .NET runtime environment tracks all references to objects allocated on the heap. Periodically, it checks whether some objects on the heap no longer have any references to them. If there are any such objects, they are *garbage collected*—that is, freed. This scheme for freeing heap allocations is different than the scheme employed by COM. COM employed a *reference counting* mechanism to track references to objects. When a reference to an object was copied, the copier would call the `AddRef` method on the object to let it know that there was another reference to it. When a piece of code was done with a reference to an object, it called the `Release` method on the object. When the number of references to an object reached zero, the object would free itself.

The advantage of the COM scheme is that all objects are *deterministically finalized*. That is, an object is freed at the very moment that the last reference to it is released. On .NET, in comparison, an object will not be freed until sometime after the last reference is released—that is, the next time the garbage collector runs. Deterministic finalization is advantageous because an object may be holding on to references to other objects itself, some of which may be scarce (such as a database connection). In that case, as soon as you free an object, you want the resources it holds to be freed as well. Even if the garbage collector runs every few milliseconds, that may not be fast enough to prevent resources from being used up.

The advantage of the .NET scheme is that it is very difficult to get the COM scheme right. Many thousands of hours have been spent in the software industry as a whole tracking down `AddRef/Release` problems. It is very easy when programming against a COM object to forget to do an `AddRef` when you copy a reference, resulting in a crash if the object is finalized too early. It is also very easy to forget to `Release` a reference once you are done with it, resulting in memory leaks and objects hanging around forever and never releasing their resources.

Another advantage of the .NET scheme is that it easily solves the problem of circular references—in other words, a situation where object A has a reference to object B and B has a reference to A. Once a circular reference has been created, in COM the developer has to explicitly use some other mechanism to break the cycle and finalize the object. However, because the .NET runtime environment knows about all references between objects, the garbage collector can determine when a set of objects that contain circular references are no longer referenced outside the cycle and finalize all the objects at once.

By and large, all of the problems with the COM scheme mentioned earlier have been hidden from Visual Basic developers by the compiler except for circular references. In most cases, the compiler would correctly insert `AddRef` or `Release` calls into the compiled code to manage the references. Thus, the fact that .NET employs garbage collection does not buy Visual Basic as much as it buys programmers who write in other .NET languages, although there are still benefits such as circular reference finalization.

Unfortunately, there is no easy way to have deterministic finalization and garbage collection coexist within the same type system. A full discussion of this issue is beyond the scope of this appendix, but the core problem can be boiled down to a single question: Is the type `Object` deterministically finalized or garbage collected? If it is garbage collected, then casting an instance of a deterministically finalized object to `Object` would have to cause the instance to lose its deterministic finalization property (once it was typed as `Object`, `AddRef`/`Release` would not be called). Given that there are many situations (such as collections) where instances need to be cast to `Object`, this is not a workable solution. If `Object` is deterministically finalized, then effectively all types must be deterministically finalized, which means that garbage collection goes out the window. One could work around the question of `Object` by splitting the type system into two completely separate camps, garbage-collected types and deterministically finalized types, but then there would have to be two different root `Object` types that would cause every type that takes `Object` (such as collections) to have two versions: one for deterministically finalized types and one for garbage-collected types.

The end result is that there is no solid replacement for deterministic finalization in Visual Basic .NET. An interface, `IDisposable`, has been added to the .NET Framework that a class should implement if it holds on to precious resources that should be disposed of as soon as possible, but the onus is on the developer to correctly call the `Dispose` method when he or she is done with the instance. C# added another piece of syntax, `using`, to help formalize the call to `Dispose`, but we did not feel that `using` was exactly the right solution for Visual Basic developers. We expect to address this situation in a better way in a future release.

Let **and** Set **Assignment**

Visual Basic has historically distinguished between value assignment (`Let`) and reference assignment (`Set`). While this is a useful distinction in many situations, one of the reasons it was truly necessary in Visual Basic had to do with parameterless default properties. Objects in previous versions of Visual Basic can expose a default property that has no parameters. In that case, the default property is considered the "value" property of the object (indeed, in most cases the parameterless default property is named `Value`). Because of this, there have to be two forms of assignment that indicate whether you are assigning the "value" of an object or assigning the actual reference to an object (see Listing A.9).

Listing A.9 `module1.bas` *(VB6)*

```
Sub Main()
    Dim x As Integer
    Dim f1 As Field
    Dim f2 As Field

    Let x = f1         ' Assigns the value of the field
    f2 = f1            ' Assigns the value field f1 to the
                       ' value of f2
    Set f2 = f1        ' Assigns the reference to the field
End Sub
```

COM distinguished between the `Let` and `Set` style of assignments, allowing properties to be defined with both kinds of accessors (see Listing A.10).

Listing A.10 `class1.cls` *(VB6)*

```
Property Set foo(Value As Variant)
End Property

Property Let foo(Value As Variant)
End Property
```

The problem is that .NET does not distinguish between the Let and Set types of assignment, so properties can define only one kind of assignment accessor. The reason has to do with the fact that most programming languages do not make a distinction between types of assignment and, to be honest, the majority won out. It would have been possible for Visual Basic to define both types of accessors but expose only one to other languages, but this was very problematic. If you had an Object property that could take values and references, which one should be exposed? No matter which one was chosen, it would be wrong in many cases. The reverse problem would occur with properties defined in other languages.

After much deliberation and consideration of alternatives, we decided the simplest way was to drop the distinction between the Let and Set forms of assignment. This meant that properties could define only one kind of assignment accessor. It also meant that parameterless default properties had to be removed from the language. Although parameterless default properties were useful, they could also be obscure and confusing, so this was not considered a huge loss.

Late Binding

Late binding is the mechanism by which resolution of a method call can be deferred until runtime. Essentially, when making a call on a variable typed as Object, the compiler will emit a call to a helper with all the relevant information about the method call. At runtime, the helper will resolve which method (if any) to call and then make the call itself.

The first challenge in implementing late binding was adapting to the change from COM to .NET. In COM, late binding was handled by a component called OLE Automation through an interface called IDispatch. IDispatch relied on the information specified in a *type library* that described a class and was either compiled into or accompanied a COM component. In contrast, .NET late binding is done through a component called *reflection*. Whereas IDispatch and type libraries were not easily accessible to previous versions of Visual Basic and were considered more of an internal implementation detail, reflection is a full-fledged part of the .NET Framework. Reflection allows inspection of the type information that is part of every .NET executable (i.e., the equivalent of a type library compiled into the executable). It also has some mechanisms for doing late binding, but they are extremely simple. They really only allow you to inspect the methods that an object has and then invoke one of them at runtime.

Because we needed to express the full set of Visual Basic binding semantics, we had to write special helpers that sit on top of reflection to do that binding. When a late-bound helper is invoked, it first goes through much the same process as the compiler does at compile time to determine which method to call. The runtime binder considers inheritance and name hiding and does overload resolution. It understands Visual Basic's conversion rules and knows which calls are legal and which are not. It is a relatively complex piece of code.

Another challenge had to do with reference parameters. `IDispatch` was built using variants, which, as noted earlier, have the ability to store pointers in them. This meant that when a late-bound call was made, Visual Basic could pass `ByRef` variants to `IDispatch` for each argument. Then, if the actual parameter of the method being called was declared `ByRef`, the pointer could be passed in and the method would work as expected. Because .NET does not have a real equivalent to `ByRef` variants, we had to employ the same copy-in/copy-out mechanism that we used for `ByRef Object` parameters, with an additional twist.

When making a call to an early-bound method, it is possible for the compiler to know which parameters are `ByRef Object`s and which are not. Thus, it can figure out which arguments, if any, need to be passed using copy-in/copy-out semantics. When making a late-bound call, however, it's impossible to know until runtime which parameters are `ByRef Object`s. Thus, there is no way to know whether to generate code to do the copy-out. The ugly, but unavoidable solution is to pass an array of `Boolean` values corresponding to the argument list to the late-binding helper. Once the late-binding helper has determined which method it is going to call, it sets each element to `True` that corresponds to a `ByRef` parameter. The compiler generates code to check the element for each argument that could do a copy-back (i.e., ignoring literals, read-only fields, and so on) and then does a copy-back if the element has been set to `True`.

The change in the locus of identity from interfaces in COM to classes in .NET affects late binding, too. In COM, you would late-bind to the particular interface that you happened to have in your hand when you made the call. However, because .NET sees only instances of classes, it is never possible to have an instance of an interface in hand. This means that it is not possible to late-bind to interfaces, only classes. If a class `Foo` implements an interface `Bar` using a private member, there is no way to late-bind to that interface member. This is an inescapable result of the design of the .NET type system.

`On Error` and Structured Exception Handling

The `On Error` style of error handling has always been built on top of exception-handling mechanisms provided by the system. With Visual Basic .NET, we decided to expose this underlying structured exception-handling mechanism directly to programmers. Structured exception handling has two advantages over `On Error`-style error handling. First, its structured nature encourages more discriminating and precise use of exception handling, which can in some cases result in more optimized assembly output. Second, structured exception handling gives a much-finer-grained control over which exceptions are handled and when. This is not to say that `On Error`-style error handling does not have advantages over structured exception handling. For example, there is no equivalent to `Resume` or `Resume Next` in structured exception handling.

Implementing `On Error`-style exception handling on top of structured exception handling is a relatively straightforward task (except for `Resume` and `Resume Next`, which we'll discuss in a moment). Any method that contains an `On Error` statement is wrapped in a `Try` statement around all the code in the method. Then, a `Catch` handler is added that catches all exceptions. Each `On Error` statement sets a value in a local variable that indicates which `On Error` statement is currently active. When an exception occurs, the `Catch` handler switches on that local variable to determine where to go to. Consider Listing A.11 as an example.

Listing A.11 test.vb **(VB.NET)**

```
Module Test
    Sub Main()
        Dim i As Integer

        On Error Goto Foo
        i = 20
Foo:
        On Error Goto Bar
        i = 30
Bar:
        On Error Goto 0
        i = 40
    End Sub
End Module
```

It is equivalent to Listing A.12.

Listing A.12 test.vb **(VB.NET)**

```
Module Test
    Sub Main()
        Try
            Dim i As Integer
            Dim CurrentHandler As Integer

            CurrentHandler = 1    ' On Error Goto Foo
            i = 20
Foo:
            CurrentHandler = 2    ' On Error Goto Bar
            i = 30
Bar:
            CurrentHandler = 0    ' On Error Goto 0
            i = 40
        Catch e As Exception Where CurrentHandler > 0
            Select Case CurrentHandler
                Case 1
                    Goto Foo
                Case 2
                    Goto Bar
            End Select

            Throw    ' In case something goes wrong.
        End Try
    End Sub
End Module
```

`Resume` and `Resume Next` are slightly more complex cases. When compiling a method that contains a `Resume` or `Resume Next` statement, the compiler adds a local that tracks which statement is being processed. Code is inserted after each statement to increment the local. When an exception occurs and a `Resume` or `Resume Next` statement is executed (either through an `On Error` statement or on its own), the local is loaded (and incremented with `Resume Next`) and then a `Select` statement is executed to jump to the statement indicated by the local. No example is provided here because of space considerations, but the process works very much along the lines of the Listing A.11/A.12 example.

It's important to note that this can be done only by the compiler and not by the .NET runtime environment—even if the .NET runtime environment had a resume mechanism, it could work only based on IL instructions, whereas the `Resume` statement works based on statements. There's no way for the .NET runtime environment to know where the "next" statement or "current" statement begins and ends.

Events and Delegates

Events in COM and .NET are implemented very differently, even though they have virtually the same functionality. In COM, a class that sources events exposes one or more event interfaces. An event interface contains callback methods to handle each event that the class exposes. Another class that wishes to handle the events sourced by the class would then implement the event interface with the various event handlers that it wished to use. The class that was handling the events would then provide this event interface to the class that sourced the events (called a *connection point*), and the sourcing class would invoke the appropriate methods when the event was raised.

In .NET, events are built around *delegates*, which are essentially managed function pointers. A delegate contains the address of a method and a particular instance of the containing class if the method is an instance method. A delegate can invoke the method to which it points, given a list of arguments. Delegates are *multicast*, which is to say that a single delegate can point to more than one method. When the delegate is invoked, all the methods to which the delegate points are called in order.

The semantics of the `AddressOf` expression were extended slightly in Visual Basic .NET to make working with delegates easier. The `AddressOf` operator can be applied to any method and produces, essentially, an unnamed delegate type representing that method's signature. The .NET type system does not actually support unnamed delegate types, so this is merely a compiler trick—the result of an `AddressOf` expression must ultimately be converted to a named delegate type. The compiler then inserts an instantiation for the correct delegate type at the point of conversion. If the target delegate type is not specified (by converting the `AddressOf` expression to `Object`) or is ambiguous (as is possible in overload resolution), an error will result.

An event, then, is made up of three things in .NET: a delegate type that defines the signature of the event, a method to add a new handler for the event, and a method that removes an existing handler for the event. When a class wishes to handle an event raised by a class, it first creates a new delegate of the type of the event on the method that will handle the event. It then passes this delegate to the add handler method of the event. The add handler method combines the delegate being passed in with all the other delegates with which it has been called to handle the event. When the class that sources the event raises the event, it simply invokes the delegate with the appropriate parameters, which calls each handler in turn. If a class wishes to stop handling the event, it creates another delegate on the handler that it wants to stop having called and calls the remove handler method with the delegate. The remove handler method then removes the particular delegate from the delegate list that it is maintaining for the event.

Visual Basic .NET significantly simplifies the process of defining and handling events. Although we give you access to most of the low-level definition of events, most of the time you don't need to bother with the inner guts. For example, you can declare an event with just a signature, and the compiler will define the event delegate for you under the covers. Also, if you declare a field with the `WithEvents` modifier, you can then declare methods in the class with the `Handles` clause, and the compiler will automatically call the add and remove event methods for you. Consider Listing A.13.

Listing A.13 `class.vb` *(VB.NET)*

```
Class Raiser
    Public Event E()

    Public Sub Raise()
        RaiseEvent E()
    End Sub
End Class


Class Handler
    Public WithEvents R As Raiser

    Public Sub New()
        R = New Raiser()
    End Sub

    Public Sub DoRaise()
        R.Raise()
    End Sub

    Public Sub HandleE() Handles R.E
    End Sub
End Class
```

It is equivalent to Listing A.14.

Listing A.14 `class1.vb` *(VB.NET)*

```
Class Raiser
    Public Delegate Sub EEventHandler()
    Public Event E As EEventHandler

    Public Sub Raise()
        RaiseEvent E()
    End Sub
End Class

Class Handler
    Private RLocal As Raiser

    Public Property R As Raiser
        Get
            Return RLocal
        End Get
        Set (ByVal Value As Raiser)
```

continues

```
                    If Not RLocal Is Nothing Then
                        R.remove_E(new EEventHandler( _
                                        AddressOf HandleE))
                    End If
                    RLocal = Value
                    If Not RLocal Is Nothing Then
                        R.add_E(new EEventHandler( _
                                        AddressOf HandleE))
                    End If
                End Set
            End Property

            Public Sub DoRaise()
                R.Raise()
            End Sub

            Public Sub HandleE()
            End Sub
        End Class
```

There are some details, such as the add and remove methods of the event, that Visual Basic .NET does not allow you to define for yourself. This may be changed in future versions of the compiler, as there are some advanced scenarios where this ability may be desirable.

Language Cleanup

As should be clear by now, moving to the .NET platform entailed some radical changes to the Visual Basic language. On top of the language changes, there were a number of programming model changes (such as the move from Visual Basic forms to .NET Windows Forms) that significantly changed the way that code is written in Visual Basic .NET. Because of the magnitude of the changes necessitated by .NET, it was clear that code from Visual Basic 6.0 would not be 100% forward compatible. Some migration and rewriting would be necessary to get code to compile, and even more would be necessary to fully move it to the .NET way of doing things.

Given this situation, the Visual Basic team decided to take the opportunity to make a few changes in the language that were not required by moving to .NET. Each of the changes was in response to specific feedback or user experiences that the team had gathered over the years, and each was considered by the Visual Basic team to be an improvement to the language when balanced against the cost of additional conversion requirements. For the most part, the changes involved removing support for anachronistic parts of the language. Examples of this would be the `Def` statements (such as `DefInt`) and `Gosub`. Selected on both feedback and experience, the pieces of the language that were dropped were ones that were rarely used by developers (and in some cases apparently largely forgotten!) and did not provide significant programmer benefits. A few of the other changes corrected quirks, such as changing `Wend` to the more regular (and grammatical) `End While`. Most of these corrections are automatically handled by the migration tool and by the editor (i.e., when the programmer presses Enter after starting a `While` statement, `End While` is pasted in automatically).

Probably the most significant change was the redefinition of the `Integer` and `Long` types to 32 bits and 64 bits, respectively, and the addition of the 16-bit `Short` type. The primary problem with a 16-bit `Integer` type is that the .NET platform imposes performance penalties on 16-bit integers. There is no IL representation for a 16-bit integer on the stack—only 32-bit and 64-bit integers. This means that working with 16-bit integers puts code at a significant disadvantage, because every operation involves a conversion to catch overflow. For example, if `a`, `b`, `c`, and `d` are all 16-bit integer variables, the expression `a = (b + c) * d` results in two separate 16-bit conversion instructions (after the addition and the multiplication) to catch overflow. This overhead is nontrivial. When doing performance testing on early incarnations of the Visual Basic .NET compiler, Visual Basic performed at a disadvantage relative to other languages. Much of that disadvantage was directly attributable to the fact that the test was written using `Integer`. Once a search and replace on `Integer` with `Long` was done, the slowdowns vanished. The fact that `Integer` is the semantically default integer type made this issue a significant one.

The other main consideration was the fact that the .NET world is inherently multilanguage. In previous versions, Visual Basic and C++ inhabited totally separate worlds. To move data between them or make cross-language calls was difficult at best. By and large, the Visual Basic developer had the easier time of it than the C++ developer—as long as the developer kept in mind that `int` was the same as `Long`, for the most part `Declare` statements would work. But because Visual Basic and C++ lived in such separate worlds, Visual Basic constantly lagged behind the curve. The Win32 world was so isolated and relatively incompatible that to take advantage of new system features often required utilizing "black magic" coding until the next version of Visual Basic was released.

Part of the promise of .NET is that all languages now have a simple, straightforward way of dealing with one another because they all work in the same world. Moving forward, new API sets will be rolled out as managed code, and when they do—with no intervention by any guru or wizard—those APIs will be immediately and fully usable by Visual Basic. By reducing the cross-language friction even more than has already been done by the .NET platform, we further encourage the connection between Visual Basic and the platform and the other languages on .NET.

New Features

Compared to the dizzying array of features necessitated by the move to .NET, the list of other new features in Visual Basic .NET is relatively modest. In general, we focused on addressing a few complaints about missing features and useful semantics. Among the things added that fall into this category are the following:

- Short-circuiting Boolean operators `AndAlso` and `OrElse`. Because the current `And` and `Or` operators cannot short-circuit (because they are used as binary operators as well as logical operators), we added two new logical operators that *will* short-circuit. Although it was possible to work around their absence, short-circuiting logical operators quickly became indispensable in practice.
- Initializers. Initializers on locals are mainly a typing convenience, but initializers on class-level data members are very handy as they obviate the need for defining a constructor in many cases.
- Compound operators. Again, these operators are mostly a typing convenience, allowing you to say "x += 1" instead of "x = x + 1".

Future Directions

Given the amount of language change that developers must digest in Visual Basic .NET, the principal plan for the language in the future is stability. Having made significant compatibility breaks with this version, we are now returning to a much more conservative stance regarding changing the behavior of existing code, restricting ourselves primarily to fixing obvious bugs. As much as possible, we wish to allow people time to make the conversion from Visual Basic 6.0 (and earlier versions) without imposing any additional concepts or new learning on them.

There were, however, some features that did not make it into Visual Basic .NET that we are strongly considering for the future. Many have to do with improving compatibility with Visual Basic 6.0, such as reintroducing arrays with nonzero lower bounds. Some have to do with .NET features that we don't fully support, such as operator overloading and unsigned types. And still others are just perennial feature requests, such as bit-shifting operators. Although it is impossible to say whether any of these features will or will not be in a future release, this discussion gives a general idea of the kinds of things that are under consideration.

For the long term, the two primary goals of the Visual Basic language have always been functionality and simplicity. As the .NET platform itself moves forward and adds features, it is important that the Visual Basic language evolve to continue to provide access to many, if not all, of those features. And, just as the language today abstracts concepts such as events to a simpler level, a focus of the language design is always on making the complexities of programming as straightforward as possible. With the introduction of concepts such as inheritance and overloading, there is no question that the Visual Basic .NET language has taken on a new degree of complexity. Finding ways to simplify that complexity for the common programmer in future versions is an area of particular importance.

Conclusions

Moving Visual Basic from COM to .NET was a demanding, yet rewarding experience. There is no question that the move entailed a great number of changes in the language—changes that will take time to fully assimilate in the Visual Basic programming community. It also entailed a great deal of change in the structure of the compiler itself and in ways to think about compiling the language. By adding features such as inheritance and over-loading to the language, however, Visual Basic has become a much more powerful language than it has been in the past.

By far, the greatest benefit in moving to .NET is the .NET platform itself. With the .NET runtime environment, Visual Basic for the first time has easy access to a huge realm of functionality that was either off-limits in the past or very difficult to access. And with the amount of continuing investment that Microsoft and other companies are making in the .NET platform, this advantage will only continue to grow over time. The .NET platform is a broad, solid foundation for a whole range of applications. To provide a point of entry to this platform for Visual Basic programmers has been an exciting challenge over the past few years, and we think it will continue to yield rewards far into the future.

■ APPENDIX B ■

C#

Eric Gunnerson

History and Design Goals

C# (pronounced "see sharp" or "sea sharp") is a new language developed to run on the .NET Common Language Runtime (CLR).

A Brief History of C++ and C#

All languages make a trade-off between simplicity and power. Of the Microsoft languages, Visual Basic has placed a higher priority on simplicity and productivity than on power. Visual C++, on the other hand, provides a tremendous amount of power, but it's also a more complex and less productive language.

The Visual C++ team has talked about a "simpler C++" for a number of years. Such a language would be like C++, but would be much simpler and more productive to use. We explored a few ideas of what "simpler and more productive" might mean, but it wasn't clear what the right mix of features would be—or who the target audience should be.

As the .NET project coalesced out of a number of Microsoft projects, it became clear that the .NET environment would provide many of the features to build a "simpler C++" and that the new platform would have a large target audience. It was also clear that there should be a C++-based language for the .NET platform.

What wasn't clear was what that language should be. After considerable discussion, two possibilities emerged.

The first possibility was to modify the C++ language to support the .NET runtime environment. When doing this, either one could go the minimalist approach, extending the C++ language with extensions in the usual manner, or one could go whole hog and build in .NET support at the syntax level, adding new constructs and modifying existing ones.

The second possibility was to develop a language in the spirit of C and C++, but without some of the baggage associated with the existing languages.

It turns out when you talk to programmers about languages, they have some very strong ideas of what a language should be. One of those ideas is that C++ should be C++ and that you shouldn't monkey with the syntax in a non-C++ way.[1] Discussions with developers made it clear that people saw the benefits of a language that was "native" to the .NET way of doing things and that they did not want us to "bastardize" C++ to be that language.[2] They did, however, want to be able to use their existing C and C++ code from the .NET world.

The decision was therefore made to pursue both avenues. The C++ team extended the C++ language to work in the .NET world, and the C# team designed a new language.

C# Design Goals

The *Perl Reference Manual* says something like "Perl is a language for getting things done." While C# doesn't subscribe to this philosophy to the same

---

[1] It's very interesting that you can show someone a bit of syntax in C#, and he or she will say, "That's cool!" If you show the same person the same bit of syntax and say it's in C++, he or she will say, "You broke C++!"

[2] To be clearer, they didn't want us to modify C++ and still call it C++.

extent that Perl does,[3] it is at its core a pragmatic language. It contains powerful abstractions such as properties, along with "get the job done" features such as unsafe code.

The C# design philosophy can be summarized in a few design goals.

Be Comfortable for C++ Programmers

C# is targeted at C++ programmers, and it therefore needs to be comfortable for programmers used to C++. To meet this goal, the C# syntax is based on the C++ syntax, with changes made only when necessary. "When necessary" is obviously in the eye of the beholder, but it's fair to say that we either needed to see a clear benefit to the change or needed the change to work with the runtime.

Fit Cleanly into the .NET Common Language Runtime

Because C# runs only on the Common Language Runtime, there is no need for any abstraction between the language and the runtime environment. Therefore, the abstractions that appear in the language are largely those of the runtime itself, and the user doesn't need to keep two different models in mind.

Simplify the C++ Model

Although C# is a child of C++, working in the Common Language Runtime and making the programmer more productive required a fair number of changes from the C++ way of doing things. Some of the simplifications include the following:

- Getting rid of the separate header file and the preprocessor
- Getting rid of memory management issues, by using a reference-based system instead of a pointer-based system, along with the runtime garbage collector

Provide the Right Amount of Flexibility

It's very important that there be enough flexibility in the language to support the code that people need to write, but it's also important that there

---

3   I don't think any language does to the extent Perl does…

isn't too much flexibility, as additional flexibility usually means additional complexity. Making a language more complex to give the user another option isn't always a good thing; you have to weigh the improvement in the option versus the increased complexity of the language.

Support Component-centric Development

The only business of C# is the creation of components. C# directly addresses some of the issues surrounding the creation of components, including versioning, design-time information, and more.

The C# Type System

Reference Versus Value Types

The type system of the Common Language Runtime is divided into two worlds. Reference types are heap-allocated types and are used for most objects. Value types are either stack-allocated or allocated as part of another object; they are used for the predefined numeric types and other types that "feel like data."

This two-type system presents a problem for languages such as C#, which wish to present a unified type system where possible. If reference types and value types remained in separate worlds, it wouldn't be possible to write something like the following:

```
int value = 55;
double precision = 0.35;
Console.WriteLine("Result: {0}, {1}", value, precision);
```

For this code to work would require an overload of `WriteLine` that took a `string`, an `int`, and a `double`.

The runtime environment provides a way to make a value type look like a reference type, known as boxing. A box is simply a reference type wrapper for a value type that allows it to be passed around like any other reference type, as a parameter of type `object`.

C# chooses to make boxing as transparent as possible, so there is no explicit box operation; when a user uses a value type in a location where boxing is required,[4] the compiler automatically generates the boxing code. This allows the user to write something like

```
Console.WriteLine("Result: {0}, {1}", value, precision);
```

without caring whether the arguments are reference types or value types.

Once a value type has been boxed, the instance is opaque from the C# standpoint; there is no difference between a boxed integer, a boxed double, and a boxed user-defined value type. This simplifies the user model, but it also means that there is no way to modify the value of a boxed instance without unboxing it to the original type, modifying the value of the original type, and reboxing it. This has some performance implications when storing boxed value types in collection classes.

User-Defined Types

In C#, reference types are written using the `class` keyword, and value types are written using the `struct` keyword. Although value types inherit implicitly from type `object`, they do this only through boxing. Value types are therefore intended for writing types such as complex numbers, BigNums, or vectors.

C# also allows defining interfaces with the `interface` keyword, and enumerated constants and bit flags can be defined using the `enum` keyword.

Component-Oriented Development

Because C# is designed to develop components, it has many features that make developing and using components easier.

Properties

Users like simplicity when they deal with objects. When dealing with a button on a form, for example, users like to write code such as

```
cancelButton.caption = "Cancel";
```

---

[4] Either by assignment to type `object` or by casting it to an interface.

where the caption field of the button is directly accessed. This is also efficient code, as the field is directly modified.

Unfortunately, this simple model makes things more difficult for the user. The point of updating the caption on a button is to actually change the caption. Because the user is directly modifying the field, however, the framework author is forced to add another step to the process:

```
cancelButton.caption = "Cancel";
cancelButton.Paint();
```

This is nonoptimal, as it forces the user to remember to call `Paint()` to make the change happen.

Another option for the framework author is to use the property design pattern. Instead of exposing a caption field, the author exposes the functions

```
string GetCaption();
void SetCaption(string caption);
```

where the `SetCaption()` function performs the `Paint()` operation for the user. The user then writes

```
cancelButton.SetCaption("Cancel");
```

This approach works, but instead of working with a simple field, the user of the `Button` class now needs to find the `Get` and `Set` functions, figure out that they're related, and write slightly more verbose code.

Properties in C# allow the framework author to use the property pattern while allowing the user to use the simple field model. The author of the button class would write the following property:

```
public string Caption
{
    get
    {
        return caption;
    }
    set
```

```
    {
        caption = value;
        Paint();
    }
}
```

The user could then write the following code:

```
cancelButton.Caption = "Cancel";
```

Thus, properties provide a considerable simplification when dealing with components.

Design Choice

The runtime environment also provides considerable flexibility in the way that properties can operate. In C#, however, they're exposed as "virtual fields." Although the author of a property writes code for the get and set accessors, and the compiler emits these as get and set methods, from the user's perspective a property is something that behaves like a field.

As a consequence, accessibility specifiers such as `public` and modifiers such as `virtual` and `abstract` can be applied only at the property level, not at the accessor level. While this complicates some useful idioms—the most common being the "public get protected set" idiom—the simplification in the user model is important.

Indexers

It's sometimes useful to be able to use a class like an array. In the .NET Framework, for example, there is a class called `ArrayList`, which is a dynamically sized array. To get and set the values in an `ArrayList` would require a couple of functions:

- object GetItem(int index);
- void SetItem(int index, object value);

Like the property design pattern, this feature makes using the code more complex, but more importantly, it makes an `ArrayList` work differently than an array. To allow the array model to be used by other classes, C# allows the user to write an indexer:

```
public object this[int index]
{
    get
    {
        return items[index];
    }
    set
    {
        items[index] = value;
    }
}
```

which then allows the user to index an *ArrayList* directly.

Design Choice

The runtime environment supports parameterized properties, which are simply properties that take parameters. In Visual Basic .NET, a class can have more than one parameterized property, and there's nothing special about such properties.

In C#, a parameterized property is exposed as a virtual array, allowing an object to be indexed as an array. A collection class, for example, is made up of its elements, and therefore indexing to get the elements is a good model.

C# supports only a single parameterized property, though it can be overloaded with different parameter types.

Operator Overloading

C# supports operator overloading to allow users to create types that operate in the same manner as the types directly supported by the runtime.[5] Users can overload unary operators, binary operators, and comparison operators. Additionally, they can overload `true` and `false` to support nullable types.

---

[5] In fact, the `Decimal` type is a user-written type; it's not directly supported by the execution engine.

Design Choice

Operator overloading adds a fair amount of complexity to a language, but it's invaluable in creating types that work like the built-in ones. Perhaps the best example of such types is the SQL data types, which work like the built-in types but also support the SQL concept of nullability, both for expressions and comparison.[6]

Attributes

Attributes allow the user to annotate code with information that is stored in the metadata and is then available for query at runtime.

```
In C#, attributes are written in square brackets:
[MarshalAs(UnmanagedType.LPTStr)]
```

If an attribute has no parameters, the parentheses can be omitted:

```
[NonSerialized]
```

If an element has multiple attributes, they can either be written in separate sets of square brackets or appear as a comma-separated list within a single set of brackets.

To resolve the name of an attribute, the C# compiler will first look for a class derived from `System.Attribute` that has the exact name. If that class is not found, the compiler will append `Attribute` to the name and try again.

In some locations, the element to which the attribute applies is ambiguous. In a usage such as

```
[MyAttribute("Value")]
public int MyMethod();
```

the attribute could apply either to the method or to the return value. To eliminate the ambiguity, C# specifies the default element for all ambiguous cases, and then allows the user to specify a different element if desired:

---

[6]   In other words, if you compare two `SQLInt` instances, and they're both null, they won't be the same; by SQL rules, `null != null`.

```
[returnValue: MyAttribute("Value")]
public int MyMethod();
```

Delegates

Delegates are used to encapsulate a function to call and (for instance methods) a specific instance to call upon. In C#, all delegates are expressed as multicast delegates.

Design Choice

The C# language provides special syntax to make it easier to perform delegate operations. The "`+=`" operator is used to combine delegates, and the "`-=`" operator is used to remove a delegate from another.

In other words, when the user writes

```
myDelegate += new MyEventHandler(myRoutine);
```

the compiler converts it to

```
myDelegate = (MyEventHandler)
        Delegate.Combine(myDelegate,
                new MyEventHandler(myRoutine));
```

The compiler performs a similar replacement with "`-=`" and `Delegate.Remove()`.

Events

Events can be thought of as properties on top of delegates, providing options both to control what happens in the accessor and to limit access to the underlying backing variable.

In C#, there are two ways to deal with events. In the simple event syntax, the user simply writes

```
public event MyEventHandler OnClick;
```

This statement declares a private delegate named `OnClick` and creates the event `OnClick`, writing the appropriate thread-safe `add_OnClick()` and `remove_OnClick()` functions. The user of a class can hook up to an event using the sam "+=" and "-=" operators as are used with delegates, although for an event the operators call `add_OnClick()` and `remove_OnClick()`.

The simple syntax works well for most cases, but does not provide sufficient control for advanced users. The auto-allocated delegate field is not a good choice for objects that support lots of events, but typically have few delegates hooked to them.[7]

C# therefore provides an advanced syntax. In this syntax, the user writes the add and remove functions, using a syntax similar to properties:

```
public event MyEventHandler OnClick
{
    add
    {
        // add code here
    }
    remove
    {
        // remove code here
    }
}
```

In this variation, the user is responsible for allocating space to store the delegate, writing appropriate add and remove code, and making the operations thread-safe.

Unsafe Code

C# allows the user to use a limited version of "inline C" to write pointer-based code.

To safely use pointers in a garbage-collected (GC) environment, there needs to be a mechanism to prevent GC-tracked objects from being relocated by the garbage collector. The runtime environment allows objects to be pinned in place, then exposed in C# in a declarative manner using the `fixed` statement. The example in Listing B.1 uses an unsafe context to sum up the bytes in a byte array.

---

[7] The Windows Forms controls are an example.

Listing B.1

```
static unsafe int DoSum(byte[] byteBuffer)
{
    int length = byteBuffer.Length;
    int sum = 0;
    fixed (byte* pBuffer = byteBuffer)
    {
        byte* pCurrent = pBuffer;
        while (pCurrent < pBuffer + length)
        {
            sum += *pCurrent;
            pCurrent++;
        }
    }
    return sum;
}
```

The fixed statement pins the byteBuffer instance in place so that its address can be safely obtained, and then the code inside the fixed block uses traditional pointer arithmetic. At the end of the fixed block, the byteBuffer will be unpinned, and fixed generates a try-finally block to ensure that this happens.

The use of pointers in an unsafe block prevents the IL verifier from verifying that this code is safe, and the machine security policy will prevent the execution of such code in scenarios such as downloaded code. In the current versions of C#, this issue is handled at an assembly level, so any use of unsafe code within an assembly marks the entire assembly as unsafe.

There are three main scenarios where unsafe code is typically used: advanced interoperability, dealing with existing structures, and performance extremes.

Advanced Interoperability

Some native and COM interfaces use pointers in their definitions in a manner that is not supported by the data marshaller. In these cases, being able to use pointers as part of COM Interop enables this code to be used directly from C# without having to write a wrapper using the Managed Extensions to C++.[8]

---

[8] Sometimes such a wrapper may still be required, and using the Managed Extensions can often be easier than using the equivalent unsafe code in C#, especially in complex cases.

Dealing with Existing Structures

Disk files may contain structures with a specific definition, or network protocols may define a specific block structure for a message. Using unsafe code allows a structure to be overlaid on top of a buffer read from the disk or network, instead of requiring the programmer to code reading each field individually.

Performance Extremes

In some cases, the overhead of accessing data through the managed environment may be too high, or an existing library may expect the power user to access data directly using pointer arithmetic. In such cases, it's important to consider the scenario carefully, as using pointers isn't always the best (or fastest) choice.

Neat Things

`foreach`

Like Visual Basic .NET and Perl, C# provides a `foreach` statement, which can be used to enumerate over objects that implement `IEnumerable`.

Design Choice 1

When writing containers that store value types, using the `IEnumerable` design pattern has an unfortunate side effect. Because `IEnumerable.GetEnumerator` returns an `IEnumerator` and `IEnumerator.Current` is of type `object`, the only way to return values from an enumerator is as an object. For value types, this means that the `Current` property boxes the value type and then returns it to the client, which immediately unboxes it. This boxing and unboxing is unfortunate from a performance standpoint.

To get around this problem, C# supports an alternative way of doing enumerators. If a class returns a type from `GetEnumerator()` that matches `IEnumerator` exactly except in terms of the type of the `Current` property, the compiler will use that class for enumeration.

To interoperate with other languages, containers that take this approach would typically provide a strongly typed version for use from within C#

and implement `IEnumerable` privately for interoperability with other .NET languages.

Design Choice 2

In the `foreach` statement, there is an "implicit explicit" conversion. For example, when the user writes

```
foreach (string s in listItems)
```

there is an implicit explicit conversion from the type of `IEnumerator.Current` to the type declared in the `foreach` statement. As the target type must be specified explicitly in the `foreach` statement and there is no reasonable cast syntax, the simplification of having this happen automatically without a cast is justified.

`switch` **on String**

To support a common user scenario, C# allows the user to write a `switch` statement based on string values (see Listing B.2).

Listing B.2

```
switch (command)
{
    case "run":
        RunAway();
        break;
    case "stop":
        StopDoingThat();
        break;
    case default:
        NotMyFault();
        break;
}
```

For small numbers of cases, the compiler will take advantage of the string interning[9] feature during runtime. The compiler calls

---

[9] String interning is the method the runtime environment uses to keep a pool of constant strings. There is only one instance of a specific string in the intern pool.

`String.IsInterned()` with the `switch` variable and returns a reference to the interned string, if the string was previously interned, or null. If the return value is null, the string can't be any of the case labels, because, as constant strings, they're all interned. If the return value isn't null, the returned string instance is compared with the instances of each case label to see if there is a match.

For large numbers of cases, the compiler switches to a hash table implementation.

`params` Arrays

One problem faced when writing libraries is dealing with methods that can take a variable number of parameters. The simplest way to deal with this issue is to write overloaded methods:

```
int Process(object param1);
int Process(object param1, object param2);
int Process(object param1, object param2, object param3);
```

Unfortunately, this approach doesn't work very well if you need to pass 12 parameters. Another option is to write an overload that accepts an array:

```
int Process(object[] values);
```

That allows the user to pass any number of parameters, but the user must now write code like the following:

```
Process(new object[] { 133, 13333, "Hi", "There", "Mom"});
```

This code is not only ugly; it's different than other usages of `Process()`, so it complicates the user model.

In C#, if the user decorates the definition of the function with the `params` keyword,

```
int Process(params object[] values);
```

the compiler will take a call like

```
Process(133, 13333, "Hi", "There", "Mom");
```

and automatically generate the temporary object array for the user.

Because this transformation adds some overhead, a typical design pattern is to write specific overloads for the most common cases (often for a maximum of three parameters), and then use parameters to handle any calls with more than three parameters.

XML Comments

In addition to the normal C++-style comments, C# allows the user to write comments in XML. Such comments are written using three slashes:

```
/// <summary>
/// Square a number
/// </summary>
/// <return>The squared number</return>
public double Square(double number)
```

When code with XML comments is compiled with the /DOC compiler switch, the compiler ensures that the XML comments are valid XML, validates any parameter names mentioned, and writes the XML comments to an output file. For each block of XML that is written, the compiler will generate a globally unique name for the element with which the XML is associated. A post-processing program can then reflect over an assembly, generate information about the classes, and integrate the XML comments to generate the final documentation. Additionally, the Visual Studio IDE presents the XML comment information in IntelliSense if the generated XML file has the same name as the assembly and lives in the same directory.

A Stack Component Example

The example in Listing B.3 implements a simple stack component in C#. It demonstrates the use of component-oriented features such as properties, indexers, and XML comments. A more complete example would also implement the ICollection and IList interfaces.

Listing B.3

```
using System;

/// <summary>
/// A general-purpose stack class
/// Not thread-safe
/// </summary>
class Stack
{
    const int sizeIncrement = 10;
    private int count = 0;
    private object[] values = new object[sizeIncrement];

    /// <summary>
    /// The number of elements in the stack
    /// </summary>
    public virtual int Count
    {
        get
        {
            return count;
        }
    }

    /// <summary>
    /// Remove the top element from the stack
    /// and return it
    /// </summary>
    /// <returns>The top element</returns>
    public virtual object Pop()
    {
            // Stack is empty
        if (count == 0)
            throw new InvalidOperationException();
        else
        {
                // Return top of stack
            count—;
            object ans = values[count];
            values[count] = null;
            return ans;
        }
    }

    /// <summary>
```

continues

```csharp
/// Push an element onto the stack
/// </summary>
/// <param name="o">The object to add</param>
public virtual void Push(object o)
{
        // Expand the stack if required
    if (count == values.Length)
    {
        int newSize = values.Length + sizeIncrement;
        object[] newValues = new object[newSize];
        for (int i = 0; i < values.Length; i++)
            newValues[i] = values[i];

        values = newValues;
    }
    values[count++] = o;
}

/// <summary>
/// Indexer to peek into the current
/// contents of the stack
/// </summary>
public object this[int index]
{
    get
    {
        return(values[count - index - 1]);
    }
}

/// <summary>
/// Produce a string representation of the stack
/// </summary>
/// <returns>The string representation</returns>
public override string ToString()
{
        // Convert all stack items to strings
    string[] args = new string[count];
    int index = 0;
    for (int i = count - 1; i >= 0; i—)
    {
        args[index] = values[i].ToString();
        index++;
    }
        // and join them together
```

```
            return String.Join(", ", args);
        }
    }

    class Test
    {
        public static void Main()
        {
            Stack s = new Stack();
            for (int i = 1; i <= 15; i++)
            {
                s.Push(i);
            }
            Console.WriteLine("Stack s = {0}", s);
            Console.WriteLine("Stack[0] = {0}", s[0]);
            Console.WriteLine("Stack[5] = {0}", s[5]);
            while (s.Count > 0)
                Console.WriteLine("Popped {0}", s.Pop());
            Console.WriteLine("Stack s = {0}", s);
        }
    }
```

Future Directions

When thinking about the future of a language, there's always a tension between the desire to add new features and the desire to keep the language simple.[10] There are a lot of possible features that could be added to C#, but only some of them will make the cut. At the time of this writing, we're focused on shipping the initial version of C# and haven't spent much time discussing which features will be added in the future.

One feature that we'd like to have, however, is generics (otherwise known as parameterized types). C# does have a limited type of genericity, in that every type can be stored as an object. This allows the creation of collection classes that can store any type. This approach works, but there are a few unfortunate consequences. Consider the following code:

```
ArrayList arr = new ArrayList();
arr.Add(1);
```

continues

---

[10] This idea is sometimes expressed as "Simplicity is a feature."

```
arr.Add(2);

int value = (int) arr[0];
```

Because the integers 1 and 2 are value types, they have to be boxed to be stored in the `ArrayList`, which stores only values of the type `object`. When the values are boxed, this requires an extra heap allocation for the box, which has some performance implications.

A second issue is the cast to `int` when accessing the value. Having to use this feature adds a bit of ugliness to your code, but more importantly, there has to be a runtime check to see whether the item from the `ArrayList` is really an integer. In other words, this code is runtime type-safe, but not compile-time type-safe.

If you had generics, you could write something like the following:

```
ArrayList<int> arr = new ArrayList<int>();
arr.Add(1);
arr.Add(2);

int value = arr[0];
```

In this case, there are no boxing and no casts.

C# and Standardization

Work on a C# standard began under the auspices of ECMA in September 2000. In addition to Microsoft, there was active involvement by Intel, Hewlett-Packard, IBM, Fujitsu, Plum Hall, and others. The technical work on C# and on CLI (a subset of the CLR) was completed in October 2001.

In December 2001, the ECMA general assembly voted to approve standards for C# and CLI. It also voted to start a fast-track process to get ISO approval for the standards.

Conclusions

The initial response to C# has been quite favorable. A fair portion of the .NET Framework is written in C#, and our developers have found the language to be well suited to the task of developing such a large framework.

Although I don't get as much time to write code as I once did, I'm really happy with how easy it is to write code in C#. I hope you enjoy using it as much as we enjoyed creating it.

If you're looking for more information on C#, you can find the language specification at `http://msdn.microsoft.com/net/ecma`. Also, you can find lots of interesting information at `http://www.gotdotnet.com`.

You might also be interested in my book, *A Programmer's Introduction to C#*, from Apress.

■ APPENDIX C ■

Python for .NET

Mark Hammond

A Brief Overview of Python

Python is a dynamic, object-oriented language. Now more than 10 years old, its popularity has been slowly growing to the point where it often ranks highly in polls for most popular programming language, and many books and companies are dedicated to its support. Although Python has a UNIX heritage, it is very much at home on the Windows platform, with support for many Windows-specific services, including COM, Active Scripting, and NT Services.

This appendix describes an exploratory implementation of the Python language for the .NET Framework. It introduces Python and the existing Python implementations, and then describes the scope and utility of the Python for .NET compiler. Finally, the limitations in the existing compiler and an alternative implementation strategy are discussed.

Portions of this appendix have been taken from various documents distributed with the Python for .NET compiler and from the official Python Web site (http://www.python.org).

Appendix C credit: Mark Hammond.

About Python

Python is a dynamic, high-level, interpreted, interactive, object-oriented language that is often compared to Tcl, Perl, Scheme, or Java. First publicly released in 1991 under a very liberal license, Python has since grown to generally rank very highly in programming language surveys.

Python combines remarkable power with very clear syntax. It has modules, classes, exceptions, very high-level dynamic data types, and dynamic typing. There are interfaces to many system calls and libraries, as well as to various windowing systems (X11, Motif, Tk, Mac, MFC). New built-in modules are easily written in C or C++. Python is also usable as an extension language for applications that need a programmable interface.

This extensibility has allowed developers to build interfaces to native system services. Microsoft Windows provides an excellent case in point; extensions to Python on Windows have been developed that allow Python to use COM/ActiveX and much of the native Win32 API, including obscure features such as Services, Overlapped IO, IO Completion Ports, and so forth.

Python Implementations

Until a few years ago, there was exactly one implementation of the Python language. This implementation, written in C, is the cornerstone of all Python development; it is the only official implementation of the language.

In 1998, the first version of JPython (since renamed Jython) was released, an implementation of the Python language written in (and certified as) 100% pure Java. This release was significant for two reasons. First, it forced the Python language to make a clear distinction between Python-the-language and Python-the-implementation; until then, the implementation itself was considered the de facto language specification, even though a formal specification already existed. Second, Jython opened the Python door to a whole new range of programmers and solutions, as Python could now be used in almost any Java program.

At this time when this appendix was written, the original C implementation and Jython were the only two mainstream implementations of

Python. Some smaller implementations have been started, but none has gathered enough critical mass to be used in the general Python community.

The Python for .NET implementation of Python is but a fledgling, created in early 1999 by Mark Hammond and Greg Stein. Although continuing maintenance is performed by Mark, either additional support or a grass-roots open-source effort will be required before this implementation could be considered viable. The implementation can be found at `http://starship.python.net/crew/mhammond/dotnet`.

Terminology

The term *Python* will often be ambiguous in this document. Therefore, the following conventions are used:

- *CPython:* The original, existing implementation of Python written in C, currently at version 2.2
- *Jython:* An implementation of Python that targets the Java Virtual Machine
- *Python for .NET:*[1] The implementation of Python that targets Microsoft .NET; the topic of this appendix

Whenever the term *Python* is used alone, it will refer to the Python language specification[2] rather than a specific implementation.

Python for .NET

Python for .NET is a completely new implementation of Python. Although many facilities could be implemented simply by extending Python (that is, by using the existing CPython implementation and writing an extension module), there were two primary reasons for creating a completely new implementation:

---

[1]   Our preferred name for this project is simply *Python.NET*, but the issue of using the trademarked *.NET* in this manner, plus the existence of the *python.net* Internet domain makes this issue murky. Therefore, we have adopted the safe *Python for .NET*.

[2]   `http://www.python.org/doc/current/ref/`.

- Full integration with .NET. The only effective way to have another .NET language derive from a Python implemented class is for Python to use .NET facilities when creating classes.
- Contractual obligations. The initial port was done under contract to Microsoft, largely to prove to Microsoft that the .NET CLR was indeed capable of supporting a large number of languages.

An alternative strategy that could be employed is discussed later in this appendix.

Current Status

The current state of the compiler and the runtime systems shows that it is possible to have compiled Python programs fully supported within the .NET Framework. Most of the basic infrastructure is in place, with full bidirectional cross-language support (i.e., Python can inherit or call objects created in other languages, and other languages can inherit from or call objects created in Python).

There are three categories of problems that preclude Python for .NET from being truly useful to a large number of people:

- There is no support for some of the features of .NET that other frameworks will require, such as custom attributes, PInvoke, or ASP.NET. This means that Python for .NET users are not currently able to write classes that interact with tools requiring those features. Related topics are the mismatch between the class/instance semantics, module/package semantics, and exception systems.
- The speed of the current system is so low as to render the current implementation useless for anything beyond demonstration purposes. This speed problem applies to both the compiler itself and the code generated by the compiler. Given that part of the appeal of Python programming is a quick edit-compile-run cycle, the speed issues severely limit the utility of Python on this platform. Some of the blame for this slow performance lies in the domain of .NET internals and `Reflection::Emit`, but some of it is due to the simple implementation of the Python for .NET compiler.

- There is no support for some Python features that some programs will require. Most of these are fairly obscure, but are a limitation. Examples include string formatting; core language features, such as long integers, complex numbers, and built-in object methods; and the standard Python library.

If these issues are addressed, we feel that Python for .NET would become a viable, interesting technology to use within .NET.

Architecture

The Python for .NET implementation consists of three semi-discrete areas: the compiler, the runtime, and the library. Although there is obviously significant interaction between these parts, each has a distinct architecture.

The Compiler

The Python for .NET compiler is written using CPython. It compiles Python source code and uses the .NET `Reflection::Emit` library to generate a .NET assembly. The COM Interoperability features of .NET are used to access the `Reflection::Emit` library.

This particular strategy was chosen to minimize the implementation time. Python's parser is built into the CPython runtime, and the existing Python2C project[3] had infrastructure we could borrow. Greg Stein was involved in the Python2C project and so provided the expertise needed to get up and running quickly.

The key benefits to this approach are the rapid implementation of a simple compiler and the rapid development obtained by coding the compiler in CPython.

The primary drawback is the speed of the compiler. Much of the abstract syntax tree manipulation code is also written in Python code, and as this is one of the most CPU-intensive areas of the compiler, we suffer a significant speed penalty. However, the core Python2C code has been integrated into a standard Python module, and it is hoped that there will be general

---

3   `http://lima.mudlib.org/~rassilon/p2c/`.

improvements in the speed of this library as more users turn to this standard module.

Further, the use of `Reflection::Emit` via COM is also causing some performance problems. Some of these problems are due to the speed of the Python COM bindings, but `Reflection::Emit` itself and/or the COM Interoperability layers are costing significant time as well.

Although currently implemented using CPython, it is envisioned that in the future this compiler will be capable of running under Python for .NET. This will allow the dynamic Python language features, such as `exec` and `eval()`, to be exploited by having the compiler invoked at runtime. However, the functionality provided by the Python for .NET compiler must be enhanced and a number of existing C-implemented Python modules must be ported before this is possible.

Python for .NET Runtime

Due to the dynamic nature of Python, the compiler will often generate code that references the Python for .NET runtime. Even for a simple Python expression such as "`a + b`", if the types of the variables are not known by the compiler, it will generate code to ensure that Python for .NET determines the correct semantics at runtime.

One of the most important jobs of the runtime environment is to ensure that the Python language semantics are faithfully implemented. For this reason, the design and implementation of the Python for .NET runtime borrows heavily from the CPython implementation. The Python for .NET runtime is written in C#.

The Python for .NET runtime defines a .NET interface (`IPyType`) that captures Python's semantics. The definition of this interface is almost identical to the existing CPython `type object`, which is the object primarily responsible for object semantics in CPython.

The `IPyType` interface defines the semantics for a Python type independent of an object instance. For example, the type definition for a string or integer defines the behavior of strings and integers without reference to a specific string or specific integer. Thus, to operate on any .NET object, the Python runtime needs two components: an instance of an `IPyType` interface that describes the Python semantics (such as defining string or integer semantics) and the .NET object itself (that is, a reference to the specific string or integer being operated on). For this reason, the Python for .NET runtime defines a `PyObject` structure (that is, a C# value type), which consists of references to an `IPyType` interface and a .NET object. Almost all runtime functions work with `PyObject`s.

The Python for .NET runtime also exposes an API for use by the compiler, which works primarily with `PyObject` structures. It provides a function for creating a new `PyObject` at runtime, given nothing except an anonymous .NET object reference. The compiler will frequently generate calls to create these `PyObject` structures (often storing the result in a variable) and pass these `PyObject` structures back into the runtime environment as needed.

The Python Library

The role of the Python for .NET library is to implement the standard Python library—the modules Python guarantees will be available to a program at runtime. Python programs reference library modules with the `import` statement.

One of the biggest challenges with a new implementation is this library. In general, there are two distinct categories of library modules in the existing CPython implementation:

- Extension modules are written in C/C++. They take advantage of the CPython runtime system to provide new facilities for Python.
- Python modules are written in Python. In general, these modules make use of the facilities provided by the extension modules written in C. For example, Python has an `os` module written purely in Python. It still makes use of the C-implemented functions in a different extension module native to the platform.

As the CPython API is defined in terms of the CPython implementation (that is, the extension module interface is specific to an implementation rather than part of the language specification), it is not practical to port existing C/C++ extension modules to the .NET implementation while having the CLR consider these modules verifiable. For this reason, there is a two-stage approach to implementing the Python library for .NET:

Reimplement all standard Python extension modules. These modules can be reimplemented either by creating an extension module in C# or by implementing these modules in Python and thereby taking advantage of the .NET Framework facilities.

Compile existing Python extension modules under the .NET compiler. Assuming that all extension modules available for CPython have been re-implemented for .NET, and that the compiler is capable, all existing Python modules should compile under the new implementation.

At the time of this writing, the library for the Python for .NET implementation is quite sparse, and only enough modules required to run basic tests have been implemented. It is hoped that this library will grow as use of the compiler expands.

Using Python for .NET

Unlike CPython, Python for .NET provides no interactive session. Thus, all Python programs must be saved as `.py` files and compiled using the Python for .NET compiler. By default, the compiler will generate an executable that can be run, but compiler options allow a variety of options. Invoking the compiler with a `-help` option will show all supported options.

The compiler itself can be downloaded from the official Web site (`http://www.python.org`). CPython, the Python for Win32 extensions, and the .NET SDK (for the C# compiler) are all required; see the `readme` file for more information.

Example: Hello World

The simplest Python program is

```
print "Hello, world"
```

Assuming this code is saved as `hello.py`, we can compile the program simply by executing the following command:

```
C:\source> python C:\Python.Net\compiler\cpy.py hello.py
```

This statement will compile the source code and create `hello.exe`. We can execute this program to see the result:

```
C:\source> hello.exe
Hello, world
C:\source>
```

Using .NET Objects

The Python for .NET compiler recognizes a special COR[4] namespace, which identifies .NET objects. Thus, any object whose name is prefixed with COR is assumed to be a reference to an external .NET object. For example, the .NET Base Class Library defines a `System.Collections` namespace, which contains a `Queue` class. A Python program could create an instance of this `Queue` class with the following code:

```
q = COR.System.Collections.Queue()
```

Any namespace can be specified. It is your responsibility to add any dependent modules (other than from the .NET Base Class Library) using the `/ref` compiler option.

Once instantiated, the `Queue` object can be used naturally. For example,

```
q.Enqueue("Hello there")
print q.Count
```

calls the `Queue`'s `Enqueue` method and fetches the `Count` property.

Method Signatures and Overloads

If a public signature is generated, the compiler still needs to determine the .NET types to use in the function signature. To this end, the compiler uses a number of hints before defaulting to a basic, default signature.

The first thing the compiler does is look for some type hints in the Python source code. As the basic CPython parser is used, no syntactic changes to the language could be made, so the compiler looks for variables

---

[4] This name is a throwback to the early days, before .NET was named .NET.

of a special name inside the function to provide type information. It recognizes two variables:

- _com_params_ is a string with a comma-separated list of .NET type names.
- _com_return_type_ is a string that holds the name of the .NET return type.

In both cases, the type name should be a fully qualified name and may be any .NET type in any referenced assembly.

For example, the Python code

```
def func(self, name, num):
    _com_params_="System.String, System.Int32"
    _com_return_type_="System.Int32"
    ...
```

will generate a function with the .NET signature similar to what would be generated by the C# compiler for

```
Int32 func(string name, Int32 num)
```

This feature is useful in a number of situations:

- When the base class from which you are implementing contains overloaded virtual methods you wish to implement. These methods all have the same name, but differ in terms of the number and types of parameters. This allows you to specify exactly which version of the method you are overloading.
- When you are implementing a class you expect other language to inherit from and wish to specify the exact signatures that should be used by subclasses.

Other Examples of Compiler Techniques

The compiler test suite shows a number of other techniques that can be used by the compiler. Examples include type conversion, arithmetic conversion, and use of the standard Python types. The test suite can be found in the `compiler\suite` directory of the distribution.

Limitations of Python for .NET

In this section, we devote some space to the limitations on the Python for .NET system.

Performance

Probably the biggest single issue with Python for .NET is the performance of both the compiler and the runtime. The speed of the runtime system must be the more critical issue, as the fastest compiler in the world would not be used if the generated code is too slow to be useful.

Only a small amount of effort has gone into analyzing the performance of the runtime system, mainly due to the lack of (free or cheap) performance analysis tools available for .NET. Without such tools, making performance-related changes is fruitless, as their effectiveness is difficult to measure.

Not withstanding the tuning of the runtime system, the simple existence of the runtime accounts for much of our performance problem. When simple arithmetic expressions take hundreds or thousands of Intermediate Language (IL) instructions (via the Python runtime environment) to complete, performance will always be a struggle.

We discuss type-related performance in more detail later in later sections.

Closed World Syndrome

Competing for the title of biggest single issue would have to be interoperability with existing Python code. Python itself is a very simple language, deriving much of its power from its library. Although the standard library (the modules provided with Python) is very rich, it is the vast array of extension modules provided by third parties that really provide the power. Indeed, most Python books and Internet queries relate to using various modules, rather than the language itself.

The existing Python for .NET system does not allow any leveraging of existing Python code. Although much of the standard library can be ported to .NET, it would not be reasonable to attempt to cover every Python module available.

Although .NET has its own rich class library, it does not solve the problem. There is not 100% overlap between the .NET and Python libraries, and lots of existing Python code already exists that references these various external modules—module dependencies often run quite deep.

Class and Instance Semantics

Although support for basic classes works fine, there are a number of areas where Python and .NET semantics collide—the most obvious being multiple inheritance (supported by Python, but not by .NET). Other, more subtle examples include the ability of a Python subclass to avoid calling a base-class constructor or to reference `self` (the moral equivalent of `this` in C#) before calling any constructors at all.

Unfortunately, many of these semantics are used regularly in Python programs, so simply not supporting them in Python for .NET would raise a significant compatibility hurdle.

It was apparent that the existing simple design would not support the required semantics, so no attempt was made to extend it as far as needed. However, with a clever design of the Python for .NET class system, and borrowing from Jython, it should be possible to get a very close match to the defined Python semantics.

Type Declarations or Inference for Speed

Python code does not have type declarations. However, all Python objects have a distinct type, so Python is not a typeless language. As an example, consider the following two Python statements:

```
a = "hello"
a = 7
```

Although the Python variable `a` has not been declared, after the first statement it references a Python string object. After the second, it references a Python integer object. At any point in time, the variable has a specific type.

As a result, the compiler is rarely able to generate efficient code. The compiler makes no attempt to track variable assignments and types, so it always generates code for the general case. Thus, simple arithmetic operations take many orders of magnitude more Intermediate Language instructions (including calls into the Python for .NET runtime system) than would be required if the types of the variables were known.

There are two general approaches to this issue—type inference and type declarations. Type interference would involve the compiler tracking assignments and the types of objects. Although good results would be possible using local analysis, the dynamic nature of Python and the modular compilation unit would prevent this approach from working completely effectively. Type declarations would involve explicit declarations or other hints being added by the user. However, Python does not define syntax for these features.

Type Declarations for Semantics

There are certain situations where type declarations are required to capture certain .NET semantics rather than for speed reasons. The most obvious example is method overloading—the ability to define a class with multiple methods of the same name, each differing in terms of the number or types of parameters. As Python does not support type declarations, it has no way to express such constructs. Therefore, some syntax[5] was invented to allow expression of overloaded methods.

Although this is an adequate workaround for Python implementing overloaded methods and functions, it does not provide the facility to nominate the overloaded method when actually making a call. For example, given the Python statement

```
myobject.Foo(a)
```

and the fact that `Foo` is an overloaded method, the compiler has no way to determine the correct function to call, nor does the user have the ability

---

[5] Technically, it is not a syntax change—the compiler recognizes assignment to a specially named variable and reacts accordingly.

to nominate it. In this situation we rely on .NET reflection to select the appropriate function at runtime, but this has performance implications and simply does not work when attempting to call base class methods or constructors.

Possible .NET and Python Enhancements

As can be seen from the previous section, there is still plenty of work to be done before we take full advantage of .NET given the current state of both .NET and Python. Therefore, we limit this section to a brief discussion of the possibilities and save further analysis for when the existing implementation could be considered of usable quality.

Type Declarations

There has been discussion in the Python community about adding optional type declarations to a future version of Python. However, for similar reasons as outlined here, no consensus has been reached, and no concrete implementations have been delivered. If Python ever does gain such capabilities, it is expected that there would be support for all of our type declaration requirements—both declaring the signature when implementing a method and selecting which signature you wish to call.

Once we have syntactic support, the compiler will need to be enhanced to take advantage of the declarations. Indeed, this is probably the biggest issue preventing Python from moving forward with concrete syntax proposals. It is still not clear anyone has the time or inclination to enhance the CPython runtime system to take full advantage of them, so the syntax enhancements would be pointless. If a commitment from the Jython or Python for .NET projects is made to support these enhancements, it may help accelerate the acceptance of these proposals into the Python language specification.

Dynamic Language Support

Due to Python's dynamic nature, there are some Python features that are difficult to map into .NET semantics. A simple example is the ability for a Python object to add attributes at runtime—although no declaration or other reference to the attribute can be seen by source code analysis, reference to the attribute will succeed at runtime. Python provides many other ways to change object behavior at runtime that are not captured by .NET.

To support this capability, the compiler will often emit special symbols or code specific to Python. At runtime, if these features are found, they are used; in this way, Python can take advantage of these features. This allows Python code compiled in a separate compilation unit (that is, a unit that exists in a separate assembly) to still provide these dynamic Python semantics when the caller is Python.

This dynamic capability is analogous to `IDispatch` support in COM—the ability for a language to dynamically determine or expose an object model at runtime. .NET leans much more toward compile-time determination of these attributes, in a clear drive for speed. However, the very nature of Python and scripting languages in general is that their users have made a conscious decision to trade execution speed for these runtime features—although possibly not as much execution speed as Python for .NET is currently costing them.

It is clear that such dynamic features may preclude use of certain other .NET features. For example, the performance penalty associated with allowing dynamically created methods to be used as virtual methods may mean they are not supported as virtual. However, there is still enough utility in the feature overlap that would make this a useful, but optional .NET addition.

It should also be noted that there are many languages with dynamic features comparable to Python. However, with Python and every other such language needing to invent its own dynamic solution, these languages are not able to share such features, even when it would make sense to be able to do so. Formalization of these features in .NET would allow multiple dynamic languages to interoperate in a natural manner.

Alternative Implementation Strategies

Python for .NET

An alternative implementation strategy for Python for .NET would be to leverage CPython and attempt to implement .NET support as a regular

Python extension module. This was not considered at the outset of the project, as a primary motivation for Microsoft's involvement was to prove that the .NET runtime system and Intermediate Language were capable of supporting the language. The existing implementation demonstrates that this is indeed true, so now that the focus must switch to providing the best compatibility and/or interoperability with CPython, this idea warrants consideration.

A full analysis of this option is beyond the scope of this appendix. However, there are a number of obvious limitations with this approach:

- Python code would not be verifiable. Thus, it would be impossible to write trusted content in Python.
- Other .NET languages would be unable to inherit from (or otherwise treat as a class) Python objects. It is quite likely that the reverse is possible: CPython programs would be able to inherit from .NET classes. This may be a trade-off worth making. Additionally, enhancements to .NET could assist in this goal.
- Any other .NET tools that require .NET support, such as possibly ASP.NET or the Windows Forms designer tool, would not support Python.

To all intents and purposes, this option is supported today using existing Python and .NET facilities. The .NET COM Interoperability features mean that many .NET features are available today. Indeed, the compiler itself depends on this to be able to use `Reflection::Emit`.

The Compiler
A number of alternative strategies were considered for the compiler.

Use a Different Intermediate Language
This solution would involve compiling the Python source code and generating some other .NET-compatible language rather than .NET Intermediate Language. The most likely target language for this scenario would be C#.

It was decided that the Python compiler should target .NET IL if at all possible. It was felt that this would provide the tightest integration with the

.NET Framework, particularly in areas such as debugging and diagnostics. As there appeared to be no significant impediment to using IL directly, this option was rejected.

Use the Unmanaged Emit API

The "unmanaged emit API" is a traditional, C-style DLL in the standard Windows tradition. The `Reflection::Emit` library is a set of .NET classes. Both APIs are designed to take .NET IL and create .NET assemblies.

This solution would involve using the "unmanaged" .NET API instead of the .NET classes. However, there were two reasons why this option was rejected:

- The advice of the Microsoft staff was that the `Reflection::Emit` APIs are the new official way of creating assemblies. The unmanaged API existed only to provide a solution to the boot-strapping problem; you can't create a managed .NET API for compilers until you have compilers to write the API in!
- Accessing these unmanaged APIs from Python code was more difficult than accessing a COM API.

Using the `Reflection::Emit` classes appeared to offer the shortest implementation time, so this alternative was chosen over the unmanaged option.

The Runtime

There were no identified alternatives to the basic scheme of having a .NET runtime implement many of the Python semantics. Although improvements to the compiler would mean less reliance on the runtime system, it is believed that the compiler will always require the runtime for some operations.

There are, however, a number of different implementation strategies possible. The first version of the compiler always works with .NET object references, rather than the `PyObject` structure as defined earlier in this appendix. However, this meant that any given `Object` had its `IPyType` interface looked up many times throughout its life, which had a large performance impact. Performance testing showed that using a value type (instead of a .NET class) provided the best performance.

The Microsoft support staff used their internal testing tool to determine that the `IPyType` interface lookup for a given .NET object is the biggest hot spot in the runtime. However, as these performance tools are not available to the Python for .NET project, meaningful tuning work is not possible. Hopefully, accessible performance analysis tools will appear soon, allowing further analysis of the runtime performance.

The Library

The Python for .NET compiler and runtime have been designed to allow arbitrary .NET assemblies to be used as Python modules. Thus, it should be possible to write the standard library in any language. The modules written in Python and compiled by the .NET compiler could have been written in C#. However, it was felt that writing the library in Python wherever possible would provide significant benefits, as witnessed in CPython.

Another strategy that has not been investigated would be to port the existing C modules to managed C++ or C#. This has not been explored, partly because the managed C++ compiler was previously not stable enough for serious use, but primarily because it seemed a huge and improbable task. It should be investigated, as there is a huge body of existing C code that is otherwise useless in the Python for .NET environment.

The only other identified strategy would be to attempt to have the compiler inline all the standard library calls. Although this is done for some common built-in functions, it was not considered a viable option for the entire standard library and would place too great a burden on compiler maintenance.

Conclusions

Python is a very popular dynamic language often categorized as a scripting language. It has a number of dynamic features that make it very attractive in certain problem domains, but these very dynamic features are the ones that cause the most friction with .NET.

The intentions with this project were to establish that the Microsoft .NET Framework was capable of supporting the Python language and to suggest ways that Python and .NET could be more tightly integrated in the future. On this basis, the project can be considered a complete success; a working version of the language has been delivered and, as this appendix shows, some real insights into the future possibilities have been gained.

There is, however, still significant work required to make Python truly useful on the .NET platform. We look forward to the day when future versions of Python are an excellent choice for many developers working with .NET.

◾ APPENDIX D ◾

Perl and the .NET Runtime

Jan Dubois

P ERL IS ONE of the most popular dynamically typed scripting languages. It was created by Larry Wall and publicly released for the first time in 1987. The current version, Perl 5, was released in 1994 and is still under active development, with Perl 5.8 being released in summer 2002.

Perl copied the best features from other languages such as C, awk, sed, sh, and BASIC. It is especially powerful for text manipulation and rapid development, which made it an ideal language for Web development (it has often been called "the duct tape of the Internet"). Another major advantage of Perl is the Comprehensive Perl Archive Network (CPAN), a distributed archive of more than 2000 modules for most common (and not so common) programming tasks.

We have used two approaches to bring Perl to the .NET runtime: the "Perl for .NET Research compiler" and the "PerlNET component builder."

Appendix D credit: Jan Dubois, Senior Developer, ActiveState. Copyright © 2002, ActiveState. All rights reserved. ActiveState, Perl Dev Kit, PerlNET, and Visual Perl are trademarks of ActiveState SRL.

371

Perl for .NET Research Compiler

The first approach was to create a full Perl compiler, generating verifiable .NET Intermediate Language (IL) code and supporting all features of the Common Language Specification (CLS).

The implementation phase of this project started in early 2000. The major parts of the project were the parser, the code generator, and the runtime support library.

The Parser

Perl syntax is especially difficult to parse, as it doesn't have a context-free grammar. Parts of already-compiled code may be executed during compile time, altering the way additional code is being parsed: Both the `use` statement and `BEGIN` blocks are executed as soon as they are completely parsed.

As parentheses on function calls are optional in Perl, the function's prototype determines the interpretation of the following tokens. A famous example by Randal Schwartz shows this:

```
time /3 ;#/; print "hello";
sin /3 ;#/; print "goodbye";
```

The first line takes the output of the `time()` function and divides it by 3. The `#` sign starts a comment and the print statement is ignored. The second line computes the sinus of the result of a pattern match: sin(/3 ;#/). The print statement is executed normally. Both `time()` and `sin()` are built-in functions, so their prototypes are known at compile time. But for user-defined functions, the prototypes cannot in general be determined without actually executing the code in `BEGIN` blocks and `use` statements. We therefore decided to use the existing Perl interpreter itself to parse Perl.

The Code Generator

The standard Perl distribution includes the `B` module that provides access to the opcode tree and the `B::CC` module that turns the opcode tree into C source code. The generated source code still needs to be linked to the Perl interpreter library, which contains the implementation for all the Perl opcodes.

We used the `B::CC` module as the basis for generating .NET code. The initial plan was to generate IL directly. But in early 2000, the `Reflection/Emit` API was still under heavy development. After learning that the Python for .NET compiler had to be modified for each biweekly drop of .NET beta code, we decided to generate C# code as our *intermediate language*. That way, tracking the changes to the `Reflection/Emit` API was punted to the Microsoft code and we could concentrate on the Perl-specific challenges of the code generator.

Interface Specification

Perl is an untyped language. Methods don't have prototypes, and even the number of arguments is in general not known until runtime: All arguments are passed in via the `@_` array. This makes it impossible to generate a strongly typed interface for a Perl class automatically. We introduced a comment convention that allowed users to annotate their Perl source code with a C#-like interface declaration (see Listing D.1).

Listing D.1

```
=for interface
    int MyMethod(str Arg1);
    int MyMethod(str Arg1, str Arg2);
=cut

sub MyMethod {
    my($arg1,$arg2) = @_;
    $arg2 = "default" unless defined $arg2;
    # …
}
```

As the example in Listing D.1 demonstrates, it is possible to create multiple .NET signatures for the same Perl method. We would create both an overloaded "outer" .NET `MyMethod()` method and an "inner" `MyMethod()` implementation to which all the outer methods would delegate. Unfortunately, the .NET debugger exposes this implementation detail.

Typed Variables

Perl already has some minimal support for declaration of typed variables. It is used so far only for the experimental "pseudo-hashes." We used this language feature to support native .NET types (see Listing D.2).

Listing D.2

```
use namespace 'System.Text';
my StringBuilder $str = StringBuilder("Hello");
my Int32 $len = $str->{Length};
```

In the example in Listing D.2, the code generator would create variables of the corresponding .NET type and not the normal Perl scalars. Primitive operations on value types would also be generated directly without calling out to the Perl runtime library.

Using typed variables creates much more efficient code, but is no longer compatible with "normal" Perl. It is obviously also not possible to assign objects of different types to these typed variables without throwing an exception.

The Runtime Library

The runtime library implements the Perl-specific data types—Perl scalars, arrays, hashes, and objects—as well as the internal bookkeeping for the Perl execution environment. This library was implemented in C#.

Status

The Perl for .NET Research compiler is not a full implementation of the Perl programming language. It does support the following features:

- Instantiation of .NET objects
- Accessing of .NET methods and properties
- Implementation of .NET classes
- Typed Perl variables
- Recursive function calls with local variables
- .NET Platform Invoke (PInvoke) support
- Cross-language inheritance (Perl can be used for both base classes and derived classes.)
- .NET exception handling

Sample code for these features is available on the Web at `http://www.` `activestate.com/Corporate/Initiatives/NET/Samples/`.

Problems

The implementation of the Perl for .NET Research compiler exposed a number of problems with this approach. The most significant related to execution speed, full language support, and compatibility with existing extensions.

Execution Speed   The generated code is surprisingly slow (more than 10 times slower than the normal Perl interpreter). Part of the problem is that both the generated code and the runtime library are all verifiable managed code. Perl often already "knows" the actual type of a Perl scalar object and accesses its internals directly. In the .NET environment, we always have to "prove" to the runtime system that the object is, indeed, of the correct type (by a runtime cast operation) before being allowed access to it. The accessor then uses a virtual method call to modify the internal state of the object.

In the traditional Perl interpreter, these operations are just two pointer indirections away. The structures have been laid out carefully, so that field offsets are always the same, independent of the scalar "type." These internal representations have been optimized over many years; the .NET implementation could definitely be improved a lot, too. But even when using typed variables, the code ran more slowly than standard Perl did.

Full Language Support   Another problem area is compatibility between "normal" Perl and Perl for .NET. Some features would just need a lot of additional implementation work, such as regular expressions. But other features are virtually impossible to implement with this approach—for example, the string form of the `eval` statement and the runtime `require`.

Both features need to reenter the parser and code generator at runtime, which is already difficult, but not impossible with the current design. They would also need to have access to the current opcode tree, because new code would have to be compiled in the correct lexical context, providing access to lexical variables in outer scopes and potentially creating new closures. The opcode tree, however, is no longer available.

Compatibility with Existing Extensions   Perl's utility lies not only in the language itself, but also in the vast amount of readily available modules from CPAN. As noted earlier, more than 2000 modules are available for all the common programming tasks developers face every day. Many of these modules are not written in plain Perl but also contain some low-level glue code in XS (a C preprocessor-like extension language). This XS code makes assumptions about the internals of the Perl interpreter, such as the layout of the data structures. For this reason, XS extension modules need to be recompiled for different versions of the Perl interpreters.

All of these XS extensions are unavailable to the Perl for .NET Research compiler: XS code is compiled to C, which will not compile to managed .NET code. The internals of the Perl for .NET runtime environment are so significantly different from the "normal" Perl interpreter as to make automatic translation impossible. Furthermore, the XS mechanism exposes all internal Perl interpreter functions, not just the documented XS extension API. A lot of the modules on CPAN do use additional APIs beyond the documented set. Emulating them all in a Perl for .NET API would be impossible.

PerlNET Component Builder

We presented the Perl for .NET Research compiler to the public during the Microsoft Professional Developers Conference (PDC) in summer 2000 and a week later at the O'Reilly Open Source conference.

Some of the feedback we got included the following:

- What is the point of modifying Perl in such a way that normal Perl code won't run on Perl for .NET and Perl for .NET code (using typed variables) won't run on "normal" Perl? Aren't you just creating a new syntax for C#?
- Compiled Perl code should run faster than interpreted code, not slower!
- If I can't use my existing Perl code with Perl for .NET, then this may just as well be a different language. Without access to CPAN modules, this technology doesn't work for migrating any of our existing code.

At the O'Reilly conference, it was also announced that work on Perl 6 would start soon. Perl 6 will be a complete redesign from the ground up, making it easier to extend the language and to target different execution environments. Ideally, this redesign should make it easier to produce an efficient compiler for Perl 6 to .NET conversions.

As it will obviously take several years to implement a complete redesign, we decided to try a different approach to bring Perl 5 to the .NET runtime environment. The goal was now full syntax compatibility, full support for CPAN modules, and normal execution speed. To achieve these goals, we had to sacrifice generation of verifiable managed code.

Interface with Standard Perl Interpreter

The new approach runs all Perl code using the normal Perl interpreter in unmanaged code outside .NET. The PerlNET component builder reads the interface specification inside the Perl comments described earlier and generates managed .NET proxy objects for the Perl code. These proxies are bona fide .NET classes, carrying all the .NET metadata about the component.

A class constructor of the proxy is responsible for compiling the corresponding Perl code once the first instance of a PerlNET component is instantiated. The proxy method transports all parameters over to the unmanaged Perl stack and dispatches the corresponding Perl method. Upon return of the Perl method, the proxy extracts the return value from the Perl stack and converts it into the correct .NET type.

The PerlNET approach avoids the disadvantages of the Research compiler: All Perl code runs at normal speed, the syntax is 100% compatible with "normal" Perl, and it supports all the same extensions.

However, there are some new disadvantages as well: PerlNET assemblies are pretty heavyweight. Each assembly creates an instance of the unmanaged Perl interpreter (but all instances of all classes within a single PerlNET assembly share the same interpreter). Moving data between Perl and other .NET languages is also more expensive: Everything has to be marshaled back and forth via PInvoke or COM Interop.

Challenges

The PerlNET approach presents a number of interesting challenges.

Efficient Data Marshalling

How can data be passed back and forth with minimal overhead? How can we make sure that a managed object is not garbage collected when it is being passed to unmanaged code and no managed reference remains?

PerlNET uses PInvoke to transfer control from managed to unmanaged code. Passing value types is efficient: The bit pattern is copied verbatim.

Reference types are marshaled via the `System.Runtime.InteropServices.GCHandle` type (as `System.IntPtr` integers). On the Perl side, they are held in a .NET wrapper class. This wrapper manages the lifetime of the `GCHandle`. Once the reference count of the wrapper goes to zero, it calls back into .NET to release the `GCHandle`.

In the other direction, PerlNET uses a custom COM interface and COM Interop to call back from Perl into the .NET proxy. Perl variables are always marshaled by address, as integers. A managed wrapper class has knowledge about the Perl data structure layout and can extract values if and when needed. If the Perl variable is just passed back to another Perl method, it only puts the address back on the Perl stack and increments the reference count. As we are already interfacing with unmanaged code, we are no longer verifiable anyway and can now manipulate Perl structures directly by using "unsafe" managed code.

This approach also has advantages when the Perl variable is being used on the managed side. For example, to translate a Perl variable containing a string into a `System.String` object, the proxy extracts the string address out of the Perl variable and then calls the following `System.String` constructor:

```
unsafe public String(sbyte* value, int startIndex,
                     int length, Encoding enc);
```

Even a Unicode string (stored by Perl in UTF-8) can be directly transformed into a .NET `String` object without any intermediate copies.

Method Overloading

As shown earlier, Perl doesn't have the concept of method overloading. For overloaded PerlNET methods, we create the .NET methods with the correct signatures, but all proxies will call the same Perl method. In most cases, the Perl method doesn't even need to differentiate based on argument type, as all variables are typeless. The code for `foo(int x)` and the code for `foo(short x)` are normally the same. In case the method does need to discriminate based on parameter type, the `System.Reflection` mechanism can be used to determine actual types.

In the other direction, calling .NET methods from Perl, PerlNET uses reflection to determine the correct method to call. Currently, the argument types must match one of the overloaded signatures; otherwise, a runtime exception is thrown. We have been discussing the implementation of a multimethod dispatch mechanism, but in practice the need for it has not been proved.

Exception Handling

Perl not only keeps the execution state on a primary parameter/return stack, but also maintains several additional status/context stacks. One example is the scope stack, which registers cleanup/restore actions to be performed at scope exit. PerlNET needs to make sure that .NET exceptions will not unwind the unmanaged stack without also unwinding the additional "private" stacks of the Perl interpreter.

For this reason, PerlNET will always set up an exception handler before calling back into .NET code. If the .NET code throws an exception, PerlNET catches it and rethrows it as a Perl exception. This approach ensures that all Perl stack maintenance is performed properly.

PerlNET also sets up a Perl exception handler whenever the proxy calls from managed code into Perl. The Perl-level exception is then converted into a .NET exception and rethrown by the proxy code.

Thus, even without user-level exception handlers, an exception is bounced back and forth between managed and unmanaged code, making sure that all cleanup happens in the right sequence. The only downside of this mechanism is that the `Stacktrace` property of the exception doesn't show the full back trace, but only the trace from the last point where the exception has been rethrown.

Supported .NET Features

Even though strictly speaking PerlNET doesn't run Perl code on the .NET runtime system, it nevertheless integrates it very closely. All of the following features are supported:

- Constructors and inheritance
- Methods including overloading
- Fields, properties, and indexers
- Events (delegates)
- Enumerations
- Exceptions
- Custom attributes
- Namespaces
- PInvoke

PerlNET Status

The PerlNET component builder is one component of the ActiveState Perl Dev Kit (found at http://www.ActiveState.com/PDK).

PerlNET fully supports cross-language inheritance. Perl can be used for both the base class and the derived class. Windows Forms applications can be implemented completely in Perl.

PerlNET, together with "Perl for ASP.NET," lets you write ASP.NET pages and Web services in Perl. For more information, see http://aspn. ActiveState.com/ASPN/Downloads/PerlASPX.

The "Visual Perl" plug-in provides integration with the Microsoft Visual Studio .NET IDE. It can be found at http://www.ActiveState. com/VisualPerl.

Example: A Windows Forms Application

The example program in Listing D.3 implements a simple Windows Forms application. The HelloWorldForm class inherits from the System.Windows.Forms.Form base class. It adds a text box and a button to the form.

When the user clicks the button, a message box displays the text from the text box.

Listing D.3

```perl
package HelloWorldForm;
use strict;
use PerlNET qw(with AUTOCALL);

use namespace "System";
use namespace "System.Windows.Forms";
use namespace "System.Drawing";

=for interface
    [extends: Form]
    [STAThread]
    static void Main();
    private field TextBox textBox;
    private void Click(any sender, EventArgs Args);
=cut

sub Main {
    my $self = HelloWorldForm->new;
    Application->Run($self);
}

sub HelloWorldForm {
    my $this = shift;

    with(my $textBox = TextBox->new(),
        Text     => "Hello Windows Forms World",
        Location => Point->new(16, 24),
        Size     => Size->new(360, 20),
        TabIndex => 1);

    with(my $button1 = Button->new(),
        Text     => "Click Me!",
        Location => Point->new(256, 64),
        Size     => Size->new(120, 40),
        TabIndex => 2);

    $button->add_Click(EventHandler->new($this, "click"));
```

continues

```
my $h = SystemInformation->CaptionHeight;
    with($this,
        Text                 => "Hello Windows Forms World",
        AutoScaleBaseSize => Size->new(5, 13),
        ClientSize           => Size->new(392, 117),
        MinimumSize          => Size->new(392, int(117 + $h)),
        AcceptButton         => $button1,
        textBox              => $textBox);

    $this->{Controls}->Add($_) for $textBox, $button;
}

sub click {
    my($this, $sender, $args) = @_;
    MessageBox->Show("Text is: '$this->{textBox}->{Text}'");
}
```

Conclusions

PerlNET brings the Perl 5 language to the .NET platform. It is especially useful for migrating legacy applications to .NET and making the abundance of CPAN modules available to.NET developers, even those preferring a different programming language.

The design process for Perl 6 has progressed quite a bit. Some of the design goals focus on support for optional strong typing and for implementation in multiple virtual environments such as the Java Virtual Machine and the .NET runtime. Ideally, a fully native implementation of Perl 6 using IL will be available in a few years.

Interested readers can view the PerlNET reference documentation at `http://aspn.activestate.com/ASPN/Perl/Reference/Products/PD K/PerlNET/Reference.html`.

■ APPENDIX E ■

Component Pascal on the CLR

John Gough

T HIS APPENDIX DEALS with another of the Project~7 languages, *Component Pascal*, which we sometimes abbreviate as just *CP*. The resulting compiler is named *Gardens Point Component Pascal* and is available under an open source license.[1]

Unlike some other language projects, it was an explicit objective from the beginning that the compiler should implement the *whole* of the language with exact semantics, or as close to the exact semantics as the *CLR* permitted. Thus, it was not an option to "leave out" inconvenient parts of the language that did not map easily to the underlying primitives of the *CLR*. Neither was it an option to gratuitously make additions to the language simply on the basis that the *CLR* facilitated such constructs. It was intended that the project should be a significant test of the ability of the run-time to provide for languages with somewhat different features from Microsoft's own languages.

Appendix E credit: © KJ Gough 2002.

[1] The Gardens Point compilers are named in honor of the scenic spot on the Brisbane River where the Queensland University of Technology is located.

A fundamental decision that must be made for every new language on the *CLI* is whether to produce verifiable code. Languages whose definitions do not enforce a high level of type safety must either produce unverifiable code or enforce conformance to a type-safe subset of the language. Component Pascal is a type-safe language, and the choice was made to produce 100% verifiable code. The advantage of producing verifiable code is that users of such code enjoy stronger guarantees from harmful behavior. This may be a critical issue in applet-like scenarios.

The architecture of the compiler is conventional (Figure E.1). A scanner and parser build an abstract syntax tree for the whole compilation unit, and semantic checking is performed during attribution of this tree. Finally, a tree-walker writes a file containing the textual form of the *Common Intermediate Language* (CIL). The *IL* assembler `ilasm` is invoked to transform this file into a program executable file. As usual, the *CIL* form of the program

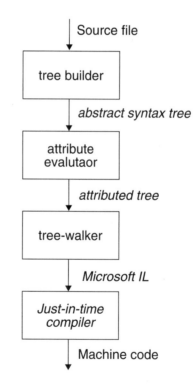

Figure E.1 *Architecture of the Gardens Point Component Pascal compiler*

is finally executed after being transformed by a *just-in-time compiler* at program load time.

As it turned out, it was possible to map the whole of the language to the *CLR* without compromising the exactness of the semantics, except in some minor points that are discussed later in this appendix. The final product does provide for some optional language extensions. These are included simply to allow components created using Component Pascal to interact more effectively with other components conforming to the Common Language Specification. The extensions include the implementation of interface types and some primitive support for structured exception handling.

This appendix discusses the issues involved in implementing a language such as Component Pascal on the CLR. This is not a trivial problem. Although the CLR was explicitly designed to support a wide range of languages, it was nevertheless necessary to implement a single object model that would suit most languages. Furthermore, the objective of producing verifiable code disallows certain tricks that would otherwise be available.

About Component Pascal

Component Pascal is an object-oriented language of the Pascal family. Its ancestors are *Pascal, Modula-2,* and *Oberon.* The language is almost a strict superset of *Oberon-2.* Listing E.1 is the canonical *"hello world"* program for Component Pascal, shown in the so-called publication format.

Listing E.1

```
module Hello;

   import CPmain, Console;
begin
   Console.WriteString("Hello CP World");
   Console.WriteLn;
End Hello.
```

The object-oriented features of Component Pascal include single implementation inheritance, with explicit annotations that control the extensibility of types and of methods. Compared to other members of the Pascal family, the signatures of procedures are more expressive, with *Ada*-like annotations specifying whether particular reference parameters carry values *into* the invocation (in mode), *out* of the invocation (out mode), or in both directions (var mode). The purpose of all these annotations is to allow a higher level of compile-time checking of source code and to provide stricter invariants for program analysis.

The Type System

As with other Pascal-family languages, the type system is based on statically declared types. The available type constructors are *records*, *pointers*, and *arrays*, as well as the usual built-in types. There are no union types (i.e., no variant records), and no subrange or enumeration types.

In common with all other Pascal dialects, the definition of an array includes a declared length. Unlike C-family languages, where all arrays of characters are declared as "char []", in Pascal two arrays are the same type only if they share the same type definition, including the length attribute. There are significant semantic consequences of this difference.

Pointers may be declared with bound types that are array or record types. There is also an open array construct in which a pointer type is bound to an array of indeterminate length. A variable of such type may refer to an array of dynamically determined length, corresponding to the one-dimensional arrays native to Java and C#.

Statically typed, non–object-oriented languages usually include a union construct, so as to allow a primitive kind of type polymorphism. Object-oriented languages have more advanced facilities for polymorphism and are able to avoid the notoriously error-provoking union construct. Most modern languages, including Java, C#, and Component Pascal, do not have a union construct.

In Component Pascal, the record types are extensible. Record type definitions may declare that they extend some existing record type, provided that the original type declared that it was extensible. The new type is said to be an extension of its base type. Pointers to such extensible types have subtype polymorphism. That is, a variable declared to be of some particular pointer type may contain a reference to an object of the declared type or to an object of any direct or indirect extension of that type.

The code fragment in Listing E.2 declares an abstract record type Figure as well as an extension of that type named Circle. The type name in parentheses in the record declaration of the Circle type specifies the base type, Figure, that the new type extends.

Listing E.2

```
type

    Figure = abstract record (* no fields *) end;
    Circle = record (Figure)
                x, y, radius : REAL;
             end;
```

It is possible to declare static variables and local variables that are of array or record types. These structures are allocated implicitly. Variables of pointer type are initially `nil`, and they require an explicit call of `new` to allocate the variable instance.

Procedures may be declared as being "bound" to a particular record type. Such type-bound procedures correspond to methods in the usual object-oriented terminology. Methods are inherited by all extensions of a particular type, unless the subtype declares a method with the same name and signature to *override* the inherited method. Thus, in the example in Listing E.2, methods declared on the `Figure` type will be inherited by `Circle` and all other extensions of the base type.

An inherited method may specify a return type that differs covariantly from the return type of the method that it overrides. That is, the return type of the method bound to the subtype may be a subtype of the return type of the method that was overridden.[2]

Just as record types may be extended only if they are declared to be extensible, so methods may be overridden only if they are declared to be extensible. The default is thus for types to be *sealed* and for methods to be *final*.

The basic, built-in types include signed integers ranging from 8 to 64 bits, and two floating-point types REAL and SHORTREAL corresponding

---

[2] This rather fine point is mentioned here because the implementation of such covariance is one of the real challenges of mapping to the CLR.

to IEEE `double` and `float`, respectively. The `CHAR` type corresponds to 16-bit Unicode characters.

Statements

Component Pascal contains the usual assignment, procedure call, loop, and choice statements. The loops include pre- and post-tested loops, a structured `for` loop, and an endless loop construct. The choice statements include an "`if, elsif, else, end`" construct, and a multiway `case` statement corresponding to the familiar `switch` of C-family languages.

An unusual feature of the language is the presence of a "type case" statement. This statement, which begins with the keyword `with`, is a multiway branch where the target branch selected depends on the *type* of the selecting variable. In many common situations, this statement is very convenient because within the selected code the selecting variable is known to be of the selected type and may be referenced without the repeated use of a narrowing cast as would be required by many other languages.

Static procedures may be nested within other procedures and within methods. Such procedure declarations may be nested to any depth, and the code in such nested procedures may access the local variables and arguments of the lexically enclosing procedures. The efficient implementation of such nonlocal addressing is a significant challenge for the compiler writer who chooses to target the *CLR.*

Recall that in Pascal-family languages arrays have a statically known fixed length. Array values may thus be assigned to variables of the same array type, as they are necessarily of the same length. Similarly, it is possible to assign entire values of the record type if the record type is not extensible. It is a characteristic of the Pascal languages that assignments have *value semantics.* That is, when arrays or records are assigned, a *copy* of the value on the right-hand side of the assignment statement is created at the destination location. Similarly, when pointer values are assigned, a value copy of the pointer is created. Of course, this value copy will be an *alias reference* to the bound value of the original pointer, and both pointer values will reference the same object.

Module Structure

The main structuring construct of Component Pascal programs is the *module*. In this language, modules correspond to compilation units, and identifiers are made visible across module boundaries by explicit *export* and *import* statements.

At the top of a module is a list of all modules whose public names are to be visible in that module. Such imported names are known by their fully qualified denotations, although there is a facility for creating short "alias" names for commonly used module names. There is nothing corresponding to the `using` statement that in C# imports names and makes them accessible unqualified by a prepended namespace identifier.

Every name that is declared at the outer lexical level in a module may be optionally marked for export. In the case of variables, the export may be *full* or *read-only*. In the case of record declarations, individual fields may be private to the current compilation unit, fully exported, or exported in read-only mode.

Notice that the visibility of names and the accessibility of features are controlled only on a module-by-module basis. There is nothing corresponding to either the `private` or `protected` modes of some other object-oriented languages.

Modules in *Component Pascal* have an optional *body*. The body, if it exists, is executed just once, when the module is loaded at runtime.

Mapping to the CLR

The most important mappings to be decided upon, when implementing a new language on the *CLI*, are the mapping of compilation units onto the class and assembly structure of the *CLI* and the mapping of the types of the language onto the types of the *Common Type System (CTS)*.

Mapping the Program Structure

In the *CLI*, classes and other named entities have their visibility controlled at the boundaries of assemblies. There may be additional rules for controlling *accessibility*, but the assembly boundary is the one that counts to the *CLI*. The use of namespaces, seemingly fundamental to programmers, has no representation at runtime. At runtime, classes have only fully qualified *dotted names*, with everything up to the last "dot" corresponding to what programmers like to think of as the namespace. A compiler may therefore perform arbitrary "name-mangling" transformations to map the hierarchical naming structure of a source language to the dotted names of the *CLI*.

In Component Pascal, each module is a compilation unit, and modules define the boundaries of visibility control. It thus seemed natural to map modules to assemblies, so that each compilation results in a separate assembly. Although this seems a natural choice, there are other possibilities.

The Synthetic Static Class

As well as defining an assembly, each module implicitly defines a *synthetic static class*. This is a class with only static methods, but no instance constructors. The class is given a made-up name and provides a mechanism to encapsulate the body of the module. Recall that the body of a module needs to be executed exactly once, when the module is loaded. This behavior is exactly what is provided by the static (class) constructor of a class. When the synthetic static class is demand-loaded, the class constructor performs any initialization specified in the module body. The guarantees of the *CLR* ensure that the class will be loaded before any access to the static data of the module is required.

Any static data of the module become static data of the synthetic class, and ordinary (that is, non–type-bound) procedures of the module become static methods of the class.

Nested procedures are implemented by static methods of the synthetic class, but in this case the names are mangled so as to ensure uniqueness in the flattened name-scope of the class. In the case of procedures nested inside type-bound procedures, the nested procedure becomes a static method of the class to which the enclosing (dispatched) method is bound.

Controlling Visibility

Classes in the *CLI* are either private to an assembly or public. These two levels of visibility correspond precisely to the nonexported or exported possibilities of Component Pascal. This provides a natural mapping for defining the visibility of types.

Class members in the *CLI* have a variety of possible accessibility attributes. As it turns out, only two are used here. Static variables of a module are mapped to static fields of the synthetic static class. If the variable is exported, it has `public` accessibility. If the variable is not exported, it must be given `assembly` visibility, because it must be accessible to all code in the module. The use of `private` in this case would be too restrictive, as the code of type-bound procedures would be unable to access such fields.

The mapping of variables with read-only export is an interesting problem, as there is no direct support for it in the *CLI*. In the current version of the compiler, such variables are public. The *Component Pascal* compiler knows that such variables must not be modified and enforces the guarantee. However, a component written in another language would permit modification of the value, as the compiler would be unaware of the (non-standard) attribute. A more secure implementation would be to map read-only variables to *properties* that export a *getter* method but no *setter* method. This would enforce security at the cost of a small runtime overhead.

Static procedures, like static variables, become members of the synthetic static class. They are declared with either public or assembly accessibility, depending on whether they are exported.

Mapping the Type System

The built-in types of *Component Pascal* map naturally to a subset of the types of the *CLI*. The character and floating-point types map directly, with the longer signed integers also corresponding directly. Although the *CLI* provides a full range of unsigned types, the *Common Language Specification* standardizes use of signed types, except for the 8-bit type, for which, perversely, the unsigned type is standard. This is the only slight problem with the *Component Pascal* mapping, as in *Component Pascal* the 8-bit number type is signed. It follows that Component Pascal programs must not export procedures with 8-bit formal parameters, if they are to be *CLS*-conformant.

The type constructors of Component Pascal generate *records*, *pointers*, and *arrays*. Somehow these have to be mapped onto the reference classes, value classes, and dynamically allocated arrays of the Common Type System. In the *CTS*, value classes have value assignment semantics, while both arrays and reference classes have assignment with alias (reference) semantics. One thing becomes immediately apparent: Some types with value semantics in Component Pascal will need to be implemented by reference objects in the Common Type System. Consider just two examples. Arrays in the CTS are always dynamically allocated, and hence are reference types. Value classes in the CTS are necessarily `sealed`, so any extensible record type must be implemented as a reference class in the *CTS*.

Reference Surrogates

The mechanism by which structures with value semantics in some source language are implemented by means of reference objects in an implementation framework has been described as *reference surrogacy*. In effect, a dynamically allocated object in the implementation framework is created to act as a surrogate for an object with value semantics in the source language program. Whenever an operation in the source code requires value copies to be made, the code in the implementation framework does whatever field-by-field or element-by-element copying is required to maintain semantic consistency with the source language view. Similarly, values that are implicitly created in the source code may require explicit invocations of `new` in the implementation framework, if they are implemented by reference surrogates.

There are two cases that require reference surrogates in Component Pascal. We consider each in turn.

Arrays   All arrays in the *CTS* are dynamically allocated, so that all *Component Pascal* arrays must be implemented by reference surrogates. Here we sketch out the main elements of the trickery that achieves the correct semantics.

Suppose that a particular program has a procedure with a local variable of array type. The source code might be written as follows:

```
procedure Foo();
        var localA : array 8 of char;
begin
        ...
```

As is usual for local variables, the array automatically comes into existence when the procedure is invoked. In conventional settings, this is done by reserving space for the array in the activation record of the procedure. However, in the case of the *CLR*, the surrogate array must be dynamically allocated from the garbage collected heap, so the implementation of the procedure will require code in its prolog to create the object. The prolog code will be equivalent to that arising from the following C# statement:

```
char [] localA = new char[8];
```

Note that in this example the `localA` in the C# fragment is a *reference* to the 8-long array, while in the *Component Pascal* source the variable is the array.

When an *entire assignment* of such arrays takes place, the compiler will generate object code that performs an element-by-element copy. This copy is performed by an inline loop in the current version of the compiler. In the case of multidimensional arrays, because the subarrays will in turn be implemented by reference surrogates, the copy operation will become a nest of loops as deep as the number of array dimensions.

Figure E.2 is a diagram of the runtime representation of a two-dimensional array. In this case, the diagram is for an array with the following *Component Pascal* declaration:

```
var bar : array 8,4 of integer;
```

A paradoxical aspect of the reference surrogate mechanism is demonstrated for the pointer types. Suppose that some type T is a value type in the source language, but is implemented as a reference surrogate type. The par-

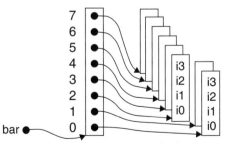

Figure E.2 *Runtime representation of a two-dimensional array*

adox is that the types `T` and `pointer to T` share the same runtime representation! The difference between the two cases is not the runtime structure that is used to represent the values, but rather the way in which allocation and assignment are translated into object code. For the pointer type, initialization consists of loading the variable with `nil`; for the value type, an explicit object must be dynamically created as discussed earlier. To translate assignment, in the pointer case, the reference is simply copied by a single Intermediate Language instruction. For record and array values, to achieve proper value semantics, the destination and source surrogate references must be loaded and a datum-by-datum copy performed.

Extensible Records   The case of extensible records is similar to that of arrays. Corresponding to each extensible record type, a reference class is declared to the *CLR*. Instances of this class are used as reference surrogates for the value record. As before, the magic is not in the type declaration but rather in the way in which the operations of the source language are translated for the runtime environment.

Value records that are implicitly created in the source code require explicit allocation of a surrogate from the heap at runtime. For assignment, it is necessary to perform a field-by-field copy, including even inherited private fields. Because the code requiring the copy does not in general have access rights for all inherited fields, it is necessary to call the public `copy` method of each supertype.

Pointers to extensible records are implemented by the same runtime class as their bound type. As is the case with arrays, the distinction between the pointer and its target lies in the different translation of the code for initialization and assignment.

Static Record Types

Record types that are sealed and do not extend any other type have the opportunity to be implemented as value classes in the *CTS*. There are advantages in doing so, because the operations for initialization and entire assignment are primitives of the runtime and do not involve object creation. The C# compiler uses such classes to implement `struct`s. The *Component*

Pascal compiler uses such classes for record types that neither are extensible nor extend any other type.

However, a small issue arises for *Component Pascal* that does not arise for C#. In the case that a particular record type R is implemented as a value class, how is the type `pointer to R` to be implemented? There are two clear possibilities. First, it is possible to use the built-in `box` instruction to copy the value records to the heap as needed. Second, it is possible to define a corresponding reference class for each defined value class. The argument against the first method is that every system-boxed value will be of type `System.Object` and will require a narrowing cast at each unboxing site. The disadvantage of the second method is the cluttering of the type-name scope with extra (possibly unused) class declarations.

The *Component Pascal* compiler uses the second method. For every suitable record type R, two *CTS* declarations are made. One is for the value class R and the other is for the reference class boxed_R. As a slight optimization, anonymous record types that occur only as pointer-bound types are implemented as reference classes, as in this case it is never possible to create an *unboxed* instance of the class.

It follows that the *Component Pascal* programmer neither knows nor needs to care whether a particular type is really implemented as a value type or as a reference surrogate. The compiler will make a choice depending on the way in which the type is used, and it will generate code so that the proper source semantics are achieved.

A final point has to do with the fact that the reference classes are *self-describing* while the value classes are not. For the self-describing types, it is possible to find out the runtime type of an object using reflection. However, in a *Component Pascal* program, the user is not required to know whether a particular type is implemented as a reference type or a value type, so how is the user supposed to know if it is permissible to call a reflection method? The answer is simple. When the program uses the TYPEOF() primitive, the *compiler* knows whether the parameter is implemented as a value object or a reference surrogate. If the parameter is a value type, then the compiler knows what the exact type is (this is the reason that the compiler knows that using a value type is permitted); otherwise, the compiler generates a runtime call to the reflection library.

Dispatched Methods

Both value and reference classes may have instance and virtual methods bound to them. Because value classes are necessarily `sealed`, the use of virtual methods on such types is of limited utility. In *Component Pascal* procedures may be bound to record types, whether the types are extensible or not. The type-bound procedures of CP thus map in a very natural way to the runtime facilities.

Consider the type-bound procedure (dispatched method) declared as follows:

```
procedure (in thisFig : Figure)Serial() : INTEGER, new;
begin <<procedure body> end Serial;
```

`SerialNum` is a method bound to the object type `Figure`, takes no other arguments, and returns the `INTEGER` type. The `this` object of the method is known as `thisFig` within the method. Unlike in most object-oriented languages, the `this` is named by the user just like any other formal parameter. In the preceding example, the method is declared to be `new`, meaning that it does not override any inherited method but is not marked as `extensible`. The method is thus final. The compiler will recognize that this particular choice of attributes allows the method to be optimally implemented as a (nonvirtual) instance method. As in other aspects, the *user* specifies the desired semantics, and the *compiler* determines the mapping to the CLR that best achieves that result.

A small curiosity has to do with the fact that in *Component Pascal* methods are associated with `record` types. The receiver value (the `this` value) in the source may be defined either as a reference parameter of the record type or as a value parameter of the corresponding `pointer` type. If the *Component Pascal* record is implemented as a reference surrogate, there is no problem, as both types are represented by the same reference class. However, if the record type is implemented as a value class, the record and the pointer types are represented by different types at runtime. This simply causes confusion for users who cannot resist the urge to read the assembly language.

Semantic Challenges

Almost all of the features of Component Pascal were mapped to the *CLR* without difficulty and provide the exact semantics expected for the source language. Once the necessity for reference surrogates is accepted, the rest follows in a natural way.

There are a small number of language constructs that pose design issues for the implementation. A few of these are discussed here. None of these turns out to be a show-stopper, but all create challenges of different levels of seriousness.

Nonlocal Addressing

In Pascal-family languages, nested procedures are able to access the local variables and parameters of their enclosing procedures. Such access is called *nonlocal addressing*. Curiously, C-family languages do not have nested procedures but may have nested blocks with local data. The implementation problems in the C-language case are trivial, as all data within a function lie within the same activation frame.

The issue with nonlocal addressing in the CLR is that there is no native mechanism to support it. Indeed, there is no legal way to refer to the local data of any method other than the currently active one. There are a small number of possible approaches to solve the problem, and the *Component Pascal* compiler uses the author's favorite one. Procedures that declare data that are accessed nonlocally define a heap-allocated data structure to hold the variables in question. An object of the type is allocated on entry to the procedure. A reference to this object is passed as an additional, hidden parameter to all nested procedures. In deeply nested cases, these *explicit heap-allocated records* (*XHR*) form a linked list. Because the compiler knows the relative nesting depths of each piece of code, it is able to generate object code to traverse the chain to access the data of any enclosing procedure.

There is some minor runtime overhead caused by the excess object creation in this approach, and it works exactly in *almost* every case. The pesky exception is the mercifully rare case where a nested procedure wants to access a reference parameter of an enclosing procedure, and the parameter type is an unboxed value type (that is, the type is *not* a reference surrogate).

The dilemma is how to place the incoming parameter in the *XHR*. If the incoming *reference* is copied into the *XHR*, it must be declared as an unmanaged pointer type, and the program will not be verifiable. Alternatively, if the *value* pointed to by the reference is copied into the *XHR* and copied back out when the nested call returns, the code will be verifiable, but the semantics will be inexact. Truly an exquisite dilemma!

Structural Compatibility of Delegates

Delegates are the *CTS* versions of type-safe function pointers. Although delegates are most often used to implement the event-handling model used by *GUI* programs on .NET, they are also well suited to implement the *procedure variable* types of *Component Pascal*. However, there is a slight semantic constraint. We would like delegates to be assignment compatible if they represent methods with the same signature. Instead, they are compatible only if the two types have the same *type name*. It is always possible to program around this constraint, but it nevertheless represents a slight semantic inaccuracy in the language implementation. Future versions of the runtime system will support the required *structural compatability*, so the problem will eventually go away.

Covariant Function Types

Methods in *Component Pascal* may be declared with covariant return types. That is, an overriding method may return a type that is a narrowed version of the return type of the method that it overrides. This language feature is not supported by the runtime environment.

It is possible to overcome this constraint by using a limited form of *type erasure*. In summary, the compiler produces code that promises to return the non-covariant type, so as to keep the verifier happy. However, the *Component Pascal* compiler knows that the real return type is narrower, and it casts the return values as necessary. This trick has a low overhead and precise semantics. The only problem is that in a mixed-language environment a compiler for a different language might try to subclass the type and override the covariant method. If the compiler for the other language did not understand the covariance metadata, it might allow the overriding method to return an incorrect type. This could cause an unexpected class cast exception in the *Component Pascal* component.

Conclusions

For the most part, the objectives of the Component Pascal project were well realized. The compiler, except for the small issues discussed earlier, implements the language accurately and produces good-quality, verifiable code. The compiler is written in Component Pascal and compiles itself successfully. It started off as about 20,000 lines of code in its initial form, but has been steadily growing as more special-case code is added to improve code quality. There are a number of utilities and other tools that are distributed with the compiler.

Compatibility Extensions

As hinted at the beginning of the appendix, some optional language extensions were added to *Component Pascal* to allow full access to the facilities of the base class libraries. The most important of these is the facility to declare that record types implement defined interfaces. There is also a limited level of access to the exception-handling facilities of the runtime environment. This last enhancement is almost a necessity, as many library methods signal failure by throwing an exception that the caller is expected to catch.

For example, we might wish to declare that the `Circle` type not only extends the abstract base type `Figure` but also implements an interface type `ClosedFig`. This interface might offer a method `getArea` that other extensions of `Figure`, such as `Parabola`, do not possess. The extended syntax is given in Listing E.3.

Listing E.3

```
type
        Circle = record (Figure + ClosedFig)
                            x, y, radius : REAL;
                    end;
```

Of course, it is insufficient to simply introduce new syntactic mechanisms unless the compiler enforces the semantics that come as part of the package. In this case, the compiler allows programs to contract to provide certain implementation features that are not normally part of Component Pascal programs. The compiler must enforce such contracts by, for example, rejecting the program in Listing E.3 if it does not define an acceptable getArea function bound to the Circle type.

Another necessity to facilitate use of the base class libraries is some way of invoking constructors with arguments. *Component Pascal* itself has only the "no-arg" constructors that are implicitly invoked by *Component Pascal's* new() function. In *Component Pascal* one typically first creates the object and *then* sets any fields, as required. However, this is impossible for some library classes, as certain fields of the object may be marked initonly and can be set only by the constructor. The solution in this case is for the program to access the constructor as though it were a value-returning object factory function. Of course, the compiler knows from the metadata that the call is actually to a constructor and is, therefore, able to generate correct code.

A final, and somewhat controversial, extension was to enhance the symbol table mechanisms of the language to allow access to name-overloaded methods from the libraries. This extension is controversial because *Component Pascal* does not allow method overloading, and it may be argued that programmers accessing overloaded methods from within a non-overloaded language may be more prone to making errors. On balance, it was decided that this language extension was less problematic than the alternative of defining tables of name translations.

All of these language extensions are optional. The compiler may be run so as to recognize the standard language, or it may be run so as to allow the *compatibility extensions* described here.

As well as being useful as a production compiler, the Component Pascal compiler is used as a vehicle for research on language implementation. There are ongoing projects that use the compiler for research in the implementation of generics (*parametric polymorphism*) and use the metadata facilities in unusual ways.

Performance

The quality of the code produced by the Component Pascal compiler is comparable to that from Microsoft's C# compiler. It even outperforms C# in one special case: At the time of writing, the *Component Pascal* compiler's implementation of multidimensional arrays outperforms the library-based multidimensional code used by C#. Unfortunately, future versions of C# will undoubtedly reverse the situation by inlining the library code.

In both cases, because of the great (and improving) technology of the just-in-time compilers, the final code quality is often very close to that of the best native-code compilers.

Notes

The wider issues of mapping particular programming language constructs to the *CLR* are dealt with in the book *Compiling for the .NET Common Language Runtime* by John Gough (Prentice-Hall, 2002). The figures in this appendix are reprinted, with permission, from that book.

As noted, *Gardens Point Component Pascal* is an open source compiler. Various distributions of the compiler, including all the source code, are available from `http://www.plasrc.qut.edu.au/ComponentPascal`.

The official definition of the Component Pascal language may be obtained from *Oberon Microsystems* at the URL `http://www.oberon.ch/resources`. This site also has some interesting discussion papers regarding the design of the language.

■ APPENDIX F ■

Hotdog: Compiling Scheme to Object-Oriented Virtual Machines

Pankaj Surana

T HE HOTDOG SCHEME compiler tests the feasibility of compiling an
advanced functional language to an object-oriented virtual machine
(VM); in particular, the compiler targets the .NET Common Language Runtime (CLR) and the Java Virtual Machine (JVM). As both are ported to more
platforms and increasing numbers of programmers write more libraries,
these VMs present an attractive alternative to compiling directly to the
hardware. However, the compiler must somehow cross the semantic gap
between functional and object-oriented languages. The Hotdog compiler
aims to translate Scheme to code approximating the output of an object-
oriented compiler, rather than exploiting the idiosyncrasies of a particular
VM implementation. The overall performance of Scheme programs compiled to these VMs tends to be better than that of a Scheme interpreter, but
falls short of optimizing Scheme native-code compilers.

Introduction to the Hotdog Scheme Compiler

There has been a booming interest among members of industry in object-oriented programming and virtual machine technology. Sun's introduction of the Java [3] programming language has gradually led programmers to write vast libraries for the Java Virtual Machine [5]. Other companies have built compatible Java Virtual Machines, porting them to more and more platforms. From supercomputers to embedded devices, Java appears to be everywhere. Not to be outdone, Microsoft has developed a competing language, C# [1], and virtual machine, .NET CLR [2], which will certainly draw lots of programmers and industry support. In the future, software development is sure to be dominated by these two languages and virtual machines.

With so much happening in industry, it would be prudent for other language communities to come along for the ride. The Hotdog compiler aims to compile the Scheme [4] programming language to both virtual machines. This would immediately make Scheme portable across a vast range of devices and operating systems. Furthermore, it would give Scheme programmers access to an enormous and still growing library of code. Finally, Scheme programs will share in the progressive performance improvements made by virtual machine technology. Both the Java Virtual Machine and the .NET Common Language Runtime offer convenient, though imperfect, platforms for the Scheme language.

Scheme, Briefly

Scheme offers a simple model for computation. It avoids the "feature creep" of other programming languages, leaving only a few constructs required for an advanced language. Even the syntax is stripped bare of superfluous characters, leaving only pairs of parentheses to demarcate an expression. Simplicity does not imply, however, that Scheme is any less powerful than more popular languages. On the contrary, because Scheme provides only the essential primitives required of an advanced language, programmers are free to combine these primitives in ever more powerful ways. Scheme is an extremely versatile language suitable for any programming task.

Scheme provides a suite of primitive value types. Boolean, character, and string types are no surprise. A symbol type is a name, similar to an interned string. A port type represents input and output devices. A vector type is a fixed-size heterogeneous array of values. Drawing from its LISP heritage, a pair type is a two-element vector. A procedure type represents code without a name, commonly referred to as a closure.

In Scheme, the number type is more complicated. To remain independent of hardware limitations, numbers are expected to support values of nearly unbounded size and precision. Scheme ignores implementation details such as fixed and floating-point numbers; instead, it is concerned with the exactness of a number—whether a number is written exactly or is an approximation of a number. These distinctions and conversions between numbers are handled automatically.

In the ascetic spirit of Scheme, a procedure named call-with-current-continuation, or call/cc, can be used to implement all known sequential control structures. A signature feature of Scheme, a continuation is often described as "the rest of the computation." For example, given the expression "(3 + 4) * 5," when computing "3 + 4" the continuation at that point is a function that takes the result of the addition and sends it to "x * 5." Because continuations are first class, one could replace that continuation with another, causing execution to suddenly jump to another point in the program. Continuations can be used to implement complex escape routines, threading systems, generators, and more. Because they are so novel and powerful, special compiler and runtime support are used to implement continuations.

Scheme is a latently typed language. Because type checking is performed dynamically at runtime, it is commonly referred to as a dynamically typed language. All values have a fixed type, but the types are not statically declared; instead, the types are checked at runtime. The program will compile and execute until it attempts to perform an illegal operation on some type—perhaps adding a character and number together. This offers greater power and flexibility, albeit without the extra safety of statically typed languages.

Object-Oriented Virtual Machines

The Java Virtual Machine and the .NET Common Language Runtime have enough in common that, for the purposes of this Scheme compiler, they can be described together. Both are designed to support the efficient execution of a statically typed, object-oriented, byte-code language. Although Java and C# are the preferred programming languages for both runtimes, they are really compiled to a high-level, stack-based, byte-code language. For the most part, both byte-code languages are similar enough that little extra work was needed to support both VMs as back ends for the Hotdog Scheme compiler.

Both VMs execute the byte-code instructions at runtime. The byte code is first verified to confirm that it complies with the type and safety protocols of the virtual machine. Although some VMs interpret the instructions, the fastest VMs dynamically compile the instructions into native machine code with a just-in-time (JIT) compiler. All virtual machines support garbage collection, but it is tuned for the allocation patterns of typical object-oriented programs. Finally, the type system, instruction set, and runtime system offer explicit support for object-oriented programs: classes with methods and fields, virtual method dispatch on a single receiver object, single inheritance, reflection, and so on. Although these features are crucial to supporting Java and C#, they complicate the compilation of fundamentally different languages.

For many languages, including Scheme, a significant difference between the CLR and JVM runtimes is the JVM's failure to support proper tail recursion. Briefly, tail recursion is when the last instruction in a routine is a method call. Because the stack frame of the calling routine is no longer required—after all, it will simply return the value it receives—it should be removed. Functional languages often express loops as recursive function calls, which allow for more powerful constructs than the primitive "do-while" statements in imperative languages. Without proper tail recursion, however, this style will consume all the provided stack space and raise an exception. Although tail calls can be faked on the JVM, this process exacts an enormous performance penalty.

Implementations

The principal rule for Hotdog's compilation strategy is "keep it simple." Rather than exploit the idiosyncratic behavior of a particular VM implementation, Hotdog attempts to generate code that mimics a Java or C# compiler. The JIT compilers, given only a few microseconds to compile a method, are designed to optimize patterns found in common Java and C# programs. An aggressive JIT compiler can inline method calls and field accesses, remove array bounds checks, and optimize method dispatch. As the VMs and JIT compilers will only strive to improve the performance of object-oriented programs, the performance of Hotdog Scheme will, along with that of Java and C#, be carried forward by every improvement in virtual machine technology. Attempts to fool the VM will sacrifice these gains.

Closures

The heavy use of closures in Scheme makes its implementation critically important. A closure is a data structure containing executable code and its associated environment. Unlike conventional languages, it is not necessarily attached to a name. Instead, it can be used like any other data type: passed as an argument, stored in a variable, or even deallocated when it is no longer needed. In fact, there are no named functions or methods, as are common in conventional languages such as C, Java, and C#. In Scheme, global names can be bound to closures, Boolean values, strings, or anything else. If the name is bound to a closure, then it can be applied like a function. This flexibility allows for particularly powerful programming techniques.

Although there is no structure analogous to a closure on either VM, there are a number of possible implementation strategies using the provided object-oriented features. Whereas some implementations attempt clever encodings, Hotdog opts to generate code that can be clearly understood by the JIT compiler. Ideally, the JIT compiler will be able to recognize and optimize Hotdog's simple object-oriented code patterns, producing faster code than is possible with a more aggressive implementation.

General Implementation

A closure is implemented as a subclass of a general `Closure` class, where one (or more) of the `apply` methods is overridden to supply the closure's body of code (see Listing F.1). The subclass also implements a class constructor method that takes the closure's environment and stores it within the class instance. Every instance of this class is a closure with a different environment.

Listing F.1 *The* `Closure` *class is the parent of all Scheme closures*

```
class Closure
{
  Closure (Environment e) {}
  object apply () { error() ;}
  object apply (object x1) { error() ;}
  object apply (object x1, object x2) { error () ;}
  object apply (object x1, object x2, object x3)
               { error() ;}
  object apply (object x1, object x2, object x3, object x4)
               { error (); }
  object apply (object x1, object x2, object x3, object x4,
               object x5) { error() ;}
  object apply (object x1, object x2, object x3, object x4,
               object x5, Pair rst) { error() ;}
}
```

The number of arguments supported by the closure class is arbitrary. The example `Closure` class in Listing F.1 shows only five arguments, followed by a `Pair` argument. If the number of arguments in a Scheme closure exceeds the hard limit set by the `Closure` class, then Hotdog packages the remaining arguments into a list and passes that list as the final argument. The preamble to the Scheme closure will unpack the list and assign the remaining arguments to local variables before execution of the body begins. It is likely that adding more arguments will improve performance and allow for further optimizations, but the compiler must be able to handle any number of arguments.

The `Closure` class implements every `apply` method with an error function. If a Scheme closure is applied with the wrong number of arguments, it will not have implemented that `apply` method; therefore, the runtime environment will call the `apply` method on the `Closure` class, which will report the error. This is usually an unrecoverable error in a Scheme program, and execution will fail.

Environments

When a Scheme closure is allocated, an environment is given to the class constructor. The environment is implemented as an array of objects. As modern VMs can optimize array range checks, array accesses can be quite cheap. However, because all environment values are coerced to the `Object` type, every use must be preceded by a type coercion. Also, because small values must be boxed, they must be unboxed again before use. As Scheme is latently typed, these costs are usually mitigated by special optimizations and runtime tricks in Scheme virtual machines. Unfortunately, neither object-oriented VM offers any way to reduce this overhead.

Variable Argument Lists

Scheme supports variable argument lists, which, like C's `printf` function, allow an arbitrary number of arguments to the closure (see Listings F.2 and F.3). Hotdog generates a single private method named `exec`, with the same number of fixed arguments, plus an extra argument to accept the variable arguments as a list. Then, every `apply` method with at least the number of required arguments is implemented, each one packaging the extra arguments into a list and sending them to the `exec` method. Because the caller does not know the signature of the closure it is calling, it can assume the closure will do the right thing with the arguments it sends.

Listing F.2 *A closure that accepts three or more arguments*

```
(lambda (x y z . rst) body ...)
```

Listing F.3 *Implementation of a closure with three or more arguments*

```
class lambda1 : Closure
{
  lambda1 (Environment e) {}
  object apply (object x1, object x2, object x3) { ... }
  object apply (object x1, object x2, object x3, object x4)
            { ... }
```

continues

```
object apply (object x1, object x2, object x3, object x4,
              object x5) { ... }
object apply (object x1, object x2, object x3, object x4,
              object x5, Pair rst) { ... }
object exec  (object x1, object x2, object x3, Pair x4)
              { body ... }
}
```

For many Scheme procedures, this implementation of variable argument lists can be quite costly, as it allocates a list for every call. For example, the arithmetic procedures accept zero or more arguments, which means simply adding two numbers will involve boxing the numbers and calling the "+" procedure. The "+" closure's `apply` method, which takes two arguments, will then pack both numbers into a list and call the `exec` method. This method will unpack the list, check the types of both numbers, unbox both, and, finally, add them. As several important Scheme procedures use variable argument lists, this technique can seriously degrade the overall performance of a Scheme program.

Case-Lambda Special Form

To provide better support for variable argument lists, Hotdog adds compiler support for a "case-lambda" special form (see Listing F.4). It allows one to define a closure with multiple entry points. In terms of classes, it allows one to write code for each `apply` method. The VM will quickly dispatch to the correct `apply` method, where user-written code can handle the arguments immediately. If the case-lambda form uses a variable argument list, then the compilation strategy described earlier applies.

Listing F.4 *Use of case-lambda form*

```
(define +
  (case-lambda
    (() 0)
    ((x) x)
    ((x y) (%primitive-add x y))
    ((x y . rst)
      (let ((sum (%primitive-add x y)))
    (if (null? rst)
      sum
      (+ sum (car rst) (cdr rst)))))))))
```

Compiling the case-lambda form in the presence of the `Closure` class, which has a fixed number of `apply` methods, requires special care. If an arm of the case-lambda uses more fixed arguments than the `Closure` class can provide, then extra dispatching code is generated in the final `apply` method. For example, if a case-lambda has one arm that takes eight arguments and another arm that takes nine arguments, both will end up calling the last `apply` method, which takes only five arguments and a list containing the remaining arguments. The compiler must generate code in this `apply` method that unpacks the list, checks the total number of arguments provided, and executes the correct arm of the case-lambda. Therefore, the last `apply` method will contain code for all case-lambda arms with more than five arguments. This situation is further complicated by an arm of a case-lambda that accepts more than five fixed arguments and a variable argument list, but the compilation strategy is an obvious extension of that discussed earlier.

Small Values

Because Scheme is latently typed, every value must be passed in a uniform way. This means, for example, that the parameters to a method must be able to accept all Scheme types. To do so, most Scheme systems pass around a pointer to a heap-allocated value. In many respects, this approach is similar to the general collection classes in Java and C#, which take items of type `object`. To make a collection of integers, all the integers must be boxed and coerced to the object type before they can be inserted into the collection. When an object is extracted from the collection, the type must be coerced before it can be used. This process results in a significant performance hit.

Scheme runtime systems generally solve this performance problem by encoding small values directly in the pointer. Because pointers are word aligned, a valid pointer will have the low bits set to 00. A Scheme runtime system will use those low bits to tag small values. For example, if the low bit is set to 1, then the remaining 31 bits contain an integer. The integer does not need to be heap allocated, type checking is a simple bit check operation, and arithmetic can be done directly on the encoded value. Similarly, Boolean values and characters can be encoded, with additional tags, directly in the pointer. The runtime and garbage collector know to check a pointer before following it into oblivion.

Unfortunately, the object-oriented VMs do not allow one to tinker with the object pointers. Each pointer is sacrosanct, because the garbage collector, runtime, and byte-code verifier require it to be valid. As a result, all small values must be boxed before passing them around. This incurs a significant overhead, as illustrated by the general collection classes. In fact, a simple numeric program written in Java or C# with boxed integers will demonstrate a performance gap compared to an unboxed version of the same program. This is a critical performance problem for latently typed languages on an object-oriented VM.

This performance gap can be reduced somewhat by preallocating a range of small values. At initialization time, the Hotdog Scheme runtime system will box all ASCII characters, the integers from 1 to 1000, and the Boolean values true and false. At runtime, a special routine is used to box a small value. This routine first checks whether a preallocated value is available and, if so, returns it. If no preallocated value is available, it boxes the integer as it normally would. Avoiding allocation for the most commonly used numbers and characters improves performance noticeably. These values must still be unboxed to be used, which invokes a type check on the object before extracting the value. Therefore, there is still a performance penalty paid for numbers on the object-oriented VMs.

Dynamic Type Checking

As a latently typed language, Scheme remains unconcerned about the types of values being used until the program explicitly attempts to interact with a value. For example, the only time Scheme cares that a value really is a number is when one tries to add two numbers together. Of course, the programmer is often concerned about the types in a program; therefore, a program may explicitly check the type of a value during execution using type predicates. Therefore, all the types will be handled in the same way until a definite action on the type takes place.

To layer this notion of types atop the object-oriented VMs, all objects must be handled as object types. This technique, called type erasure [6], replaces all type declarations with the object type. Whenever a type-specific operation is performed, such as reading from an input port, the object must first be cast to the correct type before the operation begins. If the coercion fails, it is a runtime error. The return value for a successful operation must also be coerced to the object type.

Although this implementation meets the needs of a latently typed language, it does not match the behavior of statically typed object-oriented languages. Consequently, most object-oriented VMs do not attempt to optimize dynamic type checking. In addition, where Scheme is concerned with the immediate type of an object, object-oriented languages are interested in the type hierarchy. That is, Scheme wants to know whether an object is a closure, whereas the object-oriented languages want to know whether an object is, or is a child of, a closure. Although this is fine if the object really is a closure, if it is not then the VM checks the object against each parent type, all the way back to the root type. Checking whether an object is a child of a type implies additional work that is completely unnecessary for Scheme. Because dynamic type checking occurs continuously in a Scheme program, any overhead is too much overhead.

Limitations

There are a few problems with implementing Scheme on an object-oriented VM. First and foremost, it is difficult to implement first-class continuations. The Hotdog Scheme compiler does not implement call/cc, because it tries to generate code that the VMs will recognize. One could generate Scheme code that maintained a separate stack in the heap, using the runtime stack for computation only. A Scheme program would simply tail-call from one continuation to the next. This is how many languages implement continuations, with specialized runtime systems to support a program stack in the heap. This would be impractical for Scheme on an object-oriented VM.

Scheme runtime systems, like those in many other languages, often have an interactive command line where expressions can be executed dynamically. Although this approach would be feasible on an object-oriented VM, it has some problems. Closures in Scheme are data types that are garbage collected like any other types when they are no longer referenced. On the VMs, however, closures are methods on classes. Once created, they stick around until the program ends. For lengthy sessions in an interpreter, memory would slowly be consumed by discarded closures.

The Hotdog Scheme compiler does not currently support an interactive environment.

Performance Improvements

The Hotdog Scheme compiler is relatively simple, but it still leaves room for many enhancements. The current implementation will generate a large number of classes, one for each closure in a Scheme program. This results in larger memory overhead, as each class takes up some space in the VTABLE. Because every closure is implemented as a virtual method on a subclass of the `Closure` class, the VM may not be able to inline code. Furthermore, the environments lose any type information that might be deduced at compile time. All these features can be improved somewhat by extending the base implementation.

Although Hotdog treats all closures as the same, many of them can be optimized away. A closure is used to treat a body of code as a first-class object, but that is not always needed. Whenever a closure is known not to be first-class, it can be implemented as a private instance method within the enclosing closure class, sharing the same environment. Then all calls to the closure can be direct calls to the private method. This will reduce the number of closure classes and environments, replace a virtual dispatch with a direct call, and expose that method call to the JIT compiler, which may be inclined to inline it directly in the caller.

While environments coerce all their values to objects, performance can be recovered to some degree. If the compiler can infer some of the types of the environment values, it can unpack the environment and unbox small values, storing them in private instance fields. This needs to be done only in the class constructor; therefore, the performance hit will be taken only when the closure is allocated, not on every execution.

Often within a closure, the same value is repeatedly type-checked before an operation is performed. Because type checks can be expensive, repeated checks on the same value can be reduced, checks can be lifted out of loops, or, when the byte-code verifier is turned off, many can be removed completely. The last technique produces much faster code, but a program still needs some type checks. These can be optimized on the CLR by comparing the type tokens, as extracted by reflection. This will avoid the penalty, described earlier, when a type check fails.

Alternatively, all Scheme objects can be wrapped in a special class. This class could serve as a union of Scheme primitive data types, with an integer tag to discriminate among the types. Unfortunately, this technique would create a substantial allocation overhead, as every object would require two allocations: one for the value and one for the Scheme wrapper class. It might be possible, however, to use this trick just for small values. It remains to be seen whether it would deliver better performance for small values.

Conclusions

The Hotdog Scheme compiler is capable of compiling a nearly complete subset of the Scheme programming language to both the Java Virtual Machine and the .NET Common Language Runtime. The compilation strategy strives for simplicity, generating code that somewhat resembles typical object-oriented programs. There is still room for improvement, but performance on various JVMs and beta versions of the CLR are similar— somewhere between native-code Scheme compilers and pure Scheme interpreters.

Even if the performance of Hotdog does not reach that of optimized, native-code compilers, there are still valid reasons to continue development of the compiler. First, programmers will have access to a large and growing library of code. Second, programs will be portable to a wide range of operating systems and devices. Third, programmers will have access to tools and development environments for the VMs. Finally, many applications are I/O bound, making the Scheme program less relevant to the overall performance of a program. As both the JVM and the CLR grow in popularity, advanced languages, including Scheme, may find these runtime environments a reasonable platform for their languages, and they may find a large audience willing to try them out.

References

[1]   ECMA TC39/TG2, "C# Programming Language."

[2]   ECMA TC39/TG3, "Common Language Infrastructure."

[3]   James Gosling, Bill Joy, and Guy Steele, *The Java Language Specification*, 2nd ed., Boston: Addison-Wesley, 2000.

[4]   Richard Kelsey, William Clinger, and Jonathan Rees (eds.), "Revised(5) Report on the Algorithmic Language Scheme."

[5]   T. Lindholm and F. Yellis, *The Java Virtual Machine*, Reading, MA: Addison-Wesley, 1996.

[6]   Martin Odersky and Philip Wadler, "Pizza into Java: Translating Theory into Practice," *ACM Symposium on Principles of Programming Languages*, January 1997, 132–145.

▛ APPENDIX G ▪

Functional Languages for the .NET Framework

Nigel Perry

HOSTING FUNCTIONAL LANGUAGES in object-oriented environments, such as the .NET Framework, so that they interoperate well with other languages presents a number of problems. In this appendix, we describe methods to address these problems and introduce Mondrian, a new functional language specifically designed for such environments. The appendix concentrates on the programmer's view of Mondrian's types, functions, and interlanguage calling mechanisms. We compare these to traditional functional languages and describe how they appear to other languages on .NET. Mondrian implementation issues are not dealt with in depth.

Although this appendix is not a tutorial on functional programming, it is intended to be accessible to nonfunctional programmers. In doing this, we aim to introduce to those readers who are unfamiliar with functional

Appendix G credit: Nigel Perry, Department of Computer Science, University of Canterbury, Christchurch, New Zealand, nigel@cosc.canterbury.ac.nz. This work was started while the author was on sabbatical at Utrecht University. Many thanks go to Erik Meijer, the original team leader, and Arjan van IJzendoorn team researcher at Utrecht. The work was supported with grants from the Dutch Government and Microsoft Corporation.

417

languages to some of the benefits of using the .NET Framework and CLR to write parts of their code in Mondrian.

The advantages of hosting functional languages on the .NET Framework are many. For existing functional-language programmers, they include access to large libraries and interlanguage working opportunities. Other-language programmers gain access to the expressive power of functional languages without needing to convert whole projects to the paradigm.

There are also benefits for language implementers; including "free" garbage collection and access to the .NET Framework to provide language support services. Interested readers are referred to [1].

Unfortunately, using the Common Language Runtime (CLR) raises problems for functional languages. The type systems of the two paradigms are quite different. The CLR provides a system based on subtyping (inheritance), overriding ("polymorphism"), and immediate ("strict," "applicative order") evaluation. Functional languages are typically based on parametric polymorphism and just-in-time ("nonstrict," "normal order") evaluation. These two are rather different, especially from a programmer's standpoint.

Mondrian has been designed to bridge this divide. In this appendix, we show how traditional functional language constructs map to those in Mondrian, using Haskell [2] as our reference, and how Mondrian constructs appear to other CLR-hosted languages. Mondrian itself is still in development, and its final syntax and semantics may change. We restrict ourselves primarily to types, functions, and interlanguage calling issues.

We do not argue the relative merits of functional and object-oriented languages—there is plenty already written on that subject—but rather work from the basis that both have their merits. We also do not consider multi-paradigm languages, such as O'CAML [3]; rather, we see the benefit of targeting the CLR as allowing multi-paradigm programming without the need to design multi-paradigm languages. Each may have its place, but we leave that for others.

A Brief Introduction to Mondrian

Mondrian [4, 5] is a new functional language specifically designed to fit well into object-oriented virtual machine environments, such as the .NET Framework. The semantics of the language will be familiar to functional-language programmers: It is a simple, nonstrict language. The I/O system is based on monads [6] and follows the design of Haskell [2]. A number of things are unusual, however, including the type system, exception handling, concurrency support, and syntax.

The Type System

The type system is based on those used by object-oriented languages, with the addition of parametric polymorphism. This type system makes Mondrian rather different from traditional functional languages. While it retains the expressive power, it is more easily accessible through interlanguage calling to other languages executing under the .NET Framework. Discussion of the type system from the programmer's perspective forms the major part of this appendix.

Some of the ideas in Mondrian can be seen in earlier language designs such as Pizza [7] and GJ [8] for Java, and Generic C# [9] for the .NET Framework. These language designs all extend an underlying object-oriented language by introducing concepts more common in functional languages. Mondrian takes an different approach—it is a functional design adapted for an object-oriented environment.

Exception Handling

Exceptions are an integral part of the CLR and are the standard method through which routines in the .NET Framework report and handle errors. Mondrian provides proper support for such exceptions. Constructs are provided both to generate and to handle exceptions: Exceptions produced by other CLR-hosted language code called from Mondrian can be caught, and other languages calling Mondrian can catch its exceptions.

Mondrian is not the first example of a functional language with exception handling. For example, exception handling has been added to Haskell [10]. Nevertheless, Mondrian is unusual in its complete integration with an exception system provided by an object-oriented virtual machine environment.

Concurrency Support

Threads and synchronization primitives are also an integral part of the CLR and .NET Framework. Following on from our previous work, such as

Concurrent Hope+C [11], Mondrian provides full support for CLR threads and synchronization primitives. In a multithreaded program, the individual threads can be written in any CLR-hosted language, including Mondrian, and synchronize with, and pass data between, one another.

The Syntax

The syntax of Mondrian is unusual in that it looks more like C# and less like traditional functional languages. This design was chosen to make the language more accessible to object-oriented programmers keen to exploit the expressive power of functional languages through interlanguage calling from imperative object-oriented code.

Mondrian is also a minimalist language,[1] rarely providing two ways of doing something, and often providing simpler expression forms than current functional languages offer. For example, although Mondrian supports pattern matching, a cornerstone of most functional languages, only a single level of data can be matched at a time.

To give an idea of how Mondrian looks, Listing G.1 is a simple function that calculates the roots of the quadratic equation $ax^2 + bx + c = 0$.

Listing G.1

```
class Pair { r1 : Double; r2 : Double; }

roots : Double -> Double -> Double -> Pair;
roots = a -> b -> c
   let
       d    = b * b - 4 * a * c;
       root = sqrt d;
       a2   = 2 * a;
   in if d < 0
       then
           Pair(-1, -1)
       else
           Pair( (-b + root)/a2, (-b - root)/a2 );
```

---

[1] The language is named after the Dutch abstract painter Pieter Cornelis Mondrian (1872–1944). In his later work, Mondrian limited himself to small vertical and horizontal strokes.

Types in Mondrian

The Mondrian design tackles the mismatch between traditional functional language type systems and that of the CLR by identifying ways of mapping the former onto the later. A syntax has been defined that looks familiar to the object-oriented CLR programmer, so that task of interlanguage working is simplified.

In the following discussions, we visualize CLR code fragments by using C#. Although using CLR Intermediate Language (IL) would be more language-neutral, C# is far easier to read yet still follows the CLR model closely.

Primitive Types

Primitive types appear in all languages in much the same way, and Mondrian is no different. Unusually for a functional language, Mondrian directly supports strings through the CLR primitive `System.String` type. However, the more typical "list of characters" model for strings is, of course, provided in Mondrian and standard functions to convert between the two models are provided.

The CLR provides both value ("unboxed") and reference ("boxed") versions of primitive types. To easily support parametric polymorphism, functional language implementations often restrict themselves to reference versions of primitive types, and this is the approach we have taken with Mondrian. Other CLR-hosted languages' code must therefore box values of primitive types when calling Mondrian code. Doing this is usually easy; indeed, the C# language handles it automatically so programmers never need be concerned with it.

Type Products

The product, or tuple, type is widely used in functional languages. For example, a type for a coordinate might be expressed in Haskell as

```
type Coord = (Float, Float)
```

or alternatively by a record declaration such as

```
data Coord = Cd { x, y :: Float }
```

An equivalent of both of these in the CLR type system is a *field-only* class:

```
class Coord { Float x; Float y; }
```

The mapping is straightforward and could be used by functional languages running on the CLR. However, to reduce the apparent gap between Mondrian and other languages running on the CLR, we chose to use the *class* construct directly.

The use of the class construct also simplifies accessing objects that have been created by other CLR-hosted languages. Any CLR object can be viewed as a product and its fields accessed, just as with Mondrian-created products. However, to access the methods of a CLR object from a functional language requires a different mechanism; this need is addressed later in the discussion of interlanguage calling.

Field-only classes are not commonly used by object-oriented programmers. Usually, at least a constructor method is defined, and often access methods, to separate the interface and implementation. Rather than direct field access, it is expected that Mondrian programs will provide access functions and these will be used by other languages. Access methods are, of course, good object-oriented programming style, so defining and using them is not an issue. They have additional benefits when integrating functional and nonfunctional languages on the CLR, as explained later.

Type Unions

Tagged unions are central to functional languages. They provide for both simple enumeration types and more complex variant and recursive types. The key role of tagged unions is reflected in the provision of *pattern matching* to provide simple and concise access to their components. For example, in Haskell a list of integers can be expressed as follows:

```
data IntList = Nil | Cons Integer IntList
```

A Haskell function to determine the length of an IntList might be defined as

```
length Nil = 0
length Cons h t = 1 + length t
```

or equivalently as

```
length l = case l of
            {  Nil       -> 0;
               Cons h t -> 1 + length t
            }
```

Union types are not provided by the CLR type system; rather, subtyping through a class inheritance mechanism is provided. A rough equivalent of the union type can be modeled in the class/subclass model by defining an abstract class to represent the type, together with one subclass for each of the variants. For example, `IntList` could be modeled in C# as follows:

```
abstract class IntList {};
class Nil extends IntList {};
class Cons extends IntList
{    head: Integer;
     tail: IntList;
};
```

These two models are *not* equivalent: The union type provides only a single level of variants and the number of variants is fixed. In the subtyping model, it is possible both to subclass the variants, creating a multilevel tree of variants, and to extend the number of variants. The consequence is that not all type hierarchies of CLR classes can be viewed as tagged unions by functional languages such as Haskell.

The Mondrian design addresses this lack of equivalence by using the class/subclass formulation directly. It produces a more flexible type system than traditional functional languages while also increasing the compatibility with other CLR-hosted languages.

Mondrian, following its minimalist approach, also provides pattern matching through its `switch` expression. Only one level of matching is supported—for example, patterns such as "`Cons h1 (Cons h2 t)`", which would be valid in Haskell, are not supported. The `length` function given earlier might be written in Mondrian as follows:

```
length = l -> switch(l)
                {  case Nil           : 0;
```

continues

```
                  case Cons{t = tail;}: 1 + length t;
       }
```

Parametric Types

In a functional language, our list example would usually be defined using a *parametric* type that can represent lists of any type. For example:

```
data List a = Nil | Cons a (List a)
```

In Haskell this type represents an *homogenous* list—that is, all members of the list will be of the *same* type. Uses of parametric types are checked at compile time.

The CLR does not support parametric types, an issue noted by others in the context of nonfunctional languages [9]. A standard object-oriented approach to providing something similar to parametric types is based on the existence of a unique supertype, called Object in both Java and C#, for all classes. Using this supertype, *heterogeneous* generic types may be defined. For example, a list could be defined as follows:

```
class ListNode
{   Object head;
    ListNode tail;
};
```

Parametric types are very important in the functional programming model, being a key constituent of the higher-order programming that gives the paradigm much of its expressive power. Given this importance, parametric types are directly supported by Mondrian. However, the syntax adopted is a more object-oriented style:

```
abstract class List<a> {};
class Nil<a> extends List<a> {};
class Cons<a> extends List<a>
{   head : a;
    tail : List<a>;
};
```

Types such as these can be statically checked, using the same methods as found in traditional functional languages. This means, for example, that a `List` value is guaranteed to be homogenous and type casts are never needed; indeed, Mondrian does not provide type casts at all. However, when viewed from another CLR-hosted language, the type parameters will not exist, and the `Object` type will appear instead:

```
abstract class List {};
class Nil extends List {};
class Cons extends List
{   head: Object;
    tail: List;
};
```

To other CLR languages, values of this `List` type are not guaranteed to be homogenous, and uses of `head` may need to be cast to the appropriate type:

```
Integer anInt;
Cons node;
node.head = anInt; // OK
anInt = (Integer)node.head; // cast required
```

This is the standard object-oriented programming style when dealing with heterogeneous types. Thus, the Mondrian design succeeds in presenting an appropriate model to both the functional and the nonfunctional programmer.

■ NOTE

Implementation-oriented readers will notice that there is a hidden cost in supporting Mondrian's parametric types on the CLR. In a traditional functional language, implementation parametric types are checked at compile time. In our CLR implementation, uses of parametric types are checked at runtime. This is not a drawback of Mondrian per se, as this cost is paid by all CLR-hosted languages when generic structures are created. Should direct support for generics be added to the CLR (as proposed, for example, by [9]), then this would benefit Mondrian along with other CLR-hosted languages. For more details on Mondrian implementation issues, see [1].

Functions in Mondrian

In object-oriented languages, functions are members of classes, whereas functional languages normally follow the traditional module and function model. This difference has a fundamental effect on the styles of programming in the two paradigms.

For example, in a functional language, as in many non–object-oriented imperative languages, a sorting function typically takes a comparison function as an argument. In Haskell, the declaration of such a function might be

```
Sort :: (Integer -> Integer -> Boolean) -> IntList
          -> IntList
```

In the object-oriented model, the replacement for a function value is usually an object with a well-known method. This approach is refined in some languages by specifying an interface, rather than a class, type for the comparison argument. In this style, the sorting example in C# becomes

```
interface CompareOperation
{  Boolean Compare(Integer a, Integer b);
}
static IntList Sort(CompareOperation op, IntList l);
```

The need to create special classes, or implement interfaces, to produce function "values" obfuscates the code. As for parametric types, function values are key to the expressive power of functional languages, and such obfuscation is not acceptable. Mondrian, therefore, requires an approach that supports function values clearly, while also supporting easy interworking with other CLR-hosted languages.

Monomorphic Functions

As suggested by the sorting example given earlier, a function in a functional language could be compiled into an class with a well-known method. A function "value" would then become an object reference that can be treated like any other reference type. This includes passing functions as arguments, returning them as function results, and storing them in data structures.

From the functional language perspective, the programmer sees the usual functional model and the expressive power of the languages is not obscured. Other CLR-hosted language programmers see a CLR object with a standard method name. For example, the Mondrian function

```
length :: IntList -> Integer
```

could be compiled to

```
class length
{ Integer Eval(IntList l) { … }
   …
}
```

This approach presents an appropriate model to CLR-hosted language programmers if the Mondrian function being called is indeed a function *value* returned by some computation. For example, in C#:

```
length lenFun;
int len;
IntList aList;
lenFun = <some object>.<some method>(…);
len = lenFun.Eval(aList);
```

However, for statically defined Mondrian functions, the code wouldn't be as clear:

```
int len;
IntList aList;
len = (new length()).Eval(aList);
```

For this reason, our approach in Mondrian is to provide two well-known methods; an *instance* method for use when calling a dynamic function value, and a *class* method for use when calling a statically defined function:[2]

---

2 Some readers might be concerned over the efficiency of this technique. The static method does not simply encapsulate an object creation and instance method application. A Mondrian function is a method-only class and, as such, has no state. This means that only one instance is ever required; the Mondrian compiler takes advantage of this fact and allocates a single (hidden) instance. The Apply method simply calls the Eval method on this compiler-allocated instance.

```
class length
{  Integer Eval(IntList l) { … }
   static Integer Apply(IntList l) { … }
   …
}
```

> ■ **NOTE**
> The CLR directly supports viewing object/method pairs as function values with its *delegates*. It may be thought that for other CLR-hosted languages using delegates would provide them with a simpler model for accessing Mondrian functions. Unfortunately, however, delegates appear to be close to, but are not quite at, what is required to support the general function values required by functional languages, which include those described in the following sections. Therefore, we do not intend to exploit them in Mondrian at present.

Polymorphic Functions

Polymorphic functions are provided by using a combination of the strategies for parametric types and monomorphic functions detailed earlier. This means that static type information is lost, just as for parametric types, and therefore runtime checks may be needed. For example, the Mondrian function declared as

```
length : forall a . List<a> -> Integer;
```

is compiled to

```
class length
{  Integer Eval(List l) { … }
   static Integer Apply(List l) { … }
   …
}
```

> **⁙ NOTE**
>
> Runtime checks are not *always* required. The length of a list is independent of the type of items in the list, so in the example function the loss of static type information on the kind of the list does not result in any redundant runtime checks.

Partial Applications

Many functional languages allow a function to be partially applied (or *curried*); that is, a function may be applied to fewer arguments than it requires, and the result of such an application is itself a function, which expects the remaining arguments. This is another feature that adds to the unique expressive power of functional languages and needs to be provided cleanly by Mondrian. Indeed, because a partially applied function is just a function value, functional programmers never need to know when applying a given function whether it is the result of an earlier partial application. The ideal for a CLR-hosted functional language design is to allow other CLR-hosted language programmers to use partially applied functions just like standard ones, so they too need not be concerned over the difference.

To explain how Mondrian achieves this goal, we need to delve a little deeper beyond the programmer's view and look at the implementation. A typical implementation of partial applications on a standard machine uses *closures* or *thunks*. A closure is simply a structure containing the values of the already-supplied arguments ("the environment") and a reference to the original function. When a closure is applied, the compiler emits code that merges the arguments from the call site with those from the environment, and then calls the functions.

An obvious parallel to a closure in an object-oriented environment is an object with instance variables to store the environment. The code usually emitted by the compiler to apply the closure can be placed into a method of this same object. The technique is easiest explained by an example. The Mondrian code fragment

```
times : Float -> Float -> Float;
...
addTax = times 1.125;
withTax = addTax 54;
```

can be compiled into the following pseudocode:[3]

```
class partialTimes
{  Float a1;

   partialTimes(Float a1) { this.a1 = a1; }

   Float Eval(Float a2) { return times.Eval(a1, a2); }
}
...
addTax = new partialTimes(1.125);
withTax = addTax.Eval(54);
```

This is the model we have adopted for Mondrian. The nonfunctional CLR-hosted language interface to a partial application, addTax in the preceding example, is identical to other function values produced by Mondrian code, so our goal is achieved.

The ability to create a partially applied method is not a standard object-oriented language feature. If an object-oriented programmer wishes to achieve the same effect, he or she must create a utility class, just like the partialTimes class produced automatically by the Mondrian compiler in the preceding example. Other CLR-hosted language programmers can utilize this technique to create partially applied Mondrian functions if they so choose. However, in typical use, we would expect only Mondrian code to actually produce partial applications.

Just-in-Time Evaluation

Just-in-time (JIT) evaluation, usually termed *nonstrict evaluation* by the functional language community,[4] involves delaying the evaluation of an

---

3   We have simply omitted some implementation "noise" to make the approach clear.

4   The buzz-speak "just-in-time evaluation" is credited to Erik Meijer. We use it here as the term "JIT" is well understood in the object-oriented community whereas "nonstrict evaluation" is not.

expression until its value is actually required. JIT evaluation is another key attribute that contributes to the expressive power of functional languages, and as such it is supported by Mondrian.

For functional programmers, JIT evaluation is transparent, in the sense that they never need be concerned whether a given value is actually a "real" value or whether it is a "JIT expression" that will be automatically evaluated if the value is needed.

A trivial example (a more realistic one is included later in this appendix) to demonstrate the impact of JIT evaluation is the definition of a function to implement the same functionality as the following C# expression:

```
ans = (x != 0) ? y/x : 0;
```

This expression avoids a divide-by-zero exception if x has the value 0. However, if we define a C# method to replace the conditional expression,

```
Integer fif(Boolean pred, Integer thenVal, Integer elseVal)
{   return pred ? thenVal : elseVal;
}
ans = fif(x != 0, y/x, 0);
```

then a divide-by-zero exception is thrown if x has the value 0, as the division is always performed *before* the call to fif. However, if this same code is expressed in Mondrian,

```
fif :: Boolean -> Integer -> Integer -> Integer;
fif = pred -> thenVal -> elseVal ->
          if pred then thenVal else elseVal;
… ans = fif (x != 0) (y/x) 0 …
```

then no exception is thrown. Instead, the function argument (y/x) is evaluated just in time, which in this example is *never* if x has the value 0.

The Implementation of JIT Evaluation

If the following information appears confusing (JIT evaluation is easier to implement than to describe, and this appendix isn't really about implementation), just skip to the next section.

To understand how other CLR-hosted languages can handle JIT values produced by functional languages, such as Mondrian, we need to again peek below the normal programmer's view and look at the implementation. JIT evaluation is not new; indeed, it was provided by Algol 60 under the title *call-by-name*, and its implementation strategy has not changed: Use a *closure*. Recall that closures were used to represent partial applications earlier in this appendix. An expression can be viewed as a *function* whose arguments are the values of the variables in the expression. A JIT expression can then be viewed as a function call that hasn't been made yet or, alternatively, as a *"partial" application* where all the arguments have in fact been supplied, but the actual call has not been made. To obtain the value of a JIT expression, the "partial" application is evaluated.

Accessing JIT Values from Other CLR-Hosted Languages

The provision of JIT evaluation, as described above, raises an apparent problem for other CLR-hosted languages. What *exactly* is the value of a field of an object created by a functional language? Returning to our coordinate example,

```
class Coord { Float x; Float y; }
```

what is the value of x? It could be a `Float` value, or it could be a reference to a JIT function object that will return a `Float` value when its `Eval` method is called. Accessing such a field is going to be rather involved and will require both testing and casts; the type of the field cannot even be `Float`.

Fortunately, good object-oriented programming style comes to the rescue. It is bad practice to allow direct access to instance variables of classes; rather, access methods should be used as mentioned in the section "Type Products." As access methods are written in Mondrian, the Mondrian compiler handles automatically any JIT values that are present. When a programmer using another CLR-hosted language calls a Mondrian access function, a real value will be returned.[5]

---

[5] For functional programmers, the return value is technically a reference to a value in WHNF, which for primitive types is the same thing. For structured types (objects), further access functions will need to be called to access their fields, so JIT values will again be handled automatically.

However, should a programmer using another CLR-hosted language attempt to bypass the access methods and refer to the fields directly (which may be public so other Mondrian modules can access them), then the programmer may not get the expected result...

Calling Other CLR-Hosted Languages

The discussion so far has centered on how various functional-language features can be adapted in such a way that data and functions can be easily accessed from other CLR-hosted languages. This is only one half of the picture—functional-language programmers also need to be able to access code written in other languages.

The fundamental issue in this case is independent of the CLR and the .NET Framework. Functional languages are "stateless" (no updateable variables), while object-oriented languages are fundamentally about state—the prototypical "object" encapsulates some state (its instance variables) and provides access to it via its methods.

Fortunately, this issue has been well researched, as it is essentially the same issue as supporting I/O, and a language with no I/O would be useless! A number of successful I/O techniques have been developed over the years, including continuations [12] and monads [6], the latter having now been adopted as standard in Haskell. To a functional language, calling a method in an object-oriented language is just the same as performing an I/O operation [13].

Following Haskell, Mondrian uses monadic I/O. The standard "Hello" program may be written as follows:

```
main : IO Void;
main =
{  PutStr("Please enter you name: ");
   name <- GetStr();
   PutStr("Hello there " + name);
}
```

To support calling other languages CLR-hosted languages, which must by the nature of the CLR provide an object-oriented interface, we introduce two constructs in Mondrian:

- create, which takes the specification of a class constructor and produces a monadic version of it,
- invoke, which performs the same operation for methods

We explain these constructs by using examples. The simple program in Listing G.2 executes on the CLR and produces a single random number by calling the .NET Framework's System.Random.

Listing G.2

```
// define a monadic constructor for System.Random
dotnetRand : IO<System.Random>;
dotnetRand = create System.Random();
// define a monadic interface to the Random.Next method
nextRand : Integer -> System.Random -> IO<Integer>;
nextRand = invoke System.Random.Next(Int32)
main =
{  gen <- dotNetRand;
   num <- nextRand 10 gen;
   putStrLn ("Random 1..10: " + show num);
}
```

This approach fits seamlessly into the monadic system, giving functional-language programmers access to other languages using a model with which they are familiar.

The Power of .NET: A Multilanguage Example

We conclude this appendix by working through a complete, though small, example of how the .NET Framework enables different languages to be combined to solve a problem.

Many programming courses cover the generation of prime numbers using an algorithm known as "the Sieve of Eratosthenes." Primes are useful in many applications, including hashing algorithms and cryptography, so being able to generate them easily is useful on a practical level.

The Sieve of Eratosthenes in C#

The method in Listing G.3[6] is an implementation of the Sieve of Eratosthenes in C#.

Listing G.3

```
static void PrintPrimes(int limit)
{   int[] sieve = new int[limit];
    // initialize array
    for(int i = 2; i < limit; i++) sieve[i] = i;
    // find primes
    for(int cursor = 2; cursor < limit; cursor++)
    {   if(sieve[cursor] != 0)
        {   System.Console.WriteLine( cursor );
            // "sieve" the array
            for(int j = cursor + 1; j < limit; j++)
                if(sieve[j]%cursor == 0)
                    sieve[j] = 0;
        }
    }
}
```

This method will generate and display all the primes up to a certain value—call it N. However, what if you need to generate N primes? To do so using the formulation in Listing G.3, you need to start with an array large enough to hold the Nth prime, and to determine that size you need to *know* the Nth prime, which you will not until the program has been run.

Constructing a C# program that can produce N primes, rather than all primes _N, is a lot more involved. It is possible, however, and concurrent programming and threads can help [14].

The Sieve: Combining Mondrian and C#

The problem with the formulation of Eratosthenes's algorithm in Listing G.3 is that an array is a fixed-size structure. What we really need is a dynamic structure that is *as large as needed*. Furthermore, we can't easily quantify how large in advance; this size is a dynamic function of the algorithm.

---

[6] We use the common idiom of using division to check for multiples. A "true" sieve uses index incrementing and involves no division, but the method shown here is more widely known.

This is one of the many areas where just-in-time evaluation provides benefits. In Mondrian, we can define the list of *all* the integers _N as follows:

```
from : Integer -> List<Integer>;
from = n -> n :: from (n + 1);
```

A call such as "from 2" returns all the integers _2. That is a very long list (2,147,483,647 items, followed by an overflow exception!). Attempt to write from in C#, and you will probably run out of memory rather quickly, and certainly before the call ever returns. However, Mondrian uses just-in-time evaluation, so from returns rather quickly. No items in the list are actually generated until you *need* them; once you've used an item and moved on, the CLR's garbage collection can reclaim the storage and reuse it for subsequent items. In short, you have an (almost) infinite list in a finite amount of space. The from function is so useful it is provided as standard in Mondrian.

Another useful function is filter:

```
filter :: forall a. (a -> Boolean) -> List<a> -> List<a>;
filter = pred -> elems ->
            switch(elems)
            {   case Nil:
                    Nil;
                case Cons{h = head; t = tail}:
                    if (pred h)
                    then h :: (filter pred t)
                    else filter pred t
            };
```

This function removes all elements from a list for which the function pred returns false. Again, due to just-in-time evaluation, this function does only as much work as is needed. The filter function is also provided as standard by Mondrian.

Using from and filter, we can implement the Sieve algorithm rather easily (see Listing G.4).

Listing G.4

```
// remove all multiples from a list
sieve : List -> List;
sieve = xs ->
   switch (xs)
   {  case (y::ys):
         y :: sieve (filter (notMultiple y) ys);
   };
notMultiple : Integer -> Integer -> Boolean;
notMultiple = x -> y -> not (y % x == 0);
// the "infinite" list of primes
primes : List Integer;
primes = sieve (from 2);
```

The code in Listing G.4 handles the generation of primes, but we also need to be able display them. C# is good for generating user interfaces, so we'll use it rather than Mondrian. The C# method in Listing G.5, `Print-Primes`, calls the Mondrian function `primes`, defined in Listing G.4, and the standard Mondrian list accessor functions, `hd` and `tl`, to display `count` primes starting from the `N`th one.

Listing G.5

```
void PrintPrimes(int N, int count)
{  // list of all the primes...
   Object longList = primes.Apply();
   // skip to first desired prime
   while(-N > 0)
   {  longList = tl.Apply(longList);
   }
   // display primes
   while(count- > 0)
   {  System.Console.WriteLine( hd.Apply(longList) );
      longList = hd.Apply(longList);
   }
}
```

A Glimpse into the Future: Improving the Interface

Although the preceding example is easy to follow, it lacks the "feel" with which object-oriented programmers are familiar. This stems from the mismatch between the object-oriented object/method view and the functional data/function model. An object-oriented prime generator would probably be written in "iterator" style—that is, as a class with one method to obtain the current prime and another method to advance to the next prime. The iterator style can be provided by wrapping the accesses to Mondrian functions within another class (see Listing G.6). `PrintPrimes` could then be written as shown in Listing G.7.

Listing G.6

```
class Primes
{  Object longList;
   public Primes()
   {  longList = primes.Apply();
   }
   public Integer Current()
   {  return (Integer)hd.Apply(longList);
   }
   public void Next()
   {  longList = tl.Apply(longList);
   }
}
```

Listing G.7

```
void PrintPrimes(int N, int count)
{  // allocate a prime generator
   Primes primeGen = new Primes();
   // skip to first desired prime
   while(—N > 0)
   {  primeGen.Next();
   }
   // display primes
   while(count— > 0)
   {  System.Console.WriteLine( primeGen.Current() );
      primeGen.Next();
   }
}
```

Future work will examine the automatic generation of wrapper classes such as these from code written in Mondrian.

Conclusions

We have described a method for supporting nonstrict functional languages on the .NET Framework, by introducing a language, Mondrian, that uses it. Although there is quite a gap between the functional and object-oriented computational models, the method is straightforward.

Calling functional code from object-oriented languages is not as seamless as the reverse process. Traditional functional languages have no concept of "object" and "method," and certainly no concept of the state that an object typically embodies. This means that without making significant additions to the functional languages, they are unable to present an object-oriented "view" of themselves to object-oriented clients.

For example, an object-oriented client would expect an abstract data type (ADT) to be represented by a class with instance methods for manipulating its values. However, under our strategy, which follows the functional data model, an ADT is represented by a *data-only* class and a *set* of method-only classes.

In our future work, we hope to explore the design space for extending functional languages to provide object-oriented–style access to functional code. However, at this stage, we have no plans to explore the integration of object-oriented and functional approaches into a single language. Rather, we plan to explore multilanguage, multi-paradigm programming on the .NET Framework as an alternative to designing multi-paradigm languages.

Our experimental language Mondrian is available for free download [4]. Also available is a demonstration version of the Glasgow Haskell Compiler modified to use Mondrian as a compilation route for executing on the .NET Framework.

References

[1] N. Perry and E. Meijer, "Implementing Functional Languages on Object-Oriented Virtual Machines," in preparation, see www.mondrian-script.org for further details, 2001.

[2] S. P. Jones, J. Hughes, et al., "Report on the Programming Language Haskell 98," http://www.haskell.org, Haskell Committee, 1999.

[3] D. Rémy and J. Vouillon, "Objective ML: An Effective Object-Oriented Extension to ML," *Theory and Practice of Objects Systems* vol. 4, 1988, pp. 27–50.

[4] "Mondrian," http://www.mondrian-script.org.

[5] E. Meijer, N. Perry, and A. v. IJzendoorn, "Scripting .NET Using Mondrian," *ECOOP*, 2001.

[6] P. Wadler, "Comprehending Monads," *Lisp and Functional Programming*, Nice, 1990.

[7] M. Odersky and P. Wadler, "Pizza into Java: Translating Theory into Practice," *24th ACM Symposium on Principles of Programming Languages*, Paris, 1997.

[8] G. Bracha, M. Odersky, et al., "Making the Future Safe for the Past: Adding Genericity to the Java Programming Language," *OOPSLA 98*, Vancouver, 1998.

[9] D. Syme and A. Kennedy, "Design and Implementation of Generics for the .NET Common Language Runtime," *PLDI 2001*, Snowbird, Utah, 2001.

[10] S. Marlow, S. P. Jones, and A. Moran, "Asynchronous Exceptions in Haskell," *4th International Workshop on High-Level Concurrent Languages*, Montreal, Canada, 2000.

[11] P. Burgess, N. Perry, and R. Pointon, "The Concurrent Massey Hope+C Functional Language System," Massey University, 1999.

[12] N. Perry, "Functional Language I/O," Imperial College, University of London, 1988.

[13] N. Perry, "I/O and Inter-language Calling for Functional Languages," *Proceedings of the IX International Conference of the Chilean Computer Society and XV Latin American Conference on Informatics*, Chile, 1989.

[14] J. N. Magee, "Primes Sieve of Eratosthenes," http://www-dse.doc.ic.ac.uk/concurrency/book_applets/Primes.html, Imperial College, 1998.

■ APPENDIX H ■

Active Oberon for .NET: A Case Study in Language Model Mapping

Jürg Gutknecht

A CTIVE OBERON IS a substantial evolution of the programming language Oberon. It distinguishes itself by a novel object model and by its integration into the .NET language interoperability framework.

The three concepts characterizing Active Oberon are: (1) *active object* types, (2) a single and unifying notion of abstraction called *definition*, and (3) a *static module* construct. These concepts are, in fact, powerful combinations of concepts: Active objects integrate active behavior with reactive message handling; definitions unify the units of usage, implementation, and inheritance; and modules represent both package and static object. The rigid concept of class hierarchy has been sacrificed in Active Oberon in favor of a more flexible concept of *aggregation* that is based on a generalized IMPLEMENTS relation. The relations IMPORTS and REFINES are used to specify static module dependencies and to derive new definitions from existing ones, respectively.

Appendix H credit: Jürg Gutknecht, ETH Zürich.

Active Oberon also features a *block statement* that is used to group sets of statements sharing certain processing attributes—in particular, the handling of exceptions. Finally, a USES *clause* allows the use of namespaces within a module without qualification.

This appendix is a report on a work in progress. We divide our presentation into three parts: (1) a short recall of the history of programming languages developed at the ETH, (2) a conceptual overview of Active Oberon's object model called the *Active Object System (AOS)*, and (3) a discussion of the mapping of the AOS into the *Common Type System (CTS)* exposed by .NET.

History of the ETH Programming Languages

Oberon [1] is the latest member of the Pascal family of compact programming languages. From its ancestors Pascal and Modula-2, it inherits a concise, highly expressive, and self-explanatory syntax, strictly enforced data types, and a module concept. In addition, Oberon features polymorphism based on record type extension. Active Oberon [2] is an evolution of Oberon combining the "spirit of Oberon" with the newest component technology. We aim at using Active Oberon in lectures on both small-scale and large-scale programming. Active Oberon for .NET is a first implementation of the new language.

The Active Object System

An Extended Concept of Object Types

Active Oberon for .NET propagates a "new computing model" [3] that is based on a dynamic population of communicating *active objects* or *agents*. The corresponding language construct is an upgraded variant of an object type declaration with an optional body for the specification of *intrinsic behavior*. By convention, the body of an *object type* is run automatically as a separate thread as a side effect of the creation of an instance.

Ordinary (passive) objects are considered as active objects with an empty intrinsic behavior. They often take the role of *shared resources*. Figure H.1 depicts the new computing model. It shows a collection of self-manag-

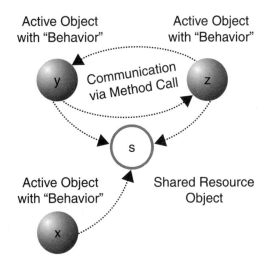

Figure H.1 *Sample scenario of communicating objects*

ing objects. Some objects (like x and y) are "active"; others (like the shared resource s) are "passive." It is worth noting that no driver processes are needed in our scenario to remote-control the evolution of objects. Participating objects communicate via method calls as usual.

The code fragment in Listing H.1 outlines a scenario of actors in a hypothetic multimedia production scripted in Active Oberon.

Listing H.1

```
TYPE

  Link = OBJECT
    VAR next: Link; x, y: INTEGER
  END Link;


  Figure = OBJECT
    VAR next: Figure; first: Link;


    PROCEDURE NEW (path: Link); (* constructor *)
    BEGIN first := path
    END NEW;
```

continues

```
        PROCEDURE Display (X, Y: INTEGER); (* method *)
          VAR cur: Link;
        BEGIN
          IF first # NIL THEN cur := first;
            WHILE cur.next # NIL DO
              DrawLine(X + cur.x, Y + cur.y, X + cur.next.x,
                       Y + cur.next.y);
            cur := cur.next
          END
        END
        END Display;


      END Figure;


    Movie = OBJECT
      VAR stopped: BOOLEAN; first, cur: Figure; X, Y: INTEGER;


        PROCEDURE NEW (orgx, orgy: INTEGER; video: Figure);
                    (* creator & initializer *)
        BEGIN X := orgx; Y := orgy; first := video
        END NEW;


        PROCEDURE Stop;
        BEGIN stopped := TRUE
        END Stop;


    BEGIN { ACTIVE } (* modifier *)
      stopped := FALSE; cur := first;
      WHILE ~stopped DO
        cur.Display(X, Y); cur := cur.next (*cyclic list*)
        X := (X + 1) MOD Scene.W; Y := (Y + 1) MOD Scene.H
      END
    END Movie;
```

Note first that no explicit pointers appear in the declarations. In Active Oberon, the keyword OBJECT is used to declare object types that are implicitly pointer-based. Further note that three kinds of objects participate in the Movie scenario: instances of type Link are pure "records" or "structures";

instances of type `Figure` are ordinary "passive" objects; and instances of type `Movie` are "active" objects.

Although the members of a typical active object scenario are largely autonomous, they are rarely truly independent of one another. As an immediate consequence, synchronization is required that necessarily manifests itself in temporary "passivation" of individual objects. On this low level of abstraction, the exhaustive enumeration of passivation conditions is surprisingly short:

- An unsatisfied precondition for continuation
- Competition for a shared resource object
- A lack of processors

From the perspective of the object concerned, the first two situations necessarily arise synchronously and are governed by Active Oberon language constructs, while the third situation may arise asynchronously and cause preemption. The language constructs governing the synchronous cases are as follows:

- `AWAIT c`
- `BEGIN { EXCLUSIVE } … END`

The `AWAIT` statement takes a scope-local Boolean condition `c` and blocks continuation while `c` is unasserted. The block statement in combination with the `EXCLUSIVE` modifier automatically guarantees mutual exclusion within the block.

Figure H.2 summarizes our explanations by showing the time evolution of the scenario depicted in Figure H.1. Note that the thread of activity of each participating object in this figure is represented by a distinguished direction. Also note that object y is passivated twice, for different reasons. Its first passivation occurs when it tries to access the shared resource s (which is blocked by object x at that time). Object y is passivated a second time while awaiting condition c, which is finally established by object z. In both cases, the scheduling is managed completely by the system. This is different from notification-oriented synchronization that fully relies on a fair behavior of the involved peer threads.

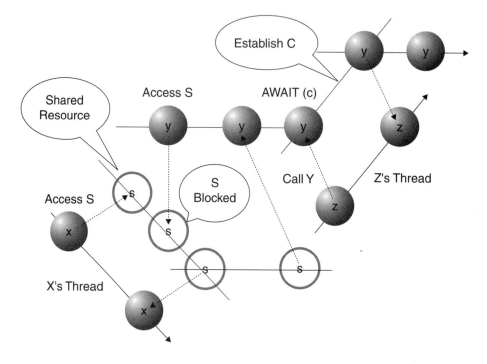

Figure H.2 *Evolution in time of an Active Object scenario*

A Unified Concept of Abstractions

Active Oberon introduces an abstract concept called *definition*. It roughly corresponds to an *abstract class* in C++, Java, and C# or, in other words, to an interface with optional state space and optional method implementations.

Note that, unlike the languages mentioned above, Active Oberon syntactically separates the notions corresponding to concrete and abstract classes because, in spite of their formal similarity, they are embodiments of radically different principles. Abstract classes (definitions) are descriptions of abstract concepts to be processed at compile time, while concrete classes (object types) are descriptions of objects to be instantiated at runtime.

Two relations apply to definitions:

- IMPLEMENTS
- REFINES

If an object type *implements* a definition, it commits itself to implement all previously unimplemented methods of this definition and to either accept, complement, or override existing implementations. Every definition implemented by an object type represents a *facet* or *role* of this type, and the entirety of implemented definitions constitutes the type's *API* (application programming interface).

Viewed from the client/server perspective taken in Figure H.3, definitions expose *units of service* to clients. For example, *D* is an abstraction of a service provided by object *s*, and *E* is an abstraction of a service provided by both objects *s* and *t*, with potentially different implementations. Object *x* is a client of *s*, making use of service units *D* and *E*. Objects *y* and *z* are clients of *s* and *t*, respectively, using the same service unit *E*, albeit with potentially different interpretations.

While definitions in Active Oberon appear as coherent facets or units of use to clients, their specification need not be self-contained but can be derived from a base definition by *refinement*. For example, Figure H.3 reveals that definition *D* is actually a refinement of base definition *D0*.

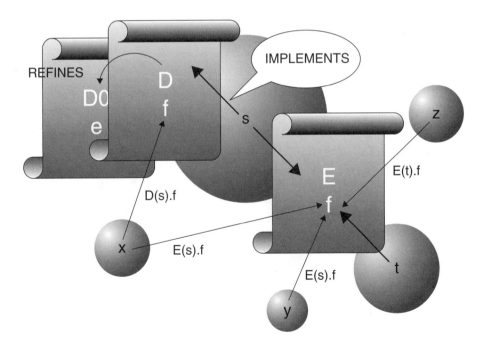

Figure H.3 *Client/server scenario in Active Oberon*

The full semantics of refinement are intricate and may well include topics such as weakening preconditions and strengthening postconditions in the future. For the moment, it suffices to think of refinement as adding variables, methods, and implementations to an existing definition.

Perhaps the most obvious advantage of our object model over traditional object-oriented systems is *symmetry*. Facets, roles, service units, and so on can uniformly be modeled as definitions in Active Oberon, ready for implementation in any combination by any concrete object type. In a traditional object-oriented language such as Java, two different ways exist for a concrete class to build on an abstraction A:

- Subclassing A and inheriting from it
- Implementing A, possibly by delegating standard work to some "helper class"

Of course, unless multiple inheritance is supported, the superclass option is applicable to at most one "main" abstraction per class.

While in some cases the distinction of a main abstraction is quite natural, it may be artificial in others. To give an example: Assume that some GUI framework supports two abstractions `Figure` and `Sensor` (mouse-sensitive area) and an object type `Control`. Then the question arises of whether a control is primarily a figure that in addition happens to be a mouse-sensitive area or primarily a sensitive area that happens to be represented as a figure. Both `Figure` and `Sensor` qualify equally well as the main abstraction and can equally well serve as the base class of the class `Control`. If `Figure` is chosen as the base class, then `Sensor` must be modeled as an interface to be implemented by `Control`, possibly assisted by some helper class `SensorImplementation`. If `Sensor` is chosen as the base class, then `Figure` must be modeled as an interface, possibly plus a helper class `FigureImplementation`. Figures H.4(a) and (b) illustrate the two asymmetric design patterns. Both are definitely inferior to the symmetric Active Oberon pattern depicted in Figure H.5, which consists of two definitions `Figure` and `Sensor` plus an object type `Control` that implements those definitions.

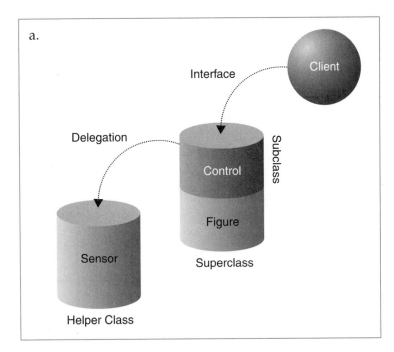

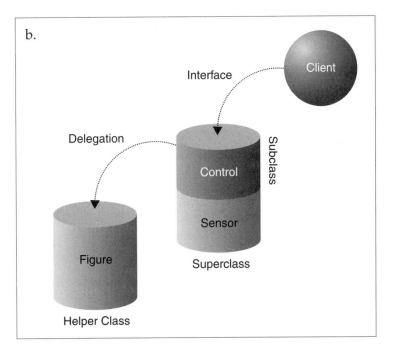

Figure H.4 *(a) Asymmetric design pattern number 1 for class* `Control`*;*
(b) Asymmetric design pattern number 2 for class `Control`

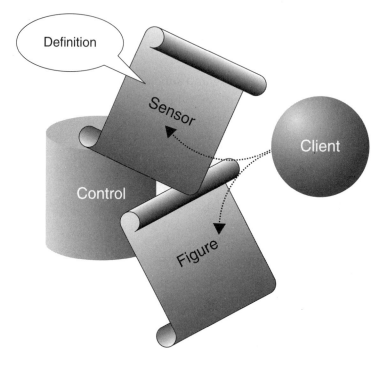

Figure H.5 *Symmetric design pattern for class* `Control`

The most negative aspect of enforced asymmetry is an inherent ambiguity and lack of a "canonical form" for the presentation and use of abstractions. This can easily be confirmed when reading, for example, any tutorial on concurrent programming in Java. The controversial choice is between (1) extending the class `Thread` and (2) implementing the interface `Runnable`. Even the most sophisticated explanations of a conceptual difference between options 1 and 2 are much less convincing than the sheer pragmatic reason of using variant 2 whenever the class to be made concurrent already extends some other base class such as `Applet`.

A second significant advantage of our object model is the "lightweight" way of object usage. Clients need not be aware of the full "type" of a server object, but merely need to know the signatures of the services they actually use. Obviously, such a minimum-knowledge model is particularly beneficial in cases that involve remote-service objects whose full specifications are locally unavailable.

We should note at this point that Active Oberon embodies an object model that in many ways resembles that of the original COM. In particular, the two models coincide in their interface-oriented object view and in the nonuse of polymorphic typing and subclassing. However, they differ in the form of implementation support. While COM carefully avoids any form of implementation inheritance and refers to "hand-knitted" methods as *delegation* and *aggregation*, Active Oberon inherently supports multiple inheritance of predefined standard functionality *at compile time* (in contrast to languages such as C++ and Eiffel, which support multiple inheritance at runtime). As a matter of fact, we could roughly characterize Active Oberon as "COM plus built-in aggregation."

It is also worth noting that the concept of definition could well be generalized. A more progressive version of this concept would, for example, allow HTML documents and XML tags to be viewed as definitions and thereby provide a cleaner and more powerful way of scripting.

Let us now get more technical and assume a configuration as caricatured in the Active Oberon code in Listing H.2.

Listing H.2

```
DEFINITION I; (* pure interface *)
  PROCEDURE { ABSTRACT }  f (..); (*abstract method *)
END I;
DEFINITION D;
  VAR x: X; (* public state variable *)
  VAR { PROTECTED } y: Y; (* protected state variable *)

  PROCEDURE { ABSTRACT } e (..); (* abstract method *)
  PROCEDURE { ABSTRACT } f (..);
  PROCEDURE g (..): ..; (* standard implementation *)
    VAR u, v: U;
  BEGIN.. RETURN ..
  END g;
  PROCEDURE { FINAL } h (..); (* final implementation *)
  BEGIN .. f(..); ..
  END h;
END D;
DEFINITION D1 REFINES D;
  VAR { PROTECTED } z: Z; (* new protected state variable *)
```

continues

```
PROCEDURE e (..); (* standard implementation *)
BEGIN .. x ..
END e;
PROCEDURE g (..); (* new standard implementation *)
BEGIN .. RETURN D.g(..) + ..
END g;
PROCEDURE { ABSTRACT } k (..);(* new abstract method *)
END D1;
TYPE A = OBJECT IMPLEMENTS I, D1;
  ..
PROCEDURE f (..); IMPLEMENTS I.f, D1.e;
BEGIN .. D1.x ..
END f;
PROCEDURE f1 (..); IMPLEMENTS D1.f;
BEGIN .. D1.e(..); ..
END f1;
PROCEDURE k (..); IMPLEMENTS D1.k;
BEGIN
END k;
  ..
END A;
```

We immediately observe the following:

- x is the only public state variable in D and D1. y and z are *protected variables* whose access is restricted to refining definitions and implementing object types.
- A meets its obligations by providing implementations for I.f, D1.f, and D1.k.
- A customizes the implementation of method D1.e.
- Within D1 and A, qualification is used to identify members of a different scope. For example, D1.x and D1.e in A refer to the variable x and to the standard implementation of e in D1, respectively.
- In this example, A IMPLEMENTS D1 implicitly implies
  A IMPLEMENTS D.

Let us now assume that a second refinement D2 of definition D exists and that A is supposed to implement both D1 and D2. Then we are faced with a more complex case of intersecting chains of refinement (see Listing H.3).

Listing H.3

```
DEFINITION D2 REFINES D;
  PROCEDURE k (..); (* new method *)
  BEGIN ..
  END k;
END D2;
TYPE A = OBJECT IMPLEMENTS I, D1, D2;
  ..
  PROCEDURE f (..); IMPLEMENTS I.f, D1.e;
  BEGIN ..
  END f;
  PROCEDURE f1 (..); IMPLEMENTS D1.f;
  BEGIN ..
  END f1;
  PROCEDURE f2 (..); IMPLEMENTS D2.f;
  BEGIN ..
  END f2;
  PROCEDURE p (..); IMPLEMENTS D2.g;
  BEGIN ..
  END p;
  PROCEDURE k (..); IMPLEMENTS D1.k, D2.k;
  BEGIN ..
  END k;
  ..
END A;
```

In this case, the definitions implemented by A (D1 and D2) have a common root (D), and some semantic clarification is needed. First, we declare D's state space to be shared by D1 and D2; that is, x refers to the same instance of the variable wherever it occurs in either D1 or D2. Second, we point out that the implication A IMPLEMENTS D1 ⇒ A IMPLEMENTS D is no longer unconditionally true. By convention, this implication holds if and only if, for each method of D, the identification of its implementation is unambiguous. In our example, A does not implement D because the identification of f's implementation is ambiguous. We note in passing that this convention is compatible with the more general semantic model based on "dominants" [4, 5] and is adapted by C++, for example.

We can best illustrate this rule by an example. Assume that our Sensor abstraction features a method called Handle. Further assume that ButtonSensor and PenSensor are refinements of Sensor providing individual implementations of `Handle`. Finally, assume that `ButtonPen-Control` implements both refinements simultaneously. Then, a necessary and sufficient condition for `ButtonPenControl` to also implement the abstract `Sensor` definition is a reimplementation of `Handle` (most probably based on `ButtonSensor.Handle` and `PenSensor.Handle`).

Let us now briefly change our perspective and turn to the client's site. In accordance with the "lightweight" view of objects by clients are *polymorphic declarations* that emphasize the desired facets of servers rather than their full "type". For example,

```
a: OBJECT { D1, D2 }
```

defines an object variable or parameter a with guaranteed implementations of the definitions `D1` and `D2`. The following would then be a possible scenario of use:

```
.. D1(a).f(..); D2(a).k(..); .. := D1(a).x; ..
```

Alternatively, a could be declared completely generically and be used under the safeguard of an `IMPLEMENTS` clause:

```
a: OBJECT
IF a IMPLEMENTS D1, D2 THEN
    .. D1(a).f(..); D2(a).k(..); .. := D1(a).x; ..
END;
```

Note that type-specific object variable declarations are still possible in Active Oberon. However, they are essentially used only in combination with *abstract data types* and external operators. For example,

```
TYPE T = OBJECT ... END;
PROCEDURE "@" (x: T): T ;
PROCEDURE "#" (x, y: T): T;
```

defines an abstract data type T featuring two operations @ and #.

A Concept of Static Modules

In combination with a static *import* relation, the *module construct* is a simple but extremely useful tool for structuring large software systems according to the principle of separation of concerns. If augmented by guaranteed version compatibility between importing and imported modules, the module/import combination is in addition an ideal framework for maintaining large software systems.

In Active Oberon for .NET, modules have dual semantics of *package* and *static object*. More precisely, an Active Oberon module is both

- A package representing simultaneously a namespace and a compilation unit
- A static object together with the following conventions of instantiation:
  - The object initializer is represented by the module body.
  - As a precondition of instantiation, all imported modules (that is, their static objects) must be created and initialized in a compatible version.

For example, the module declaration in Listing H.4 defines the following items:

- A package M consisting of three object types M.A, M.X, and M.Y.
- A static object M whose state variables are a, s, and t, whose methods are F and G, and whose initializer is the BEGIN ... END block at the end of the module text. In addition, the import clause requires modules L and N to be initialized and ready for delegation before M is instantiated.

Listing H.4

```
MODULE M;
  IMPORT L, N;
  TYPE
    A = OBJECT { PUBLIC } END A;
    X = OBJECT { PUBLIC }
      VAR { PUBLIC } a: A;
      VAR x: X;
      ...
```

continues

```
    : END X;
      Y = OBJECT ... END Y;
    VAR { PUBLIC } a: A;
    PROCEDURE { PUBLIC } F (t: T): A;
    VAR s, t: T;
    BEGIN ...
    END F;
    PROCEDURE G (a: A);
    BEGIN ...
    END G;
  BEGIN (* module initialization *)
      ... N ... (* delegate work to module N *)
  END M.
```

By default, the elements of a module scope are private to the module. However, the PUBLIC modifier may be used to declare any module element as "exported"—that is, as visible from the outside. In Listing H.4, the object types A and X are public, while Y is private. Further, the members a and F of the static object M are public, while s, t, and G are private.

By convention, the members of object type scopes are private to the enclosing module. However, public object types may declare public members again by simply adding a PUBLIC modifier. For example, in object type X, state variable a is public, while x is private.

It is worth noting at this point that "static" module objects distinguish themselves from "ordinary" Active Oberon objects in only one point: They are created and managed by the system rather than by application programs. As a consequence, Active Oberon modules can implement definitions exactly as object types can and, correspondingly, they can equally be used by clients via definitions.

In concluding these explanations, we emphasize that the system is expected to guarantee version compatibility between L, M, and N at both compile time and runtime.

The Mapping to the Common Type System

Recapitulation of the .NET Interoperability Framework

From an interoperability perspective, the main constituents of the .NET language framework are as follows:

- A component packaging model
- A compile-time naming hierarchy
  - A *namespace* is a qualified set of names.
- A runtime deployment hierarchy
  - An *application* is a logically connected set of assemblies described by a configuration script (in XML).
  - An *assembly* is a deployment unit consisting of a collection of modules described by a manifest.
  - A *module* is either a portable executable (DLL or EXE file) or a container for additional resources such as fonts and pictures.
- A virtual object system called CTS (Common Type System)
  - The CTS supports the well-known object concepts of *class, subclass, interface, static class member, instance class member, abstract method, virtual method, sealed (final) method, virtual call, static call,* and *interface call.*
- A stack engine model
  - The stack engine model operates on an abstract execution stack. *MSIL* is a comprehensive intermediate language covering all three .NET models so that, in the end, the task of implementing a language for .NET simply amounts to compiling the language to MSIL.

    In the case of Active Oberon, the compiler uses a simple recursive descent strategy [6], with the benefit of a built-in mapping to the stack engine model. No substantial problems have arisen from this choice, and MSIL has proved to be a very suitable target. However, our additional constraints of single-pass compilation and, in particular, the "declare before use" obligation made our task more difficult. Obviously, this obligation is awkward in combination with a scenario of active object types mutually referring to one another. Also, a fine point worth mentioning in connection with expression compilation is the problem of constant folding. It can be caricatured as follows. When compiling an expression of the form X op Y (where X and Y are subexpressions and op is an operator), the recursive descent essentially proceeds as

```
Operand(X); Get(op); Operand(Y); Operator(op)
```

under assumption of the following semantics: Procedure `Operand` parses an operand and emits code for its evaluation on the stack, procedure `Get` reads and saves the operator, and procedure `Operator` emits the operator to the stack. Obviously, this may lead to premature code emission if X and Y are constant expressions. An improved version of `Operand` would fold constants instead of emitting code until it encountered a nonconstant element. However, in the case of a constant X and a nonconstant Y, this strategy leads to emitting Y first, which, of course, is not a problem if either op is symmetric or a *swap-stack-top* instruction is available in MSIL. Unfortunately, no such instruction exists, and we must leave constant folding to the JIT.

Returning now to a more conceptual level, we first observe that languages within the .NET Framework typically take dual roles as *consumers* and *producers* of components. Correspondingly, the primary tasks language implementers for .NET are confronted with can be summarized as follows:

- Mapping their language to the .NET model (preferably to the official .NET Common Language Specification)
- Mapping the .NET model (at least the CLS) to their language

In the following sections, we shall discuss these tasks in the special case of Active Oberon. For this purpose, we first recall the main constructs supported by Active Oberon and their connecting relations:

- Constructs: Module, object type, definition
- Relations: IMPORTS, IMPLEMENTS, and REFINES

Table H.1 summarizes these ideas.

Modules and definitions are the only compilation units in Active Oberon. Object types are not compiled separately, so their declarations need to be wrapped in some module scope.

TABLE H.1 Constructs and Relations Supported by Active Oberon

Construct	Relation	Construct
Definition	REFINES	Definition
Object type	IMPLEMENTS	Definition
Module	IMPLEMENTS	Definition
Module	IMPORTS	Module

Mapping Modules

Let us first concentrate on the compilation of modules—in particular, on the compilation of our exemplary module M. The result is a cascade as shown in Figure H.6: an assembly M containing a portable executable M, containing (1) a collection of sealed classes A, X, and Y corresponding to the object types declared in M and (2) a sealed class M corresponding to the static object associated with M.

The sealed class M is sometimes called the *module class*. It is static in the sense that all its methods are static. Note in particular how the module's initialization code is compiled into the constructor of the module class. In detail, the activities given in Listing H.5 are performed exactly once at instantiation time of the module class.

Listing H.5

```
FOR each module N imported by M DO
  Check version of N;
  IF compatible with version expected by M THEN
    Load and initialize static object N
  ELSE throw loading exception
  END
END;
Initialize static object M
```

When compiling an Active Oberon module, the compiler implicitly generates a .NET namespace for later use by any .NET language. Concretely, in the case of our exemplary module M, a namespace M is generated

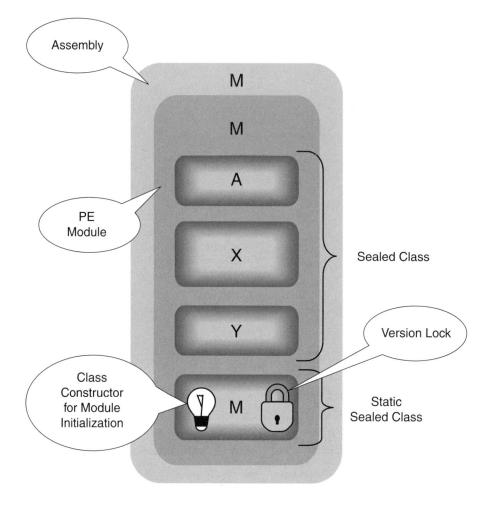

Figure H.6 *Compilation result of an Active Oberon for .NET module*

containing members M.A, M.X, M.Y, and M.M (the static object associated with M). The elements of the module object can be accessed by qualification as usual. For example, method F of M is referred to in general as M.M.F. Within Active Oberon, the shortcut notation M.F is considered equivalent to M.M.F.

Let us now turn to *definitions*, the second kind of Active Oberon compilation units. Remembering that definitions are abstractions, it is natural to compile each definition into an abstract .NET class, with the immediate advantage that refinement (at least a simple form of it) harmoniously maps to class extension in .NET.

However, this approach is infeasible with the IMPLEMENTS relation, at least in the case of multiple definitions implemented by the same object type. The mapping of the IMPLEMENTS relation to .NET is, in fact, a most intricate problem. It essentially amounts to finding a mapping from a restricted form of "multiple inheritance" to single inheritance plus interfaces.

Mapping Definitions

For the sake of concreteness, let now A be an object type in Active Oberon, and let D be any definition implemented by A. We already know that A is mapped to a sealed .NET class. For the mapping of the IMPLEMENTS relation, we can identify three modeling options:

- Declare D as the base class of A
- Aggregate D with A
- Integrate D with A

We already mentioned the first option at the end of the previous section. It is simple to implement but is restricted to one definition per object type. The second and third options are replicable arbitrarily.

In detail, several possibilities exist for *aggregating* D with A. Our favorite one is subsumed by a transformation of D into a pair consisting of an interface I_D and a static class C_D, constructed according to the following rules:

1. Transform each state variable of D into a property signature—that is, a pair (get, set) of abstract methods.
2. Define I_D as the set of property signatures constructed in 1 plus the method signatures of D.
3. Transform each method of D into a static method by (a) adding a reference parameter of type A to its signature and (b) consistently replacing accesses to D's state variables in the implementation by accesses to the corresponding properties of the object passed as a reference parameter.

4. Define C_D as the set of the static methods constructed in 3.
5. Extend A's state space by D's state variables.
6. Have A implement I_D—that is, implement the property signatures constructed in 1 and D's methods, either by explicit implementation or by delegation to C_D.

It is probably best to demonstrate this procedure with a concrete example. Let T be any data type, and let D and A be declared as shown in Listing H.6.

Listing H.6

```
DEFINITION D;
  VAR x: T;
  PROCEDURE f (y: T);
    VAR z: T;
  BEGIN x := y ; z := x
  END f;
  PROCEDURE { ABSTRACT } g(): T;
END D;
TYPE
  A = OBJECT IMPLEMENTS D;
    PROCEDURE g (y: T) IMPLEMENTS D.g;
      VAR z: T;
    BEGIN z := x; x := y
    END g;
  END A;
```

Then, the result of the transformation formulated in C#, .NET's *canonical language*, is as shown in Listing H.7.

Listing H.7

```
public interface ID {
  int x { get; set; }
  void f(int y); /* implemented by SD.f */
  void g(int y);
}
public class SD {
  public static void f(D me, int y)
  { int z; me.x = y; z = me.x; }
}
```

```
sealed class A: ID {
  int D_x;
  public void g(int y) { int z; z = x; x = y; }
  public void f(int y) { SD.f(this, y); } /* delegation */
  public int x { get { return D_x; } set { D_x = value; } }
}
```

It is worth emphasizing that within the Active Oberon language domain:

- The exact identity of each method called is known when A is compiled.
- D is never instantiated and does not have to be precompiled.

Consequently, our third modeling option relies on lazy code generation and takes D as a source code template to be *integrated* with A at compile time. The obvious advantage of this method is direct access to D's state variables without virtual calls; the disadvantage is unavoidable multiplication of runtime code.

Our current solution of preference is "optimized aggregation" or, more precisely, aggregation plus

- Mapping of one of the definitions implemented by A to A's base class; and
- Trusting the JIT optimizer to draw benefit from A's seal.

Interoperability

Language interoperability is .NET's highlight and major strength, and language implementers on .NET are well advised to apply special care regarding both the *consumer perspective* and the *producer perspective* of their language.

Taking a producer perspective in our case of Active Oberon, we first recall that the compilation units are *modules* and *definitions*. From a compilation view, they share the following characteristics:

- Each compilation unit defines its own namespace.
- The result of each compilation is an assembly.

TABLE H.2 Compilation Results

Result from the Compilation of a	Outer Shell	Inner Shell	Contents
Module	Assembly	PE module	One sealed class for each object type declared in the module One static sealed class representing the static module object
Definition	Assembly	PE module	One sealed static class representing the set of preimplemented methods One interface representing the signatures of the state variables and methods

From the earlier discussions, we can easily understand the summary provided in Table H.2.

In the interest of interoperability, it could obviously be reasonable to offer options for the following:

- Unwrapping the static module object from its namespace
- Compiling definitions into abstract classes

Let us now switch to a consumer perspective. In an interoperable environment, the Active Oberon compiler must obviously be prepared to accept components produced by foreign languages. The abstract vehicle provided by .NET for this purpose is the *namespace*. Active Oberon supports the use of foreign namespaces within the current module scope via full qualification or, alternatively, via aliasing. For example, the statement

```
IMPORTS P.M AS M;
```

opens a symbolic portal M to the namespace P.M, and allows the use of its ingredients with simplified qualification by M.

A complication arises due to the fact that there is not in general a one-to-one correspondence between namespaces and deployment units. Command-line hints specifying the assemblies required for the next compilation provide a temporary solution.

However, the crucial questions from a consumer's view are these:

- What are the reusable components?
- How can they be used?

The answers are simple in essence: The reusable components are .NET interfaces and .NET classes, and each can be used by Active Oberon either as an abstraction or as a factory for the creation of service objects. Table H.3 clarifies this point.

Note an important technical fine point: The definitions derived from foreign (non-Oberon) classes are precompiled and cannot be mapped to an *(interface, static class)* pair as explained earlier. Instead, they must be mapped to a base class. As a consequence, at most one definition derived from a foreign class can be implemented per object type.

The code excerpt in Listing H.8 sketches the implementation of a generalized 15-puzzle in Active Oberon for .NET. Module `Puzzle` defines two object types: `PuzzleForm` and `Launcher`. `PuzzleForm` implements (and inherits from) definition `System.Winforms.Form`. Because this definition is derived from a foreign class, it must be mapped to `Puzzle.PuzzleForm`'s base class. `Launcher` is an active object with an intrinsic behavior. The next section explains how such behavior is mapped to .NET.

TABLE H.3 Reusability of Components

.NET Component	Active Oberon Entity If Used as Abstraction	Active Oberon Entity If Used for Instantiation
Interface	Definition	—
Abstract class	Definition	—
Concrete class	Definition	Object type

Listing H.8

```
MODULE Puzzle;
  USES System, System.Drawing, System.WinForms; (* name-
spaces *)
TYPE
  PuzzleForm = OBJECT IMPLEMENTS System.WinForms.Form;
    VAR nofElems: INTEGER; …
    PROCEDURE MoveElem(pbox: System.WinForms.PictureBox;
      dx, dy, nofSteps: INTEGER);
    VAR i, j: INTEGER; loc: System.Drawing.Point;
    BEGIN …
    END MoveElem;
    PROCEDURE TimerEventHandler(state: OBJECT);
    BEGIN …
    END TimerEventHandler;
    PROCEDURE Dispose() IMPLEMENTS
                         System.WinForms.Form.Dispose;
    BEGIN …
    END Dispose;
    PROCEDURE NEW(image: System.Drawing.Image;
               (*  constructor *)
    title: System.String; subDivisions: INTEGER);
    BEGIN …
    END NEW;
  END PuzzleForm;
  Launcher = OBJECT
    VAR target: System.WinForms.Form;
    PROCEDURE NEW (t: System.WinForms.Form);
                 (* initializer *)
    BEGIN target := t
    END NEW;
    BEGIN { ACTIVE }
          System.WinForms.Application.Run(target)
  END Launcher;
VAR puzzle: PuzzleForm; launcher: Launcher; …
BEGIN
  WRITELN("Puzzle implemented in Active Oberon for .net");
  …
END Puzzle.
```

Mapping Active Behavior

Probably the main profit we can gain from the active object construct in
Active Oberon is its conceptual influence on the mindset of system

builders. In terms of functionality, it is basically equivalent to object constructs that support the implementation of a `run()` method.

In particular, when compiling an active object type, we can easily mimic the active object construct in the .NET Framework by proceeding as follows:

- Map the object type's body to a method plus a field:
  ```
  Method void body() { ... }; Field Thread thread;
  ```
- Map the generator NEW(x) to the following pair of statements:
  ```
  x.thread = new Thread(new ThreadStart(body));
  x.thread.Start()
  ```

Two active object topics still remain to be discussed: mutual exclusion and assertion-oriented synchronization [1]. Regarding mutual exclusion, the mapping is simple:

- Translate each mutually exclusive block statement `BEGIN { EXCLUSIVE }` ... `END` within an active object scope into a critical section on .NET bracketed by `Monitor.Enter(this); ...; Monitor.Exit(this);`.
- The mapping of assertion-oriented synchronization is more complex. Consider a statement `AWAIT(c)` within any object scope, where c is a local Boolean condition. Then, this would be one possible solution:
  - Translate `AWAIT(c)` into a loop of the form `while !c { Monitor.Wait(this); }`.
  - Automatically generate a `Monitor.PulseAll(this);` call immediately before the exit of every critical section.

Obviously, this topic will need further investigation and optimization, in particular when efficiency matters.

Language Fitting

We should not conclude this section on the mapping of Active Oberon to .NET without mentioning a few minor adjustments of the original Oberon language that should be regarded as a tribute to making the revised language fit optimally in the .NET interoperability scheme.

- **Delegates**   We extended Oberon's concept of procedure variables to *method variables* that are able to represent arbitrary method values of arbitrary object instances and are no longer restricted to global procedure values. No language changes were necessary. The compiler now simply allocates a pair of pointers *(code pointer, object base)* for every method variable.

- **Value Types**   Besides the ordinary reference types, the .NET object system supports value types. In Active Oberon, value types are called *record types*. Record types are declared in form of the well-known RECORD ... END construct. Their members are called *fields*. Methods in record types are not supported, nor is boxing.

- **Overloading**   We extended Oberon to support method overloading. In the case of ambiguity, we require calls of an overloaded method to explicitly specify the desired signature as, for example, in

  ```
  u := MyModule.MyOverloadedMethod{(S, T): U)}(s, t)
  ```

  with s, t, and u of types S, T, and U, respectively.

- **Base Method Calls**   Because Oberon does not support subclassing, no special construct is provided for base method calls. However, calls of method implementations in definitions are possible from within the implementing object type simply by using their exact and fully qualified names.

- **Exception Handling**   Active Oberon provides a rough form of exception handling. The corresponding throw/catch pair of constructs is
  - A built-in THROWEXCEPTION procedure
  - An extended form of the block statement:

    ```
    BEGIN (* regular code )
      EXCEPTIONALLY ( summary exception handling code *)
    END
    ```

- **Namespaces**   Oberon does not provide an explicit namespace construct. However, module packaging can nevertheless be achieved simply by using a qualified module name. For example, a module M that is a member of a module package P could be called P.M.

- **Assemblies**   Except in the case of Active Oberon modules, there is no guaranteed one-to-one correspondence between namespaces and deployment units in .NET. In Active Oberon, command-line arguments serve as locating hints to the compiler. If the `System` namespace is imported, then `mscorlib` is automatically located.

- **Procedure Nesting**   Because access to intermediate variables is unsupported by .NET, the current Active Oberon compiler does not allow nested procedures.

Summary and Conclusions

This appendix is a report on a joint project with Microsoft Research whose goal is the implementation of Oberon as a research language on the .NET interoperability platform. We took the opportunity and slightly revised the original Oberon language and its object model. Our two conceptual main achievements are (1) a unified notion of *active objects* that subsumes (passive) objects and concurrency, and (2) a unified concept of abstraction called *definition* that subsumes the concepts of base class and interface.

The current version of the Active Oberon for .NET compiler uses a simple and fast, one-pass, recursive-descent strategy. It is reflectively programmed in Active Oberon for .NET and is able to self-compile. It makes use of .NET's `System.Reflection` API for internalizing imported classes and interfaces but still produces textual MSIL code. Also, in some cases the current compiler relies on explicit hints provided by the programmer, with "forward" declarations being the most prominent example.

We are currently developing a second version of the Active Oberon compiler. It is again based on the recursive-descent parsing strategy, but will generate a more elaborate intermediate data structure that can serve as a basis for the following improvements:

- Resolve mutual references in the source code without the need for forward declaration
- Generate native MSIL code via the `System.Reflection Emit` API
- Apply the definition mapping rules in their full generality

Also, in the course of a different, local project, we are currently implementing Active Oberon on a custom flyweight system kernel called Aos

[7, 8], running natively on Intel SMP and StrongARM systems. In the end, this effort will allow us to compare the efficiency of the two runtimes and fine-tune our implementations.

Some preliminary benchmarks have shown the JIT optimizer to generate about 50% more efficient native Intel code in comparison with our native (nonoptimizing) Oberon compiler.

We have concentrated in this appendix on the object model, because this topic is most intimately related with "programming in the large" and with interoperability, and because it still harbors ample research potential. However, we should not forget that, quantitatively, the translation of executable statements into the stack engine is still the dominant part of the compiler. In this respect, we have little to criticize: The stack engine is well designed and allows our one-pass, recursive-descent algorithm to emit MSIL code naturally. A minor fine point is a missing instruction for swapping the two topmost elements on the stack. Such an instruction would be beneficial for constant expression folding by the compiler.

A more radical and definitely worthwhile thought revolves around a new API for compiler writers based on a parse tree data structure instead of on MSIL code. Not only would such an API factor out the reflection parts from each compiler, but it would also take the burden from compilers of maintaining their own symbol table. As a net effect, language implementation on .NET would be quite easy, and doors could be opened for the implementation of hundreds of small, special-purpose languages.

Acknowledgments

My thanks go to Microsoft Research, in particular to James Plamondon, Pierre-Yves Saintoyant, Brad Merrill, Jim Miller, Dan Fay, Erik Meijer, and Don Syme for launching, managing, and supporting this project, for inviting us to participate, and for hosting us in the devlabs.

My sincere thanks go also to my collaborators Thomas Frey, Philipp Kramer, Hanspeter Högger, Karel Skoupy, and Ben Smith-Mannschott for their competent help with the implementation of the compiler, and to Patrick Reali for pointing out an optimization of my previous solution for aggregating definitions.

I highly appreciated the profitable comments by Damien Watkins, Andrew Kennedy, and the reviewers of a previous version of this appendix. Last but not least, I gratefully acknowledge Brian Kirk's vital interest in Active Oberon and his constructive comments.

References

[1]   N. Wirth, "The Programming Language Oberon," *Software—Practice and Experience*, 18:7, 671–690, July 1988.

[2]   J. Gutknecht, "Do the Fish Really Need Remote Control? A Proposal for Self-Active Objects in Oberon," *JMLC '97*, 207–220.

[3]   R. Milner, "Computing and Communication—What's the Difference?," The Computer Laboratory, Cambridge University, June 1999, speech given on the occasion of Tony Hoare's retirement in Oxford.

[4]   B. Stroustroup, private communication, ETH Zürich, November 2000.

[5]   G. Ramalingam and H. Srinivasan, *A Member Lookup Algorithm for C++*, IBM T. J. Watson Research Center, P.O. Box 704, Yorktown Heights, NY, 10598, USA.

[6]   N. Wirth, *Theory and Techniques of Compiler Construction*, Addison-Wesley, Reading, MA, April 1996.

[7]   P. Muller, "A Multiprocessor Kernel for Active Object-Based Systems," *JMLC 2000*, 263–277.

[8]   P. Reali, "Structuring a Compiler with Active Objects," *JMLC 2000*, 250–262.

Glossary

This glossary provides definitions of .NET Framework terms. Its major purpose is to provide a single source of definitions for terms in the .NET Framework used in this book.

Accessibility   A test to verify that at a given point in a program, a CLI `tool` can access a program element represented by a name. The first part of this test determines whether the name is visible. If it is visible, then the second part of the test determines whether it can be accessed—for example, read or written to.

Application   An executing process that consists of one or more application domains, which themselves consist of one or more assemblies. At least one assembly must have an external entry point; use of this entry point triggers (or causes a hosting environment to trigger) the creation of an initial application domain. Applications may also contain unmanaged code and resources, such as bitmap images.

Application Domain   An application consists of one or more application domains. Application domains act like subprocesses within a process, by providing boundaries. An application domain isolates objects created by one application domain from those created by another application domain. An assembly is loaded into an application domain; the application domain is the smallest part of a process that can be unloaded.

Array   Values whose members, called elements, are accessed by an index rather than by name. An array has a rank that specifies the number of indices needed to locate an element (sometimes called the number of dimensions) within the array. It may have either zero or nonzero lower bounds in each dimension.

Assembly   The unit of deployment and versioning in the .NET Framework. It establishes the *namespace* for resolving requests for types and determines which types and resources are exposed externally and which are accessible only from within the assembly. An assembly includes an assembly manifest that describes the assembly's contents.

Assembly Manifest   Metadata describing which modules and resource files are part of a particular assembly, which types are exported, and which other assemblies are referenced. The metadata may also specify which security permissions are required to run, which additional permissions are optionally requested, and which permissions the assembly refuses.

Assertion [Security]   A way of ensuring that a method has access to a particular resource, even if the method's callers do not have the required permission. During a stack walk, if a stack frame asserting the required permission is encountered, a security check for that permission will succeed without proceeding further. To perform an assertion of a permission, code must not only have that permission, but also be granted the `SecurityPermission.Assertion` permission. Unwise use of assertions can create security holes, so they should be used only with the utmost caution.

Base Framework   A core part of the Framework Class Library. It provides fundamental classes, such as `Object` and `String`. The Base Framework and the CLR form part of the CLI.

Boxing   Converting a value of a value type to a value of an object type, which means that the object type will carry full type information at runtime and will be allocated in the garbage collected heap. The

IL instruction set's `box` instruction converts a value type to an `Object` by making a copy of the value type and embedding it in a newly allocated object.

Built-in Data Types Types provided by the CLR's type system. They include value types, such as `Int16` and `Int32`, and reference types, such as `Object` and `String`. The IL supports these types with specific instructions.

CLS See *Common Language Specification.*

CLS Compliant CLR elements that publicly expose only language features that are present in the Common Language Specification are said to be CLS compliant. "Publicly exposed" means elements are visible outside their assembly. For example, a method may be CLS compliant if it uses only CLS-compliant types in its parameter list; the same method may use non–CLS-compliant types within its body, as they remain hidden within the assembly. CLS compliance can apply to classes, interfaces, components, tools, and more.

CLS compliance comes in three forms: CLS Consumer, CLS Extender, and CLS Frameworker. To provide a simple example of how CLS compliance affects these different categories, following is Rule 1 from the CLS:

- Boxed value types are not CLS compliant.

This means that:

- CLS Consumers do not need to be able to consume boxed value types.
- CLS Extenders do not need to provide a mechanism that produces boxed reference types.
- CLS Frameworkers do not use boxed value types in their publicly exposed forms.

(See the ECMA specification for all the CLS rules, including this example.)

CLS Consumer Languages and tools that allow developers to use (consume) types defined in CLS-compliant frameworks. CLS Consumers may not be able to create new CLS types, however.

CLS Extender Languages and tools that allow developers to use types defined in CLS-compliant frameworks and to extend these frameworks—for example, by inheriting from types defined in the framework and/or defining new interfaces. CLS Extenders always satisfy at least the same requirements as CLS Consumers for any CLS rule; that is, they satisfy a superset of the rules for Consumers.

CLS Frameworker Languages and tools that allow developers to create entire CLS-compliant frameworks for use in the CLI. CLS Frameworkers satisfy all the requirements of CLS Consumers and Extenders for any CLS rule.

Code Access Security (CAS) An evidence-based security system that allows evidence to be evaluated by a policy to decide which permissions should be granted. Evidence can consist of any information about an assembly, including the location of origin of the assembly, signatures on the assembly, and so forth. Permissions are granted to assemblies as the finest-grained unit of trust for code.

Coercion An attempt to transform a value of one type into a value of another type. Widening coercions preserve information. An example of a widening coercion is a conversion from `Int32` to `Int64`. Narrowing coercions sometimes lose information. An example of a narrowing coercion is a conversion from `Int64` to `Int32`.

COM Interoperability (COM Interop) The mechanism within the runtime environment that allows COM and the CLR to interact.

Common Intermediate Language (CIL) A language used as the output of several compilers and as the input to a JIT compiler. It defines an abstract stack-based execution architecture. The CLR may include several JIT compilers for converting CIL to native code.

Common Language Infrastructure (CLI)   The combination of the Common Language Runtime, Base Framework, and other libraries. The CLI is the major component of the ECMA standard.

Common Language Runtime (CLR)   The type, metadata, and execution systems provided by the .NET Framework, which supplies managed code and data with services such as cross-language integration, code access security, object lifetime management, and debugging and profiling support. By targeting the CLR, compilers and other tools can offer these services to developers.

Common Language Specification (CLS)   A subset of the .NET Framework's features that are supported by a broad set of compliant languages and tools. CLS compliance is only applicable to the publicly exposed aspects of types. CLS-compliant languages and tools are guaranteed to interoperate with other CLS-compliant languages and tools. For example, the type `Int32` is CLS compliant, so languages and tools expect that other CLS-compliant languages and tools will know how to correctly use this type.

Contract   A guarantee between a definer and a user. An example of a contract is the methods in an interface type. In adding the interface type to its definition, a type agrees to the contract specified by the interface type. Contracts vary from strictly enforceable, such as verifying that a function's signature conforms to a contract (syntax correctness), to assuming consistent behavior among classes implementing a common contract (semantic correctness). Semantic contracts are more difficult to specify and verify.

Custom Attributes   A means by which developers can provide user-defined metadata to any program element.

Debug   To observe the execution of a program and modify its values and execution. .NET provides debugging services for this purpose.

Declarative Security Check   A security check that is invoked by storing required permissions in the metadata of the component. Developers write declarative security in the form of custom attributes.

There are many different forms of declarative security: link demand, inheritance demand, demand, assert, deny, permit only.

Demand   A security operation performed by trusted code protecting a resource: The demand causes the system to check whether all callers have the specified permission or permissions via a stack walk. A demand succeeds if all callers have the permission(s), subject to possible overrides; otherwise, a security exception is raised.

Demand Set   The permissions that an object requires its callers to have.

Denial (of Permission)   A way in which a method can prevent its callers and itself from exercising the privilege represented by a permission (unless it is explicitly asserted). If a method on the call stack denies Permission A, a stack walk checking for Permission A will fail unless a valid assertion is found on the stack between the method that does the denial and the method that initiated the check for Permission A.

Events   Events encapsulate the idea of "notification" by providing three operations: register to be notified when the event occurs; remove registration for notification; and announce that the event has occurred. Events can be considered a form of "syntactic sugar"; at a fundamental level, they are function calls.

Exact Type   A type that defines all the methods and fields of a particular value. For example, a value may be an instance of an object type that implements many interface types, such as `String`. The object type (in this case, `String`) is the exact type for any values of that type.

Exceptions   A runtime error-reporting mechanism that requires programs to handle raised exceptions or have their stack unwound until each exception is handled (caught) or the thread terminates.

Executable File   A file in Portable Executable (PE) format that can be loaded into memory and executed by the operating system loader. It can be either an .EXE or a .DLL file.

Execution System   The runtime system that the CLR supplies and uses to control execution of managed and unmanaged code. The execution system takes as input either Intermediate Language (IL) code or precompiled native code, as well as the metadata associated with the code. The execution system is responsible for loading and unloading code, IL verification, memory management, security, exception handling, and laying out objects.

Fixup [File Format]   An entry in a PE file that will be modified later by the linker or when the entry is loaded into the execution engine. When a CLR PE file is generated, some of the information needed during execution might not be available (for example, the address of a static field that is defined in another module). The PE file is emitted with a "fixup" for that information, and the correct information is supplied at a later time.

Garbage Collection (GC)   The process of transitively tracing through all pointers to actively used objects to locate all objects that can be referenced and then arranging to reuse any heap memory that was not found during this trace. The CLR's garbage collector also arranges to compact the memory that is in use to reduce the working space needed for the heap.

GC   See *Garbage Collection.*

Grant Set [Security]   A set of permissions that indicates which operations or resources an assembly is authorized to access. An assembly requests authorization for certain privileges and is granted authorization based on the security policy.

IL   See *Common Intermediate Language.*

Imperative Security Check   A security check that occurs when a security method is called within the code that is being protected. This type of check can be data-driven and can be isolated to a single location within an object or method. For example, if the name of a file to be protected is known only at runtime, then an imperative security check can be invoked by passing the file name as a parameter to a security method. See also *Declarative Security Check.*

Inheritance Demand [Security]   A permission that is required to subtype a particular class, as specified in the metadata for the class. When applied to a method, it demands the permission to override the method.

Instance Fields   Fields for which each value of a type contains its own copy; also known as data members in other languages/environments.

Instance Methods   Methods invoked on a value rather than a type. These methods receive a `this` pointer to access instance fields of the value, but the `this` pointer may sometimes be null.

Interface Type   A partial specification of a type; that is, a specification that may cover some, but not all, aspects of a type. Interface types may be supported by many different exact types, and exact types may implement many different interface types. Interfaces thus specify a contract that must be satisfied by any class that promises to implement the interface.

Intermediate Language (IL)   See *Common Intermediate Language.*

Interoperability   The mechanisms within the runtime environment that allow the CLR to interact with other application models. These other applications may be unmanaged code that can be accessed via PInvoke or COM components accessed via COM Interop.

JIT   Just in time. A phrase that describes an action that is taken only when it becomes necessary, such as JIT compilation or JIT object activation. By convention, the term "JIT" alone is used to refer to a JIT compiler.

JIT Compiler   A compiler that converts IL into machine code when the code is required at runtime; also known as a "JITter." The CLR may supply more than one JIT compiler.

Library   A set of types that provide the abstraction and implementation of a service. Such libraries are often called class libraries, but they are not limited to containing only classes. In fact, they can be assembled using any CLR types, including classes, interfaces, and value types. A set of libraries can be combined into a profile.

Lifetime   The time beginning when an object is allocated in memory and ending when the last reachable reference to the object is removed, at which point the garbage collector can delete the object from memory.

Link-Time Demand [Security]   A demand that results in a security check at JIT time to permit access to a method. Unlike a runtime demand, only the immediate caller of the method needs the permission.

Load Instructions   IL instructions that load values, such as local variables, onto the execution stack.

Locals [Execution System]   Locations allocated on the stack by a method for its own storage purposes. They include local variables declared by the user as well as temporary locations for storing intermediate values (i.e., when the compiler runs out of registers).

Location [Execution System]   An area in memory where a value can be stored and a *location contract* that specifies a type that can be stored. The location contract designates how the value stored in that location can be used. For example, a location may specify that it holds a reference to an interface type. A value stored in that location can be accessed only as if it is of that interface type, even though its exact type may provide more functionality. Only one value can be stored in a location at any point in time.

Managed Code   Code that supplies the metadata necessary for the CLR to provide services such as memory management, cross-language integration, code access security, and automatic lifetime control of objects. All code based on IL executes as managed code.

Managed Pointer   A pointer to a field inside a garbage-collectible object, typically created by a compiler for temporary use (for example, a pointer to a particular character within a garbage-collectible string). The garbage collector must be able to update all internal pointers when it compacts the heap. For garbage collection to operate correctly, an object reference to the whole object must exist (somewhere visible to the garbage collector) whenever there is an internal pointer to it.

Member (of a Type)   A constructor, field, method, property, or event. The member may be either static or an instance. A nested class is a not a member of the enclosing class.

Metadata   Data (or information) about data. In the CLR, metadata is used to describe assemblies and types. It is stored with them in the executable files, and is used by compilers, tools, and the runtime system to provide a wide range of services. Metadata is essential for runtime type information and dynamic method invocation. Many architectures/systems use metadata—for example, type libraries in COM provide metadata.

Method   A callable set of execution instructions. Methods specify a contract; that is, they have a name, a number of parameters, and a return type. Clients that need to call a method must satisfy the contract when calling the method. Several kinds of methods are possible, such as instance and static.

Module   A single PE file. When the file contains a manifest, it becomes an assembly and can be loaded by the CLR type loader. When the file has no manifest, it must be part of an assembly to be loaded. Modules written in different source languages can be collected into a single assembly.

Native Code   Code that has been compiled to processor-specific machine code.

Object-Oriented Programming   A programming style based on the concepts of identity, classification, inheritance, polymorphism, and information hiding. The earliest example of this style was Simula 67.

Object Reference   A reference to an object allocated on the garbage-collected heap. Object references are reported to the garbage collector so that they can be modified if the objects to which they refer are moved onto the heap.

Object Types   A subset of the reference types. Object types are referred to as classes in some programming languages. Values (instances) of an object type are called objects. Object types are exact types; that is, they completely specify all the functionality (contracts) that a type implements.

Override [Security]   A security override that dynamically changes the evaluation of a subsequent security demand. An assertion may cause a demand of the specified permission to succeed prematurely, whereas a deny or permit-only operation can cause a demand to fail where it otherwise would not. See *Assertion, Denial,* and *Permit Only* for more details.

Parameter Area [Execution System]   The part of the method's stack frame (activation record) used to store parameters being passed to methods that it calls.

PE File   Portable Executable file. The file format used for executable programs as well as files to be linked together to form executable programs.

Permission Class [Security]   A class that controls access to a resource by supporting authorization checks.

Permission Object [Security]   An instance of a permission class that represents access rights to resources. It encapsulates the permission state into one manageable unit that can be persisted, passed through policy mechanisms, or stored in memory. A permission object can be used to perform a request or a demand for authorization.

Permit Only   By placing a permit-only restriction on a permission or permissions, a method can prevent its callers and itself from exercising the privileges represented by other permissions it might have (unless explicitly asserted). If a method on the call stack does permit-only Permission A, a stack walk that checks for Permission A will succeed but a demand for Permission B (which the code otherwise had) will fail unless a valid assertion is found on the stack between the method that does the denial and the method that initiated the check for Permission B.

A permit-only operation is similar to a deny operation. Where the denial specifies the permission(s) to be denied, however, the permit-only operation specifies the only permission(s) that pass—a demand for any other permission fails.

Platform Invocation Services   Functionality to enable managed code to call unmanaged native entry points.

Platform Invoke (PInvoke)   See *Platform Invocation Services.*

Pointer Types   A subset of the reference types. Pointer types can point at data or code. They are represented as addresses. Three kinds of pointers exist: managed pointers, unmanaged pointers, and unmanaged function pointers.

Portable Executable (PE)   See *PE File.*

Privilege [Security]   The right of a user to access a protected resource or function.

Profile (noun)   A specification of a set of libraries, each of which represents one or more services, and a set of requirements on IL, that provides a useful programming base. An example is the Kernel profile.

Profile (verb)   To measure the execution of a program, usually for the purpose of improving performance by identifying the source of performance loss.

Properties   At a fundamental level, set and get methods, often accessing just the contents of a field of an object. Properties allow some languages to expose syntax that looks like field reference/assignment but that actually turns into method calls. Indexed properties allow syntax that looks like array subscripting and turns into calls with arguments; unlike in true arrays, the subscripts may be of any type (not just integers).

Reference Types   One of the two basic types in the type system. Reference types are the combination of an address in memory (its identity) and the sequence of bits located at that address.

Reflection   The ability to provide type information at runtime, typically so that a client can discover the members (methods, fields, properties, events, and nested types) of a type. Reflection also allows these members to be referenced at runtime, and it permits new types to be defined. Newly defined types can then be saved to disk, as well as allowing instances to be allocated and more.

Runtime   See *Execution System.*

Security Hole   An unprotected entry point into an otherwise secure computer, component, application, or other online resource.

Security Manager   A class used to initiate security checks and interrogate security information in the execution environment.

Security Object   An object that .NET allocates on the stack frame of methods that uses overrides, such as Assert and Deny, that require frame-specific security information. The security object is defined and used by the security system; it is never directly used by the compiled code.

Security Policy   The active policy on the client's computer that programmatically generates a granted set of permissions from a set of requested permissions. A security policy consists of several levels that interact; by default only permissions granted by all layers are allowed to be granted.

- Enterprise level: security policy distributed across many machines of an enterprise

- Machine level: security policy applied to all managed code on the machine

- User level: security policy applied to all managed code run by the corresponding user

- Application domain level: security policy applied to all managed code in an application domain

Security System   The system that implements most aspects of both role-based and code access security, including functionality such as stack walking. It provides the basic API for performing the imperative CAS functions such as Check, Assert, and Deny.

Stack Frame [Execution Engine Architecture]   The portion of the stack associated with an individual method call invocation.

Stack Walk   The process of proceeding through the call stack, examining each stack frame. In .NET, stack walks are performed for several reasons, including garbage collection and security checks.

Static Fields   Fields for which there is only one field per type rather than one field per value (as with instance fields). Some programming languages refer to them as class fields (or class variables).

Static Methods   Methods invoked on a type rather then a value. Some programming languages refer to them as class methods. Static methods do not receive a `this` pointer.

Store Instructions   IL instructions that store values from the execution stack into locations, such as local variables.

`this` Pointer   A pointer to the object instance on whose behalf the current instance method is executing. It allows access to the fields of a value on which a method is invoked. Not all methods have a `this` pointer (see *Static Methods*). The `this` pointer may be `null`.

Trusted Computing Base (TCB)   The hardware, firmware, and software that protect a computer system by enforcing a security policy. For systems using .NET, the TCB includes all of the security code (such as the `Permission` classes and the Security Manager) as well as some parts of the execution system (such as the verifier).

Type   A definition from which values can be instantiated. The CLR type system understands two fundamental different types: value types and reference types. Types may have static, instance, and virtual methods; static and instance fields; events; and properties.

Typed Reference   A built-in data type that represents a type/value pair. Typed references describe local variables and parameters only.

Type Loader (Class Loader)   The facility that loads the implementation of a class into memory, checks it for consistency, and prepares the class for execution.

Type Safety   A technique for ensuring that all access to memory is done in such a way that the type system cannot be circumvented. Type safety is facilitated by making sure that every reference is typed and that every type reference only ever references a type that is assignment compatible with its type. Using only strictly typed references allows the execution engine to validate all assignments to a reference and guarantees that both the reference and the object it references are strictly compatible. An example of type-safe access is the use of only publicly exposed methods to access values; an example of unsafe type access is the use of pointers to directly modify the fields of values. Although the CLR provides facilities to ensure type safety, they may or may not be used.

Type System   A system that provides developers with a number of types and with the facility to define their own types. It consists of two fundamentally different types: value types and reference types. Examples of built-in types include `Int32`, a value type, and `Object`, a reference type. Developers may define their own value and reference types. The type system is shared by all compliant languages, tools, and the CLI.

Unboxing   Converting a value of an object type into a value of a value type. While every value type can be boxed (that is, converted into an object type), not all object types can be converted into value types.

Unmanaged Code   Code that was created without knowledge of the conventions and requirements of the CLR. Unmanaged code executes in the .NET environment with minimal services (for example, no garbage collection, limited debugging, no declarative security). Unmanaged code does not have metadata describing it.

Value   An instance of any CLR type.

Value Type   A data type that fully describes a value by specifying the sequence of bits that makes up the value's representation. Type information for a value type instance is not stored with the instance at runtime, but rather is available in metadata. Value types are similar to the type `int` in C++ and Java. Instances of value types can be treated as objects by using boxing.

Verification   The process of examining IL to ensure that it conforms to a specific set of rules defined to prove that the code is type safe. The CLR can verify IL.

Virtual Method   A method whose resolution is not determined until runtime; even then, the resolution depends on the type of the value receiving the method invocation.

Visibility   A Boolean test to verify that if a name is used at a point in a program, the compiler can resolve the name—that is, find the element being referred to. Visibility is the first question that needs to be answered to determine whether the programming element is accessible.

Suggested Reading List

Following is a list of some of the books referenced in this text or those recommended by the authors:

- J. Gough (2002). *Compiling for the .NET Common Language Runtime (CLR)*, Englewood Cliffs: Prentice-Hall.
- M. Henning and, S. Vinoski (1999). *Advanced CORBA Programming with C++*, Boston: Addison-Wesley.
- B. LaMacchia, S. Lange, M. Lyons, R. Martin, and K. Price (2002). *.NET Framework Security*, Boston: Addison-Wesley.
- S. Lidin (2002). *Inside Microsoft .NET IL Assembler*, Redmond: Microsoft Press.
- J. Richter (2002). *Applied Microsoft .NET Framework Programming*, Redmond: Microsoft Press.
- W. R. Stevens (1992). *Advanced Programming in the UNIX Environment*, Reading: Addison-Wesley.
- C. Szyperski (1998). *Component Software—Beyond Object-Oriented Programming*, Boston: Addison-Wesley.

Index

informIT